To Bob
with love
Christmas 1988

ARCTIC ORDEAL

"... *gentle elevations, and dales wooded to the edge of the stream,*" 2 July 1821 [Coppermine River]

Arctic Ordeal

THE JOURNAL OF JOHN RICHARDSON

SURGEON-NATURALIST WITH FRANKLIN

1820–1822

Edited by C. Stuart Houston
Illustrated by H. Albert Hochbaum
Appendixes by John W. Thomson (Lichenology)
and Walter O. Kupsch (Geology)
Foreword by W. Gillies Ross

McGill-Queen's University Press
Kingston and Montreal

©McGill-Queen's University Press 1984
Reprinted 1985
ISBN 0-7735-0418-4
Legal deposit 4th quarter 1984
Bibliothèque nationale du Québec
Printed in Canada

Designed by Beth Earl

First published in Great Britain in 1984 by
Alan Sutton Publishing Company Limited
30 Brunswick Road
Gloucester GL1 1JJ
ISBN 0-86299-201-x

Canadian Cataloguing in Publication Data

Richardson, John, Sir, 1787–1865.
 Arctic ordeal: the journal of John Richardson, surgeon-naturalist with
 Franklin, 1820–1822

ISBN 0-7735-0418-4

 1. Northwest Territories – Description and travel – To 1900.* 2. Arctic regions –
 Discovery and exploration – British. 3. Scientific expeditions – Arctic regions.
 4. Natural history – Northwest Territories. I. Houston, C. Stuart (Clarence
 Stuart), 1927– II. Title

FC3961.1.R52A3 1984   917.19′2′041   C84-098530-4 G650.1820 R52 1984

Contents

Maps

Maps 2–8 are superimposed on National Topographic Services Maps; see Acknowledgments, pp. xvii-xviii.

Tables

Foreword

Franklin's overland expedition of 1819–22 was the first to travel and chart a section of the northern coast of mainland Canada, which until then was known to Europeans only at the two widely separated points reached by Hearne (1771) and Mackenzie (1789). The expedition established fundamental geographical relationships which strongly influenced the remainder of the search for the Northwest Passage. As Franklin and his men were setting up their advance base at Fort Enterprise in preparation for the descent of the Coppermine River to the coast, Edward Parry's two ships were returning to England, having sailed westward through Lancaster Sound, Barrow Strait, and Viscount Melville Sound to the meridian of 113°48″ w near Melville Island. Although tough multi-year ice at the western extremity of this corridor had proved impenetrable, Parry's voyage conclusively established the existence of the important Lancaster Sound gateway into the Arctic Islands, among which other passageways to the west were likely to exist. Franklin's explorations of 1821, and the work of subsequent overland expeditions, enticingly revealed a sea route parallel to Parry's track but farther south, along the mainland coast. It only remained, then, for a maritime expedition to link Parry's gateway with Franklin's mainland coast, and to sail on to Bering Strait and the Pacific.

Curiously enough, it was Franklin himself who set out in 1845 to close the gap between the two charted regions and complete the Northwest Passage, but by the greatest of ironies his entire expedition met with disaster at the threshold of the relatively easy coastal route he had explored in 1821.

The overland expedition of 1819–22 has always excited great interest because of the narrow line it trod between survival and catastrophe. The fact that only nine of the twenty members of the party returned alive from the Barren Grounds, along with the probable occurrence of cannibalism, the murder of one member, and the execution of another (by John Richardson, the author of this journal), has given this enterprise a macabre fascination. The tragic events have also raised questions about the expedition's techniques of travel and subsistence, the adequacy of its leadership, and the relationship between officers and men. Clearly these concerns bear directly on the entire phenomenon of arctic exploration during the nineteenth century.

Unlike Franklin's narrative, Richardson's journal was not written for public consumption. It is a personal record of events and it provides us with another valuable perspective. As Dr Houston has already edited for publication the private journal of Hood, we now have at our disposal three accounts of this interesting and controversial expedition of discovery with which we can assess the effectiveness of the operation, from the naval bureaucracy down to the nine voyageurs who gave their lives for a cause they did not understand.

W. Gillies Ross
Bishop's University

Preface

The four officers of the first Arctic Land Expedition, John Franklin, John Richardson, George Back, and Robert Hood, each kept a daily journal. Franklin, who lost his journal when his canoe upset in Belanger Rapids on 14 September 1821, was given access to the other three accounts and quoted Richardson extensively, sometimes verbatim, in his *Journey ...* (1823);[1] surprisingly, he made little use of Back's diary. Franklin then returned the journals to the families of the officers. Hood's journal of the expedition's first year was published in 1974 under the title *To the Arctic by Canoe* and reproduced his fine watercolour paintings.[2] Back's unpublished journal, which covers the journey from beginning to end, is in the McCord Museum, McGill University, and has recently been transcribed completely; it offers additional corroboration and much insight into personalities and events. Traill, one of Franklin's biographers, had access to the continuation of Franklin's journal which he resumed after the accident, and his book reproduced two sample pages, scrawled semi-legibly in pencil, recording the events of 3–7 November.[3]

John Richardson's journal, written during the tragic last year of the expedition, became the property of his widow at Grasmere when Sir John died on 5 June 1865. On Lady Richardson's death it was passed on to Major-General John Booth Richardson, Sir John's oldest living son.[4] Next it went to the general's only child, Captain John Franklin Richardson in Lincolnshire.[5] In 1966 a part of the captain's estate was sold by Dawson's of Pall Mall, London.[6] Dr Robert E. Johnson, Richardson's biographer, encouraged the University of Illinois to buy the collection of seventy-two books, manuscripts, and reprints for its renowned Rare Book Room, including the holograph journal, and copies of Richardson's publications on the flora and fauna of what is now western Canada, each corrected in his own hand. It is a happy coincidence that John Richardson's journal begins on 21 August 1820, while Hood's journal ends on 13 September (Table 1). Since the

TABLE 1 First Franklin expedition: dates* and principal locations

Year		Entire expedition	Franklin	Back
1819	Gravesend, England	23 May	Journal begins	
	Stromness, Orkneys	4–16 June		
	York Factory	30 Aug.–9 Sept.		16 June: Journal begins
	Cumberland House	23 Oct.–31 Dec.		
1820	Cumberland House		1–18 Jan.	1–18 Jan.
	Fort Chipewyan		26 Mar.–18 July	26 Mar.–18 July
	Fort Resolution	25–27 July		
	Fort Providence	29 July–2 Aug.		
	Fort Enterprise		20 Aug.–9 Sept.	20–29 Aug.
			15 Sept.–31 Dec.	10 Sept.–18 Oct.
	Fort Providence			2 Nov.–8 Dec.
	Fort Resolution			10–24 Dec.
1821	Fort Chipewyan			2 Jan.–9 Feb.
	Fort Resolution			20 Feb.–5 Mar.
	Fort Providence			7–10 Mar.
	Fort Enterprise		1 Jan.–14 June	17 Mar.–14 June
	Point Lake camp		21–25 June	21–25 June
	Mouth of Coppermine	14–21 July		
	Point Turnagain	16–22 Aug.		
	Mouth of Hood R.	26–31 Aug.		
	Belanger Rapids		14 Sept. (Journal lost)	
	Obstruction Rapids	26 Sept.–4 Oct.		
	Hood's tent (15 mi ssw of Obstruction Rapids)			
	Fort Enterprise		11 Oct.–16 Nov.	9–11 Oct.
	Roundrock Lake			12–30 Oct.
	Akaicho's camp (moving every few days)		26 Nov.–1 Dec.	4–14 Nov.
	Fort Providence		11–15 Dec.	21–24 Nov.
	Fort Resolution		19–31 Dec.	27 Nov.–31 Dec.
1822	Fort Resolution	1 Jan.–27 May		
	Fort Chipewyan	2–6 June		
	Cumberland House	28–30 June		
	Norway House	4–7 July		
	York Factory	14 July–7 Sept.		10 Aug.: Journal ends
	London, England	21 Oct.		

*Gaps in dates reflect periods spent in travel

Richardson	Hood
	Journal begins
1 Jan.–13 June	1 Jan.–13 June
13–18 July	13–18 July
20 Aug.–9 Sept.	20–29 Aug.
21 Aug.: Journal begins	
15 Sept.–31 Dec.	10 Sept.–31 Dec.
	15 Sept.: Journal ends
1 Jan.–30 Apr.	1 Jan.–14 June
7 May–4 June	
10–25 June	21–25 June
7–23 Oct.	Death 20 Oct.
29 Oct.–16 Nov.	
26 Nov.–1 Dec.	
11–15 Dec.	
19 Dec.: Journal ends	

two officers were involved in separate expeditions to Point Lake after 29 August, there are only eight days of overlap. Furthermore, Richardson's journal deals with fifty-one days not reported by Franklin.

While Richardson was at Fort Resolution, York Factory, or both, he almost certainly recopied his field journal, for it is not sufficiently tattered or weather-beaten to have been written in the field. The existence of an earlier version is also indicated by an occasional remark such as "see p. 82 rough notes."

My wife and I have made a typewritten copy of Richardson's journal, typed page for page and line for line, and this has been deposited in two libraries: the Rare Book Room, University Library, University of Illinois at Champaign-Urbana, and the Shortt Library of Canadiana, Special Collections, University of Saskatchewan. Spelling, punctuation, and use of upper- and lower-case letters have been transcribed as faithfully as possible; only two words cannot be deciphered with reasonable certainty.

The last half of Richardson's journal, pages 263 to 383 by his count (when numbering his pages he omitted numerals 124–33, inclusive), is devoted to tedious and detailed descriptions of birds, mammals, and fish. As a sample, his description of the Yellow-billed Loon is given in full in Appendix A. In the text that follows, I have not included these descriptions. When such passages intrude upon the narrative of his first 222 pages, they have been omitted, with a notation as to their presence in the original; later descriptions are indicated within the appropriate appendix.

In this book I have reproduced Richardson's journal with his misspellings, abbreviations, and inconsistencies. Richardson often omitted apostrophes and his punctuation was erratic. In the space of a few pages he might use several spellings of the same word – moschetoes, musquitoes, and mosquitoes, for example. He regularly used long dashes in place of periods; I have substituted periods. In places where Richardson used "ditto," "do," or ditto marks in his tables, the words intended have been substituted, to avoid confusing the reader. He often reversed grave and acute accents on French words. Latin names have been placed in italics, as Richardson himself always did in publication. Words beginning with upper-case letters in mid-sentence have been converted to lower case. His summation of courses and distances for each entire day, corrected for magnetic declination, is given following the detailed but uncorrected courses and distances of each "leg" of the day's journey. I have moved these forward from a table to the daily account. Parentheses are Richardson's in every instance; square brackets indicate an insertion by the editor.

SOME ABBREVIATIONS COMMONLY USED BY RICHARDSON

az. azimuth; chr. chronometer; Cuv. Cuvier; en. fr. in French; geog. geographic; lat. latitude; long. longitude; pr. per; Reg. An. *Le Règne Animal* by Cuvier; st. statute; ther. thermometer; var^n variation.

we at length made a fire – It was not sufficient, however, to warm the whole party, much less to thaw our shoes, and no tripe de roche being gathered we had nothing to cook.
Course SbW by compass – Distance 5½ miles.

Sunday October 7th 1821

Cold & clear weather – Left the encampment about nine and a little before noon came to a pretty extensive thicket of small willows – Here Mr Hood, John Hepburn, and myself determined to remain, and our tent being pitched Mr Franklin read prayers and took a very affectionate leave of us – His baggage consisting only of a single blanket, and the officers journals, added very little to the mens loads, which were now reduced to their personal clothing and a single tent. No tripe de roche to day – Drank an infusion of the Ledrum palustre.

The melancholy circumstances attendant on the deaths of Mr Hood and Michel (who returned to us, on the 9th) and the other painful occurrences, until the 29th of this month when after a most distressing journey Hepburn and myself reached the house, have been detailed in an account drawn up and transmitted home, I shall not therefore enter upon a subject so harrassing to my feelings here – but proceed at once to

Monday October 29th 1821 –

When we entered Fort Enterprise, in the dusk of the evening, and had the melancholy satisfaction of embracing Mr Franklin. No language that I can use, being adequate to convey a just idea of the wretchedness of the abode, in which we found our commanding officer, I shall not make

A page from Richardson's journal

VARIABLE SPELLINGS ACCORDING TO WRITER

Fort Enterprise (Richardson)   Fort Enterprize (Hood)
Akaicho (Richardson)   Akaitcho (Franklin)   Ekeicho (Back)
Cascathry (Richardson)   Keskarrah (Franklin)
Semandrè (Richardson)   Samandre (Franklin)
Benoit (Richardson)   Bennoit (Franklin)

Site of the bear kill, 5 August 1821

Acknowledgments

The existence of Robert Hood's journal was made known to me by Mrs Ruth Horlick; its owner, Richard G. Birch, kindly allowed me to prepare it for publication in 1974. Dr Robert E. Johnson, Richardson's biographer, first informed me of the existence of Richardson's journal, which detailed the events of the first Franklin expedition beyond Fort Enterprise where Hood's journal had ended. This journal has been the property of the University of Illinois at Champaign-Urbana since 1966. On my visit there on 1 December 1978 I received the warm encouragement of Mrs Mary Ceibert, rare-book librarian, and of Dr Johnson. Robert W. Oram of the University of Illinois gave permission to prepare the journal for publication. With my interest in Franklin's journeys rekindled, my wife Mary and I, based on Bathurst Inlet Lodge, were happy to participate in a ten-day "Following Franklin" exploration of Bathurst Inlet in August 1979.

Since I began to work on Richardson's journal I have enjoyed the co-operation and assistance of librarians at the University of Saskatchewan, Saskatoon, and the University of Michigan, Ann Arbor. Facilities for transcribing the microfilm copy of Richardson's journal were provided by the former institution. In 1981 I was able to use four months of my sabbatical leave to work on notes and commentary to accompany the published journal. Mrs Shirlee Anne Smith of the Hudson's Bay Company Archives, Provincial Archives of Manitoba, Winnipeg, was very helpful and gave me permission to quote from unpublished trading-post journals of the 1820s. Mrs Pamela Miller of the McCord Museum, McGill University, provided a microfilm copy of George Back's journal, and Conrad Graham and Shirley Thompson of the same institution gave permission to use relevant quotations from Back's journal.

The Surveys and Mapping Branch of Energy, Mines and Resources Canada gave permission to superimpose courses and distances from Richardson's journal on 1:250,000 National Topographic Services [NTS] maps. These maps,

© Her Majesty the Queen in Right of Canada, reproduced in the journal, are Map 2: Winter Lake 86A, 1962; Redrock Lake 86G, 1977; Indin Lake 86B, 1974; Point Lake 86H, 1962. Map 3: Hepburn Lake 86J, 1977; Sloan River 86K, 1977; Dismal Lakes 86N, 1977; Coppermine 86O, 1979. Map 4: Kikerk Lake 86P, 1982; Hepburn Island 76M, 1966. Map 5: Arctic Sound 76N, 1965; Rideout Island 76O, 1982; Tinney Hills 76J, 1982; Elu Inlet 77A, 1965; Mara River 76K, 1965; Richardson Islands 77B, 1976. Map 6: Kathawachaga Lake 76L, 1964; Mara River 76K, 1965; Arctic Sound 76N, 1965; Hepburn Island 76M, 1966. Map 7: Contwoyto Lake 76E, 1964; Lac de Gras 76D, 1977; Point Lake 86H, 1962; Winter Lake 86A, 1962. Map 8: Wecho River 85O, 1981; Carp Lakes 85P, 1979; Yellowknife 85J, 1960; Hearne Lake 85I, 1980.

The illustration of an 1820s compass is reprinted from the *Encyclopaedia Britannica* (14th ed., 1942), 6: 171, by permission of Encyclopaedia Britannica, Inc.

Appendixes explaining geology and early lichen names were contributed by Walter O. Kupsch and John W. Thomson, respectively. Specialized assistance concerning arctic tree-ring chronology was provided by Gordon C. Jacoby; mammal and dressed meat weights, by Peter Flood, Jack Howard, and Orville Pritchard; fish, by F.M. Atton and W.B. Scott; plants and lichens, by W.J. Cody, Charles D. Bird, John H. Hudson, and John W. Thomson; Yellow-billed loon, by Henri Ouellet; other birds, by W. Earl Godfrey; Eskimo words and igloo construction, by Robert Williamson; Finan McDonald, by William Ormsby; male breast secretion, by Gwen Gotsch, reference librarian, La Leche League International, Franklin Park, Illinois, who lent an unpublished term paper by Helen I. Gates. Shirley Stacey drew Map 1, lettered maps 2 through 8, and drew the plan of an igloo based on a sketch by Dr Richardson. W. Gillies Ross kindly wrote the Foreword.

Margaret Belcher, H. Albert Hochbaum, Stanley C. Houston, Robert E. Johnson, Joan McGilvray, David Norton, W. Gillies Ross, and J. Frank Roy offered constructive criticism and assistance with major sections of the manuscript. Mrs Joan Matlock typed the manuscript. Rosemary Shipton provided skilful and sympathetic help in the final editing process.

The completion of this project would have been impossible without the help of my wife Mary. In her demanding role as research assistant, she has matched every hour that I have spent working on Richardson's journal. She searched library holdings, checked references, read microfilm, compiled the index, and became an expert in deciphering the 1820s handwriting of Hood, Richardson, and Back.

I am particularly indebted to H. Albert Hochbaum of Delta, Manitoba, artist, author, and keen Franklin enthusiast. He shares with us his beautiful sketches with their authentic flavour of the Arctic where Franklin and his men trod, and where Dr Hochbaum himself has spent many seasons. His illustrations in this book are from field sketches he made in the Western Arctic between 1969 and 1983. All the Hood River and Bathurst Inlet sketches result from visits to the places on the anniversary dates of Richardson's and Franklin's visits there.

Financial support for publication was given by the Social Science Federation of Canada, using funds provided by the Social Sciences and Humanities Research Council of Canada; Associated Medical Services, Inc. and the Hannah Institute for the History of Medicine; Walter S. Bailey and the W.B. Saunders Company of Canada; the President's Fund, University of Saskatchewan; and the Canada Council under its block grant program.

"… A high hill adjoining to our encampment …" 3 August 1821

Introduction

After Britain's victory over Napoleon at the Battle of Waterloo in 1815, the underemployed British navy fixed some of its attention on the three unachieved goals in arctic exploration: the Northwest Passage, the Northeast Passage, and the North Pole. In these explorations first priority was allotted to the Northwest Passage, since there was still a hope of finding a practical commercial route for trade with the orient. In 1818 Captain John Ross was sent to re-survey Baffin Bay and seek a passage to the west, while Captain David Buchan and Lieutenant John Franklin made an unsuccessful attempt to sail north to the pole from Spitzbergen.

In 1819 Lieutenants William Edward Parry and Matthew Liddon were instructed to follow the Northwest Passage by sea. Encountering most favourable conditions, Parry penetrated west to Melville Island at 113° longitude, the most successful arctic sailing voyage ever. At the same time, the first Arctic Land Expedition, as it was then called, led by John Franklin, was dispatched to the mouth of the Coppermine River to trace by canoe the northern coast of the continent to the east. The expedition was "undertaken by order and under the auspices of his Lordship ... the right honourable The Earl Bathurst, K.G., one of His Majesty's principal secretaries of state."[1]

Franklin's instructions were comprehensive. As he stated in the introduction to the narrative of his journey: "... the main object of the Expedition was that of determining the latitudes and longitudes of the Northern Coast of North America, and the trending of that Coast from the Mouth of the Copper-Mine River to the eastern extremity of that Continent ... to ascertain correctly the latitude and longitude of every remarkable spot upon our route ... register the temperature of the air, at least three times in every twenty-four hours; together with the state of the wind and weather, and any other meteorological phenomenon ... the dip and variation of the magnetic needle, and the intensity of the magnetic force."[2] Further, the expedition was to study the land, the natives, the natural history, the aurora borealis, and the mineralogy, with specific instructions to visit and explore the source of copper near the Coppermine River.

John Franklin was born at Spilsby, Lincolnshire, on 16 April 1786, attended Louth Grammar School, and joined the navy six weeks before his fourteenth birthday. Although he was to become a hero, with promotion to captain after the first Arctic Land Expedition and a knighthood after the second, opinions differ concerning his capability as a leader. He combined some very positive qualities with certain obvious limitations. He was a plodding naval officer, lacking imagination and insight, yet he was doggedly determined, calm in danger, and cheerfully buoyant.[3] He was deeply religious, thoughtful of others, singularly simple and affectionate, a man who was never known to be provoked into using a harsh or hasty word.[4] Even Vilhjalmur Stefansson, perhaps his most outspoken critic, admits that Franklin's personality was "one of great charm ... tolerant, kindly and pious."[5] In his physical constitution, as described by H.D. Traill, Franklin seems to have been little suited to the rigours of arctic expeditions. He "owed least of all men to any peculiar advantages of bodily constitution ... His circulation was slow and his vitality, therefore, easily lowered. He suffered all his life, and even in England, from cold hands and feet."[6] Yet Traill credits him with "unrivalled fortitude" in the face of his "unexampled sufferings" on the first expedition, and uses the adjective "unsurpassed" in describing his leadership.

The most famous of Franklin's officers was Dr John Richardson, who served as surgeon and naturalist. Richardson was born at Dumfries, Scotland, on 5 November 1787, the first of twelve children of brewer Gabriel Richardson and his wife, née Anne Mundell. A precocious boy, John learned to read at four years of age and was apprenticed to his surgeon uncle at the age of thirteen. In the winters during his apprenticeship he studied at Edinburgh, obtaining his licence from the Royal College of Surgeons on 17 February 1807. He was then appointed as assistant-surgeon with the Royal Navy, where he served through a good part of the Napoleonic wars until 1813. After some months of attending lectures he was posted as surgeon with the Royal Marines in actions against the United States in the War of 1812–14; from Halifax he was sent to Montreal, St Jean on the Richelieu River, and Quebec City, and before news of the armistice reached them his battalion occupied an island just north of the Georgia-Florida boundary. After the wars, Richardson went on half-pay and resumed studies at Edinburgh. Having completed a thesis on Yellow Fever, he obtained his MD degree in August 1816. At the same time, he studied natural history under Professor Robert Jameson. He practised in Leith, the port of Edinburgh, for about two years, until his appointment to Franklin's first overland arctic expedition in search of the long-sought Northwest Passage.[7]

When the secretary of the admiralty communicated with Richardson on 25 March 1819 about the expedition, he wrote: "... if you feel disposed for such an expedition, and think that your health and qualifications are suitable for the

John Richardson

undertaking, and you could be ready to set out from England by the first week in May, I request you to state to me whether you could undertake to collect and preserve specimens of minerals, plants, and animals, in order that I may lay it before Lord Melville, for his consideration and approval."[8] On 24 April 1819 Richardson wrote from London to his father: "My duty will be to collect minerals, plants and animals. The country has never been visited by a naturalist, and presents a rich harvest. My knowledge of these subjects is very limited, but I am endeavouring to extend it by the opportunities afforded me here, and if I succeed in making a good collection, I have no doubt of my promotion on my return."[9]

Richardson was a true generalist. In the days when few people other than medical doctors had training in botany and zoology, almost every British and American exploring expedition hired a doctor to act both as surgeon and naturalist. While some were good surgeons and indifferent naturalists and some were keen naturalists but indifferent surgeons, Richardson proved himself to be proficient in both fields.

The other officers assigned to the expedition were George Back and Robert Hood, the midshipmen. They were chosen because of their demonstrated artistic ability combined with navigational skills, and were to make sketches, paintings, and maps to record the new country visited.

George Back was born at Stockport, Cheshire, in 1796, entered the navy in 1808, and was a prisoner of the French from 1809 through 1814. He then resumed service in the navy and served under Franklin on the *Trent*'s arctic voyage in 1818.

Robert Hood was born at Portarlington, Queens County, Ireland, in 1797 and joined the navy in 1811. When he was examined in October 1816, the captains remarked of his logbook, "... journals which we have never seen surpassed."[10] Throughout the first Franklin expedition, Hood made most of the observations of latitude, longitude, and magnetic variation, studied the electrical phenomena associated with the aurora borealis, and each evening mapped accurately the progress of the day's journey. He can be appreciated fully only from his journal, which was published in 1974.[11]

John Hepburn and Samuel Wilks were the ordinary seamen attached to the expedition. Hepburn had been taken prisoner by an American privateer and then transferred to a French trading vessel during the Napoleonic wars. Wilks, "unequal to the fatigue of the journey," was discharged at Cumberland House in the spring of 1820 and returned to England.

These naval men were sent to carry out a difficult task with totally inadequate resources. In accepting the leadership of the expedition, Franklin perhaps too readily succumbed to the temptation of fame and career advancement. As commanding officer he should have recognized that the Admiralty was attempting to promote this first visit by white men along the northern coast of North America "on the cheap." A navy man, Franklin was unfairly given an overland assignment, inappropriate to his training and previous experience.

Instead of providing transport for the party in a navy ship, the Admiralty purchased accommodation in the annual Hudson's Bay Company supply ships, *Prince of Wales*, *Eddystone*, and *Wear*, which also carried a group of Selkirk settlers. They embarked from Gravesend on 23 May 1819, stopped twelve days in the Orkney Islands, and, after a trying journey in which the *Wear* and *Prince of Wales* were severely damaged, arrived at York Factory on 30 August.

The first Franklin expedition arrived by mischance in the worst possible year. The large North West Company and the smaller Hudson's Bay Company were virtually at war with one another, seizing each other's men and goods, and consequently they had fewer supplies and less manpower to place at Franklin's disposal. Richardson wrote home from Fort Enterprise: "... intrigue and violence have a powerful sway. The contests of the rival Fur Companies have been carried on in a disgraceful and barbarous manner ... we still hear of wars and rumours of wars at the posts below."[12] George Simpson, the new governor of the Hudson's Bay Company and a recent arrival at Fort Chipewyan, was preoccupied with company concerns. The needs of the explorers were a second priority to him, and he berated at least one of his juniors for giving the amount of help he did.[13]

After little more than a week at York Factory, the exploring party, consisting of John Franklin, John Richardson, midshipmen George Back and Robert Hood, English seamen John Hepburn and Samuel Wilks, and four Orkneymen, began their inland journey on 9 September. The men had a tough job tracking the heavy York boats upstream against the current to the first height of land at the Painted Stone portage on 3 October. They stopped at Norway House on 6–7 October, hauled their supplies around the Grand Rapid on 10–12 October, and reached Cumberland House in freezing weather on 23 October 1819. On 18 January 1820 Franklin, Back, and Hepburn set out from Cumberland House on snowshoes, travelled up the Saskatchewan River to Carlton, then across country to Green Lake and Ile-à-la-Crosse, and reached Fort Chipewyan on Lake Athabasca on 26 March. Richardson and Hood remained at Cumberland House for the winter, to collect specimens and study the Indians. Many of Hood's watercolours, which were subsequently kept by the family in the attic of a coachhouse in Tipperary, Ireland, for nearly 100 years, were done that winter when his brush sometimes froze to the paper. He depicted five species of birds not described to science at the time they were painted.[14]

While waiting for northern rivers to clear of ice, Richardson made a trip upstream to Fort Carlton. The original post journals in the Hudson's Bay Company Archives in Winnipeg reveal that Richardson left Cumberland on 1 May and reached Fort Carlton with J.P. Pruden on the evening of 10 May; Richardson left with Mr Hutchinson on 26 May and arrived back at Cumberland on 30 May.[15] This visit persuaded Richardson that Carlton was one of the best sites in North America for studying birds.[16]

Richardson and Hood left Cumberland House with a crew of voyageurs on 13 June 1820. Their foreman, Louis St Jean, drowned in Otter Rapids on the Churchill River, but the others rejoined Franklin, Back, and Hepburn at Fort Chipewyan on 12 July. Franklin discharged three voyageurs and retained sixteen others who were willing to undertake the arduous and dangerous northern journey. He hired three voyageurs' wives, who brought three children with them, to make moccasins and clothing at the winter residence. The four Orkneymen who had accompanied Franklin thus far declined to go farther than Fort Chipewyan. Franklin's comparison of the prudence of the Orkneymen with the fearlessness of British seamen is revealing: "… they minutely scanned all our intentions, weighed every circumstance, looked narrowly into the plan of our route, and still more circumspectly to the prospect of return. Such caution on the part of the northern mariners forms a singular contrast with the ready and thoughtless manner in which an English seaman enters upon any enterprise, however hazardous, without inquiring, or desiring to know, where he is going, or what he is going about."[17]

The augmented and consolidated expedition left Lake Athabasca on 18 July 1820. They stopped at Fort Resolution on the south shore of Great Slave Lake from 25–27 July, where they were joined by the interpreter Pierre St Germain. Upon reaching Fort Providence on the north shore on 29 July they hired Willard-Ferdinand Wentzel, the North West Company's clerk in charge of Fort Providence, a second Copper Indian interpreter, Jean Baptiste Adam, and a seventeenth voyageur. The voyageurs were Jean Baptiste Belleau, Emanuel Connoyer, Jean Baptiste Parent, Joseph Forcier, Pierre Dumas, Joseph Gagné, Solomon

Belanger "le gros," Jean Baptiste Belanger "le rouge," Joseph Benoit, Régiste Vaillant, Ignace Perrault, Antonio Vincenza Fontano, Gabriel Beauparlant, Mathew Pelonquin, Michel Teroahauté, Joseph Peltier, and François Semandrè. Weakness and "biliary calculi" (gallstones), respectively, caused the discharge of Belleau and Connoyer during the first winter.[18] Wentzel had hired a number of Copper Indian hunters and their chief Akaicho; these Indians, with their families, were loosely associated with the expedition for the next eleven months, the hunters accompanying Franklin from Fort Providence to the Arctic Ocean.

The first twenty days of August were spent in an arduous trip up the Yellowknife River chain, with many portages; the expedition arrived at Winter Lake on 20 August, the day that Richardson's journal begins.

In a letter home, Richardson described their choice of wintering location:

We arrived here on August 20, and finding it a fit place for a winter residence immediately commenced the requisite buildings. Beyond this spot, which is situated two and a half degrees to the northward of Fort Providence, the country is destitute of wood, its vegetable productions consisting solely of various species of moss upon which the reindeer feed. The abundance of this kind of food attracts these animals in great numbers to the barren hills in the summer season, but during the winter they retire to the woods, partly for shelter from the inclemency of the weather and partly because the snow being loose is more easily removed in their search after the moss. In fine weather, however, they pay occasional visits to their favourite pastures on the barren grounds.

That we may be as much advanced as possible when the return of summer permits us to resume our journey, we have fixed our abode upon the verge of the woods, and indeed we could not have selected a more convenient or beautiful spot. The surrounding country is finely varied by hill and dale and interspersed with numerous lakes connected by small streams. One of these lakes, which we have named Winter Lake, discharges its waters by a moderately sized river, whose sheltering banks are clothed with wood. Amidst this wood, on a small and rather elevated plain, we have erected Fort Enterprise, and the situation is such that while we have an extensive southern prospect down the wooded banks of the river, the nakedness of the northern country is hid by a clump of trees on the rising ground in our rear.

Winter Lake supplies us with fish, but our staple commodity is the reindeer. We are just in the track of their visits to and from the woods and some are daily killed within sight of the house.

We have managed, notwithstanding the diminutive size of the trees, to construct a stately dwelling. It is fifty feet long, and twenty-four wide, and consists of three bedrooms and a common hall. We have besides a large kitchen behind, a storehouse on one wing, and a house for twenty men on the other. If to this you add a few Indian lodges scattered in the foreground you may picture to yourself Fort Enterprise, and conclude that it makes a very respectable appearance.

The buildings are framed of logs and plastered on the outside and inside with clay. With the latter material also the roof is covered and the chimneys constructed. The windows are closed with thin parchment made of reindeer skin, and our chairs and tables are formed by the hatchet and knife, tools which the Canadians use with great dexterity.[19]

Wentzel had been "appointed to settle the Indians required for leaders, guides and hunters to the expedition" and he related in a letter written at the time to the Hon. Roderick McKenzie that he had "so far succeeded as to have collected the choicest hunters of the Red Knife Tribe, as well as the most powerful leaders and knowing men amongst them."[20] Akaicho had a special role as adviser and Indian personnel officer. Owing to the lateness of the season, he refused to accompany the expedition to Point Lake in September 1820, forcing the explorers to restrict themselves to two small parties which reconnoitred the next summer's route as far north as the lake.

Included in the equipment brought from England were such scientific instruments as magnets, three sextants, two azimuth compasses, several artificial horizons, twelve thermometers, a theodolite,[21] a sympiesometer (barometer), a dipping needle,[22] a transit instrument, and an electrometer. Each officer carried a compass, a spy-glass, and a chronometer.[23] In addition to Bibles, prayer books, and scripture commentaries, the officers brought blank leather-bound notebooks in which to record daily events. Large sheets of paper allowed them to protract the course of each day's journey. They also brought manuals on navigation and astronomy, books of exploration written by Hearne and Mackenzie, and at least three natural history texts: the 1817 four-volume edition of *Le Règne Animal* by Cuvier in French, *Lichenographia Universalis* by Erik Acharius in Latin, and *Flora Lapponica* by Wahlenberg. Richardson probably packed Jameson's three-volume geology and at least one medical or surgical text as well.

Food from England, carried all the way to Fort Enterprise, included arrowroot, portable soup, two cases of chocolate, two canisters of tea, two barrels of flour, and three cases of preserved meats.[24] Unable to carry all the supplies, the explorers left behind stores of bacon, flour, rice, and tobacco at York Factory on 9 September 1819;[25] another 1200 pounds of sugar, biscuit, tea, rice, and portable soup at Rock House on the Hayes River on 17 September 1819;[26] and about 640 pounds of mouldy pemmican at Methy Portage on 8 July 1820.[27] Unknown amounts of goods were purchased in the Territories at Cumberland House and Carlton House; five bales of "assorted stores," including a share of "the ammunition absolutely required for the support of his post" from McLeod at Ile-à-la-Crosse on 28 June 1820;[28] seventy pounds of meat and a little barley from

Edward Smith at Fort Chipewyan on 18 July;[29] three fishing nets, a gun, a pair of pistols, and 550 pounds of dried moose meat at Fort Resolution on 26 July 1820,[30] and 200 dried reindeer tongues probably at Fort Providence.[31]

On 2 August 1820, when the expedition left Fort Providence on the north shore of Great Slave Lake, their arsenal included four fowling-pieces, a few old trading guns, eight pistols, two barrels of gunpowder, 140 pounds of ball and small shot, and twenty-four Indian daggers.[32] In addition to cooking utensils such as kettles and pots, there were packages of knives, chisels, axes, nails, fastenings for a boat, looking glasses, nine fishing nets of different meshes, beads, needles, blankets, and a few yards of cloth.

Ten "pieces," another 750 or 800 pounds of stores, were sent from York Factory with the fur company canoe parties in the autumn of 1820. Five "pieces" of ammunition and tobacco were left on the shore at Grand Rapids by unco-operative North West Company men, while five "pieces," including three kegs of spirits, a keg of flour, and thirty-five pounds of sugar were brought on by Hudson's Bay Company men.[33]

George Back made a 1200-mile trek on snowshoes to obtain further stores. At Fort Resolution, "though their united list did not furnish the half of what was required," Robert McVicar of the Hudson's Bay Company gave Back "in many articles ... the whole he had in his possession."[34] The sixty pounds of ball, a barrel of gunpowder, two rolls of tobacco, and some clothing carried by the seven voyageurs who left Fort Providence on 26 December 1820 and arrived at Fort Enterprise 15 January 1821 were likely from this source, as were the additional forty pounds of tobacco which were brought by six voyageurs on 4 March. Back also purchased at Fort Chipewyan four sledge loads of unspecified material, brought by four voyageurs to Fort Enterprise on 4 April. Back's journal entry of 17 March proudly recorded that he had "succeeded in the procuration of supplies beyond [Franklin's] most sanguine expectations."

Each of the voyageurs thus made at least one round trip on snowshoes from Fort Enterprise to Fort Providence, nearly 200 miles away, and most went on to Fort Resolution, 100 miles farther, on the south shore of Great Slave Lake. Beauparlant went with Back an additional 280 miles to Chipewyan. The two Belangers made the trip from Fort Enterprise to Providence twice, the last time on 17 April, to take the first instalment of completed journals, charts, drawings, observations, and letters for transmission to England. These long and arduous extra journeys were all undertaken as part of a voyageur's job.

At Fort Enterprise on 23 November 1820 the officers received letters and enjoyed the luxury of London newspapers. These came from England on the 1820 Hudson's Bay ship *Eddystone* that left London on 12 May and arrived at York Factory on 15 August, bringing more Selkirk settlers and the first missionary to the Northwest, the Rev. John West. The mail and newspapers were carried by North West Company canoes to Great Slave Lake and were finally brought from Fort Resolution by Belanger. From the newspapers the officers learned of the death of the demented King George III on 29 January of the previous year, but they dared not tell the Indians that the great king across the seas was dead.

The expedition was augmented by the arrival of two Eskimo interpreters during the winter of 1820–1. Augustus and Junius, from the west coast of Hudson Bay about 200 miles north of Churchill, accompanied the fur brigade that left Fort Chipewyan on 1 October and reached Fort Resolution on 8 October 1820.[35] The two Eskimos were living there in an igloo when George Back met them on 10 December 1820. They accompanied Mr Wentzel and Pierre St Germain to Fort Enterprise, where they arrived on 25 January 1821.

When the expedition left Fort Enterprise on foot in June 1821, they were heavily laden. As Richardson tells us, fifteen porters (fourteen voyageurs and one interpreter) of the advance party leaving the fort on 4 June carried sixty-four pounds of gunpowder, sixty-eight pounds of shot and ball, seven fishing nets, and a "considerable quantity of line."[36] They carried two tents for the four officers and two more tents for the sixteen men. Provisions included two bags totalling perhaps 160 pounds of pemmican, 400 pounds of fat, eighty pounds of dried meat, a cask of portable soup (eighty pounds?), and a box of arrowroot, weight unknown. For the Eskimos they hoped to meet they also carried ice chisels, hatchets, other iron tools, and a bale of additional presents.

Three men had dog-sledges that carried a double load of about 160 pounds. Seven men dragged sledges, and five carried their loads on their backs. A single load consisted of eighty pounds, without counting personal baggage of clothing, blankets, and boots totalling about forty pounds more. For example, Hood's buffalo robe probably weighed ten pounds and Beauparlant carried fire steels, flints, awls, fish-hooks, rings, beads, and a glass.[37]

From the advance party on Point Lake, Richardson sent a light-hearted letter on 9 June 1821 to George Back with the main party at Fort Enterprise:

> Amongst these hills you may observe some curious basins, but nowhere did I see anything worthy of your pencil. So much for the country. It is a barren subject, and deserves to be thus briefly dismissed.
>
> Not so the motley group of which we were composed. It afforded ample scope for the ablest pencil or pen, and whether character or humour were most kept in view, would, in the hands of genius, produce a picture not in many respects inferior either to Chaucer's Pilgrims or Hogarth's Guards. The party was composed of twenty-three individuals, all marching in Indian file, but variously grouped according to their physical strength and the heaviness of their burdens. Belanger "le gros," exulting in his strength, was foremost in the rank. Belanger "le rouge" followed close behind; whilst little Perrault completed the trio, and formed the first triangle in the picture. Adam came next, but at a respectful distance. His over-loaded sledge could not keep pace with the others, and he had frequently to lug along another with the "butin"[38] of his beloved Angelique. I need not trouble you with an account of

the rank maintained by the rest of the party. You know their various characters and powers, and can arrange them correctly. Roulante came tumbling along in the rear, the snow sometimes too deep to admit of her legs reaching the bottom, but the rotundity of her body was such that she never sank beyond a certain depth. In such cases it was admirable to see the dexterity with which she drew her extremities into her enormous corporation, and came rolling like an avalanche along the surface of the snow. Dumas, from the love he bore to the northern, carried Ryer, and Michel, for reasons unknown, carried her "butin." The most prominent figure, however, of the whole, because the most unearthly, was mother Adam. She came striding along supported by a stick which towered over the heads of all the others; a pair of red stockings and various other articles of her garb heightened the peculiarities of her figure; and as to her gait, it was similar to nothing I had ever before seen. Sometimes I was tempted to compare her to Hecate, sometimes to Meg Merrilies. Not that she had mind enough to be a powerful sorceress, or majesty sufficient for a commanding presence, but because she appeared to be rather a creature of the imagination than a reality. Every member of her body seemed to have belonged to different individuals and to have been formed by a random association into a sort of semblance of the human form; but from the want of proper animation the extremities never acted in concert, and the distorted spine which composed the centre, now bent to this side, now to that, according as the leg which described the greater or the smaller circle was in motion, while the arms played up and down to preserve something like equilibrium, but with the involuntary and convulsive motions of the most fantastic of Shakespeare's weird sisters in the height of her frenzy.

There was another figure of a different gender, with an unwashed face, matted locks, and moustaches of the colour and strength of straw; equip him as you please and place him in any part of the file you choose.

A Canadian would have told you the whole story in few words: – "Beaucoup de misère, point de chaudières, assez de sacrés."[39] You see I am determined that you should have your share of it by engaging you in the deciphering of this scrawl. Adieu! compliments to all our messmates.

Yours sincerely,

John Richardson.[40]

Thirteen of the voyageurs returned the sixty miles from Point Lake to Fort Enterprise to bring back another load that was no doubt of similar proportions, though Franklin is less specific. They pulled the three large birchbark canoes, tents, instruments, and eighty pounds of dried meat.

Each canoe weighed 300 pounds, not counting oars and poles, and was set on a small sledge fore and aft, resting on clothing or blankets. It was dragged by three or four men and two dogs. Every officer carried his personal belongings, such as books, boots, and blankets, a knapsack on his back or a bag on each shoulder, and a rifle, but dragged no sledge. On this final trip to Point Lake each voyageur dragged nearly 180 pounds behind him, but we know from Hood's journal that these were probably Troy pounds, in total equivalent to 150 avoirdupois pounds.[41]

Akaicho had with him a personal attendant, a husky Dogrib servant. Akaicho's brother, Annoethai-yazzeh or White Capot, was the chief guide, assisted by the Hermaphrodite.[42] Franklin rarely gave the names of individual Indians, but he did quote from Richardson's journal the names of those with Richardson's advance party on 4 June. Thereafter, the names and functions of the Indians are known almost exclusively from Richardson, who took a much more personal interest in them. Richardson also provided alternate names for two of the most important Indians.

The first two hunters assigned to Richardson's advance party were Baldhead and Basil, but Little-foot caught up to the party later that first day, accompanied by two Indian women, Angélique (Adam's wife) and Roulante. Longlegs and a small party of Indians arrived at Richardson's camp on Point Lake on 14 June, followed by the larger party with Akaicho the next day, including additional hunters. On 11 June Basil returned towards Fort Enterprise to give temporary aid to the advancing parties. Baldhead and Little-foot continued hunting and by 23 June the women had pounded 200 pounds of dried meat into pemmican, an important portion of the expedition's sustenance during the sea voyage by canoe later in the summer. On 19 June Longlegs and Cascathry left to hunt in advance of the party along Point Lake. On 20 June most of the women, including Angélique and Roulante, went north, probably to Takiyuak Lake. At noon on 21 June Franklin, Back, and Hood arrived at Point Lake.

The number of Indian hunters with the main party varied almost daily. On 20 June, before Franklin's arrival, there were five hunters with Richardson; on 23 June, after two of the best hunters, Le Petit Chasseur and Thoveeyorre, had stayed back to care for their father ailing with renal colic (kidney stones), and without counting Little Singer, there were still five hunters. They were Little-foot, Baldhead, Basil, Little Hand, and Broadface. Broadface was mentioned on 8 July as the hunter "enamoured of Cascathry's daughter, Greenstockings," and presumably sleeping with her, perhaps unaware that she was already pregnant by midshipman Robert Hood.[43]

The conflict between the Hudson's Bay Company and the North West Company may have made hiring of voyageurs more difficult than in other years. Colin Robertson's letter of June 1820 gives an outsider's view of the prospects and the personnel of the expedition: "This [is] a most unfortunate juncture for an undertaking of so much hazard, in particular as regards the selection of men, for altho' open hostilities have ceased, further than the apprehension of some notorious characters, still men of known fidelity accustomed to the manners and habits of the natives are so necessary in the present contest, that I fear the

Captain's [Franklin's] portion of good men bears no proportion to those of inferior character. He appears to be an amiable, gentlemanly man, and I regret the painful situation he is placed, from the strong party spirit that at present exists in this part of the country."[44]

Eleven voyageurs made up slightly more than half the party of twenty men who participated in the exploration of the arctic shores. They were of varying backgrounds. Antonio Vincenza Fontano was from Italy, Michel Teroahauté was an Iroquois Indian, and the remaining nine were French Canadians or Canadiens, spelled "Canadians" by Richardson. Contrary to Robertson's predictions, they proved to be capable travellers. These voyageurs risked their lives for a year's salary of £60 (1200 Halifax livres), roughly double the usual salary paid to voyageurs by the fur companies prior to 1818. The bowsmen and steersmen of each canoe received £80 (1600 Halifax livres). In comparison, fur company clerks, able to read and write, received £100 per year.[45]

On the Franklin expedition the voyageurs had to work harder, in worse weather, and in much greater danger than could be expected during regular fur trade duties. Normally they had to carry heavy loads of furs or trading goods on their backs over portages – Methy Portage between the Churchill and Athabasca river systems was thirteen miles long – but such carries, interspersed as they were with canoe travel, were child's play compared to the long overland hikes they made with Franklin. Each voyageur carried from 120 to 180 pounds between Fort Enterprise and Rocknest Lake, a distance of more than 117 statute miles, yet their party averaged better than two miles per hour. On 26 June the overburdened men were too fatigued to drag the third canoe, so left it on the shores of Point Lake.

After a week of hiking along the ice of Point Lake and Redrock Lake, the officers and men finally were able to begin their summer's travel. They launched the two remaining birchbark canoes on Rocknest Lake on 1 July 1821. The canoe completed at Fort Chipewyan on 2 July 1820 is known from Franklin's account to have been 32 feet, 6 inches long, up to 4 feet, 10 inches wide, and up to 1 foot, 11¼ inches deep. The main strength of its frame came from seventy-three cedar hoops. On this expedition each canoe carried ten men, their baggage, and twenty-five "pieces" of ninety pounds each. Even allowing for the pounds being Troy pounds, these were seventy-five-pound "pieces" with a total weight of 1875 avoirdupois pounds. With eight working paddlers and two officers in each canoe, the human cargo added an additional weight, close to 1500 pounds.

The voyageurs were in their element and happiest when paddling canoes on rivers and lakes. They enjoyed shooting rapids. Their experience, skill, and judgment enabled them to descend the unfamiliar and difficult rapids of the Coppermine without any loss of equipment or supplies.

On 14 July John Richardson was the first to climb a high hill; he thus became the fourth European to view the Arctic Ocean from the mainland of North America. Samuel Hearne had been at the mouth of the Coppermine in 1771, fifty years earlier. Alexander Mackenzie and a German named John Steinbruck had reached the mouth of the Mackenzie River in 1789.

Wentzel and four voyageurs, Parent, Forcier, Dumas, and Gagné, were dispatched on 19 July to carry the dispatches, books, instruments, and some specimens back to Slave Lake for transmission to England.[46] The rest of the party were to continue along the coast with Franklin, but not one of the Indians was willing to risk the journey along the arctic coast, in spite of Franklin's promises of large sums of money. All the hunters returned from the mouth of the Coppermine with Wentzel and the four voyageurs. They were wise, for Franklin was determined to explore the arctic coastline until he met Edward Parry's sailing ships or until he reached Repulse Bay, then the northernmost mapped site on the west coast of Hudson's Bay in longitude 86°15'. Repulse Bay was on the Arctic Circle about 750 miles to the east of the Coppermine, an unrealistic goal for a summer's travel in birchbark canoes.

Up to this point the expedition had travelled within territory familiar to their guides, where game was known to be plentiful at this time of year. They had been supported by Wentzel and by capable Indian hunters. They now set out on an unknown ocean in birchbark canoes. The most heroic and most tragic days were yet to come. The dramatic story can be followed in Richardson's words.

This Introduction serves as background information necessary for an understanding of Richardson's journal. My Commentary discusses in greater detail a number of the points raised in the journal and elaborates on the significance of Richardson's many contributions.

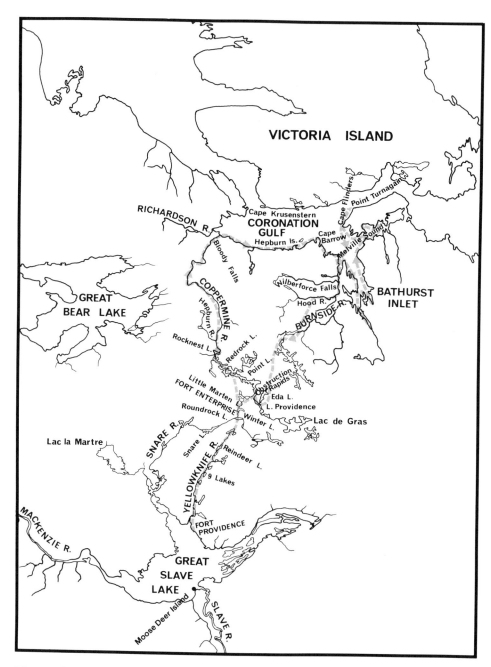

Map 1   *Great Slave Lake to Bathurst Inlet: general map of route*

Arctic Ordeal

THE JOURNAL OF JOHN RICHARDSON

SURGEON-NATURALIST WITH FRANKLIN

1820–1822

H. Albert Hochbaum
Fort Enterprise, N.W.T.
April 4, 1983

Site of Fort Enterprise, sketched from above the rapids at Winter Lake

1

FORT ENTERPRISE 1820

Monday August 21st 1820

A party was employed this morning in erecting a store-house. The spot chosen
for our intended Winter residence lies upon the sandy banks of Winter River,
here an inconsiderable stream by which Winter Lake discharges its waters into
Rock [Roundrock] Lake, a considerable body of water lying about three miles to
the South west. The banks of Winter River are ornamented with groves of the
white-spruce tree;[1] and flanked on each side by an irregular marshy plain, varying in breadth from one to three or four miles and somewhat broken by abrupt
elevations of coarse gravel and bounded by an amphitheatre of disconnected
hills. The summits of these hills are generally constituted[?] by a naked, smooth
rounded mass of gneiss rocks; their sides are very thinly covered with a loose
gravelly soil and often exhibit small mural precipices or more frequently
accumulations of large cubical stones; whilst near their bases there is often a thin
stratum of mountain peat, over which a few stunted black-spruce trees[2] are
thinly scattered.

   In every direction around us, there are lakes of various magnitudes;
indeed the bottoms of all the vallies are occupied by bodies of water, some of
them of considerable depth but which have little communication with each other
except during the floods produced in the spring by the melting snow. The sides
of the hills and all the drier spots of the vallies are clothed with a beautiful carpet
of those Lichens which form the favourite pasture of the Rein-deer.[3] It is composed principally of the *Cenomyce rangiferina, Cetraria nivalis* and *cucullata* and

1 *Picea glauca.*
2 *Picea mariana.*

3 Caribou, *Rangifer tarandus.* Throughout
Richardson's journal, "deer" refers to
caribou.

Cornicularia ochrileuca.[4] The principal shrubs are the *Vaccinium myrtilloides,*[5] *Empetrum nigrum,*[6] and *Ledum palustre,*[7] the dwarf birch[8] and a few willows.[9] The *Vaccinium vitus-idaea,*[10] *Arbutus uva-ursi*[11] and *alpina*[12] are very common and the *Andromeda polifolia*[13] and *Habenia glauca*[14] occur on almost every peaty spot. Several beautiful fish were taken today with the rod and artificial fly in a small rapid at the commencement of Winter River. They belong to a species of the genus *Salmo* ... [2½-page description of the "Blue Fish," which Richardson named Back's Grayling, *Coregonus signifer.*][15]

"The banks of Winter River ..."

4 Four species of lichen. *Cenomyce rangiferina* has been transferred to a different genus and is now *Cladonia rangiferina. Cornicularia ochrileuca* is now *Alectoria ochroleuca.*
5 Canada Blueberry.
6 Crowberry.
7 Labrador Tea, *Ledum decumbens,* used to make "country tea" or "Indian tea."
8 *Betula glandulosa* and the very similar *Betula nana.*
9 *Salix,* various species.
10 Mountain Cranberry.
11 Bearberry, *Arctostatphylos uva-ursi.*
12 Alpine Bearberry, *Arctostaphylos alpina.*
13 Bog Rosemary.
14 Possibly the White Orchid, *Habenaria dilatata.*
15 Arctic Grayling, *Thymallus arcticus.*

The stomach of this beautiful fish is generally filled with gravel or black earth. It bites eagerly at the artificial fly and deriving great power from its large dorsal fin, affords much sport to the angler. Its rectum is filled with black faeces. The ordinary length of the species is about 16 inches exclusive of the caudal fin, or about 12 inches from the snout to the anus. As an article of food it is inferior to the Attihhawmegh.[16]

Another fish closely resembling the preceding was caught at the same place. It is probably the young of the same species … The usual size of this fish is 8 inches … [1-page description of what Richardson correctly thought to be the young of the Grayling.]

Tuesday August 22^d 1820

Men employed in constructing the store house. Women splicing[17] and drying meat.

Saturday August 26th 1820

Akaicho and his hunters arrived today, having been sent for by Mr Franklin, to accompany the Expedition to the Coppermine River. They expressed so strong a dislike to the measure and urged the lateness of the season with so much positiveness, that dependant as we were upon their exertions for provision, it was deemed prudent to comply in some measure with their wishes and to modify the original plan of proceeding. Accordingly Mr F. decided upon sending M^{essrs} Back and Hood in a light canoe to ascertain the distance and size of the river, whilst the rest of the party remained behind to construct the buildings necessary for our winter's residence.

Monday[18] August 29th 1820

M^{essrs} Back and Hood set out this morning in a light canoe for the Coppermine River with 8 voyageurs and an Indian guide. They carried with them about 200 lbs. of dried Reindeer-flesh which had been prepared since the 20th. Akaicho returned to his hunting grounds.

---

16 Lake Whitefish, *Coregonus clupeaformis*.
17 Splicing the meat, "an operation that consists of cutting it into thin slices, and then exposing it to the sun or to the flame of a slow fire –

so as to thoroughly dry it – when it can be preserved for future use." George Back's journal, 5 July 1821.
18 Richardson's slip. It was Tuesday.

Abstract of the temperatures of the atmosphere for August 1820.

Extremes

Maximum (on the 21st day)	78°
Minimum (on the 28th and 30th days)	33
Least maximum (on the 26th day)	44
Greatest minimum (1st & 4th days)	64
Highest morning observation (4th & 7th)	65
Lowest morning observation (28th)	33
Highest evening observation (21st)	68
Lowest evening obs.[19] (30th)	33
Greatest range in 24 hours	69
Least range	10

Fair days	22	Clear days	14	Wind East of Mer.	15
Rain fell on	9	Cloudy days	17	West of Mer.	15
Thunder heard on	1				

Wednesday Septr 6th 1820

This evening we removed our tent to the summit of a hill three miles distant for the better observing of the eclipse of the sun calculated to occur tomorrow morning at sun-rise. Some snow fell in the afternoon, the evening was cold and we spent an uncomfortable night.

Thursday September 7th 1820 Fort Enterprise

A heavy snow storm having prevented us from observing the eclipse we struck the tent and returned to Fort Enterprise, the name given to our rising buildings.

Friday[20] September 9th 1820 Journey

Mr Franklin and I started this morning on a pedestrian excursion to the Coppermine River, under the guidance of an old Indian named Cascathry [Keskarrah] and accompanied by John Hepburn and Semandrè who carried our blankets, cooking utensils, hatchets, and a small supply of dried meat. Our guide led us from the top of one hill to the top of another, making as straight a course to the northward as the numerous lakes with which the country is intersected would permit. By noon we reached a remarkable hill with precipitous sides named by

19 In his weather tables, Richardson was inconsistent in his use of "ditto" and "do." Rather than confuse the reader I have consistently substituted, for example, "evening obs." for "ditto", in keeping with Richardson's intent.

20 It was Saturday, not Friday.

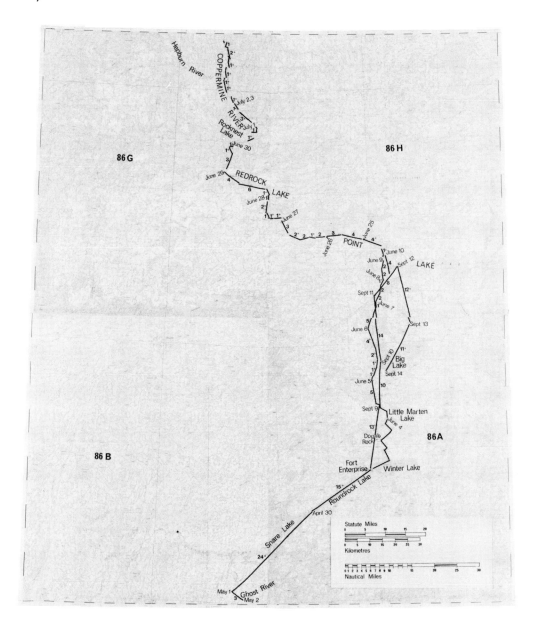

Map 2   *9–15 September 1820; 30 April–2 May 1821; 4 June–4 July 1821*

the Copper Indians Agnaatheh or the Dog-rib rock, and which M[r] F. ascertained by observation to be in Lat. 64°34′52″ north. Its longitude deduced from the Ch[r]. is 112°59′29″ w. The canoe course passes to the eastward of this rock, but we kept to the westward as being the more direct course. From the time we quitted the banks of Winter River we saw only a few detached clumps of trees, but after passing Dog-rib rock even these disappeared and we travelled through a naked country. In the course of the afternoon Cascathry killed a rein deer and loaded himself with its head and skin, and our men also carried off a few pounds of its flesh for supper, but their loads were already too great to permit them to take much additional weight. We halted for the night on the borders of a small lake which washed the base of a ridge of sand about three hundred feet high. There was a solitary and ancient pine[21] tree here which did not exceed 6 or 8 feet in height but whose branches spread themselves out for several yards, and we gladly cropped a few twigs to make a bed and protect us from the frozen ground still white from a fall of snow which took place in the afternoon. Thermometer at sunset 29° wind South-east. Our attendants having with some trouble grubbed up a sufficient quantity of the roots of the dwarf birch to make a fire, were enabled to prepare a comfortable supper of reindeer meat which we dispatched with the appetites which travelling in this country never fails to ensure. We then stretched ourselves out on the pine brush and covered by a single blanket each enjoyed a night of sound repose. The small quantity of bed clothes we carried induced us to sleep without undressing. Old Cascathry followed a different plan. He stripped himself to the skin and having toasted his body for a short time over the embers of the fire, he crept under his deer skin and rags previously spread out as smoothly as possible, and coiling himself up in a circular form, fell asleep instantly. This custom of undressing to the skin, even when lying in the open air is common to all the Indian tribes. Course NBE 13¾ miles.

Sunday September 10th 1820

Resuming our journey at day-break we pursued a northerly course, making occasional circuits however round the lakes that crossed our path. We had a bleak walk, as the day proved cold and snowy and our guide persisted in leading us over the summit of every hill that lay in our route. Cascathry having killed another deer to day attempted to carry its skin also, but soon found that the burthen was beyond his strength; he therefore spread this second skin upon a large stone until his return, making at the same time a small cache of deer's meat in its neighbourhood, that he might still farther reduce his load. We bivouacked

21 Spruce and Fir were at that time included in the genus, *Pinus*. Throughout Richardson's journal, "pine" refers to White Spruce or Black Spruce, and "cypres" refers to Jack-pine.

in the evening on the borders of a lake [Big Lake] in Lat. 61°51′45″[22] Long. 113°07′08″ West having come 10 miles in a Nth2° East course – our firewood proved still more scanty than on the preceding night, but the spot selected being dry and sandy, we slept comfortably.

Monday September 11th 1820

We set out early this morning and continued our march at a good pace. The small streams that we crossed during the two last days walk ran uniformly to the southward towards Winter Lake – but this morning after passing a remarkable sandy ridge, the course of the rivulets appeared more uncertain; they often ran towards the east or west and sometimes towards the north. We encamped in the evening in a marshy bottom, amongst a few dwarf pines and owing to the dampness of the ground passed a cold and comfortless night. Course and distance today N4°W. 14 miles. Lat. of Encampment 65°5′31″N. Long. 113°9′26″W. Fresh NNE breezes with snow during the night. Long. of enc^t corrected in the Spring 113°10′56″W.

Tuesday September 12th 1820

The morning proving foggy we had little opportunity of seeing the face of the country. The hills were steep and lay more in ridges than on the preceding days and there were fewer accumulations of sand than what we saw during yesterday's march. The country still seems however to belong to the gneiss formation. Our progress in the early part of the morning was slow and we were detained for two hours on the summit of a hill, exposed to a very cold wind, whilst our guide went in pursuit of some rein-deer. He was unsuccessful but after walking a few miles farther he pointed out the Copper mine River in the distance and we pushed forwards towards it with all the speed we were capable of. At noon we arrived at an arm of Point Lake an extensive expansion of the River. Lat. at noon 65°09′06″N. We continued our walk along the south end of the arm for about a mile farther and halted to break fast amidst a grove of pretty tall spruce trees. After this refreshment, we set out along the east side of the arm towards the main body of the lake, leaving Semandrè to prepare an encampment amongst the pines against our return. The main body of the lake runs nearly east and west and as far as we could gather from the Indians is about 50 miles long. At the spot where we approached it, it was upwards of [2] mile[s] in width,[23] apparently

22 Richardson's slip of the pen, whereby he wrote 61° in place of 64°, represented an error of three degrees of latitude or about 200 miles. The lake is now named Big Lake.

23 Richardson left the number blank. The lake was over a mile wide here, between opposing points, and in most places was much wider.

very deep with high and rocky banks. The numerous arms which spread from it on each side into the vallies between its bounding hills, give it a strong resemblance to the Missinippi or Churchill river. The temperature of its surface water was 41° that of the air being 42°. Long. & Lat. of this spot 65°13'12"N. 112°57'37" w. During our return to the encampment John Hepburn and Cascathry shot several Wavys (*Anas hyperborea*)[24] which afforded us a very seasonable supply our stock of provisions being exhausted. These birds were feeding in large flocks

Wavys feeding on crowberries

on the crowberries which grew plentifully on the sides of the hills. We reached our encampment after dark, found a comfortable hut prepared for our reception, made an excellent supper and retiring to bed enjoyed a night of sound repose. This part of the country seems to belong to the gneiss formation, but the hills are higher than those in the neighbourhood of Fort Enterprise. They stand however in the same detached manner, without forming connected ranges, and the bottom of every valley is occupied either by a small lake or a stoney marsh. On the borders of such of these lakes as communicate with the Coppermine river, there are a few groves of spruce trees, generally growing on accumulations of sand on the acclivities of the hills.

Wednesday September 13th 1820

It snowed hard during the night and the whole of the day was cold and disagre[e]able with much snow and sleet. We had a strong northerly gale and the Wavys, taking advantage of it, to quit this frozen land in search of a milder

24 Snow Geese, *Chen caerulescens*.

"… in search of a milder climate …"

climate flew over our heads in large flocks. We set out on our return to Fort
Enterprise about 10 a.m. & taking a route somewhat different from the one by
which we came, kept to the eastward of a chain of lakes. The thickness of the
atmosphere occasioned us to make frequent halts from the inability of our guide
to trace his way and ultimately compelled us to stop after a march of 12½ miles
on a s 13° East course. We encamped in lat. 64°57′50″ N., Long. 112°50′37″ W. on a
spot which afforded us plenty of dwarf birches, but they were so much frozen,
and the snow fell so thick that upwards of two hours were wasted in endeavouring to make a fire. Our efforts were at length crowned with success, and after a
good supper we laid or rather sat down to sleep for the nature of the ground
obliged us to pass the night in a demi-erect position with our backs against a
bank of earth.

Thursday September 14th 1820

After enjoying a more comfortable night's rest than we had expected we set off at
6 a.m. the thermometer then standing at 18°. An old sprain in the ankle has been
very troublesome to Mʳ Franklin for three days past. This morning it gave him
excessive pain and we got on but slowly. In the afternoon we rejoined our track
outwards and obtained a small supply of provision from Cascathry's cache. At
sun-set, we encamped amidst a number of sand hills in Lat. 64°47′40″ Long.
113°02′07″ having come 11¼ miles on a s. 26 West course.

Friday September 15th 1820

We started early this morning and pushed on as fast as we could for Fort Enterprise, our provisions being completely expended, and we arrived there soon
after sunset having walked 19 miles on a s 9° e. course.

M^{essrs} Back and Hood had returned from their excursion on the day
succeeding that on which we set out. They proceeded in the canoe a little beyond Dog-rib rock or to the NW end of Martin [Little Marten] lake when finding
the portages long and their Indian guide uncertain of the route by water, they
left the canoe altogether and performed the rest of the journey on foot. They fell
upon Point Lake a little to the eastward of where we saw it, spent several days in
tracing it and found that for 20 miles it lay nearly East and West with many deep
bays branching off from it. During our absence considerable progress has been
made in the erection of a winter house, it being now nearly roofed-in. It is
constructed like the other log houses of the country, of the rough stems of trees
rudely dovetailed into each other at the corners. Its length is 50 feet and breadth
24 and it is partitioned into a hall and three bed-rooms. The walls and roof have
to be covered with mud & the flooring is yet to be laid and the chimnies to be
built. In the mean time, we live in our tents, which are very cold habitations
although we maintain a good fire in front of them and have endeavoured to
shelter ourselves from the winds by a barricade of pine branches.

Saturday September 16th 1820 Fort Enterprise

A fishery has been established for some days in Winter Lake, but it has hitherto
been attended with little success. The fish caught are Trout,[25] Attihhawmegh,
Pike[26] and Methye.[27] The Rein-deer are now beginning to quit the barren ground
and to come into the vicinity of the house in their way to the woods, and we are
in consequence plentifully supplied with provisions by the Indian hunters.

Saturday September 30th 1820

The house being nearly ready for our reception, a heavy fall of rain took place
this morning and has washed the greatest part of the mud off the roof. An Indian
arrived from Akaicho today with a message that a party of Dog-ribs had plun-
dered a cache he had made of fat for our use.

---

25 Lake Trout, *Salvelinus namaycush*.
26 Northern Pike, *Esox lucius*.
27 Burbot, *Lota lota*.

Abstract of a register of Temperatures for September 1820. Fort Enterprise.

Extremes

Maximum (8th day)		53°
Minimum (26th)		16
Least Maximum		
Greatest Minimum		
Highest morning observation	13th	40°
Lowest morning obs.	17th	17
Highest evening obs.	8th	49
Lowest evening obs.	26th	16
Greatest range in 24 hours	17th	40
Least range	30th	05

Fair days   14 days   Clear days   8⅓   Wind easterly   15   Rain fell on   8
Hail   0   Snow   15 in all 16   Cloudy days   21⅔   Westerly   15

Sunday October 1st 1820

The following is a list of the Lichens that I have hitherto observed in the neighbourhood of Fort Enterprise.

1. *Arthonia gibberulosa*? Ach: lich. univ: p. 142. on the scaly bark of spruce trees.[28]
2. *Lecidea petraea*? *E. eccentrica.* Ach. p. 156. On rough pieces of gravel and decaying granite on the summits of hills.[29]
3. *L. lapicida y cicatricosa.* Ach. p. 159. In large patches on rolled masses of decaying granite, gneiss and mica slate.[30]
4. *L. atrovirens. a* and *y* Ach. p. 163. Very common, on granite.[31]
5. *L. tigillaris.* Ach. 164 Wahl. flor. Lapp. p. 463. On dry decaying wood.[32]
6. *L. albocaerulescens*? Ach. p. 189. In the fissures of rocks and on the shady-sides of stones.[33]
7. *L. icmadophila.* Ach. p. 191. On the drier lumps of turf in peaty marshes.[34]
8. *Gyrophora proboscidea.* Ach. p. 220[35]
9. *G. hyperborea*? an proboscidea var?[36]
10. *G. pensylvanica* Ach. p. 227[37]
11. *G. Muhlenbergii* Ach. p. 227[38]

Growing in consort. They cover the surfaces of most of the larger stones which strew the barren grounds, and are named *Tripe de Roche.*

28 *Melaspilea megalyna* (Ach.) Arn., perhaps an error in identification. Notes 28 through 64 have been supplied by John W. Thomson.
29 *Rhizocarpon petraeum* (Wulf.) Mass., but probably *Rhizocarpon grande* (Flörke) Arn., which is more common in the region but had not been differentiated in the 1820s.
30 *Lecidea fuscoatra* (Hoffm.) Ach.
31 a = *Rhizocarpon geographicum* (L.) DC; y =

32 *Cyphelium tigillare* (Ach.) Ach.
33 *Huilia flavocaerulescens* (Hornem) Hertel.
34 *Icmadophila ericetorum* (L.) Zahlbr.
35 *Umbilicaria proboscidea* (L.) Schrad.
36 *Umbilicaria hyperborea* (Ach.) Ach.
37 *Lasallia pensylvanica* (Hoffm.) Llano.
38 *Actinogyra mühlenbergii* (Ach.) Schol.

Rhizocarpon oederi (Web.) Körb.

12. *G. hirsuta.* Ach. p. 230. *Gyromium velleum* Wahl. Shady clefts of rocks.[39]
13. *Calicium chlorellum,* β *orachroium.* Wahl. p. 487. Ach. p. 235. on decaying dried wood.[40]
14. *Lecanora psoralis?* Ach. p. 376. on coarse gravel.[41]
15. *Lecanora subfusca.* Ach. p. 393. Wahl. p. 407. Admodum variat. On decaying wood, and on the scaly bark of the white spruce.[42]
16. *L. ventosa.* Ach. p. 399. On the sides of large stones in places that are overflowed by the spring floods.[43]
17. *L. rubina* β *heteromorpha* Ach. p. 412. On stones, in cracks and depressions; on rocks; and on the trunk and older branches of the white spruce.[44]
18. *L. ereutica* β *microcyclos.* Ach. p. 431. On stones.[45]
19. *Evernia prunastri?* Very defective specimens on the lower branches of old trees.[46]
20. *Parmelia olivacea.* Ach. p. 462. On the stems of the dwarf birch.[47]
21. *P. saxatilis.* Ach. p. 469. On stones and trees.[48]
22. *P. Fahlunensis.* Ach. p. 470. On stones.[49]
23. *P. caesia?* β *teretiuscula.* Ach. p. 479 *velrecurva?* p. 490. On stones and coarse gravel, also on decorticated and decaying wood.[50]
24. *P. conspersa?* γ *georgiana.* Ach. p. 487. Common on stones.[51]
25. *P. ambigua.* Ach. p. 485. On naked decaying wood and on the alder tree.[52]
26. *Cetraria juniperina* β *prunastri* Ach p. 506 Wahl. p. 432.[53] On the bark of decaying birches and stems of the *Betula nana.*
27. *C. sepincola.* Ach. p. 507. On the stems of the *Betula nana.*
28. *C. nivalis.* Ach. p. 510. On the ground. abundant.
29. *C. cucullata.* Ach. p. 511. On the ground. Abundant.
30. *C. islandica.* Ach. p. 512. On the ground in moist shady places.
31. *Cetraria?* an nova species? an odontellus? Wahl. p. 434. no root – lies loose on the ground.[54]
32. *Peltidia apthosa* β *verrucosa* Ach. p. 517. In moist places.[55]
33. *Nephroma polaris.* Ach. p. 521. In old rein deer tracks.[56]

39 *Umbilicaria vellea* (L.) Ach.
40 *Calicium trabinellum* Ach., but Richardson might have had *Mycocalicium subtile* (Pers.) Szat.
41 *Lecanora radiosa* (Hoffm.) Schaer, but that species is not North American. Richardson may have had *Lecanora muralis* (Schreb.) Rabenh.
42 *Lecanora subfusca* (L.) Ach. This is an aggregate of species. Based on the spruce bark habitat, Richardson may have had *Lecanora coilocarpa* (Ach.) Nyl.
43 *Haematomma lapponicum* Räs.
44 *Rhizoplaca chrysoleuca* (Sm.) Zopf.
45 *Acarospora molybdina* Wahlenb.
46 *Evernia mesomorpha* Nyl., since *E. prunastri* is not in that area.
47 Still known as *Parmelia olivacea* (L.) Ach., but *P. septentrionalis* is also possible.
48 Name unchanged for this species and for nos 27, 28, 29, 30, and 39.
49 *Cetraria commixta* (Nyl.) Th. Fr.
50 *Physcia caesia* (Hoffm.) Hampe.
51 Richardson probably had *Xanthoparmelia separata* (Th. Fr.) Hale.
52 *Parmeliopsis ambigua* (Wulf.) Nyl.
53 *Cetraria pinastri* (Scop.) S. Gray.
54 *Masonhalea richardsonii* (Hook.) Kärnef.
55 *Peltigera aphthosa* var. *leucophlebia* Nyl. (Acharius mentions the underside is veined.)
56 *Nephroma arcticum* (L.) Torss.

34. *Cenomyce pyxidata*. Ach. p. 534. On the ground.[57]
35. *C. coccifera*. Ach. p. 537. On the ground.[58]
36. *C. deformis*. Ach. p. 538. On the ground.[59]
37. *C. ecmocyna* δ *subulata* Ach. p. 550. β *aeomyces furcatus* Wahl. β *subulatus* p. 457. On the ground.[60]
38. *C. ecmocyna* γ? β *aeomyces gracilis*. Wahl. p. 455. On the ground.[61]
39. *Stereocaulon paschale*. Ach. p. 581. On the ground.
40. *Cornicularia ochroleuca*. Ach. p. 614. At the roots of bushes near the summits of hills. β *nigricans*? ditto[62]
41. *C. lanata*. Ach. p. 615. On stones – barren.[63]
42. *Dufourea* _____? On the ground. Not common.[64]

Friday October 6ᵗʰ 1820. Fort Enterprise

Today the house being completed, we struck the tents and took up our abode in it. It is, as has been already mentioned a log-building, the walls and roof are plastered with clay, the floors laid with planks rudely squared by the hatchet, and the windows closed with parchment of rein-deer skin. The clay froze as it was daubed on, and has since cracked in such a manner, that the wind rushes in from every quarter. Nevertheless with the aid of warm clothing, and good fires, we expect to get comfortably over the winter.

Monday October 9ᵗʰ 1820

Last night a thin film of ice formed across the river. The lakes are now firmly frozen over. We have been visited by several flocks of Snow-birds.[65]

The Rein-deer have been very numerous in this neighbourhood for 15 or 20 days past. Their horns, which in the middle of August were yet tender, have now attained their proper size and are beginning to lose their hairy covering which hangs from them in ragged filaments. The fat is at this season deposited to the depth of two inches or more on the rumps of the males and is beginning to get red and high flavoured, which is considered as an indication of the commencement of the rutting season. The horns of the Rein-deer vary not only with its sex and age, but are otherwise so uncertain in their growth that they are never alike in any two individuals. The females and young males have shorter

---

57 *Cladonia pyxidata* (L.) Hoffm.
58 *Cladonia coccifera* (L.) Willd.
59 *Cladonia deformis* (L.) Hoffm.
60 Probably *Cladonia gracilis* (L.) Willd. var. *gracilis*, an abundant species in the area.
61 Probably *Cladonia gracilis*, subspecies *turbinata* (Ach.) Ahti.

62 *Alectoria ochroleuca* (Hoffm.) Mass.
63 This name correctly applies to *Ephebe lanata* (L.) Vain., but I suspect that because Richardson says "on stones" he had *Pseudephebe pubescens* (L.) Choisy.
64 *Dactylina arctica* (Richards.) Nyl.
65 Snow Bunting, *Plectrophenax nivalis*.

and less palmated horns and generally want a broad plate which runs forward betwixt the eyes and hangs over the nose in the older males. This plate sometimes originates from the base of the right, sometimes from the left horn, and occassionally one arises from each. The old males shed their horns about the end of December. The females lose theirs, when the snow disappearing enables them to frequent the barren grounds, or about the middle or end of May. Soon after

"The horns of the Rein-deer ... are never alike ..."

this period they drop their young. The young males lose their horns about the same time with the females, or a little earlier, some of them as early as April. The hair of the Rein-deer falls in July and is succeeded by a short thick coat of mingled clove-, deep reddish-, and yellowish-browns; the belly and underparts of the neck &c. remaining white. As the winter approaches the hair becomes longer and lighter in its colours and it begins to loosen in May being then much worn on the sides from the animal rubbing itself against trees and stones. It becomes greyish and almost white before it is completely shed. The Indians form their robes of the skins procured in Autumn when the hair is short. Towards the spring the larvae of the oestrus attaining a large size, produce so many perforations in the skins that they are good for nothing. The cicatrices only of these holes are to be seen in August, but a fresh set of ova have in the mean time been deposited.

 The Rein-deer retire from the sea-coast in July and August, rut in October on the verge of the barren grounds and shelter themselves in the woods during the winter. They are often induced by a few fine days in the winter to pay a transitory visit to their favourite pastures in the barren country, but their principal movement to the northward commences generally in the end of April when the snow first begins to melt on the sides of the hills; and early in May when large patches of the ground are visible, they are on the banks of the Coppermine River. The females take the lead in this spring migration and bring forth their young on the sea-coast about the end of May or beginning of June. There are certain spots or passes well known to the Indians through which the deer invariably pass in their migrations to and from the coast, and it has been observed that they always travel against the wind. The principal food of the Rein-deer in the barren grounds consists of the *Cetraria nivalis* and *cucullata, Cenomyce rangiferina, Cornicularia ochrileuca,* and other lichens and they also eat the hay or dry grass which is found in the swamps in autumn. In the woods they feed on the different lichens which hang from the trees. They are accustomed to gnaw the fallen antlers of other deer and are said also to devour mice.

The weight of a full grown barren-ground deer,[66] exclusive of the offal, varies from 90 to 130 lbs. There is however a much larger kind[67] found in the woody parts of the country whose carcase weighs from 220 to 240 lbs. This kind never leaves the woods but its skin is as much perforated by the gad-fly[68] as that of the others, a presumptive proof that the smaller species are not driven to the sea-coast by the attacks of that insect. There are a few rein-deer occasionally killed in the spring whose skins are entire, and these are always fat, whereas the others are lean at that season. The gad-fly does not confine its attacks to the skin of the back, but deposites its ova also in the mucous membrane which lines the nostrils and fauces. This insect likewise infests the Red-deer (Wawaskeesh or Stag)[69] but its ova are not found in the skin of the Moose,[70] or Buffaloe,[71] nor as we have been informed in the Sheep[72] and Goat[73] that inhabit the rocky mountains, although the rein deer found in these parts (which by the way are of an unusually large kind) are as much tormented by them as the Barrenground variety. The herds of rein-deer are attended in their migrations by bands of wolves,[74] who destroy a great many of them.

The Copper Indians kill the rein-deer in the summer with the gun or taking advantage of a favourable disposition of the ground they enclose a herd upon a neck of land and drive them into a lake where they fall an easy prey; but in the rutting season and in the spring when they are numerous on the skirts of the woods they catch them in snares. The snares are simple nooses formed in a rope made of twisted sinew, which are placed in the apertures of a slight hedge constructed with the branches of trees. This hedge is disposed so as to form several winding compartments, and although it is by no means strong yet the deer seldom attempt to break through it. The herd is led into the labyrinth by two converging rows of poles and one is generally caught at each of the openings by

66 Barren-ground Caribou, subspecies *Rangifer tarandus groenlandicus.*
67 Woodland Caribou, subspecies *Rangifer tarandus caribou.*
68 Warble Fly, *Oedemagena tarandi.*
69 Wapiti or American Elk, *Cervus elaphus.*
70 Moose, *Alces alces.*
71 American Bison, *Bison bison.*
72 Bighorn Sheep, *Ovis canadensis.*
73 Mountain Goat, *Oreamnos americanus.*
74 Wolf, *Canis lupus.*

the noose placed there. The hunter too lying in ambush stabs some of them with his bayonnet as they pass by, and the whole herd frequently becomes his prey. Where wood is scarce a piece of turf turned up answers the purpose of a pole to conduct them towards the snares.

The Rein-deer has a quick eye, but the hunter by keeping to leeward and using a little caution may approach very near; their apprehensions being much more easily roused by the smell than the sight of any unusual object. Indeed their curiosity often causes them to come close up to and wheel around the hunter; thus affording him a good opportunity of singling out the fattest of the herd, and upon these occasions they often become so confused by the shouts and gestures of their enemy, that they run backwards and forwards with great rapidity but without the power of making their escape.

The Copper Indians find by experience that a white dress attracts them most readily, and they often succeed in bringing them within shot by kneeling and vibrating the gun from side to side in imitation of the motions of a deer's horns when he is in the act of rubbing his head against a stone.

The Dog-rib Indians have a mode of killing these animals which though very simple, is very successful. It was thus described to us by Mr Wentzel who resided long amongst that people.

The hunters go in pairs, the foremost man carrying in one hand the horns and part of the skin of the head of a deer, and in the other a small bundle of twigs against which he from time to time rubs the horns, imitating the gestures peculiar to the animal. His comrade follows, treading exactly in his footsteps and holding their two guns in a horizontal position so that the muzzles project under the arms of him who carries the head. Both hunters have a fillet of white skin round their foreheads and the foremost has a strip of the same kind round his wrists. They approach the deer by degrees, raising their legs very slowly but setting them down somewhat suddenly after the manner of a deer, and always taking care to lift their right or left feet simultaneously. If any of the herd leave off feeding to gaze upon this extraordinary phenomenon, it instantly stops and the head begins to play its part by licking its shoulders and performing other necessary movements. In this way the hunters attain the very centre of the herd, without exciting suspicion and have leisure to single out the fattest. The hind-most man then pushes forward his comrades gun, the head is dropped and they both fire nearly at the same instant. The herd scampers off, the hunters trot after them; in a short time the poor animals halt to ascertain the cause of their terror, their foes stop at the same instant and having loaded as they ran, greet the gazers with a second fatal discharge. The consternation of the deer increases, they run to and fro, in the utmost confusion, and sometimes the whole herd are destroyed within the space of a few hundred yards.[75]

75 This long account was quoted almost verbatim in Franklin, *Journey*, 243–4, and again by Richardson, *Fauna Boreali-Americana*, I: *Mammals*, now preceded by "Captain Franklin observes that..."

Wednesday October 18th 1820. Fort Enterprise

Messrs Back and Wentzel set out today for Fort Providence to make arrangements respecting supplies for next summer. They were accompanied by Beauparlant and Belanger and two Indian hunters with their wives. The small lakes have been frozen for a month past, but Winter River is as yet only partially covered with ice, and they were obliged to descend to Rock lake before they found a crossing place.

We have at present upwards of 100 deer in store, and about 800 lbs. of suet. The fishery which was carried on in Winter Lake in open water was interrupted about a week ago in consequence of the freezing of the lake. It has since been resumed, by setting the nets under the ice and it proves more productive than formerly.

Monday October 23d 1820. Fort Enterprise

A party of men sent to Akaicho's encampment on the South side of Winter Lake returned with 370 lbs. of dried meat and 220 lbs. of suet.

Thursday October 26th 1820

Akaicho and his party arrived at the house today. The deer having retired into the woods; the hunting in this neighbourhood is given up for the season.

Abstract of Temperatures for October 1820

Extremes

Maximum (1st, 18th & 19th)		37°
Minimum 15th		05°
Least maximum 29th		19°
Greatest minimum 2d		34°
Highest evening obs 3d		35°
Lowest evening obs.	14th and 22d	11°
Greatest range in 24h	18th	30°
Least range	2d	05°
Highest morning obs.	2d	34°
Lowest morning obs.	15th	05°

Fair days 18 days	Cloudy days 24⅓	Wind easterly 22⅓	
Rain fell on 3	Clear days 6⅔	westerly 7⅔	
Hail fell on 1	13 days		
Snow fell on 9			

Wednesday November 1st 1820 Fort Enterprise

The summer birds have now entirely disappeared and there remain for our winter companions, only, the Raven,[76] Cinereous Crow[77] and Ptarmigan.[78] Snowbirds and a very small bird of which we have obtained no specimens are occasional visitors.[79] The last of the water fowl that left us was a species of Colymbus ... caught in the nets about the beginning of October[80] ... [Richardson gives the first-ever description of the Yellow-billed Loon, *Gavia adamsii*, which because of its historical importance is reproduced in Appendix A.]

These birds return to this country about the end of May, make their nests of feathers on the margins of the lakes and lay two eggs.

Willow Ptarmigan in winter plumage

Yellow-billed Loon

76 Common Raven, *Corvus corax*.
77 Gray Jay, *Perisoreus canadensis*.
78 Throughout Richardson's journal the Willow Ptarmigan, *Lagopus lagopus* and the Rock Ptarmigan, *Lagopus mutus*, the smaller species that is present also in Europe, were referred to as "partridges."
79 Probably the Boreal Chickadee, *Parus hudsonicus*, but possibly the Common Redpoll, *Carduelis flammea*.
80 Yellow-billed Loon, *Gavia adamsii*.

Thursday November 16th 1820 Fort Enterprise

Winter River is now firmly frozen over, the small rapid at its commencement being all that remains open. The fishery failing, has been given up. Akaicho and his band still remain at the house and as they require rations, they encrease

Hawk-Owl

greatly the consumption of provisions. Our ball and small shot being entirely expended we are unable to equip them and send them off to their hunting grounds. The Rein-deer which had not been seen since the 26th of October made their appearance again in the neighbourhood of the house on the 12th of the present month and remained for a few days, but the want of ammunition hindered the Indians from going in pursuit of them.

Thursday November 23d 1820 Fort Enterprise

Belanger one of the voyageurs who accompanied Mr Back, returned today with letters. They had a tedious and fatiguing journey of sixteen days to Fort Providence and for the last week were nearly destitute of provision. In their way down, they killed a small owl ...[81] [1¼-page description of the Hawk-Owl]

81 Hawk-Owl, *Surnia ulula*.

November 28th 1820 Fort Enterprise

November 28th 1820 Fort Enterprise

Pierre St. Germain, the interpreter and 8 voyageurs set out this morning to bring up from Fort Providence such stores as Mr Back may be able to procure.

Abstract of Temperatures for November 1820

Extremes

Maximum 16th	$+25°$
Minimum 28th	$-31°$
Least maximum 27th	$-20°$
Greatest minimum 16th	$+18°$
Highest morning obs. 16th	$+20°$
Lowest morning obs. 28th	$-31°$
Highest evening obs. 16th	$+18°$
Lowest evening obs. 27th	$-26°$
Greatest range in 24 hours 28th	$25°$
Least range in 24 hours 4th	$4°$

Fair days 21   Cloudy days 19   Wind easterly 18¾
Snowy days 9   Clear days 11   westerly 11¼

Friday December 1st 1820 Fort Enterprise

Friday December 1st 1820 Fort Enterprise

Old Cascathry, the guide who accompanied us to the Coppermine River & has been residing at the Fort ever since, nursing his wife who is about to lose her nose by an ulcer made an offering today to the Water-spirit whose wrath he apprehends to be the cause of her malady. This offering consisted of an old knife, a small piece of tobacco, and some other trifling articles, made up into a packet and committed to the rapid with a long prayer.

Tuesday December 12th 1820 Fort Enterprise

Tuesday December 12th 1820 Fort Enterprise

We have frequently remarked, that in the cold clear nights the moisture of the breath freezes with a considerable crackling noise.

　　Akaicho with his young men and their wives left us today. We gave him a few balls which were brought from Fort Providence by Belanger. They have been a heavy drain upon our provisions during their residence at the house, and Akaicho's mother, together with Cascathry and family still remain as our guests and intend to do so all the winter.

Monday December 25th 1820

The male Rein-deer are now shedding their horns.

Abstract of Temperatures for December 1820

Extremes

Maximum 3^d day	+6°
Minimum 29th	−57°
Least maximum 29th	−52°
Greatest minimum 3^d	0°
Highest morning obs. 3^d	0°
Lowest morning obs. 29th	−52°
Highest evening obs. 3^d	+4°
Lowest evening obs. 29th	−57°
Greatest range in 24^h 21st	33°
Least range in 24 h	2°

Fair days   23   Cloudy days   11   Wind Easterly   10¾

Snowy days   8   Clear days   20   Westerly   20¼

Aurora visible on 28 nights

2

FORT ENTERPRISE: PREPARATION FOR DEPARTURE

Monday January 1st 1821 Fort Enterprise

The trees are now intensely frozen and so hard that all the large axes have given way except one. If this were to break also, we should be reduced to much distress from the want of firewood for the few small hatchets that we have remaining are quite unfit for cutting down a tree.

"The trees are now intensely frozen ..." Winter Lake, north-east shore

Friday January 5th 1821

This evening whilst we were at dinner old Cascathry came in for medicine for his wife. He received it and wrapped it up with such extraordinary carefulness that we could not help smiling at his gestures. This roused the old fellow's suspicions, and his wife afterwards fancying that it had not produced its wanted good effects, they came to the conclusion that I had intentionally given them some bad drugs. The whole night was spent in singing and groaning – next morning the whole family were crying in concert and it was not until the evening of the second day that we succeeded in pacifying them. The old woman then began to feel better and her faith in the efficacy of the medicine was renewed.

Monday January 8th 1821

Two hunters came from Akaicho to carry him a supply of ammunition when it arrives. Akaicho is encamped near Rein-deer Lake. Fine mild weather. Reindeer again seen in the neighbourhood of the house.

Monday January 15th 1821

Our men arrived from Fort Providence, with 2 kegs of rum, one barrel of powder, two rolls of tobacco, 60 lbs. of ball and some clothing. They have been 21 days on the march up and the labour they have undergone is sufficiently evinced by the collars of the sledges having worn out the shoulders of the coats. One [of] the rum kegs was broached on the way up and a considerable quantity abstracted.

Wednesday January 17th 1821 Fort Enterprise

The old male rein deer have all shed their horns.

Thursday January 25th 1821

Mr Wentzel, & Pierez St. Germain arrived from Slave Lake with two Eskimaux from Churchill, named Augustus and Junius or Tattanna and Haeootaerock. The former speaks English.

Abstract of Temperatures for January 1821

Extremes				
Maximum 7^(th) & 18^(th)	+20°			
Minimum 22^d	−49°			
Least maximum 1^(st)	−40°			
Greatest minimum 18^(th)	−2°			
Highest morning observation	+13°			
Lowest morning obs. 22^d	−49°			
Highest evening obs. 10^(th)	+12°			
Lowest evening obs. 31^(st)	−48°			
Greatest range in 24 hours	48°			
Least range in 24 hours	3°			
Fair days 21	Cloudy days 20⅔	Wind Easterly	14	
Snowy days 10	Clear days 10⅓		Westerly	17
Aurora visible on 18 days				

Monday February 5^(th) 1821

Two Indians came from Akaicho for a further supply of ammunition. Akaicho discontented with the small supply of ammunition we gave him before and displeased at not having rum sent to him. Sent him a keg of diluted spirits and some powder & shot.

Monday February 12^(th) 1821 Fort Enterprise

A party of six men was again dispatched to Fort Providence to bring up the remainder of the stores. Two hunters are to join them from Akaicho's band. Pierez St. Germain went to Akaicho now hunting to the southward and westward of the house.

On comparing the language of our two Eskimaux with a copy of St. John's gospel printed for the use of the Moravian missionary settlements on the Labrador coast, it appears that the Eskimaux who resort to Churchill speak a language essentially the same with those who frequent the Labrador coast. The Red-knives too recognize the expression *Teyma*[1] used by the Eskimaux when they accost strangers in a friendly manner, as similarly pronounced by Augustus and those of his race who frequent the mouth of the Coppermine River.

---

1 Teyma or taima in Inuktikut (Eskimo language) means "stop it" or "it is done." The somewhat similar sounding word that Richardson was trying to convey was "saimuk," sometimes rendered "chimo," which means "clasp hands." This merely described what Europeans did on first meeting – they came forward to shake hands.

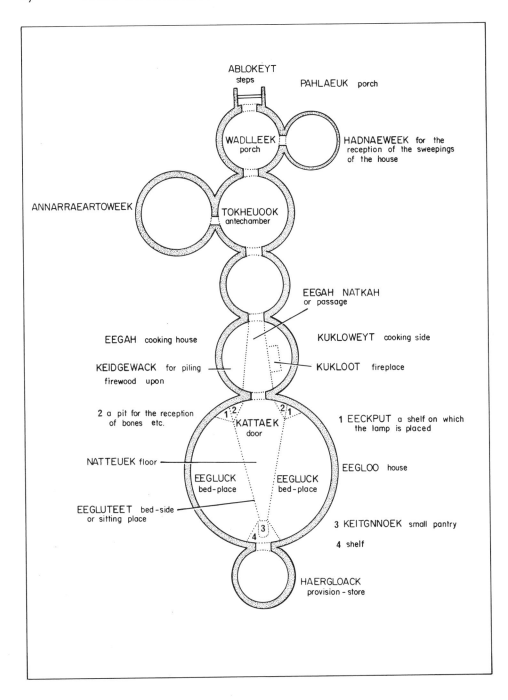

Plan of an igloo, based on a sketch by Dr Richardson

The tribe to which Augustus belongs, reside generally a little to the northward of Churchill. In the spring before the ice quits the shores they kill seal, but during winter they frequent the borders of the large lakes near the coast, where they obtain Rein-deer and Musk oxen. Augustus has never been farther north than Marble Island, but he says that Eskimaux from the Arctic sea come overland to trade with his tribe and that canoes can go to the country of these strangers by following the sea-coast. Some uncertainty exists however with respect to this northern sea and it may prove that he speaks of Chesterfield inlet which is nearly 200 miles deep.[2]

The winter habitations of the Eskimaux who visit Churchill are built of snow, and judging from one constructed by Augustus today they are very comfortable dwellings. Having selected a spot on the river, where the snow was about two feet deep, and sufficiently compact, they commenced by tracing out a circle, twelve feet in diameter. The snow in the interior of the circle was next divided with a broad knife having a long handle, into slabs three feet long, six inches thick and two feet deep, being the thickness of the layer of snow. These slabs were tenacious enough to admit of being moved about without breaking, or even losing the sharpness of their angles, and they had a slight degree of curvature, corresponding with that of the circle from which they were cut. They were piled upon each other, exactly like courses of hewn stone, around the circle which was traced out, and care was taken to smooth the beds of the different courses with the knife and to cut them so as to give the wall a slight inclination inwards, by which contrivance the building acquired the properties of a dome. The dome was closed somewhat suddenly and flatly by cutting the upper slabs in a wedge-form instead of the more rectangular shape of those below. The roof was about eight feet high and the last aperture was shut up by a small conical piece. The whole was built from within and each slab was cut so that it retained its position without requiring support until another was placed beside it; the lightness of the slabs greatly facilitating the operation. When the building was covered in, a little loose snow was thrown over it, to close up every chink and a low door was cut through the walls with the knife. A bed-place was next formed and neatly faced with slabs of snow, which were covered with a thin layer of pine branches to prevent them from melting by the heat of the body. At each end of the bed a pillar of snow was erected to place a lamp upon, and lastly a porch was built before the door and a piece of clear ice was placed in an aperture cut in the wall for a window.

The purity of the material of which the house was framed, the elegance of its construction and the translucency of its walls, which transmitted a very pleasant light gave it an appearance far superior to a marble building and one might survey it with feelings somewhat akin to those produced by the con-

2 Chesterfield Inlet is about 100 miles deep,
   though closer to 200 if one measures to the
   west end of Baker Lake.

templation of a Grecian temple reared by Phidias.[3] Both are triumphs of art inimitable in their kinds.

Annexed there is a plan of a complete Eskimaux snow-house with kitchen and other apartments,[4] copied from a sketch made by Augustus, with the names of the different places affixed. The only fire-place is in the kitchen, the heat of the lamp sufficing to keep the other apartments warm.

Wednesday February 14th 1821 Fort Enterprise

Several deer killed near the house. The men have been employed for some time past bringing in deer that were put in cache in the fall. More than half of the caches have been destroyed by the wolves and wolverenes.[5] Complaints from the Indians that M[r] Weekes the gentleman in charge of the Northwest post at Fort Providence has refused to pay M[r] Franklin's notes for goods –

Abstract of Temperatures for February 1821 Fort Enterprise

Extremes

Maximum 14th	+1°
Minima 2[d] & 3[d]	−51°
Least maximum 3[d]	−41°
Greatest minimum 16th	−12°
Highest morning obs. 14th	−7°
Lowest morning obs. 2[d], 3[d]	−51°
Highest evening obs.	−9°
Lowest evening obs.	−48°
Greatest range in 24 hours	41°
Least range	7°

Fair days 19	Cloudy days 13⅓	Wind Easterly 15½			
Snowy days 9	Clear days 14⅔	Westerly 12½			

March 4th 1821

The people returned from Fort Providence bringing a cask of flour, 36 lbs. of sugar, a roll of tobacco and 40 lbs. of ball. M[r] Franklin received a letter from M[r]

---

3 Phidias, perhaps the greatest sculptor of all time, famous for his statues of *Zeus* and *Athene*, also designed the Parthenon. He lived in the age of Pericles.

4 This complex and elongated igloo design has one more circle than the diagram in Franklin, *Journey*, p. 267. Augustus probably made his plan more sophisticated to please his enquirer, Dr Richardson. Spellings are not in accord with modern orthographical convention which would render "iglu" and "iglirq" in place of "eegloo" and "eegluck" (Professor Robert Williamson).

5 Wolverine, *Gulo gulo*.

Weekes denying that he had refused to pay any notes and asserting that Akaicho wished to leave us and had sent him a message to that effect. Pierez arrived soon afterwards and informed us that he left Akaicho in excellent humour.

March 12th 1821

Sent 4 men to Fort Providence for stores.

March 17th 1821

Mr Back arrived from Fort Chepewyan having performed since he left us a journey of nearly one thousand miles on foot.

March 23d 1821

Two Indians belonging to the band under the Hook and Long-legs brought a message from these Chiefs importing that if Mr Franklin sent them a supply of ammunition they would meet us in the summer on the banks of the Copper-mine river and bring provisions. Mr F. agreed to pay them for their provisions but could not spare them any ammunition.

St. Germain and Adam our Interpreters evince great apprehensions respecting the dangers of a sea voyage, and pretend that they engaged only to accompany us as long as the Indians remain with us. Suspect that St. Germain has endeavoured to prevent Akaicho from furnishing us with dried meat, that the want of provisions may put a stop to our journey. He was questioned today on this head, and stoutly denied the main charge but confessed that he had said some things to our prejudice.

March 30th 1821 Fort Enterprise

Akaicho arrived. He denied ever having any intention of leaving us.

March 31st 1821

Akaicho went away. Augustus accompanied him by invitation.

Abstract of Temperatures for March 1821

Extremes

Maximum 31st	+24°
Minimum 1st	−49°
Least maximum 1st	−26°
Highest minimum 30th	+8°
Highest morning obs. 31st	+10°
Lowest morning obs. 1st	−49°
Highest evening obs. 31st	+12°
Lowest evening obs. 13th	−36°
Greatest range in 24 hours 11th	64°
Least range in 24 hours	24°

Fair days 22   Cloudy days   12⅓   Wind Easterly   15¾
Snowy days 9   Clear days   18⅔   Westerly   15¼
Aurora visible on 24 nights

April 4th 1821 Fort Enterprise

The 4 men arrived with the remainder of the stores from Fort Providence.
        For some days past, the weather has been very fine, a considerable thaw has taken place and the rein-deer have appeared in numbers in the vicinity of the house. The new horns of the old males already make some show, but the young males and the females still carry their last year's horns.

April 17th 1821

The two Belangers set out for Fort Providence with letters. Same day Connoyer was discharged on account of ill health[6] and went down accompanied by an Indian named the Belly.

April 20th 1821

The fine weather in the beginning of the month and the consequent movement of the rein deer to the northward having induced the Indians to believe that the spring was commencing many of them have quitted the woods and set their snares in the neighbourhood of the house. Two or three days of cold weather,

6 Connoyer suffered biliary colic from gall-stones.

have however damped their hopes, the deer have gone to the southward again, and they now say that another moon must elapse before the wished for season commences. In the mean time they are suffering from the want of food, in consequence of their premature departure from the woods. Our fresh meat is all expended and we are now consuming the pounded meat that was laid up for our summer stock. During the winter we have occassionally obtained some varying hares and in the present scarcity of provisions they are still more sought after.

Their down is already beginning to fall off, and their rutting season is commencing. This Hare appears to be the same or nearly the same with the *Lepus variabilis* Cuv. reg. anim. p. 210.[7] It is not found in wooded districts, but frequents the barren grounds and it is said the Rocky Mountains on Mackenzie's River. It keeps principally on the dry acclivities and summits of the hills in this neighbourhood, sheltering itself under large stones and in the natural cavities of rocks, but without digging holes for itself. It eats the dried grass or hay, which is easily obtained, even in winter as the snow is drifted off from the elevated situations it resorts to; and it is also fond of the bark of the dwarf birch and of the berries of the *Arbutus alpina* which adhere to the parent plants all the winter.

As this animal is of an uniform white colour except the tips of the ears which are black, its dimensions are almost the only circumstances that require to be mentioned in a description of it. It rests like the common rabbit on the whole length of the hind leg but it walks on the toes, so that the hind and fore feet make nearly similar oval prints on the snow. The fur of its winter coat is about 2½ inches long and the skin is so extremely tender that it can scarcely be taken off entire. ... Height of the animal behind when in a sitting position, resting on the hind soles and fore paws 17½ inches. Height at the fore-shoulder when in the same position 16 inches.

The varying hare, according to the Indians brings forth only once a year and the number of its young varies from two to four. Its fur becomes white in October.

Le lapin d'Amerique Cuv. p. 211[8] which is so common about Cumberland is rarely seen in this neighbourhood and when it is found, is not above half the size of the varying hare.

The common Mouse of this country[9] belongs to the subdivision *Campagnols* Cuv. and is the same or nearly allied to the *Mus oeconomicus* (Pall.) Reg.

7 Arctic Hare, *Lepus arcticus*. Richardson throughout his journal calls this the Varying Hare or Alpine Hare but it is larger and heavier than the Blue Hare, *Lepus timidus* of the Scottish highlands and Sweden, with longer ears and more intensely black tips, which also turns white in winter. Contrary to Richardson's second-hand information, the Arctic Hare does not range west of the Mackenzie River. Cuv. Reg Anim, often only Cuv. or Cuv. Reg An, refers to the French edition of Cuvier, *Règne Animal*.

8 Snowshoe Hare, *Lepus americanus*. In North America, this species is sometimes called the Varying Hare. Richardson consistently calls it the American Hare.

9 Meadow Vole, *Microtus pennsylvanicus*. Richardson notes similarities to the common meadow mouse in Europe, then called *Mus oeconomicus*.

an. p. 193. It shows a strong inclination to domesticate itself, many of them already frequenting the house. They steal fat and make hoards of it. In general shape and appearance it strongly resembles the European domestic mouse, but is a little larger, and has a broader back. [2-page description of the Meadow Vole, *Microtus pennsylvanicus*]

April 22ᵈ 1821 Fort Enterprise

A moose deer having been killed by one of our hunters about 50 miles to the SW, Pierez St. Germain went for it with a dog sledge and returned today.

April 27ᵗʰ 1821

Our dried meat being all expended, we had nothing to eat today. During the night however a deer was brought in which had been killed by old Cascathry. Our men suffer much from Snow blindness. Ice on the lakes about 7 feet thick.

April 28ᵗʰ 1821

Mr. Wentzel and Pierez went to visit Akaicho.

April 30ᵗʰ 1821

The two Belangers returned from Fort Providence having been only 5 days on the march. The Belly who accompanied Connoyer and who had received a note upon Mʳ Weekes for some ammunition in consideration of that service complains that it was not paid. The circumstance has induced the Indians to believe that we wish to deceive them, and that their rewards will be witheld.

Abstract of Temperatures for April 1821

Extremes

Maximum 1ˢᵗ	$+40°$
Minimum 15ᵗʰ	$-32°$
Least maximum 15ᵗʰ	$-14°$
Highest minimum 1ˢᵗ	$+15°$
Highest morning obs. 1ˢᵗ	$+30°$
Lowest morning obs. 8ᵗʰ	$-20°$
Highest evening obs. 2ᵈ	$+19°$

Lowest evening obs. 15th	$-24°$	
Greatest range in 24 h 19th	$71°$	
Least range in 24 h	$22°$	
Fair days 19 Cloudy days 17	Wind Easterly	18
Snowy days 11 Clear days 13	Westerly	12

April 30th 1821

This morning I set off to visit Akaicho's encampment, in company with three men going for meat. We started at 9 a.m., and after descending Winter River and passing through a long narrow lake, termed by the natives Round Rock lake, entered Snare-lake and encamped at a Deer-pound formed this season by Akaicho. Our course and distance from the house was s 55° w, 15½ miles.

May 1st 1821

Set out at 4 a.m. and continuing our course down the lake passed the enclosures of the deer-pound, which are extensive and calculated for 80 snares. The rows of branches stuck in the snow to conduct the deer into the pound extended for two miles upon the lake. After leaving Snare-lake which is about 15½ miles long and from one to three broad, we fell upon a chain of small detached lakes surrounded by broken and well wooded hills. The ground was in general marshy, and the trees were birch[10] and black spruce. On one or two sandy hills however the white spruce grew to a larger size than we had before found it to the northward of Slave lake. The whole country belongs to the gneiss formation but the mural precipices were more frequent here than nearer Fort Enterprise. In the afternoon we arrived at an encampm[t] which Akaicho had left two days ago. There was a considerable cache of meat here. Course and distance to day s 44° w. 24½ miles.

May 2[d] 1821

Leaving the men to return to the fort with meat I followed Akaicho's trail and arrived at his encampment after walking about three miles s 54° E course.[11]

I found 7 or 8 hunters with their families living in the same tent with Akaicho. The most honourable place in the tent that is the farthest from the door was reserved for the leader and never invaded by any of the others except in his

10 Perhaps the larger Water Birch, *Betula fontin-alis* or the Alaska Birch, *Betula papyrifera neo-alaskana*.

11 This camp was about three miles south of the Ghost River and about eight miles west of Wecho Lake, at 64°00′ N, 114°10′ W.

absence. Several orphans and old people were residing with him, dependants on his bounty. Their diet was the same with that of the others and they were not badly clothed.

May 3ᵈ 1821

One of the hunters shot two birds of the genus *Falco* today. They are spring visitors and were when killed in the act of building their nest. Their skins were turned inside out and dried before I saw them, for the purpose of being sewed up in a pillow as a remedy for the headache ... It is about the size of a sparrow hawk, preys on partridges and quits this country in the winter. Buteo lagopus?[12] [7-line description of the Rough-legged Hawk]

May 4ᵗʰ 1821

One of the Indians brought in today a bird termed by the voyageurs Le perdrix du savanne.[13] Its plumage was much damaged, but as it was the first specimen of the kind I had seen in the country the following description was taken of it. [1-page description of the Spruce Grouse]
    The claws are long, awl-shaped and channelled beneath. This form of the claw shows that the Swamp partridge leads a different life from the Ptarmigan whose claws are excellently adapted for making excavations in the snow, but not for resting on trees. Its length is 15½ inches. The specimen was a cock. The hen is said to be more grey but to have a red eyelid also. They feed on the leaves of pine; the cyprès of the Canadians a species of *Pinus* being their favourite food.[14] The crop of the individual here described was filled with the leaves of the black spruce. This bird appears to be La Gelinotte noir Cuv. reg. an. p. 449.
    The small black woodpecker with four toes[15] is common in woods about the encampment, and there is another small bird called by the voyageurs Messange[16] which is also said to winter here but I did not obtain specimens of either.
    The Cinereous crow is very busy at present carrying food to its young, which according to the Indians will come abroad towards the end of the present month. These birds have much the manners of the English Magpies,[17]

12 Rough-legged Hawk, *Buteo lagopus*. It is somewhat larger than the Sparrow Hawk, *Accipiter nisus* of Europe, which in turn is larger than the American Kestrel, *Falco sparverius*, formerly known as Sparrow Hawk.
13 Spruce Grouse, *Dendragapus canadensis*.
14 Jack-pine, *Pinus banksiana*.
15 Either the Downy Woodpecker, *Picoides pubescens* or the Hairy Woodpecker, *Picoides villosus*.
16 Boreal Chickadee, *Parus hudsonicus*.
17 Magpie, *Pica pica*. The Gray Jay lays its eggs during −40° winter temperatures.

are very familiar but very cunning, and it is remarkable that though they are often watched when they carry away food, yet their nests have never been discovered by any of the Indians. Their winter hoards, however, are frequently found in the hollows of old trees or between the layers of the bark of decayed birches. These hoards contain berries and such pieces of animal food as they are able to pick up.

"The snow has melted upon the summit of some of the hills"

The hills adjoining to our present encampment consist of gneiss, very generally stratified in the saddle form.

The American hare is common here and its down is already becoming grey. The varying hare so plentiful on the barren hills about Fort Enterprise is not found here.

The trees have thawed and the sap is beginning to flow.

May 5th 1821

Today a party of men arrived from the fort for meat and as soon as the evening frost commenced I set off with them on my return. We travelled all night and as there was but little frost the sledges sunk deep in the snow, and the labour was great. The snow has nearly melted away upon the summit of some of the hills and in the swamps the low bushes are appearing, in consequence of which the difficulty of dragging the sledges is much increased. The twilight lasts the whole night. Course and distance today [not completed]

May 6th 1821

I set off in the evening, leaving the men to come on at leisure with their heavy sledges, and walking all night arrived at the Fort to break fast on the morning of the 7th. Course and distance [not completed]

     The White partridges are now very numerous and are flying and calling all night. They have lost almost all the feathers from their necks, which is the first part of their plumage that begins to change. There are two species or varieties of the White partridge, the smaller of the two frequenting the barren grounds in summer but going towards the south in winter. [½-page description of the larger of the two species of ptarmigan, the Willow Ptarmigan, *Lagopus lagopus*, a male killed on 14 April]

May 7th 1821

Large patches of ground visible on the sides of hills and other spots where the snow lay thinly. Men arrived with meat.

Willow Ptarmigan male in spring moult

May 8th 1821

A Fly seen. A party of men sent off again for meat and the women also sent to live at Akaicho's encampment to diminish the consumption at the Fort.

May 9th 1821

Mergansers seen.[18] Rein deer approaching the house.

May 10th 1821

Two gulls seen.[19] The berries of the *Vaccinium vitis idaea, Empetrum nigrum* and *Arbutus alpina* which have been covered and protected by the snow all the winter may now be gathered plentifully. The ground continues frozen, but the snow thaws rapidly in the sun-shine and many of the musci are beginning to sprout. The calyptrae of some *Jungermanniae*[20] are already visible. Considerable portions of the river broken up. The average temperature for the last ten days obtained by taking the means of the extremes is +31°75″ F.

The nets have been set since the beginning of the month but the success has been trifling. A few Methys and common trout have been caught together with a species of *Salmo* that is new to us. In Eskimaux its appellation is okeugnak by the Copper Indians it is termed Kathieh and our voyageurs have named it the Round fish.[21] [2-page description of the Round Whitefish]

This fish spawns in September. It preys on small insects.

May 11th 1821

Loons (*Colymbi*) seen today.[22]

Description of a bird of the genus *Falco* killed in Septr 1820,[23] omitted to be inserted before. It is said to remain in this country all the winter and to prey on the White Partridge. [1-page description of a Northern Goshawk]

---

18 Probably the Red-breasted Merganser, *Mergus serrator*.
19 Probably the Herring Gull, *Larus argentatus*.
20 Leafy liverworts.

21 Round Whitefish, *Prosopium cylindraceum*.
22 All four species of loon may occur here.
23 Northern Goshawk, *Accipiter gentilis*

May 18th 1821

Yesterday several ducks alighted in the rapid above the Fort, one of which being procured today proved to be a Drake of the species named by Cuvier Reg. An. p. 539 La petite Sarcelle.[24] [1½-page description of a Green-winged Teal]

May 20th 1821

The weather for the last ten days has been disagre[e]ably cold and blowing. The mean of the extreme temperatures being only 26°55″ F. The arrival of the summer birds however shows that the fine weather has set in to the southward – and we have been informed by an Indian who arrived a few days ago from Fort Providence that the snow had entirely disappeared in the neighbourhood of that post before the tenth of the month. The cold weather we have experienced proceeds from northerly winds. Except the bursting of the willow catkins there is no appearance of vegetation as yet.

May 21th 1821

A goose seen today.

May 22d 1821

Description of a Goose killed today. It is denominated by the Canadian voyageurs L'outarde and is the largest species of goose that frequents this country. *Anas Canadensis* – Le cravant. Cuv. regn. an.[25] [9-line description of the Canada Goose]

Many of these Cravants, a few white Geese, numerous flocks of Ducks and some Swans have passed today. They are all pretty fat. The most common duck that has arrived is the *Anas acuta* – Le Pilot Cuv. reg. anim.[26] [2-page description of the Pintail] *Anas hyperborea* – White goose – L'oie de neige.[27] Cuv. reg. an. p. 531. Wawee (Knisteneaux) Kangokh (Eskimaux) [5-line description of the Snow Goose] Larus? Cuv. reg. an.[28] [8-line description of the Mew Gull]

24 Green-winged Teal, *Anas crecca*.
25 Canada Goose, *Branta canadensis*.
26 Northern Pintail, *Anas acuta*.
27 Snow Goose, *Chen caerulescens*.
28 Mew Gull, *Larus canus*. This antedated by five years the "type specimen" of *Larus canus brachyrhynchus*, collected on 23 May 1826 at Great Bear Lake and described by Richardson.

Akaicho arrived today and was received according to his stipulation with a salute of several fowling pieces and the ensign flying at the flag staff. In a conference which took place in the afternoon he complained much of the treatment he had received from us and enumerated many grounds of dissatisfaction, the principal of which were the non-payment of Mr Franklin's notes by Mr Weekes from whence he apprehended that his own reward would be withheld; our want of attention to him as a chief, the weakness of the rum sent to him, the smallness of the present now offered to him and the want of a chief's clothing which he had been accustomed to receive at Fort Providence every spring and he concluded by refusing to accept of the rum and goods now offered to him. In reply to these complaints it was stated that Mr. Weekes's conduct could not be properly

Green-winged Teal drake in spring plumage

discussed at the distance we were from his fort, that no dependence might be placed in the vague reports that floated through the Indian territory, that for our part although we had heard many stories to his (Akaicho's) disadvantage we discredited them all; that the rum we had sent him being what the great men in England were accustomed to drink, was of a milder kind, but in fact stronger than what he had been accustomed to receive; and that the distance we had come and the speed with which we travelled, precluded us from bringing in large quantities of goods like the traders; that this had been fully explained to him when he agreed to accompany us and that in consideration of his not receiving his usual spring outfit his debts to the Company had been cancelled and a present much greater than any he had ever received before ordered to be got ready for his return. He was further informed that we were much disappointed in not receiving any dried meat from him, an article indispensable for our summer voyage and which he had led us to believe there was no difficulty in procuring and that in fact his complaints were so groundless in comparison with the real injury we sustained from the want of supplies that we were led to believe they were preferred solely for the purpose of cloaking his own want of attention to the terms of his engagement. He then shifted his ground and stated that if we attempted to make a voyage along the sea coast we would inevitably perish and he advised us strongly against persisting in the attempt. This part of his harangue being an exact transcript of the sentiments formerly expressed by our Interpreters induced us to conclude that they had prompted his present line of conduct by telling him that we had goods or rum concealed. And in fact he received a portion of our dinner in the manner he had been accustomed to do and seemed inclined to make up matters with us in the course of the evening provided we added to the present offered to him. Being told however that this was impossible since we had already offered him all the rum we had and every article of goods we could spare from our own equipment his obstinacy was a little shaken and he made some concessions but finally deferred giving a final answer until the arrival of Humpy his elder brother. The young men however did not choose to wait so long and at night came for the rum which we judged to be a considerable step towards a reconciliation.

May 23ᵈ 1821

Akaicho being, as he said, ashamed to show himself kept close in his tent all day. St. Germain the most intelligent of our two interpreters and the one who has most influence with the Indians being informed that their defection would be laid solely to his charge, and being threatened with punishment if evil conse-quences ensued exerted himself very much today in bringing about a change in their sentiments. It must be confessed however that the leader [Akaicho] alone appears to be seriously displeased, the rest although they decline hunting con-duct themselves in other respects with the same good humour and freedom as formerly.

May 24ᵗʰ 1821

Box one of our women went away to Fort Providence under the charge of an Old Chief who came here some days ago for medicine for his eyes. The other two women who have families prefer accompanying the Indians during their summer hunt.

Akaicho came to the house today and appeared inclined to be friendly with us, but vented his ill humour in a quarrel with Augustus about a gun.

May 25th 1821

Humpy the Leader's elder brother, White Capot [Annoethai-yazzeh] another of his brothers and one of our Guides arrived with the remainder of Akaicho's band as also Long legs brother to the Hook with three of his band. We had another formidable conference in the evening, the former complaints were reiterated and we parted about midnight without coming to any satisfactory conclusion. Humpy and the White Capot however censured their Brother's conduct. There are at present in the Indian encampment 30 hunters, 31 women and 60 children in all 121 Indians of the Red-knife or Copper nation. The rest of the nation are with the Hook on the Coppermine River, on the portages leading to Great Bear Lake.

May 26th 1821

More angry conversations with Akaicho, he still refuses to accept of the offered present. Pierez however has been busy amongst the young men and has shaken the leader's authority which was shown in the evening by their accepting of the goods set apart for them and each of them seperately declaring that they would accompany us to the sea whether Akaicho went or not.

May 27th 1821

The hunters being supplied with ammunition went out and killed three deer today, part of which we got. They expend great part of their ammunition on ducks and geese.

May 29th 1821

Akaicho finding his power on the wane, now courts our favour with an abjectness that we did not expect from him. He has taken the goods alledging when he took them that he was now convinced we had nothing in reserve. Five deer brought in. Men employed repairing the canoes.

Description of a Plover killed today.[29] Genus *Charadrius* subd. Les Oedicnemes Cuv. Reg. Anim. [1-page description of the Lesser Golden-Plover]

---

29 Lesser Golden-Plover, *Pluvialis dominica.*

May 31st 1821

Average temperature for the last eleven days 36°50″ F.

Abstract of Temperatures for May 1821

Extremes

Maximum 28th	68°
Minimum 15th	8°
Least maximum 11th	26°
Greatest minimum 28th	35°
Highest morning observ[n] 4th	52°
Lowest morning obs. 11th	20°
Highest evening obs. 28th	43°
Lowest evening obs. 19th	12
Greatest range in 24 hours	75°
Least range	23°

Fair days   23   Cloudy days   20⅔   Wind Easterly 24
Snowy days   6   Clear days   10⅓   Westerly   7
Rainy days   7   Foggy days   4

The following tables constructed in imitation of those given by Wahlenberg in his Flora Lapponica are too simple to require an explanation.

		1819	1820
	Med ex maximis	+38° 04″	+23° 41″
Autumno (mens. IX, X, XI)	minimis	+28 28	+14 30
[Autumn]	differentia	10 76	09 11

		1819–1820	1820–1821
	Med ex maximis	+02° 20″	−17 95
Hyeme (mens. XII, I, II)	minimis	−09 41	−28 62
[Winter]	differentia	11 61	10 67

		1820	1821
	Med ex maximis	+41° 49″	+19 39
Vere (mens. III, IV, V)	minimis	+23 25	−03 09
[Spring]	differentia	17 24	22 48

		1820	1821
	Med ex maximis	+66° 53	
Aestate (mens. VI, VII, VIII)	minimis	+51 38	
[Summer]	differentia	15 15	

The register of Temperatures for the remainder of this year being lost by the canoe oversetting, the temps. for July & August last year are given and hence the means for the year at Fort Enterprise may be deduced.

Tabeola methoda Wahlenbergii constructa

3

ON SNOWSHOES TO ROCKNEST LAKE

June 4th 1821

The snow having melted and run off the lakes in this neighbourhood and most of the elevated grounds being clear, the Indians have been urged for some days past to set out for the Coppermine river and collect provisions there for us, but they have evaded our request under various pretences and it is evident that they linger about the house in the hope of picking up such articles as we may deem unnecessary to take with us. Mr Franklin therefore determined on dispatching all the stores and baggage of the Expedition to Point Lake without further delay, and everything being ready I took charge of the party, and we left the Fort at 4 O clock this morning. I had 15 voyageurs with me, three of them conducting dog-sledges, seven dragging their own sledges, and the remaining 5 carrying their burdens on their backs.

The average load of each individual was about 80 lbs. exclusive of his personal baggage which might be rated at 40 lbs. more. The dog-sledges were doubly loaded. These loads consisted of two bags of pemmican and 5 bags of fat 80 lbs. each, of 80 lbs. of dried meat, a cask of portable soup, a box of arrow root, 64 lbs. of gunpowder, 68 lbs. of shot and ball, a bale of presents for the Eskim-aux, and a large quantity of ice chisels and hatchets and other articles of iron for the same people – besides 7 nets, a considerable quantity of line, the sails and other things necessary for the equipment of the canoes and two tents. Two Indian hunters, Bald-head and Basil were appointed to attend us. The former was accompanied by his wife, so that the party consisted in all of 19. We set off in high spirits, passed through Winter lake across several small lakes which Winter River forms in its course from Marten lake and along the banks of this stream where through the rapidity of the current the ice had broken up. These portages were very troublesome to those who had sledges, as they were obliged to make two trips with their loads, yet the party advanced at the rate of two miles an hour including rests. We entered Marten Lake about noon, and every one being fatigued would have put up soon after, but continued to walk on in hopes of falling in with some brush wood to make a fire with. Our search after wood however proving inefectual and some of the party becoming too tired to proceed any further we were compelled to bivouack on the exposed side of a hill, the only spot clear of snow, for although we were not more than 16 miles to the north-ward of the Fort, yet the season appeared to be at least a week later – one of the hunters who dropt behind killed a deer and part of it was brought in by a man who remained with him; the rest was put in a cache. Soon after we halted a sick Indian, Little foot[1] and his wife arrived together with Angelique and Roulante by which our party was encreased to 23. The two latter had stolen from the Fort without the knowledge of Mr Franklin as it was intended that they should accompany the Indians to diminish the consumption of provisions with our party. The want of fuel prevented our voyageurs from eating, and sleep their only resource under such circumstances being driven away by the extreme cold of the night they passed their time miserably enough.

June 5th 1821

Set off early in the morning in search of wood, and after travelling 4 or 5 miles on [the ice of] Marten lake, quitted it about a mile to the westward of the spot where the autumn party left their canoe and passing for about 5 miles over a ridge of sand hills and across some small lakes encamped at a clump of pines and birches. Our hunters killed nothing today, but just before we halted the carcase of a deer which had been strangled and partly eaten by a wolf was found. This, together with what was obtained yesterday afforded one meal to the party.

June 6th 1821

Resumed our journey at sun-rise and travelled through a series of small lakes and low grounds so deeply covered with snow, that it was difficult to distin-guish lake from land. Our path which was somewhat winding was flanked on each side almost the whole way by ranges of low sand hills interspersed with a few barren elevations of gneiss. The distances and courses per compass were as follow, NNW ¾ of a mile over a sand hill and across 2 small lakes; Nbw 1¼ swamp and lake; Nbw½w 1¼ principally lake; NWbN 1¾ swamp; NW 2¼ through a lake; NWbw½w 4½ through another lake seperated from the last by a detroit. We encamped at the foot of a high ridge of sand hills and having collected a quantity

---

1 Also known as Petit Pied and Akaiyazza.

of dry moss, principally a species of *cornicularia* which is very abundant here, we made several fires and speedily cooked a deer which was killed in the last lake through which we passed. This animal had its thigh broken by a shot from one of our hunters, but it would have escaped if two of the dogs had not been released from the sledges and allowed to go in pursuit of it. They held it at bay until the hunter came up and completed the business by stabbing it repeatedly with his knife.

June 7th 1821

Except on the summits of the hills the snow appears to have decreased extremely little in this part of the country and as we had warm weather with rain during the night we sink at least two feet at every step. Our progress in consequence was very slow. The courses are NNW 2½ miles over a high ridge of sand hills. NNW 2 through a lake. NNW ½ across a moor. NW 1 mile – lake.

   Encamped on a small eminence which scarcely afforded moss enough to make a fire, but men and dogs were so jaded that we could proceed no farther. Soon after we encamped one of the hunters wounded a deer which was caught by the dogs after a chace of a mile.

June 8th 1821

Our route today lay through a hilly tract of country, and as we followed the vallies, as much as possible, it was necessarily winding, and from the deepness and softness of the snow, very difficult. The gneiss formation seems to be continued here, but the hills are higher and the vallies narrower and deeper than in the neighbourhood of Fort Enterprise. The acclivities of many of the hills are almost precipitous. The courses and distances were NNW 2 miles through a narrow valley composed of lake and swamp. From a range of hills on the left of this valley the banks of the Coppermine river are visible. NbW 2 miles round the foot of a hill. NWbN 2 miles over a rather elevated moor. NbW 1¼ across a lake. All the vallies here seem to incline towards the river. Encamped about 1½ mile to the NNE of a small clump of pines in which we slept in our autumn excursion[2] and whose latitude and longitude was 65°05′31″ N 113°09′26″ W.

June 9th 1821

Much thaw having taken place during the night a large lake which lay in our way was so deeply covered with water that it was impossible to take the sledges

---

2 On 11 September 1820.

Eriophorum vaginatum – *Cottongrass*

through it. Our only alternative was to cross a high hill and we effected it but with much difficulty, frequently sinking through the snow amongst broken rocks up to the middle. The labour of dragging a sledge was now so great, that all the Indians deserted theirs, and many of our voyageurs, following their example, took their loads on their backs, but others were constrained to retain their sledges, their burdens being too bulky to carry. As the sledges frequently sunk into the water which in many places to the depth of a foot or more, flowed beneath the snow, everything upon them was completely soaked. The dogs were several times compelled to swim and the labour of pushing on their trains fell entirely upon their conductors. We travelled only 4 miles today but every one of the party was much fatigued. Courses and distances NW 2 miles NNW 2 miles. Encamped on the borders of Point Lake, our autumn encampment bearing WNW ½ a mile. The afternoon proved warm and fine and we were enabled to dry many of the wet things. A deer was killed today and we had plenty of wood within a reasonable distance.

June 10th 1821

In consequence of the warmth of the night the water which yesterday lay very deep on the ice had made holes for itself and run very much off, notwithstanding which we were frequently knee-deep in marching across Point Lake – after advancing about 4 miles the depth of the water rendered our further progress at this time impracticable and we put ashore and encamped in a clump of pines.

Our hunters killed 5 deer today. The mean temperature for the last ten days taken from the register at Fort Enterprise was 41°55" F^t. On the 1st of June the *Eriophorum vaginatum*[3] was in full flower at that place, whilst in the neighbourhood of our present encampment it is only now bursting forth.

Monday June 11th 1821 Point Lake

This morning 13 of the men returned to Fort Enterprise, leaving with me Adam the Interpreter and Parent to take care of the stores. I sent Basil back with them and detained Bald-head and Akaiyazza or Little-foot who is getting well to hunt here. The two Canadians were employed the whole day in drying the stores that got wet yesterday and in preparing stages for drying meat. Angelique, Roulante and the wives of the two hunters spliced two deer, and in the evening their husbands came in with intelligence of having killed two more deer.

Tuesday June 12th 1821

Adam and the 4 women[4] went off today for the deer and returned in the evening. The Indians who were hunting on the other side of the lake, returned at the same time, having killed one small deer. Several bands of deer crossed the lake today, but now that the snow has disappeared they are exceedingly wild and difficult of approach.

June 13th 1821 Wednesday

It rained hard in the night, and the day being rather unpromising, the hunters remained in the encampment. In the course of the day, the deer killed yesterday was brought home and spliced. A species of *Dufourea* of which some barren plants were found at Fort Enterprise, is very common here and is not rare in fructification.

Description of a bird killed today *Numenius borealis*.[5] [1-page description of a Eskimo Curlew]

These birds are hatching at present. One of their nests found on the ground contained three eggs of a pyriform shape, and siskin-green colour, clouded with a few large irregular spots of bright umber-brown.

---

3 Cotton-grass.
4 Angelique, Roulante, Little-foot's wife
  named Little Forehead, and Baldhead's wife.

5 Eskimo Curlew, *Numenius borealis*. The nest
  was the first known to science.

Description of a small animal which inhabits the barren grounds and burrows in sandy places, but which has much the appearance and manners of a squirrel. It is termed by the Canadians Sifler and by Hearne the ground hog.[6] [1½-page description of Arctic Ground Squirrel]

There are pretty large pouches in the cheeks. Pouches filled with berries – (seashore July 28 pouches filled with the seeds of a Polygonum).[7]

These animals when fat are considered by the Indians as delicacies and are much sought after by the Bears and Wolverenes.

"A species of Salix burst its catkins today"

Thursday June 14th 1821 Point Lake

Calm and fine weather. The thermometer rose to 56° and the snow melted fast. It now lies only under the steep cliffs. The ice on the lake is still upwards of 5 feet thick, but it is perforated in many places and the water has almost entirely run off its surface. A species of *Salix* burst its catkins today.

In the afternoon Long-legs arrived with a small party of Indians. Although they had come directly from Fort Enterprise, where their wants had been supplied as far as our means allowed, yet they made many urgent demands upon me, particular[l]y for ammunition.

6 Arctic Ground Squirrel, *Spermophilus parryii*. This species was first named and described by Richardson in 1825 (see Appendix B).

7 Knotweed.

Friday June 15th 1821 Point Lake

Thermometer rose to 60°. The streams that issue from the melting snow on the sides of the hills are now pretty large, some of them scarcely fordable, and all the low vallies are flooded.

Akaicho and the rest of the Indians arrived about noon from Fort Enterprise. He informed me that his party had been very unsuccessful in their hunts, having expended all the ammunition they received at the Fort, without killing more than was sufficient for their own subsistance; and that of course he required a further supply. I was obliged to refuse him in conformity with Mr Franklin's instructions, which were to give ammunition only in proportion to the deer brought in, and much of my time was employed in disagre[e]able altercations on this head. The *Arbutus alpina* began to flower today and most of the small birds are hatching.

Saturday June 16th 1821 Point Lake

Cold disagreeable weather in the morning, followed by heavy rain in the afternoon. The thermometer rose only to 40° and afterwards fell to 32°. Three deer that were killed yesterday by the two hunters were brought in and spliced.

Sunday June 17th 1821 Point Lake

Showers and sleet with strong NE winds in the morning, were succeeded in the afternoon by a heavy fall of snow. In the evening the weather became clear and the temperature which had not exceeded 35° fell to 30°. One of the Old Indians, the father of two of our best hunters[8] having suffered much for some days from a retention of urine, passed a pretty large calculus last night, after some medicine I had given him, and to the magical powers of which this desirable event was universally ascribed, but as I could not affirm that there were no more stones in the kidneys or bladder a conjuror undertook to ascertain the fact, and is at present shut up with the sick man in a conjuring house, where I understand they must remain without eating or drinking.

The conjuror chaunts a kind of song and occassionally bursts into a phrenzy shaking his house violently and shouting vehemently. The old man's wife and several other women are seated near awaiting the result with evident anxiety, but the male part of the tribe walk about as if unconscious of what is going on.

8 Le Petit Chasseur and Thoveeyorre.

Monday June 18th 1821

A moderately clear and fine but not a warm day. The snow which fell yesterday has disappeared. The conjuror and his patient were released from their confinement about midnight, both much exhausted.

A wolf chased a stout buck-deer across the lake today. Whilst upon the ice, they seemed to be nearly equal in speed, but the wolf was much more steady in his pace and thus obtained an advantage over the deer, which every now and then stopped to look at his enemy and then with great consternation bounded off again. When they reached the shore, the pursuer gained still more rapidly upon his prey and catching him by the flank, threw him upon his back at the first effort. An Indian, who had concealed himself, now ran forward with his knife, the wolf, which was a white one and one of the largest, sneaked off and the Indian having killed the disabled deer, the venison was brought to the encampment.

Tuesday June 19th 1821

The thermometer rose to 54°. Fine weather. Ice on the lake, honeycombed from the action of the sun. *Anemone cuneifolia*[9] in flower. A party of Indians went off to the northward.

Wednesday June 20th 1821

Fine weather. The^r 56°. The greatest part of the women and children crossed the lake today with the intention of going to the Betsee-to [Takiyuak Lake], a large lake and of passing the summer there. Angelique and Roulante went with them. We have now left at the encampment Akaicho, White Capot, 5 hunters, the old sick man, his wife and daughter in law. Cascathry and Long legs went off yesterday.

Thursday June 21st 1821 Point Lake

Two Indians arrived in the night with the agreeable intelligence that Mr Franklin and the party bringing the canoes were at no great distance and about noon I had the satisfaction of seeing them arrive. Deer were scarce in their track and consequently they had fared badly.

9 *Anemone parviflora.*

Weather fine. The dwarf birch opened its buds today. The country about Point Lake consists mostly of a species of slate which probably belongs to the transition class of rocks, as one of the highest hills in the neighbourhood seems to be composed of Grey-wacke.

An old Indian, who by the by, is considered as a hermaphrodite by his countrymen, and who remembers Mr Hearne's passing and is well acquainted with the country to the northward of the Coppermine river informs me, that directly north by compass or nearly north-east true at a considerable distance lies the Contwoyo-to or Rum lake a piece of water upwards of 50 miles in extent which gives rise to the Ana-tessy a large river [Burnside River] by which we may descend in canoes to the sea, in three days. Its course is NE true. The northern extremity of this lake is the Congecathewachaga of Hearne [Kathawachaga Lake].

The Betsee-tessy [Tree River] another river of considerable magnitude arises from a lake of the same name, [Takiyuak Lake][10] which lies to the northward of Rum Lake and falls into the sea betwixt the mouths of the Coppermine river and Ana-tessy. Many Eskimaux frequent the Coppermine river, but they are less numerous on the other two rivers.

The Hermaphrodite being better acquainted with the route than our Guides has been engaged by Akaicho to accompany us.

Situation of encampment June 21st 65°12′40″ R, 113°08′25″ Chr, Variation 43°04′20″ East.

Distance in geographical miles between Fort Enterprise and Point Lake 54½ Statute miles.

Friday June 22^d 1821 Point Lake

The^r rose to 56°. Heavy showers in the afternoon. Mr Franklin having determined to proceed with the canoes and baggage on the ice, the men were employed to day in preparing sledges and in covering their runners with iron hoops.

Akaicho confessed that a considerable portion of the ammunition he received on quitting Fort Enterprise was given to those who accompanied the women, but making a promise of behaving more faithfully in future, he received a further supply of ten rounds for each hunter with the understanding that they are to obtain no more unless they furnish us with a proportionate quantity of meat. Four deer were killed on the lake today and brought in. Long. of the encampment 113°8′25″ w. and variation 43°4′ Easterly. Latitude deduced from last years observations 65°12″40″ N.

10 The Tree River actually begins somewhat to
   the north of Takiyuak Lake, called Betsee-to
   by Richardson.

Saturday June 23ᵈ 1821

Fresh breezes from the NE, cloudy weather. Thermometer rose to 50° F.

    The old sick man believing his death to be at hand has refused to allow his two sons Le Petit Chasseur and Thoveeyorrè to leave him, and has thus deprived us of the services of two of the best of our hunters. The rest 5 in number set off in the afternoon to make caches of provision on our route and to halt for us at the first open water. Akaicho, White Capot, The Hermaphrodite, Le petit Chanteur and Akaicho's slave, a stout Dog-rib remain to accompany us on our journey. About 200 lbs. weight of dried meat were pounded today to fit it for being made into pemmican.

Sunday June 24ᵗʰ 1821

Our preparations being completed we would have commenced journey today but the weather was too stormy to admit of our venturing upon the lake with the canoes. In the afternoon a heavy fall of snow took place, which was succeeded by sleet and mist. Therᵣ rose to 39°. Wind NE strong.

Monday June 25ᵗʰ 1821

Wind ssw light. Sky clouded. Highest tempᵣ 50°. Wind evening NNE.

    Started about noon. Men heavily laden; each drags upwards of two pieces or 180 lbs. weight and their sledges are much impeded by the snow which fell yesterday and still lies on the lake. The three canoes require 6 dogs and 9 men to conduct them. Our route lay down the main channel of the lake which varied in breadth to three miles and upwards. Many extensive arms branched off to the northward of this channel and it appeared to be bounded on the south by a chain of lofty islands. The hills on each side rose 6 or 700 feet high and were rather round backed but obtuse-conical elevations, probably of trap rocks were frequent, and high and steep cliffs were very numerous. The cliffs we had an opportunity of examining consisted of greenish-grey clay slate; having a curved fracture and splitting into slates of very unequal thickness. The dip was towards the north. We put up at 8ʰ p.m. the party much fatigued, many of them affected with erythematous inflammation on the insides of the thighs attended with much hardness and swelling. Several of them were similarly affected on their arrival at Point Lake, but were recovering from the rest they enjoyed there, today's march however has rendered them worse than ever.

    Our stock of provision consists of two bags of pemmican, two of pounded meat, five of suet and two small bundles of dried meat – together with fresh meat sufficient for our supper this night. No deer were seen during the march but one crossed the lake in front of the encampment in the evening. The Indians fired several shots at it, but missed. The neighbourhood of our encampment scarcely afforded twigs enough to make a fire, the fatigue of the party compelling us to encamp at a distance from any of the clumps of wood which in this part of the lake are two or three miles asunder.

Courses per compass NWbN ½ mile, NWbW ½ W 1¼ miles, WSW 4¼ miles. Situation of Encampment June 25th 65°16'20" North (R) 113°17'40" West (R). Direct daily course corrected for variation NW, 5½ miles.

Tuesday June 26th 1821 Point Lake

Fine warm day. Ther 56° Wind ENE. Snow on the lake melting.

Started after breakfast. The lameness of the men encreased very much during todays march, many not previously affected began to complain, and one of the dogs became so tired that they were obliged to release it from the harness, under these circumstances we were compelled to encamp at an early hour having marched on a W½S course only 4 miles. As it was evident that the party could not proceed with their present loads Mr Franklin decided upon laying up the third canoe and it was accordingly properly secured upon a stage which was erected for the purpose in a small clump of wood. An additional dog was thus furnished to each of the other canoes and three men allotted to lighten the burdens of those who were most lame. Dried meat was served out for supper, but during the night the Indians killed two deer. The channel through which we marched today is bounded on the north by a very large island, beyond which the Indians inform us a large body of the lake lies.

The first specimens of *Solorina crocea*[11] that we have observed in this country, were found in the neighbourhood of the encampment.

Courses per compass SWbW¼W 4½ miles, SW¼S 3 miles, EbS½S ¾ mile. Situation of Encampment June 26th 65°16'40" North (R) 113°31'45" West (R) Direct daily course corrected for variation W½N, 6 miles.

Wednesday June 27th 1821

Morning fine and warm, but the sky afterwards becoming clouded rendered it more agre[e]able for walking. Wind ESE. Another deer was killed this morning. The full daily allowance for the whole party including the Indians exceeds two deer and as we breakfasted before starting, the loads were not much encreased by this supply of fresh meat and being distributed amongst a greater number of

---

11 A lichen, still known as *Solorina crocea*.

hands[12] we made a longer march than usual – the direct distance being 7¼ miles on a NWbW½W course, but the distance actually walked was considerably greater. Throughout the day's march the hills on each side of the lake bore a strong resemblance in altitude and form to those about Fort Enterprise and like them appeared to consist of gneiss and sienite. We observed a bed of pure chrystalline greenstone in a gneiss cliff. In the early part of our march we passed the mouth of a pretty large river which flows into the lake from the southward. We encamped amongst a few spruce trees. These clumps occur in the deeper vallies on the borders of the lake at intervals of 4 or 5 miles. The dwarf birch grows here in sheltered spots to the height of 4 or 5 feet.

A small Lemming[13] ... was killed after we encamped. [2-page description of Collared Lemming]

The individual examined was a female and had in its womb, six young destitute of hair but having their extremities fully formed. At first sight it strongly resembled the campagnol above described but its size is somewhat greater, its hair coarser and tail shorter besides the generic differences in the feet and teeth. It showed some courage when attacked and turned upon its pursuers.

Courses per compass sw 2 miles, sw½w 1½ miles, swbs 2 miles, wsw 2½ miles, wbN¾N 3 miles.

Today and yesterday we have been marching along the South and sw side of an island the extreme length of which is about 11 miles and breadth nearly as much. There are many large islands also to the southward of our track & a river of considerable size flows from thence.

Situation of encampment 65°23′15″ North (R), 113°42′02″ West (R)
Direct daily course corrected for variation NW½W 10½ miles.

Thursday June 28th 1821 Point Lake

Heavy rain during the night and in the morning, which towards noon changed into a thick fog. Served out dried meat for breakfast. Started about noon and after travelling 5 or 6 miles by a winding course, came to the end of Point Lake which discharges itself into Red Rock Lake by a channel about 100 yards wide. This was open and the canoes ran down it, whilst the sledge loads were carried across a peninsula into Red Rock lake upon the left bank of which we encamped. The borders of this lake are well covered with wood which is however of small size and consists entirely of white spruce. The rolled stones on the shore are mostly of blue or red clay slate hence its Indian name of which the above is a translation. Todays journey was extremely painful, the ice having been honey combed by the rain presented innumerable sharp points which in a very short

---

12 By the arrangements of the previous day, when they left one canoe behind.

13 Collared Lemming, *Dicrostonyx torquatus.*

time tore the shoes in pieces and lacerated the feet. The direct course and distance was NNW½W 3 miles. We were compelled to sup tonight on pounded meat and fat, an encroachment upon our sea-stores, which was made with great reluctance.

Courses per compass SW½S 1½ miles, WSW 1½ miles, NWbW½W 1 mile, NW¾N 2½ miles. Situation of the south end of the rapid which terminates Point Lake, 65°26'10" North (R), 113°59'15" West (R). This lake as was afterwards ascertained is 71 miles long from East to West. NW¼N 1 mile.

Situation of Encampment June 28th a little below the head of Red Rock Lake, 65°28'06" North (R), 113°59'10" West (R).

Direct daily course corrected for variation NNW¾W, 5¾ miles.

Friday June 29th 1821 Red Rock Lake

Cloudy weather with slight showers. Started after breakfast. The hills on both sides of this lake, which is narrow, are about 4 or 500 feet high, are round-backed, have a tolerably even outline and are covered to the tops, but not thickly, with small pines (white spruce). The acclivities of all the hills are swampy at this season. In the course of todays march we were directed by pine branches strewed across the lake to a cache of two deer made by the 5 hunters who preceded us. Akaicho judged from the appearance of this cache that it was three days old, and from the carcases being entire with the exception of a single shoulder that they had killed more animals and made other caches which we had missed from not following precisely the same route. This supply was very seasonable and our men cheerfully dragged the additional weight. In the afternoon we passed the mouth of a river apparently as large as the discharge of Point Lake. The Indians in coming from Great Martin lake [Lac La Martre] make a portage across a height of land into this river.

We encamped in the evening at the bottom of the lake and found the river which connected it with the next lake open. Strata here greenish-gray clay slate dipping WbN at an angle of 30°. Its lustre was faintly glimmering. The musk ox[14] is said to frequent this part of the country in some seasons, and this is [the] spot where Akaicho expected to find his hunters. Course and distance today NWbW½W 7 miles. Var. per obs. 47° Easterly.[15]

Courses per compass WNW 1½ miles, SWbW 6 miles, WbS 4 miles.

Situation of Encampment June 29th 65°33'06" North (R), 114°23'00" West (R). On a point of the lake composed of Clay Slates. Well wooded.

Direct daily course corrected for variation NWbW 11 miles.

14 Muskox, *Ovibos moschatus*.
15 This observation of magnetic variation was
   omitted from Richardson's table.

Saturday June 30th 1821

A fine morning. The canoes were carried a short distance across a point of land to avoid some broken ice and put into the river, whilst the Officers walked with the Indians about three miles across a neck of land through tolerably thick woods. We then embarked in the canoes and ran down a rapid which brought us to another lake wherein the ice was so much decayed as to be extremely dangerous. We traversed it however without accident although we were obliged in one instance to cross an open channel in the canoes, and in another to make a portage along the shore. The Indians here shewed some uncertainty as to our route and at first led us towards the West end of the lake, but afterwards coming in sight of a very remarkable hill, known to them by the name of Rock-nest, they recollected themselves and directed us to the NE. This occassioned us to make another dangerous traverse across the lake, the ice cracking under our feet at every step. We effected a landing on the eastern bank of the lake by ferrying the luggage on pieces of ice across an open channel which ran along the shore. Here we encamped, having come in a direct line 7 miles, on a NbE½E course. A considerable stream[16] joins the Copper mine river about a mile before it loses itself in the Rock-nest lake. With the exception of the Rock-nest and two or three adjoining hills the borders of this lake are low consisting of a long, round backed, even range of gently elevated hills clothed with wood to their very tops. The strata where we had an opportunity of examining them were composed of clay slate, having a colour intermediate between greenish grey and clove brown and a feebly glistening or glimmering lustre. The dip East at angle of 40°. Moschetoes troublesome.

The hunters killed nothing today and our stock of pounded meat was still further reduced.

Courses per compass NNW 3½ miles, WNW 1½ miles, NEbN 1 mile.

The lake of the Red Rock which is upwards of 16 miles from East to West terminates here in a rapid at the foot of which Rock Nest Lake commences. A river flows into the rapid from the Southward.

Situation of Encampment in Rock Nest Lake 65°48′06″ R, 114°21′55″ R.

Direct daily course corrected for variation N¼E 5¼ miles.

Abstract of Temperatures for June

Extremes	
Maximum on the 12th day	78°
Minimum 2^d	14°
Least maximum 17th day	35°

16 From Scotstoun Lake.

Greatest minima, 8th, 9th, 12th, & 14th days	42°
Highest morning obs. 9th	58°
Lowest morning obs. 4th	18°
Highest evening obs 12th	52°
Lowest evening obs. 2d	22°
Greatest range in 24 hours 12th	78°[17]
Least range in 24 hours	29°
Greatest daily difference of extremes 12th	36°
Least daily difference	29°

Fair days   21   Cloudy days   16   Wind Easterly 24

Snowy days   4   Clear days   14   Westerly   6

Rainy days   9 in all 9

[Detailed meteorological journal for June 1821, with 7 temperature and wind entries for most days, followed by a summary of monthly 10-day minimal mean and maximal temperatures for 22 months, September 1819–June 1821.]

The easterly winds predominate in the country to the Northward of Great Slave lake as appears on a reference to the table, and while they continue to blow, the weather is milder than during the Westerly winds. In Dec.r & Jan.y the coldest months the latter prevailed. The coldest wind in every season in this country is the NW.

Sunday July 1st, 1821 Rock Nest Lake

Fine clear weather. Recommenced our journey by dragging the canoes across the ice, into a piece of open water, which the Indians yesterday supposed to be the commencement of the river, but which proved to be merely a channel running across, amongst a range of sandy islands. In the course of the day, we crossed several such channels, making the intermediate portages, often, on detached and fragile pieces of ice, with infinite hazard, not only to the safety of the goods, but even to the lives of the men. The Indians having conducted us into a deep bay, from which they said the river issues, acknowledged that they had mistaken the route, but M.r Franklin having ascended one of the highest hills in the neighbourhood & discovered another deep bay to the northward – & two men being sent to explore this passage returned with the agre[e]able information of having seen the river issuing from its bottom – and we resumed our march after a delay of three hours. One of the dogs escaped from us here and went in pursuit of a deer, to such a distance that we were unable to recover it. Whilst we halted a white wolf chased two deer upon the ice, but was scared from his prey, when

17 The range of temperatures was 78° − 14° =
   64°, but Richardson entered the range
   incorrectly as 78°.

just ready to seize it, by the barking of our dogs, otherwise we might have had a liberal share of the products of his chase. In the course of our march through the bay, we passed close to the foot of the Rock-nest, which in one point of view bears an exact resemblance to the very remarkable hill in the neighbourhood of Edinburgh named Salisbury crags. Towards the evening we embarked upon the river, but had not descended far, before we were obliged to cut a channel through the drift ice, which had blocked up a part of it narrower then the rest. Soon after passing this barrier we came to a strong rapid, which the canoes ran with safety, after being lightened. We then encamped at the mouth of a small stream which issues from a lake that lies at a short distance from the banks of the river. Direct course and distance today NEbE½E 4 miles. The Coppermine river at this place is about 200 yards wide, 8 or ten feet deep, with a rocky bottom and strong current. Both banks are well wooded, but on the right side, at the distance of a few miles, there is a high range of very barren hills, which the Indians report to be a continuation of the barren grounds.

We were obliged this evening to make a further encroachment upon our stock of provisions, by serving out a portion of pemmican. After supper, however, Akaicho and the Little-singer who had been hunting all day, came in and informed us that they had killed two deer. A party was immediately dispatched to bring them, but they did not return before midnight.

In the night, the Little-hand and Basil, two of the hunters whom we supposed to be in advance, arrived and acquainted us that the other three, not knowing that we had passed, were still encamped on the borders of Rock nest Lake and that they themselves had come to our smoke under the idea that it was raised by Long-legs. We were much vexed at having missed the hunters when we learnt that they had three deer at their encampment, besides others in two caches which we had passed unnoticed. Akaicho's Slave was immediately despatched to inform them that we would await their arrival a little farther down the river and to desire that they would bring the meat down in the small canoe they had with them.

Courses per compass NNE 1½ miles to the Nest Rock a remarkable hill composed of Trap Rocks. NE 1 mile. Nest Rock Lake terminates here being nearly 4 miles long.[18] NbW ¼ mile, NWbN ½ mile, North ⅓ mile, West ⅓ mile.

Situation of Encampment July 1, 65°40'55" R, 114°15'00" R. Coppermine River is 160 yards wide here. A small river falls into it (from a lake to the Northward) at this place.

Direct daily course corrected for variation NE 4 miles.

101 Geographical or 117 Statute Miles is the distance the Canoes & cargoes were dragged over the Snow & ice.

18 Two entries totalling 4 or 5 miles travel on Rocknest Lake were omitted; as a consequence this lake appears too small on Franklin's map.

4

BY CANOE DOWN THE COPPERMINE

Monday July 2ᵈ 1821 Coppermine River

Strong breezes and clear weather. Sun very powerful.

    Embarked and descended a number of rapids. We were several times in danger of breaking the canoes from the want of the long poles which lie along their bottoms, and equalize the pressure of their cargoes, & the first canoe was almost filled with water, by a sudden plunge in one of the rapids. Every precaution, however, was taken by an equal distribution of the ammunition and instruments betwixt the two canoes, to guard so far as possible against an accident to either of the canoes, proving fatal to the progress of the expedition.

    The banks of the river, here, are rocky and the scenery beautiful, consisting of gentle elevations, and dales wooded to the edge of the stream, flanked on both sides at the distance of three or four miles, by a range of round-backed barren hills, upwards of 600 feet high. At the foot of the rapids, which were about two miles long, the high lands receded to a greater distance and the river flowed with a more gentle current, in a wider channel, through a level and open country, consisting of alluvial sand. In one place the passage was blocked up with drift ice, still covered to some depth with snow. A channel for the canoes was made for some way with poles and hatchets, but at length it became necessary to carry them over a piece, more compact than the rest, an operation which proved extremely hazardous from the number of perforations, which had been made in the ice, by the action of the water underneath, but which were concealed by the snow. Some of the men slipt through, but none of the baggage was lost nor did any serious accident occur.

    This part of the river being very wide was mistaken for a lake, of which the Guide had spoken as the last we should meet within our voyage to the sea and we accordingly encamped after passing through it, for the purpose of gumming the canoes, cutting poles and making other preparations for the voyage under the supposition that we should have no more ice to cross. The Guide, however, who had walked along shore, arrived in the evening and informed us, that the lake[1] he meant was further on. This damped the satisfaction we felt on having passed the ice, but two men being sent to reconnoitre the lake renewed our joy by the intelligence of there being an open channel through it.

Observed in flower today – *Dryas integrifolia*.[2] *Anemone cuneifolia. Stellaria uliginosa?*[3] *Equisetum arvense*.[4] The *epilobium spicatum*[5] is sending forth young shoots.

"Fired at a brown-bear which was upon the bank, but missed it"

Courses per compass West 3½ miles, wbN½N 1½ miles.

Situation of Encampment where we remained July 2 & 3 to fit the canoes, 65°43′28″ North by Observation, 114°26′45″ West by Chronometers. Variation 42°17′22″ East.

Direct daily course corrected for variation NW¾W, 5 miles.

Tuesday July 3ᵈ 1821 Coppermine River

The hunters arrived early in the morning. It appeared that the dog which escaped from us two days ago, came into the vicinity of their encampment, howling piteously. Seeing him without his harness, they came to the hasty con-

---

1 Another widening of the river.
2 Mountain Avens, now the floral emblem of the Northwest Territories.
3 Chickweed. Listed in Scoggan, *Flora*.
4 Common Horsetail.
5 Fireweed, *Epilobium angustifolium*.

clusion, that our whole party had perished in a rapid, and throwing away part of their baggage and leaving the meat behind them, they set off with the utmost haste, to join Long-legs. Akaicho's Slave met them in their flight but too far advanced to admit of their returning for the meat. It is now too late to send for it as it has been killed six days. The hunters in descending a rapid in their small canoe, fired at a brown-bear[6] which was upon the bank, but missed it.

Animals are very scarce in this part of the country, particularly deer, and the Indians expressed much regret at having left the meat, and were much ashamed of the panic into which they had been thrown. To remedy this evil as much as possible seven of them including the 5 hunters, the Little-singer and Slave set out with their two small canoes to hunt before us on the river, and they are in great hopes of meeting with some Musk-oxen, which they say are generally numerous, about 30 or 40 miles below our present encampment. Their canoes carry only 5 of the party, so that two of them must walk by turns along the banks, but they have promised to travel day and night until they arrive at a favourable spot for hunting. The situation of the encampment was ascertained by observation to be in Latitude 65°43′28″ N and Long. 114°26′45″ W. The variation is 42°17′22″ E.

The men have been employed all day in repairing and gumming the canoes and they have had very favourable weather for the purpose. A few trout of considerable size were taken today, with lines, but it was necessary to make another inroad on the pemmican.

Wednesday July 4th 1821

Embarked at half past 4 in the morning, descended many long rapids and passed through some shallow expansions of the river. Wherever the rapid appeared dangerous the ammunition and instruments were landed and carried along the banks. On one of these occasions as the people were re-embarking from a ledge of ice which adhered to the bank it gave way under their feet and they were precipitated into the river – but were rescued without further damage than a sound ducking, and the canoe fortunately tho' narrowly escaped being crushed by the weight of the mass which exceeded several tons.

Throughout the whole day's voyage the current was very strong marking a steep descent. The banks of the river were gravelly and latterly were bounded at a small distance by cliffs of fine sand from one to two hundred feet high. Sandy plains on a level with the summits of these cliffs extended six or seven miles backwards and were terminated by ranges of hills 800 or 1000 feet in height. The ranges were round-backed with moderately steep acclivities, but

---

6 Barren-ground Grizzly, until recently known as *Ursus horribilis richardsonii* or *Ursus richard-* *soni*, but now considered conspecific with the Grizzly, *Ursus arctos*.

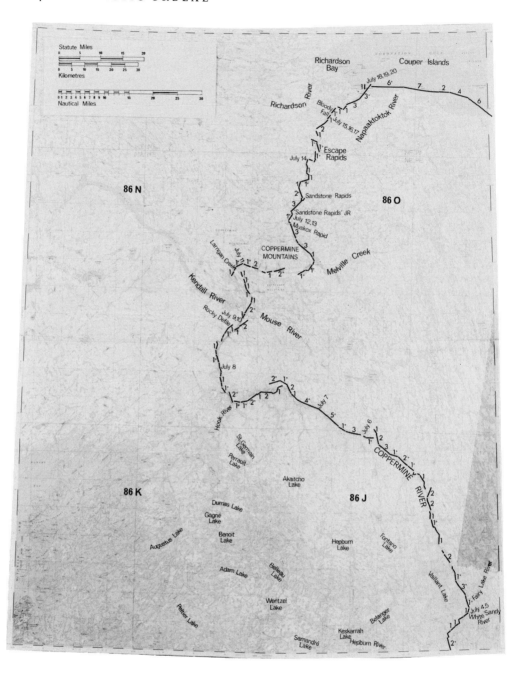

Map 3   *4–21 July 1821*

were sometimes terminated by high bluffs. The cliffs were not frequent, and we were precluded from examining such as did occur, by their distance.

After having come 21 miles on a North course we overtook the Indians at 11 a.m. and put ashore at their encampment where we found only one of them, who told us that the others were in pursuit of a band of Musk-oxen, whose tracks they had seen. In consequence of this information we pitched the tents and in the afternoon received the agre[e]able intelligence of the death of eight cows[7] of which four were full grown. A young cow irritated by the firing ran down to the river and passed close to Mr Franklin who was walking at a short distance from the encampment. He fired, and wounded it, when it instantly turned and ran at him but he avoided its fury by running to an elevated spot of ground, and some people coming in the mean time from the encampment it took to flight. The people were dispatched to bring in the meat.

Courses per compass WNW 1¼ miles, NNW ¼ mile, NWbW 1½ miles. This course terminates in a small lake formed by an expansion of the River. NWbW 1¼ miles, NNW¼W ¼ mile, NW½W 1½ miles, NW½N ¾ mile, NW½W 1¼ miles, NW½N ¾ mile, WNW ½ mile, NW¾W 2½ miles. The river again dilates here & flows round an island. SWbW ¾ mile, NNW 1 mile, NW½W ½ mile, NWbW 2½ miles, NNE ¼ mile, WNW ¾ mile, NbE ¾ mile, North 1 mile, NbE 1 mile, NW½W ¾ mile, North 1¼ miles.

The White Sandy River a rapid mountain stream joins the Coppermine River at the Encampment. It is about 50 yards wide &c.

Situation of the Encampment on the 4th & 5th 66°05′00″ North Observation, 114°25′15″ West Chr, Variation 44°00′10″ East. Sandy plains frequented by the Musk ox.

Direct daily course corrected for variation N½E, 21 miles.

Thursday July 5th 1821 *Coppermine River*

The people returned with the meat, after midnight, and have been employed all the morning splicing and drying it. *Sterna hirundo*[8] killed today. [4-line description of Arctic Tern]

Weather fine and warm. Plants in flower. *Salix reticulata*[9] very common, *Alnus glutinosa*.[10] *Andromeda tetragona*,[11] plentiful. *Draba hirta?*[12] *Phaca?*[13] *Hippophae canadensis*.[14] *Salices et carices* varii.[15]

---

7 Muskox cows.
8 Arctic Tern, *Sterna paradisaea*.
9 Net-veined Willow.
10 Green Alder, *Alnus crispa*.
11 Arctic White Heather, *Cassiope tetragona*.

12 Draba or Whitlow Grass.
13 Milk-vetch, *Astragalus*.
14 Soapberry, *Shepherdia canadensis*.
15 Various willows and sedges.

Arctic Terns

Friday July 6th 1821

The Hunters having received a further supply of ammunition set off in the night time in two small canoes and at half past five in the morning we followed them accompanied by Akaicho, White Capot and the Hermaphrodite. Morning cold and cloudy. After descending a series of rapids and passing the embouchure of the River of the Fairy Lake [Fairylake River from Takiyuak Lake] a pretty large stream whose banks are said to be much frequented by the Musk oxen the river became wider and less rapid and its sandy banks more continuous. As the day advanced the woods became thinner and more stunted and in the afternoon the barren hills approached the river's edge. The sandy banks still however appeared at intervals and in some places the river expanding considerably flowed with a gentle current over a fine sandy bottom and abounded in alluvial islands covered with willows.

The medium breadth of the stream may be stated at 300 yards but in the rapids it was diminished more than one half.

In the evening we approached several ranges of hills, which were from 12 to 1500 feet high and lay nearly parallel to the river or about NW true. These are the first hills which we have seen in this country that can be said to possess the form of a mountain range. They are in general rather round backed, but the outline is not even being interrupted by craggy eminences rather obtusely conical, one of which being examined was found to consist of Syenite. Large beds of green stone also occur in some parts of the range – but perhaps these rocks are subordinate to the clay-slate which exists here in considerable quantity, having a greenish colour and a continuous pearly lustre.

The Hunters killed a rein-deer in the morning which we picked up as we came along. One of them, who was walking along the shore afterwards fired upon two (Grizzly)brown bears and wounded one of them which instantly turned and pursued him. His companion put ashore to his assistance but did not succeed in killing the bears which fled upon the reinforcement coming up. During the delay occassioned by this circumstance we overtook them and afterwards embarking together we paddled until 7 p.m. when we put ashore and encamped at the foot of the above mentioned range. Latitude at noon 66°19′58″ N. Course and distance for the whole day NW¼N 42¾ miles. Plants observed in flower today *Pedicularis Sceptrum Carolinium*.[16] *P. hirsuta*.[17] *P. lapponica*.[18] *Silene acaulis*.[19] *Anthericum calyculatum*.[20] *Saxifraga bulbifera*.[21] *S. nivalis*.[22] *Draba aizoides*.[23] *D. alpina*.[24] *Pyrola rotundifolia*.[25] *Dryas integrifolia* very abundant. *Salices et Carices quaedam*.[26] The *Juniperus communis*[27] occurs on these hills but was not in flower.

Courses per compass, NWbN ¾ mile, NWbW½W 1¾ miles, NW½W ¾ mile [Actual site of Fairy Lake River]. WbN 3½ miles, NW½W 1½ miles.

Situation of the mouth of the Fairy Lake River which flows from the Eastward & is about 100 yards wide, but shallow, 66°07′58″ North (R), 114°05′58″ West (R).

WbN ¾ mile, NW ½ mile, W½N 2 miles, WbN ¾ mile, 66°19′58″ N. Obs. NW½N, a small island.

WbN 1 mile, NWbW¾W ¾ mile, SWbS ¼ mile, NWbW 1½ miles, NW 1 mile, NWbW ½ mile, WbN¾N 2 miles, NWbW ½ mile, NNW 2 miles, NWbW½W ¾ mile, NW½N ½ mile, WbN 1½ miles, WbS ½ mile, SWbS ⅓ mile, NWbW ½ mile, W¾S 1½ miles, West 2½ miles, a dilatation of the river with two small islands in the centre.

SW½W 1½ miles, W½S 3 miles, a small island.

NWbW 2 miles, WbS½S 1 mile, SW 1½ miles, banks on the south side low and Sandy, broken into small islands.

SWbW ½ mile, situation of Encampment at the foot of lofty peaked mountains of Granite, 66°40′05″ North (R), 115°25′43″ Chr., variation 48°00′00″ East.

Direct daily course corrected for variation NWbN 42¾ miles.

16 A Lousewort, perhaps *Pedicularis arctica* (*P. langsdorffii*).
17 Hairy Lousewort.
18 Lapland Lousewort.
19 Moss Campion.
20 *Lloydia serotina*.
21 Nodding Saxifrage, *Saxifraga cernua*.
22 Alpine Saxifrage.
23 Possibly Yellow Mountain Saxifrage, *Saxi-*
fraga aizoides, if Richardson meant this as the last saxifrage, not the first draba on his list.
24 This Whitlow Grass or Draba has no common name: *Draba alpina* is correct.
25 Probably Pink-flowered Wintergreen, *Pyrola asarifolia*.
26 Willows and sedges, various kinds.
27 Ground Juniper.

Saturday July 7ᵗʰ 1821 Coppermine River

Hoar frost in the night. Thermometer at 4 a.m. 40°.

Embarked a little after 4 a.m. and at 7 came to the Hook's encampment situated on the summit of a lofty sand cliff whose base was washed by the river. The Hook had only three hunters with him the rest of his band having remained at their snares in [Great] Bear Lake, but the size of his party was encreased by Long legs and Cascathry with his family who had preceded us. A formal conference was afterwards held with the Hook when he was decorated with a medal by Mʳ Franklin and cheerfully gave us all the provision he had amounting to 130 lbs. of pounded meat, which was sufficient to make 2½ bags of pemmican, besides a small quantity of dried meat and tongues. In return for which they received a small quantity of ammunition and notes upon the NW company to be paid in the winter. The Hook pleaded in excuse for the smallness of the supply he was enabled to give us, that he had received his usual stock of ammunition from Fort Providence but a few days ago, and that we had refused to furnish any when he sent to Fort Enterprise in the winter. Moschetoes very numerous. Several papileinaceous insects²⁸ on the wing. Men employed during the afternoon making pemmican. Weather sultry. Course and distance NWbW 8 miles.

Courses per compass, swbw 3 miles, wsw½w 1½ miles, many sand banks and low islands.

West 5¼ miles. Situation of Encampment July 7ᵗʰ, 66°45′11″ North Obs., 115°42′23″ West Chr., variation 46°07′30″ East. Sand hills covering the base of mountains of Clay Slate.

Direct daily course corrected for variation NWbW 8 miles.

Sunday July 8ᵗʰ 1821

Mʳ Franklin this morning completed his arrangements with the Hook who has agreed to remain with his party on the borders of Great Bear Lake until the month of Novʳ that he may afford us relief in the event of our returning by that route. And he has also promised to make caches of dried meat on the portages leading from the Coppermine River to Bear Lake for which he is to receive payment at the Fort whether we return that way or not. We embarked at 11 a.m. with Akaicho and the White Capot in one canoe, and Old Cascathry in the other. Broad-face, one of our hunters being enamoured of Cascathry's daughter chose to remain with the Hook. The other four with the Little Singer walked along the banks of the river, two of them however by turns conducting two small canoes down the stream.

---

28 Butterflies.

The hills in the neighbourhood of the Hook's encampment are more even in their outline than those we had previously passed but there are some high peaks in the direction of the river, some of them obtuse – others short pointed – conical. From this spot the river course lay for a considerable distance between two ranges of hills, pretty even in their outlines and round-backed but having rather steep acclivities. The immediate borders of the stream consisted either of high banks of fine sand or of steep gravelly cliffs and sometimes where the hills receded to a little distance the intervening space was occupied by high sandy ridges apparently the ancient banks of the river. The peaks above mentioned proved on a nearer approach to be the summits of a connected range of hills whose forms seemed to indicate that they were composed of gneiss and sienite. The river wound through a narrow pass in these mountains by a tortuous course running generally to the westward but sometimes even to the southward. Just where the river inclines most to the westward the Indians are accustomed to make a portage into Great Bear Lake which they accomplish with their families in two or three days. Their utmost marches when thus encumbered do not exceed ten or twelve miles.[29] The exact situation of this portage which lies in 66°45′55″ north latitude and 116°31′05″ West Longitude is marked by the junction of [a] small stream [Hook River] with the Coppermine River. After passing which the river resuming a northerly course becomes narrower and more rapid, running betwixt high and even ranges of round backed hills between whose barren acclivities and the stream there lies a series of steeply rounded clayey banks well covered with trees.

About two hours after we set out we found a deer on the banks of the river which had been killed by our hunters and soon after shot another from one of the canoes. About 6 p.m. we found some marks that had been made by a band of Indians which on being examined were found to be quite recent – and soon after, coming to others, still more recent we put ashore, encamped and made a large fire to warn them of our approach – in the hopes of obtaining supplies from them.

Course and distance wbN ¾N 21¼ miles.

Courses per compass swbw½w 4½ miles, wbs½s ½ mile, West 1 mile, a long & low island of sand.

wbN¾N 2 miles, wbs¾s 1½ miles, ssw½w 2¼ miles, swbw ¾ mile, SSE 1 mile, sbw½w ½ mile, wsw ½ mile, sw 2 miles, sbw 1 mile, s¾w 2½ miles, swbs 1¼ miles, sw½w 1¼ miles. Situation of the mouth of a small stream [Hook River] which the Indians ascend in crossing from the Copp. River to Bear Lake, 66°45′55″ North (R), 116°31′05″ West (R).

wbN½N 2¼ miles. Rapids.

wbN 1¼ miles, NW¾w ¾ mile, NWbw 1 mile, NWbN ¾ mile. Rapids

29 Per day.

NWbW ¾ mile. The River runs here in a narrow channel bounded by high hills. From the hills above the Encampment 66°52′20″ North (R), 116°35′45″ West (R), the Coppermine mountains are visible.

Direct daily course corrected NWbW ½w, 21¾ miles.

Monday July 9ᵗʰ 1821 Coppermine River

The smoke of the Indian's fire being seen late last night one of the canoes was sent down the river to them and returned about half past one this morning with a small bundle of dried meat. The band from which it was obtained consisting only of three old men with their wives they had unfortunately left a considerable quantity of pounded meat on the borders of Great Bear Lake from the want of people to carry it. Soon after embarking we came to the Indian encampment where Mʳ Franklin landed and gave their leader a note upon the NW company in return for the provision they had given us. After re embarking we continued to descend the river which was now contracted between lofty banks to about 120 yards in width. Its channel filled with large stones and current very swift. At 11 a.m. we came to a rapid [Rocky Defile Rapid] which had been the theme of discourse with the Indians for many days, and we found that although the grandeur of the scene was commensurate with their descriptions yet that their habitual love of the marvellous had induced them to exaggerate the danger of passing it exceedingly. The river here struggles through a narrow gloomy channel which it has cut during the lapse of ages in the shelving foot of a hill. The channel is bounded by perpendicular rocky walls varying in height from 50 to 150 feet, above which there is imposed an immense body of fine sand. The form of the land here would lead one to suppose that the river, at some distant period, pent in by the rock formed a long narrow lake whose superfluous waters were discharged by a magnificent cascade, and this opinion is in some degree corroborated by the figure of various sandy ridges and peaks which rise immediately above the rapid to the height of 5 or 600 feet – and bear an exact resemblance to the banks of sand which are often found in the borders of a lake. The length of this defile exceeds half a mile and our canoes after a part of their cargoes was landed ran through it without sustaining any injury. Soon after passing the rapid we met the hunters running up the east side of the river to prevent us from disturbing a herd of musk oxen which they had observed grazing upon the opposite bank. We put them across and they succeeded in killing six of these animals upon which we encamped for the purpose of splicing and drying the meat.

The country immediately below the rapid consists of sandy plains which are broken by small conical eminences also of sand and bounded to the Westward by a continuation of the mountain chain which we crossed at the Bear Lake portages and to the Eastward and Northward at the distance of twelve miles by the celebrated Copper mountains. The plains are crowned by several clumps of moderately large spruce trees (30 feet high) and there is a considerable quantity of small dry wood standing upon them. The channel of the river lies about 300 feet below their surface, its banks are steep and on a level with the water a species of syenite projects from under the superimposed bed of sand. This syenite I am inclined to think belongs to the transition series. The beds of the mountain torrents which in various places in this neighbourhood cut through the banks of the river are lined with fragments of variegated and spotted red sandstone composed principally of felspar. There occurs also a kind of quartzy sandstone, having a coarse texture and greyish white colour which frequently contains enclosed small pieces of the red kind. A brownish-red glistening stone of a very smooth compact appearance and containing small and narrow chrystals of a blueish or greenish black mineral is often found in these torrents. The basis of this porphyritic stone does not yield to the knife. We observed also some rolled masses of limestone of a wine yellow colour and very compact texture having thin layers of flinty slate intermixed with it. Long. obs. 116°27′28″ Lat 67°1′10″ Var^n 44°11′43″ E.

Course and distance today NbE 9 miles.

Courses per compass NWbW¼W ⅓ mile, NW ¾ mile, WNW 1½ miles, NW½W ¾ mile, NWbN 1 mile, NWbW½W ½ mile. Most westerly part of the Coppermine River and greatest longitude attained by the Expedition, 66°55′50″ North (R) 116°38′40″ West (R).

NWbN ¾ mile, NNW ¾ mile, Nbw 1½ miles, NbE 1 mile. Rocky defile rapid. Rocks Trap tuff. 66°58′30″ North (R). 116°34′10″ West (R).

NbE½E 1 mile, NbE 2 miles. Magnetic dip 87°31′18″ Situation of Encampment on 9th & 10th July, 67°01′10″ North (Obs.), 116°27′28″ West (Chr.), Variation 44°11′43″ E.

Direct daily course corrected NbE 9 miles.

Tuesday July 10th 1821

Sultry weather. Much annoyed by musquitoes. The drying of the meat impeded by thunder showers. Remained encamped all day. The dip of the magnetic needle was observed to be 87°31′18″.

Wednesday July 11th 1821

The Hunters having gone off last night with the intention of waiting for us at the Copper mountains we followed them this morning at three O clock and having passed the Mouse a considerable stream which after a tortuous course through the plains falls into the river on its eastern bank, we came to a wide and shallow channel which it was necessary from the rapidity of the current to descend with poles. Here we passed a cliff of clay-stone of a greyish colour and dipping NNW at an angle of 20° per compass. At half past 7 we arrived at the foot of the Copper Mountains and landing on the western bank of the River found that the Indians had killed three Musk oxen. This determined us upon encamping immediately and whilst part of the Men were employed splicing and drying the meat, another party with the Officers and Indians set out to search for Copper in the places to which the Indians had been accustomed to resort. The party employed in this pursuit consisted of 21 but after travelling for ten hours over a considerable space of ground we found only a few small pieces. The Copper mountains seem to be composed principally of felspar much iron-shot and hence of a dark reddish brown appearance. This rock has very generally an amygdaloidal structure, the cavities filled with calcareous spar and other substances; at other times it occurs in form of a simple clay stone and sometimes it has a conglomerated appearance. There are many narrow vallies in this range of the Copper mountains which are generally bounded by perpendicular walls of greenstone. One or two beds of reddish-sandstone were also met with. It would appear that the Indians search in the vallies and when they see any sparry substance, green ore or copper projecting above the surface they dig in that neighbourhood – but they have no other rule to direct them and have never found the metal in its original repository. From the small fragments we picked up I am led to believe that it occurs in veins in the amygdaloid and perhaps also disseminated through it. The minerals with which it is associated will appear from the specimens sent home. The Indians report that they find Copper often in large pieces in every part of this range which they have examined for two days walk to the NW and that the Eskimaux come hither to search for that mineral. Lat. and Long. of our encampment 67°10′50″ N., 116°19′50″ W. Course and distance NbE 9½ miles. [written in later]

Courses per compass Nbw 1 mile, Nbw½w 2¼ miles. The Coppermine River is dilated & shallow here, & full of gravelly islands & rapids.

NWbN 1 mile. Confluence of the Mouse River which comes from the Eastward. 67°05′25″ North (R), 116°22′15″ West (R).

wbN 1 mile, NWbw¾w 1 mile, NWbw½w 1 mile, NWbw 1 mile, Nbw½w 1 mile.

Situation of the mouth of a small stream [Larrigan Creek] which issues from the valley in which the Indians search for Copper, 67°10′30″ North (R), 116°25′45″ West (R).

NbE ¾ mile, NNE½E 1½ miles. Encampment at the Copper mountains July 11th. 67°10′50″ North (R), 116°19′50″ West (R).

Direct daily course corrected NbE, 9½ miles.

Thursday July 12th 1821

Embarked at 6 and proceeded down the river the Indians following by land. As we were now entering upon the confines of the Eskimaux country our guides recommended us to be cautious in lighting fires lest we should discover ourselves adding that the same reason would lead them to avoid crossing the tops of the hills. They moreover informed us that from hence to the sea the river was little else than a succession of rapids, on which account they quitted their canoes altogether. M[r] Franklin however deeming a small canoe to be absolutely requisite

"... two musk oxen being seen on the banks of the river"

should we be compelled to walk along the coast ordered two men to conduct one of them down the river. Throughout today's voyage the current was very strong but the navigation tolerably good and we had to lighten the canoes only once. The river is in many places confined betwixt perpendicular walls of brownish-red sandstone having a thin slaty structure and dipping to the northward, is everywhere to the northward of the Copper mountains narrow and flows through a channel 150 or 200 feet below the surrounding country. Another range of Trap hills similar in external form to the Copper Mountains but not so high bounds the view to the Northward and the intermediate country is uneven but not hilly and consists of a sandy superstratum which when cut through by the rivulets discloses extensive beds of red freestone. The wood has almost disappeared from the banks of the river being confined to a few well sheltered corners and the surrounding country is perfectly naked. Many large fragments of ice that have accumulated out of the reach of the stream remind us of the tardy departure of winter from this inhospitable land.

At 3 p.m. two musk oxen being seen on the banks of the river, they were pursued by a party of our men, who succeeded in killing them both. Soon after this we landed and pitched our tents amidst the vestiges of an old eskimaux encampment. The Indians arrived in the evening with a report that a bear had sprung upon them whilst they were walking in earnest conversation with each other. This attack was so sudden that they had not time to level their guns properly and they all missed except Akaicho who less confused than the others took a deliberate aim and killed it on the spot. The Indians do not eat the flesh of the Grizzly-bear themselves, but knowing that we had no such prejudice they brought us some of the choice pieces and upon trial we unanimously pronounced them to be superior to the best musk ox meat we had seen. There are some stumps of trees in the neighbourhood of our encampment which have been cut down by the stone hatchets of the Eskimaux. Course and distance NbE½E 13½ miles.

Lat. 67°23′14″ N. Long. 116°6′51″ Var^n 49°46′24″ Easterly.

Courses per compass ENE 1½ miles, NEbE 2 miles, NbE½E ¾ mile, NEbN 1 mile, NNE½E 2¼ miles, NbE½E 1¾ miles, NE ½ mile, Nbw 1½ miles, NWbN ¾ mile. Influx of a mountain Stream [Melville Creek], 67°14′00″ North (R), 115°52′45″ West (R).

wbN½N ¾ mile, wbN 1 mile, wbs 3 miles. A small island.

wbN¼N 1 mile, wbN½N 3 miles, Musk Ox Rapid, 67°20′50″ North (R), 116°03′50″ West (R).

wsw ½ mile, wNw 1½ miles. Situation of Encampment at the Sandstone Rapids July 12th & 13th, 67°23′14″ North (Obs.), 116°06′51″ West (Chr.), Variation 49°46′24″ East.[30]

Direct daily course corrected NbE½E, 13½ miles.

Friday July 13th 1821

Weather warm and fine. Temp^r in the afternoon 75°.

Junius and Augustus were sent off this morning with directions to proceed to a remarkable rapid said by the Indians to be resorted to at this season for the purpose of fishing by the Eskimaux and to endeavour to open a communication with any of that nation they might find there. They were supplied with beads looking glasses and some iron articles that they might be enabled to conciliate their countrymen by presents and to avoid exciting alarm by their appearance in the first instance they were dressed in deerskins cut out by

30 On my 1:250,000 Coppermine map #86-o, 1977 provisional edition, Muskox Rapids was printed in and then crossed out at the site of Richardson's Muskox Rapids. Muskox Rapids was used to name the next set of rapids which Richardson called Sandstone Rapids. Sandstone Rapids is placed on this map at 116°26′, just beyond Richardson's Island Portage.

one of the Indians after the fashion of the Eskimaux he had seen, which indeed varied but little from that adopted by Augustus' tribe. These two adventurous men, armed only with small pistols which they concealed about their dress set out with the utmost alacrity to perform the task allotted to them. Junius in particular was perfectly delighted at the idea of meeting a tribe that spoke his own language. They were directed to return immediately if there were no lodges at the rapid.

In the afternoon an ox coming down to the river side was killed by a party that went after it.

Saturday July 14ᵗʰ 1821 *Coppermine River*

Weather warm but windy. No intelligence of Augustus and his companion hav-ing arrived at 11 a.m., considerable anxiety for their safety prevailed amongst the party, and we embarked and proceeded down the river, with the intention of meeting them, or at least of ascertaining the cause of their delay. As the appear-ance of Indians in our suite, might induce the Eskimaux to suspect the purity of our intentions, they were requested to remain behind, until we had paved the way for their reception in a friendly manner, but Akaicho ever ready to augur misfortune, expressed his belief that our two Interpreters were killed, and that the Eskimaux warned of our appearance, were lying in wait for us. If this were the case he went on to state, although the strength of *our* party might resist any hostile attack, yet that *his* small band, seperated from us, was too weak to offer any effectual resistance and that therefore, he was resolved, either to accompany us down the river or to return at once to his lands. After much argument, how-ever, he yielded to our requests, and agreed to stay where he was, provided that Mʳ Wentzel remained with him. We therefore left that Gentleman, with a Cana-dian attendant behind.

The River during the whole of today's voyage flows between high banks of red-sandstone and is every where shoal and rapid: and as its course is very crooked much time was spent in examining the different rapids previous to running them.

Most of the Officers and men travelled by land the greatest part of this day, all well armed. The flat country here is covered with grass and is devoid of the large stones so frequent on the barren grounds but the ranges of trap hills which seem to intersect it at regular distances are barren enough.

We had been informed, that the range visible from our last encamp-ment, was the last betwixt us and the sea, which was distinctly visible from its summit; and of course, we ascended it with much eagerness, but our disappoint-ment was proportionably great when we beheld beyond them a plain similar to that we had just left, terminated by another range of trap hills between whose tops the summits of some distant blue mountains appeared. In the evening we had the satisfaction of meeting with Junius who was hurrying back to inform us that they had seen 4 Eskimaux lodges at the fall, which we now recognized to be the one described by Hearne, and that they had had some conversation with their inhabitants, across the river and had told them of the approach of white people, who would make them many useful presents. This information seemed to frighten them very much, and they would not venture to land upon this side upon which our Interpreters were, but sometimes approached near enough in their canoes to be distinctly heard. Their language differed in some respects from Augustus' but they understood one another tolerably well. Augustus trusting for a supply of provision to the Eskimaux had neglected to carry any with him, and this was the main cause of Junius' return.

We encamped in the evening on the left bank of the river having come 12 miles on NbE½E course.

Junius, after a short refreshment, returned to Augustus accompanied by John Hepburn, who had orders to remain about a mile above the fall, to arrest the canoes in their passing lest they should come upon the Eskimaux unawares.

About 10 p.m. to our great mortification, the Indians arrived. They had become impatient and Mr Wentzel did not possess authority enough to restrain them from following us.

Soon afterwards I went to the summit of a hill about 3 miles distant from our encampment, and had a view of the sea which appeared to be covered with ice and extended from NNE to NEbE. A large promontory [named Cape Hearne by Franklin] from the westward bore NE and its lofty mountains proved to be the blue land we had seen in the forenoon and which had led us to believe that the sea was still far distant. From the top of the hill, I observed the sun set a few minutes before midnight but although I remained there about half an hour it did not rise in that time. Its rays however gilded the tops of the hills, before I reached the encampment. The mosquitoes were uncommonly numerous tonight.

NWbW½W ⅓ mile, N¼W 3 miles, NNE ½ mile. Situation of the Island Portage, 67°25′25″ North (R), 116°01′10″ West (R).

NNW ½ mile, NW ½ mile, wbN¾N 2¼ miles. Small rocky Islands.

NWbN 1 mile. Range of hills, 67°30′00″ North (R), 116°00′00″ West (R).

NNE 1½ miles, NW 1 mile, wbs ¾ mile, NW 1 mile, NWbW½W ¾ mile, NWbN ¾ mile. Situation of encampment, 67°34′20″ North (R), 115°55′45″ West (R). No trees beyond this place.

Direct daily course corrected NbE½E, 12 miles.

Sunday July 15th 1821

Leaving Mr Wentzel and the Indians at the encampment we embarked at 8 a.m. A party walking on shore, to lighten the canoes. The river at this place flows between high sandstone cliffs, reddish slate clay rocks, and shelving banks of white clay and is full of shoals and dangerous rapids. In one of these [Escape Rapids], the canoes were filled with water and narrowly escaped foundering. About noon Hepburn appeared on the left bank and by his direction we put ashore in a small sandy bay at the head of the celebrated rapid of Hearne [Bloody Falls].

This rapid is a sort of shelving cascade about 300 yards in length having a descent of from 10 to 15 feet. It is bounded on each side by high walls of red sandstone upon which a series of lofty green hills rests. We found the Eskimaux encampment on a small rocky island at the foot of the rapid in the eastern side of the river and Augustus perched on an eminence on the opposite side. From him we learnt, that on his first arrival, he had called to a man whom he saw at the lodges, to come and ferry him across the river. The man immediately complied with his request and crossed the foot of the rapid with two canoes; when he approached the shore, however, he showed some degree of apprehension and could not be persuaded to land, but held a parley with the stranger at the distance of a few yards. He was then told that the white people were come; with the most favourable inclination, to his tribe. He then enquired the number of canoes that we had with us, expressed himself to be not displeased at our arrival, and desired Augustus to caution us not to attempt running the rapid. Notwithstanding this apparently favourable opening of the communication the Eskimaux that night deserted their lodges and took shelter upon an island a little further down the river. Next morning they returned and threw down their lodges, as if to give notice to any of their nation that might arrive, that, there was an enemy in the neighbourhood. They passed that night also on the island, but came occassionally to converse with Augustus, and about the time that we approached the rapid, one of the men was speaking to him from his canoe and was almost persuaded to land but unfortunately at this instant the party of our people who walked appeared on the tops of the hills, on which the man instantly retreated and shortly after, Augustus observed their whole band, consisting of 4 men and as many women, crossing over to the Eastern bank of the river. Two of the men were very tall. They left their canoes on the beach and fled. Their dogs 10 in number remained at their lodges, with all their stone kettles, hatchets, a few fish spears of copper, two small bits of iron and a considerable quantity of skins and some dried salmon, which was covered with maggots and half putrid. A great many skins of small birds were also hung up to a stage and even two mice were preserved in the same way. The fish guts also were spread out to dry, but the dogs were making great havoc amongst them. The island upon which the lodges were erected lies exactly at the foot of the rapid, and is seperated from the shore, by a narrow channel in which the Eskimaux spear great numbers of salmon. Having carried the canoes and their cargoes from the bay in which we landed to the foot of the rapid, we encamped on the very spot where the Massacre of the Eskimaux was transacted by Hearne's party. The ground is still strewed with human skulls and as it is overgrown with rank grass, appears to be avoided as a place of encampment. Augustus and Junius were put across the river in the afternoon to look for the runaways, but their search was fruitless. A few pieces of iron and some trinkets were left in their canoes and the stages of fish left in their lodges as well secured as possible from the attacks of their dogs.

Course and distance today NbE 8¾ miles.

The nets were set at the foot of the rapid and we caught some fine salmon and Attihawmeghs.

We have seen no trees today. Our firewood consists of willows and a few pieces of drift wood.

Courses per compass NE ¾ mile, NWbN½N ½ mile, WNW ½ mile, NW½W 1¼ miles, WbN 1¾ miles, WNW ¼ mile, SWbW 1¼ miles, WNW 1 mile. 67°39′35″ North Obs.

N¼E 2 miles. River broad & shallow here & full of gravelly banks.

NbW ¾ mile, NbW¾W 1 mile. Encampment at Massacre Rapid July 15th, 16th and 17th. 67°42′35″ North (Obs), 115°49′33″ (Chr.), Variation 50°20′14″ East.

Direct daily course corrected NbE, 8¾ miles.

Monday July 16th 1821 Massacre Rapid

Three men were sent up the river to obtain wood for floats to the nets. After waiting until noon for the re-appearance of the Eskimaux, Adam the Interpreter was sent with a Canadian to inform Mr Wentzel and the Indians of the state of matters and Mr Franklin was preparing to go down to the sea in one of the canoes, leaving Mr Back to wait the return of the men who were absent. Just as we were about to embark, Adam arrived in the utmost consternation, and informed us that our people were chased by a band of Eskimaux. The orders for embarking were instantly countermanded and Mr Franklin with Augustus, and an armed party went to their rescue. We met our people returning slowly and learnt that they had come unawares upon the Eskimaux who were travelling towards the rapid with their women and children, and a considerable number of dogs carrying their baggage. The women hid themselves on the first alarm, but the men began to dance and to signify by their motions a desire of peace. Our men returned their salutes by pulling off their hats and making bows but neither party was willing to approach the other. Going forward we found their baggage deserted and an old man lying behind a stone at a small distance, being too infirm to make his escape. He shewed much apprehension at first but Augustus soon calmed his fears and presenting him with a piece of iron he became very communicative. It appeared that the party to which he belonged, consisted of 8 men with their families & that they were returning from a hunting excursion with a quantity of dried meat. His dialect differed from that used by Augustus, but they understood each other tolerably well. Soon after this, Akaicho and the Indians came in sight and we learnt that they had seen the Eskimaux the day before and had endeavoured without success to open a friendly communication with them. They exhibited no hostile intentions but were affraid to come near. Akaicho keeping out of their sight followed them at a distance expecting that ultimately finding themselves inclosed between our party and his they would be compelled to come to a parley with one of us.

Massacre Rapids [Bloody Falls]

When Augustus first approached the old man he pricked at him with a brass spear and he treated Akaicho in the same way notwithstanding, he had been told that he was coming and had even expressed a desire to see him.

The countenance of the old man whose name is Terregannoeuck or the White-fox, is oval, with a sufficiently prominent nose and is in nothing very different from an European face except in the smallness of the eyes and perhaps the narrowness of the forehead. His complexion is very fresh and red and he has a longer beard than I have hitherto seen on any of the aboriginal inhabitants of America. It is between two and three inches long, thick and perfectly white. His face is not tattooed. His dress consists of a shirt or jacket with a hood, wide breeches reaching only to the knee and tight leggins sewed to the shoes all of deer skin. The soles of the shoes are made of seal skin and they are stuffed with feathers instead of socks. He was bent with age but appeared to have been about 5 feet 10 inches high. His hands and feet were small in proportion to his height. The tribe to which he belongs denominate themselves Naggeooktorrmoeoot or Deer horn Eskimaux and frequent the Massacre rapid during the present and following moons for the purpose of killing salmon. They then retire to a river which flows into the sea a short way to the westward and pass the winter in snow houses. They repair to the sea in the spring and kill seals, but they see no sea-horses or whales, although Terregannoeuck remembers one of the latter, which had been killed by some distant tribe, being driven ashore on his part of the coast, by a gale of wind, and they occassionally receive pieces of whale bone from a tribe that inhabits the country to the eastward. Deer may be killed sparingly on the coast all the year. Fish constantly in the rivers and in the sea as soon as the ice breaks up. This tribe do not make use of nets but are tolerably successful with the hook and line. The Musk-ox is found only on the banks of the rivers near the straggling woods and they do not hunt them in the winter. Their principal weapon is the bow and arrow and they get sufficiently near the deer to use it either by crawling or by leading these animals by ranges of turf towards a spot where the bowman can conceal himself. Their bows are formed of three pieces of fir, the centre piece alone bent, the end ones lying in the same straight line with the bowstring. The pieces are neatly tied together with sinew. Their canoes are similar to those we saw in Hudsons straights, but are smaller. Their cooking utensils are made of potstone and they make very neat dishes of fir, the sides being formed of thin deal[31] bent into an oval form, secured at the ends by sewing, and fitted so nicely to the bottom as to be perfectly water-tight. They have also large spoons made of the horns of the Musk ox.

We made Terregannoeuck a variety of presents, of which he seemed to hold the hatchets and other iron instruments in the highest estimation. He placed each article as he received it first on his right shoulder, then on the left and when he wished to express still higher satisfaction rubbed it over his head.

We left him, after he had promised to bring the young men to our tents, when they had recovered sufficiently from their fears, to approach the spot where they had left him, but he did not expect them to return that night. It may be remarked, that contrary to the Indian practice, he asked each of our names, as we came up, and the man who conversed with Augustus from the canoe, also demanded his name and that of Junius.

Late in the evening Augustus and Junius went to pass the night with the old man, fearing that his representations might fail in calming the fears of the young people, unless the intentions of the white people, were more fully detailed. None of this tribe had ever seen white people before, but they had heard of them.

31 A "whole deal" was a plank 1¼ inches thick, usually 3 inches wide.

Tuesday July 17th 1821 Massacre Rapid

During the night, an old woman who had concealed herself amongst the rocks, came to Terregannoeucks tent, which with the assistance of Junius and Augustus he had erected – and from her we learnt, that the rest of the party had fled to a river, a short distance to the westward where there was another party of Eskimaux fishing. The features of the old woman are remarkable for roundness and flatness. Her forehead is tattooed in two double lines which meet at the nose and are prolonged downwards. Three parallel lines run from the outer angle of each eye to the alae of the nose and three others proceed from the corners of the mouth to the angles of the jaw. The chin is bisected by one perpendicular line. Her dress differed very little from the old man's.

Mr Hood went today with a party to bring some meat which Terregannoeuck had promised us yesterday and which he said was stored up in the neighbourhood – but it proved to be too putrid for our use.

In the afternoon a party of nine Eskimaux, appeared on the banks of the river, about a mile below our encampment, carrying their canoes and baggage on their backs, but they turned and fled as soon as they perceived our tents. The appearance of so many different bands of Eskimaux, has terrified our Indian hunters to such a degree, that they have determined on leaving us tomorrow, lest they should be surrounded, and their retreat cut off. Mr Franklin endeavoured by large promises to induce one or two of them to accompany us along the coast, but in vain. Variations per az. 50°20′14″ East.

Lat. and Long. ascertained today 67°42′35″ Obs. 115°49′33″ Chr.

Wednesday July 18th 1821

At 5 O'clock a.m. Embarked and proceeded down the river, the Indians at the same time setting out on their return promising to wait three days on the Copper mountains for Mr Wentzel and 4 men that Mr Franklin intends to discharge at the sea, to reduce the size of our party and lessen the consumption of provisions. They were furnished with ammunition at their departure. After we had passed a few rapids the river became wider and more navigable for a canoe and flowed through a channel considerably below the level of a tract of alluvial sandy soil. We arrived at the mouth of the river before noon, and encamped on its western bank. The river at its confluence with the sea is very shallow and barred nearly across by sand banks, which run out from the main land on each side, to a low alluvial island, which lying in the centre, divides the channel into two. Of these the westernmost only is navigable for a canoe. The water beyond the sand banks, is of a clear green colour, and is decidedly salt. Hearne must have tasted the water of the river, when he pronounced it to be merely brackish. We saw many seals in the mouth of the river. The islands are high and numerous and shut the horizon in, on many points of the compass. The sea appears clear from the eminences on which we are encamped from NWbW to Nbw per compass; and towards the NE the land makes like a chain of islands. In every other direction the land appears continuous. The ice lies in a pretty solid field, three or four miles distant from the mouth of the river.

A few ducks were seen today, for the first time since we passed the Copper mountains. The shore is strewed with a considerable quantity of drift

Iviagiknak (like the breast of a woman) where the party probably camped at the mouth of the Coppermine River

lumber, which is principally the wood of the *Populus balsamifera*[32] and none of it of great size. The nets were set in the afternoon, M[r] Franklin proposing to make up his dispatches for England here.

Course and distance from the Massacre Rapid NE¼E 9½ miles.

Nbw¼w 1¼ miles, NEbE¼E 1 mile, Nbw 1 mile, NNE 3 miles, Nbw½w 3½ miles, NW 1 mile.

187¼ distance from Encampment July 1st below Rock Nest to the Sea

54¼   ,,   ,,   ,,   June 21 to 25 on Point Lake to July 1st.

_____   ,,   travelled along Point Lake to the northward & Eastward in autumn 1820 by Mess[rs] Hood & Back

_____   ,,   travelled along Point Lake & Providence Lake & Rapid Sept[r] 1821 to opposite where M[r] Back left off

_____   ,,   through which the Coppermine River was traced by the Expedition including its windings in geographical miles.

The distance in statute miles is _____

32 Balsam Poplar.

88°05'07" Magnetic Dip. Sea Coast. Mouth of the Coppermine River, 67°47'50" North (Obs.), 115°36'49" West (Chr.). Variation 46°26'00" East.

The most Southerly part of the Coppermine River seen by the Expedition lies in Lat. 64°50' N., Long. 112°12' W. Hence the direct line of its course which was traced is NNW½W dist. 20¾ miles geogr. or 236 Statute miles.

Direct daily course corrected NE¼N, 8 miles.

Thursday July 19th 1821 Arctic Sea

This morning Augustus and I went up to Terregannoeuck's lodge but were disappointed on finding that his affrighted family had not returned. I could obtain no additional information from the old fellow respecting the country to the eastward, for although he was sufficiently loquacious yet he was or affected to be extremely ignorant of any part except a small tract lying between the Coppermine river and another river to the westward [Richardson River], which falls into the sea at eight or nine miles distance from our encampment. He readily told us the name of his tribe, which is Keedleenoers Naggoeookto-ook and may be translated the Indians inhabiting the sea coast frequented by the deer with large antlers. He also named a small river to the eastward Nappaark-tokto-wok or Tree River³³ but he shewed a great dislike to mentioning the name of the Coppermine River and always evaded the question with much dexterity and no small degree of volubility. He attempted to persuade Augustus to remain with him, and offered him one of his daughters for a wife. These Eskimaux strike fire with two stones, catching the sparks in the down of the catkins of a willow.

In the afternoon Mr Wentzel took leave of us and set out accompanied by four men, Parent, Gagnè, Dumas and Forcier, with directions to proceed to Point Lake, transport the canoe that was left there to Fort Enterprise, where he was to embark the instruments and books³⁴ and carry them to Slave Lake. Our voyageurs seem terrified at the idea of a voyage through an icy sea in bark canoes, and have had frequent debates on the subject. The two Interpreters in particular express their fears with the least disguise and have made many urgent requests to be allowed to return with Mr Wentzel. Our stock of ammunition has been reduced by the supplies given to Mr Wentzel's party to 1000 balls and a proportion of powder rather greater. The Canadians determined to leave no means unattempted, which may tend to promote their safety, have secreted and distributed amongst themselves a bag of small shot. They hope thus to be enab-

33 The Nipartoktuak River is the first river east of the Coppermine River, less than 20 miles away; the Tree River is the fourth such river and is about 100 miles east of the mouth of the Coppermine.

34 And natural history specimens. Wentzel and the four men also carried some of Richardson's rock and plant specimens collected along the Coppermine River.

led, when provisions become scarce, privately to procure ducks and geese and to avoid the necessity of sharing them with the officers. Since we encamped at the Massacre rapid we have lived upon the produce of our nets but our stock of provision does not exceed 14 days consumption and it is of no use, to talk to a Canadian voyageur of going upon short allowance. They prefer running the risk of going entirely without hereafter, that they may have a present belly full, and if it is not given to them they will steal it and in their opinion it is no disgrace to be caught pilfering provisions.

The latitude was ascertained to be 67°47′50″ N, Long. 115°36′49″ West. Var^n 46″26′E. and dip 88°05′07″. The sun set tonight at 11^{h}30′ apparent time.

Description of a species of *Salmo* which is taken in great numbers by the Eskimaux in the Salmon leap at the Massacre Rapid. It is inferior to the English salmon in size. Shape that of the common salmon but the head is proportionably larger.[35] [1½-page description of Arctic Char]

Plies p. 220 Reg. An. en fr. Limancha

Description of a fish of the genus Pleuronectes taken in nets at the mouth of the Coppermine River.[36] [1-page description of Starry Flounder]

Friday July 20th 1821 Arctic Sea

Intended to have started at 4 this morning but were prevented by a fresh easterly wind which in the afternoon brought on a continued rain. Thunder in the afternoon. Few fish being caught today some dried meat was issued to the men.

35 Arctic Char, *Salvelinus alpinus.* Called "trout" throughout the journal. Richardson named this specimen the Coppermine River Salmon, *Salmo Hearnii.*

36 Starry Flounder, *Platichthys stellatus.*

5

BY CANOE IN THE
ARCTIC OCEAN

Saturday July 21st 1821

Saturday July 21st 1821

Foggy weather with strong winds prevented us from embarking before noon when it cleared up and we began our voyage in the hyperborean sea – and soon after landed upon an island where the Eskimaux had erected a stage of drift timber and stored up many of their fishing implements and winter sledges together with a great many dressed seal, musk ox and deer skins. Their spears headed with bone and many small articles of the same material apparently intended for some kind of game were worked with extreme neatness. We paddled all day along the coast, on the inside of a crowded range of islands, and saw but very little ice. One small iceberg was seen in the distance. It is to be recollected however that the view from a canoe is very limited. In the afternoon a rein deer being discovered on an island, we put ashore and killed it. It proved to be a fat male and was a great acquisition in the present state of affairs. We encamped on the main, at 9 p.m. Course EbS½s and distance 37 miles. The outline of this part of the coast is in general even and the shore easy of access but the Islands are high and rocky and for the most part bounded by mural precipices of greenstone and basalt which present a columnar structure. At the spot where we landed a considerable quantity of muscle shells,[1] with a little sea-weed lay on the beach. We were rejoiced to find the beach also strewed with abundance of small drift wood, none of it recent. The following plants have been collected in flower, here and at the mouth of the Coppermine River.

  Potentilla fruticosa.[2] *P* _____? *verticillari* affinis.[3] *Pedicularis Sceptrum Carolinium. Pedicularis hirsuta. Pedicularis* _____? *euphrasoides* affinis.[4] *P.* _____?

1 Mussel shells.
2 Shrubby Cinquefoil.

3 Probably *Potentilla pulchella* var. *gracilicaulis.*
4 Probably Labrador Lousewort, *Pedicularis labradorica.*

sudetica affinis.[5] *P. Lapponica. P. flammea.*[6] *Lychnis* _____?[7] *Tofielda borealis.*[8] *Statice armeria.*[9] *Anemone ranunculoides?*[10] *Carex limosa.*[11] *C.* _____? *ampullacea velvesicaria* affinis.[12] *Pyrola rotundifolia. P. secunda.*[13] *Vaccinium uliginosum.*[14] *V. vitis idaea. Silene acaulis. Azalea procumbens.*[15] *Saxifraga oppositifolia.*[16] *S. nivalis. S. tricuspidata.*[17] *S. hirculus.*[18] *S. cernua. S. hirta.*[19] *S.* _____? *groenlandicae* vel *magellanicae* similis.[20] *Primula mistassinica* (Pursh).[21] *Chrysanthemum* _____?[22] *Epilobium Latifolium.*[23] *Artemesia* _____?[24] *Pinguicula* _____?[25] *Triglochin palustre.*[26] *Achillea millefolium.*[27] *Comarum palustre.*[28] *Senecio* _____? *paledosa* vel *tomentosa* affinis.[29]

"The islands are high and rocky ..."

5 Identity confirmed by Hooker as *Pedicularis sudetica.*
6 *Pedicularis flammea* confirmed by Hooker.
7 Probably Bladder Campion, *Melandrium apetalum.*
8 False Asphodel, *Tofieldia pusilla.*
9 Thrift, *Armeria maritima.*
10 Richardson's Anemone, *Anemone richardsonii.*
11 Confirmed by Hooker as *Carex limosa.*
12 *Carex ampullacea* (John Hudson, pers. comm.).
13 One-sided Wintergreen.
14 Bilberry or Arctic Bog Blueberry.
15 Alpine Azalea, *Loiseleuria procumbens.*
16 Purple Saxifrage.
17 Prickly Saxifrage.
18 Yellow Marsh Saxifrage.
19 Probably Tufted Saxifrage, *Saxifraga caespitosa.*
20 As above, note 19.
21 Bird's-eye Primrose, though north of accepted range.
22 Chrysanthemum, *Chrysanthemum integrifolium.*
23 Broad-leaved Willow Herb, *Epilobium latifolium.*
24 *Wormwood.*
25 *Butterwort, probably Pinguicula vulgaris.*
26 Slender Arrow-grass.
27 Yarrow or Milfoil.
28 One of the cinquefoils, *Potentilla palustris.*
29 Groundsel, *Senecio lugens.*

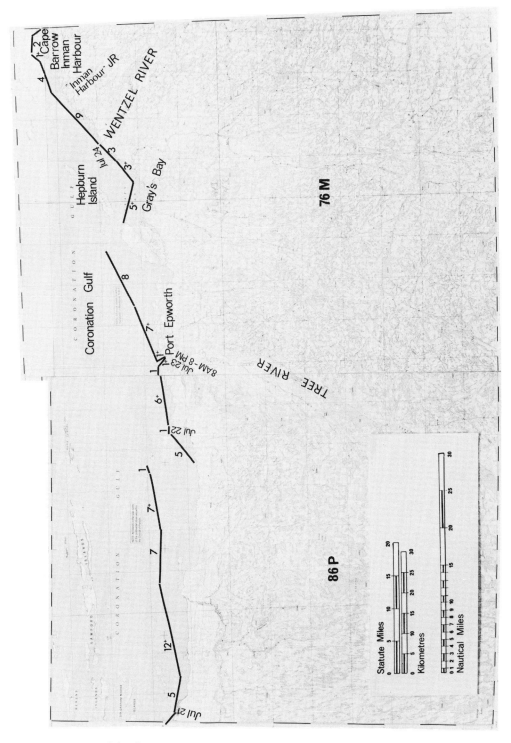

Map 4   21–24 July 1821

Epilobium spicatum. Stellaria glauca (Smith).[30] *Cerastium viscosum* (Smith).[31] *Arenaria peploides.*[32] *Crepis* _____?[33] *Hedysarum* _____? Liquorice root of Sir Alex[r] M[c]Kenzie.[34]

Weather all day very cold. The[r] varying from 40° to 45° Wind NE per compass.

Mouth of Richardson's River, 67°48'30" North (R), 115°52'30" West (R)

Cape Hearne, 68°06'40" North (R), 115°17'28" West (R)

Mouth of the Coppermine River, 67°47'50" North (Obs.), 115°36'49" West (Chr.), Variation 46°26'00" East. Couper's Isles in the offing.

NE 6½ miles, Small stream of fresh water [Nipartoktuak River] 67°45'58" North (R), 115°11'10" West (R). Between Couper's Isles & the Coast from 6 to 33 fathoms of water.

NE¼E 7 miles, NE 2 miles, NEbE½E 4 miles, E½N 6 miles.

Situation of Encampment July 21, 67°41'25" North (R), 114°29'10" West (R)

Direct daily course corrected EbS½S, 37 miles [27 miles].

Sunday July 22[d] 1821 Arctic sea

We embarked at 4 a.m. and continued our voyage along the coast – which during the morning presented the same general appearance that it did yesterday, namely a gravelly or sandy beach skirted by green fields but towards the evening the shore became exceedingly sterile and rocky and at last projecting considerably to the northward it formed a high and steep promontory. We rounded this sailing amongst many loose pieces of ice which from a distance appearing like a connected field, threw us when we first saw it into some alarm. The weather was very fine and for a few hours we were favoured with a fine fair wind. In the afternoon light variable airs, blowing alternately from the land and from the ice produced instantaneous and very striking changes of temperature. We saw some geese and ducks today and also two deer, but did not succeed in killing any. Encamped at 8 p.m. Course and distance E½S 38½ miles. Lat. obs. at noon.

NE½E 5 miles, NNE¾E 12½ miles, NE 7 miles, NEbN 7½ miles. Coast fringed with islands from 1 mile distant to as far as our view extended.

NEbN 1 mile, N½W 5 miles. Situation of Encampment July 22, 67°44'50" North (R), 112°47'50" West (R).

Direct daily course corrected E½S, 38½ miles.

---

30 Chickweed, probably *Stellaria longipes.*
31 Mouse-ear Chickweed, probably *Cerastium beeringianum.*
32 Seabeach Sandwort, now *Honckenya peploides.*

33 Hawk's-beard, probably *Crepis nana.*
34 *Hedysarum Mackenzii*, first named and described by Richardson in the Botanical Appendix to Franklin, 1823.

Monday July 23ᵈ 1821 Arctic sea

Embarking at 4 a.m. we ran with a freeze[35] breeze, for nine miles along the coast, sheltered on the outside by a compact field of ice, which left a clear channel about one mile wide. At 8 a.m. we came to a deep bay [Port Epworth] into which the Nappaarhtoktowok or Tree River of the Eskimaux discharges itself. Here we encamped and set our nets the wind having become adverse and too strong to admit of our proceeding. This part of the coast, is the most sterile and inhospitable that can be imagined. One basaltic cliff succeeds another, with a tiresome uniformity and their debris intirely covers the narrow vallies that intervene to the exclusion of every kind of herbage.

These trap cliffs, resembling in some points of view a pummice quoin,[36] whose thin edge lay beneath the contracted horizon of our canoe, were productive of considerable delay in our voyage, by frequently leading us into the bays in search of passages where none existed. About 8 in the evening the weather moderating the nets were taken up and we resumed our voyage. We caught only one attihawmegh and a few Zumards.[37]

Description of a fish caught at the mouth of the Tree river. Cottus? Crapaud de Mer.[38] [1¼-page description of Six-horned Bull-head]

Soon after starting, we discovered a rein-deer on the beach and landed the two Interpreters, who succeeded in killing it. Resuming our voyage, we were much impeded by the ice and at last being unable to penetrate a body of stream ice collected round a cape, we put ashore and encamped at 4 a.m. on the 24ᵗʰ. Course and distance (carried to the next day)

Lat. obs. at the Tree River 67°42′15″ Long. 112°30″ Varⁿ 47°37′42″ E.

NE 1 mile, NE½N 6½ miles, NE 1 mile, E¾N 1½ miles. In a bay termed Port Epworth, 67°42′15″ North (Obs.), 112°30′00″ (Chr.). Variation 47°37′42″ East.

[Mouth of] the Tree River [estimated to be] 67°40′15″, Long. 112°30′, Varⁿ 47°37′42″ E.

WNW 1¼ miles, NNE 7½ miles, NbE½E 8 miles. Eastern extremity of the peninsula which forms Gray's bay, 67°49′20″ North (R), 111°50′00″ West (R).

Tuesday July 24ᵗʰ 1821 Arctic sea

The ice seperating a little from the shore we embarked and with some difficulty effected a passage. Then making a traverse across a deep bay [Gray's Bay], we pulled up under its eastern shore the wind blowing strong from the NE per compass. The Interpreters landed here and went in pursuit of a deer, but had no success. About 7 p.m. a thunder storm coming on we encamped at the mouth of a

---

35 A fresh and cold breeze.
36 A quoin is a solid angle such as the external angle of a building.
37 Bull-heads (see footnote 38).

38 Richardson's "Six-horned Bull-head" which he named *Cottus hexacornis*. Now the Deepwater Sculpin, *Myoxocephalus quadricornis* (Linnaeus).

river and set four nets. The Eskimaux had recently piled up some drift timber here and even in the most sterile parts of the coast and in all the islands we have visited, traces of their encampments and stone fox traps have been pretty numerous. A few ducks were seen today, also some ravens and snow birds – only two or three gulls have been seen since we embarked on the arctic sea. Basaltic cliffs are numerous on this part of the coast, and they bound almost all the islands.

A large quantity of a species of *Cineraria*[39] growing in the alluvial soil at the mouth of the river. The river has been named Wentzel's River, is about 100 yards wide and discharges a considerable body of water.

Course and distance on the 23ᵈ and 24ᵗʰ ENE 31 miles.

ENE 5½ miles, West end of Hepburn's Island which is 5¼ miles long from SW to NE, 67°50′00″ North (R), 111°48′00″ West (R).

"… stone fox traps have been pretty numerous"

N½E 3½ miles, N½W 3 miles. East end of Hepburn's Island, 67°53′40″ North (R), 111°37′00″ West (R).

Encampment at the mouth of Wentzel's River, 67°52′25″ North (R), 111°29′30″ West (R).

Daily direct course [July 23 & 24 combined] corrected ENE, 31 miles.

Wednesday July 25ᵗʰ 1821 Arctic sea

Our fishery was injured by the entrance of some seals into the mouth of the river and we caught only three salmon-trout. Heavy rain with thunder during the night. Embarked at 7 a.m. Cold blowing weather. Embarked at 7 a.m. and ran for

39 Probably Marsh-fleabane, *Senecio congestus*.

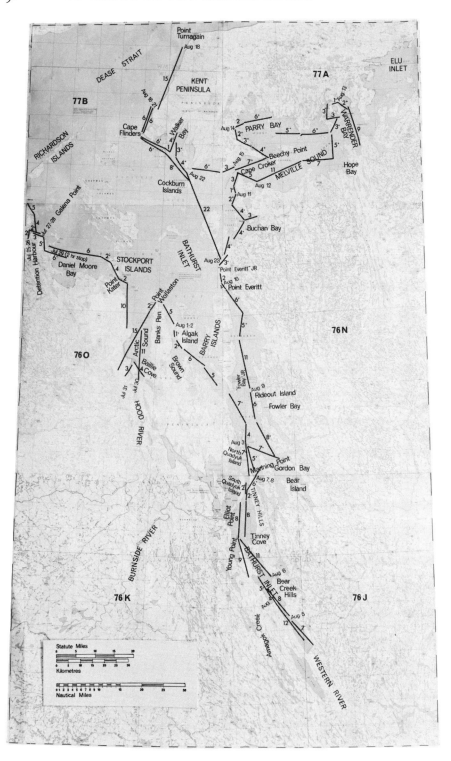

Map 5   *25 July–22 August 1821*

some time, when a thick fog coming on, we landed to breakfast. The rocks here consist of a beautiful admixture of red and grey granite traversed from North to South (true) by veins of red felspar, which were crossed in various directions by other smaller veins filled with the same substance. We reembarked after break-fast the fog continuing unabated all day, and kept as close to the main land as we could, but having to cross some bays, it became a matter of doubt whether we had left the main and were running along an island. The fog at times clearing partially away, allowed us to obtain an imperfect view of a chain of islands on the outside with much heavy brash ice[40] near us. In keeping along the land we were led first to the Northward and then away to the SE and occassionally were delayed for a considerable time in looking for channels amongst the ice, which had accumulated at various points or promontories. About 9 p.m. we entered a narrow passage and encamped. An old Eskimaux encampment was traced out on this spot.

No deer killed today. Our small stock of provisions is waning rapidly and to add to the evil part of them have become mouldy from dampness. The Cape we have rounded is named C. Barrow.

Course and distance East 28¼ miles.

North 9 miles. Inmans Harbour, 67°58′40″ North (R), 111°06′00″ West (R).

NNE 4 miles, NbW 1½ miles, NE 2 miles. Cape Barrow, 68°03′10″ North (R), 111°00′00″ West (R). Lofty Granite peaks. Jamieson's group of islands lie in the offing.

E½S 5 miles, SEbE 4 miles, SE 2 miles. Encampment at the entrance of Detention harbour 25th and 26th July, 67°53′45″ North (Obs.), 110°41′26″ West (Chr.). Variation 40°49′00″ East.

Daily direct course corrected East, 28¼ miles.

Thursday July 26th 1821 Arctic sea

Much wind and rain during the night. And a great deal of ice has drifted into the strait. Embarked at 4 a.m. and attempted to force a passage, when the first canoe got enclosed and remained in a very perilous situation for some time, the pieces of ice crowded together by the action of the current and wind pressing strongly on its feeble sides. A partial opening however occurring we landed without having sustained any serious injury. Two men having gone round the bay, it was ascertained that instead of having entered a narrow passage between an island and the main we had entered the mouth of a harbour and that it was necessary to return by the way we came and get round a point to the northward. This was however impracticable the channel by which we entered last night

---

40 Loose, crumbling ice.

being completely closed up by a dense field of drift ice. In the afternoon the weather cleared up and several men went a hunting. The ice floats backwards and forwards in the harbour moved by currents which are not regular enough to deserve the name of a tide but appear to be solely owing to the wind. An Eskimaux ice chissel and a knife of copper were found in the old encampment today, together with a small iron knife.

Friday July 27th 1821 Detention Harbour

The hunting party were unsuccessful. Embarked about noon and pulling round the harbour, landed on the opposite side and made a portage of a mile and a half across the point. Sea covered with ice as far as the eye can reach. Latitude of Detention Harbour per obs. 67°53′45″ Long. 110°41′20″ Chr. Var^n 40°49′ E.

NEbE½E 2¾ miles. Encampment at Galena Point July 27th and 28th, 67°53′12″ North (Obs.), 110°34′30″ West (R). A small vein of Galena in Syenite.

Daily direct course corrected E½N, 3¼ miles.

Saturday July 28th 1821

Several of the men went a hunting but killed nothing. We have not only made great inroads into our provision but have also the mortification to discover that the pemmican upon which our principal reliance is placed, has become mouldy. The drift timber on this part of the coast consists of pine and taccamahac[41] most probably from Mackenzie's or some other river to the westward of the Coppermine. It all appears to have lain long in the water, the bark is completely worn off and the ends of the pieces rubbed perfectly smooth.

A small vein of galena was discovered on the beach traversing granite or gneiss rocks. Last night, we had a severe frost, a pretty thick crust being formed on a kettleful of water in one of the tents – and for several nights past thin films of ice have formed on the salt water amongst the cakes of stream ice. This is what the greenland men term *bay-ice*.

The following plants were obtained on this part of the coast. *Erigeron* _____? *bellidifolia affine.*[42] *Androsace* _____? *septentrionale proximum.*[43] *Ranunculus nivalis.*[44] *Potentilla* _____?[45] *Ranunculus pygmaeus* (Wahl)[46] *Cardamine pratensis.*[47] *Astragalus alpinus*? (Wahl)[48] *Phaca* (Wahl.)[49] *Oxytropis* (Persoon)

---

41 Balsam Poplar.
42 Fleabane, possibly *Erigeron yukonensis*, which although rare is the only tall fleabane with a showy flower that resembles *E. pulchellus* (W.J. Cody, pers. comm.).
43 Pygmyflower.

44 Snow Buttercup.
45 Cinquefoil, not identifiable as to species.
46 Dwarf Buttercup.
47 Bitter Cress.
48 Alpine Milk-vetch.
49 A vetch, *Astragalus*, species not known,

floribus sulphureis.[50] *Astragalus* floribus violaceis.[51] *Hedysarum* floribus cannes-ine rubris.[52] *Phaca serida* (Wahl.) floribus violaceis.[53]

Course from Enc^t Detent. Harbour E½N 3¼. Lat. of Galena point 67°53'12" obs., Long. 110°34'30" DR.

Sunday July 28th [29th] 1821 Galena Point

Fine calm weather. Attended divine service. The ice appearing less compact we put the canoes in the water soon after noon and made an attempt to force a passage in which we fortunately succeeded although with much labour and no small hazard to our frail vessels. After coasting the shore for two or three miles we came to the entrance of a deep bay whose bottom was filled up by a body of ice so compact as to preclude all idea of a passage whilst at the same time the traverse across its mouth was attended with much danger from the approach of a large field of ice which was coming into the bay before the wind. The dread of further detention, however, prevented us from hesitating and we had the satisfaction of landing safely in an hour and a half on the opposite shore.

The hunters went in pursuit of a deer here, but missed it.

After remaining about two hours to dine or rather sup we re embarked[54] and pursued our voyage through a labyrinth of islands. The bay above mentioned has been named Moore's bay. Many seals were seen today.

Courses per compass ENE 2½ miles, SE 3 miles. Entrance of Moore's Bay, west side, 67°48'35" North (R), 110°36'30" West (R).

Moore's bay, east side, 67°47'10" North (R), 110°15'15" West (R).

Monday July 30th 1821

In the morning we again got involved in a field of ice, but after considerable delay extricated ourselves and[55] entered a deep sound and proceeded to its bottom in search of the mouth of a river, which we supposed it to receive from the colour of its waters, and the kind of wrack that was thrown upon its shores. About 10 a.m. we landed and breakfasted whilst the Hunters went in pursuit of some deer that were seen but with which they did not come up. Embarking we crossed the sound and coasting along its eastern side passed the river without perceiving it and entered a deep bay, where the water at its mouth was only

50 Locoweed, probably *Oxytropis maydelliana*.
51 *Astragalus alpinus* if blue-violet, but *A. eucosmus* if deep purple.
52 Once again this is the new species, *Hedysarum mackenzii*.
53 Possibly *Astragalus richardsonii*, in which the keel is purplish-tipped (W.J. Cody, pers. comm.).
54 At midnight according to Franklin's account.
55 They rounded Point Kater at 6 a.m., after paddling since midnight, according to Franklin.

brackish but became salt[i]er as we advanced towards its bottom. We encamped at 6 a.m.[56] and by walking across the country for two miles discovered the river [Hood River] whose mouth being barred across by low sandy islands and banks was not perceived when we passed it.

Course and distance to encampment in Baillie's cove SE¾S 41½ m.

A young rein-deer was killed in the evening. The nights are cold, but the mosquitoes are still numerous and continue their attacks even in the frosty nights, though less vigorously than formerly. They are put to rest only by a strong breeze of wind.

Courses per compass. ENE 5½ miles, NEbE½E 6½ miles, NEbE 6 miles. Channels among Stockport Isles, 67°42′50″ North (R), 109°56′30″ West (R).

Entrance of Snug Harbour from 110°02′00″ West to 109°42′00″ West (R).

EbN 2½ miles, EbS 4 miles. Point Kater. West side of Arctic Sound, 67°41′50″ North (R), 109°45′00″ West (R).

EbN 2 miles, SE½S 10 miles. Extremity of Arctic Sound. 67°30′12″ North (Obs.), 109°41′00″ West (R).

SE½S 11 miles. Encampment in Baillie's cove, Arctic sound, 67°19′10″ North (R), 109°31′45″ West (R).

Daily direct course corrected SE¾S, 41½ miles [29 & 30 July combined].

The mouth of the Hood River "being barred across by low sandy islands ..."

56 Probably 6 p.m.

Tuesday July 31st 1821 Arctic sound

Our stock of provision is now reduced so low, that it has become a matter of first importance, to receive a supply on which account we have for some time been very anxious to discover some parties of Eskimaux – and as we learnt from Terregannoeuck that they frequent the rivers at this season Mr Franklin determined on going up the one that flows into this bay, principally with the view of obtaining dried provisions and leather (of which we were in great want) from the

"… our further progress was stopped by a cascade …"

natives and also in the hope of adding to our stock by our own exertions in hunting and fishing. We therefore embarked at 4 a.m. paddled round to the mouth of the river, entered it and advanced against the current, until our further progress was stopped by a cascade. Here we encamped, set four nets and sent out a party of hunters and also the two Eskimaux to look for their countrymen. The river is from three to four hundred yards wide below the rapid but so shallow as to be scarcely navigable for a canoe. The cascade is produced by a ridge of syenite, is three or four feet in height and about 250 feet wide. A very thick bed of alluvial clay is incumbent on the syenite and forms lofty and steep banks to the river.

Our hunters did not return until after midnight. They killed a brown bear and two small deer. The two Eskimaux returned at the same time, having traced the river for 15 or 16 miles farther up without discovering any vestige of inhabitants. The nets set below the fall produced a salmon trout and some attihawmegh.

Lat 67°19'23" N. Long. obs. 109°44'40" W. Var^n 41°43'32". Dip 88°55'

Courses per compass West 4 miles, South 3 miles. Encampment at the first fall in Hood's river. 67°19'23" North (Obs.), 109°44'30" (Chr.) Variation 41°43'32" East. Dip of Mag needle 88°54'50".

Daily direct course corrected West 4½ miles

Wednesday August 1st 1821 Hood's River

Sent for the Bear. We had now an opportunity of gratifying our curiosity respecting this animal so much dreaded by the Indians and of whose strength and ferocity we had heard such terrible accounts. It proved to be a lean male, of a yellowish-brown colour, the tips of the hairs on the head and back a little hoary. Its hair was long and somewhat woolly and it was falling off and discovering a very thin coat of sleek black hair … The general appearance of the teeth indicated advanced age.

Its dimensions were as follows –	ft.	inch
Length from the extremity of the snout to the tip		
of the tail	5	8
of the tail		6
Height from the sole to the tip of the fore shoulder	2	9
of hind quarters about	2	6

Length of the hind soles 10 inch. breadth 5 inches.

Forefeet 6 inches in diameter. …

[1-page description of Grizzly Bear[57]]

The legs of the animal were long and it appeared from its extreme leanness to have been in ill health, a circumstance which prevented the voyageurs from eating of it. The officers were less scrupulous and we boiled its paws and found them excellent. Embarked at 10 a.m. and proceeding down the river took on board another rein deer which was killed last night by Credit. We then ran through Arctic sound and rounding point Wollaston its eastern extremity opened another extensive sheet of water and the remainder of the afternoon was spend in endeavouring to ascertain from the tops of the hills whether it was another bay or merely a passage inclosed by a chain of islands. Appearances rather favouring the latter opinion it was determined to proceed through it. During the delay four more deer were killed all young and very lean. It appears that the coast is pretty well frequented by rein deer at this season, but it is rather

---

57 Grizzly Bear, *Ursus arctos*.

singular that hitherto we have killed none excepting the first but young ones of last season which were all too lean to have been eaten by any but those who had no choice. We paddled along the western shore of the channel, with the intention of encamping, but were prevented from the want of drift wood on the

high basaltic cliffs

beach. This induced us to make a traverse across to an island, where we encamped at 11 p.m. and fortunately found a small bay whose shores furnished us with a little firewood. During the night we had a heavy gale of wind from the westward.

Course and distance NE 16¼ miles.

Courses per compass NbW 15 miles, coasting Banks' peninsula. North 2¼ miles. Point Wollaston, the extremity of the peninsula & Eastern point of Arctic sound, 67°34'30" North (R), 109°21'45" West (R).

EbS½S 5 miles. Encampment on an island which lies across the entrance of Brown's cove, Aug. 1ˢᵗ & 2ᵈ, 67°30'00" (R), 109°04'00" West (R).

Daily direct course corrected NE, 16¼ miles.

Thursday Augᵗ 2ᵈ 1821

Detained all day by a heavy gale of wind.

The coast which we have visited since the 25ᵗʰ July presents a considerable variety of appearance. Cape Barrow consists of steep conical craggy mountains of granite which rise so abruptly from the waters edge as to admit of few landing places even for a canoe. At detention harbour these mountains recede a little from the shore and in Moore's bay a little to the eastward the sea washes cliffs of a species of brown indurated clay, in the debris of which we found some specimens of Green copper ore. From this bay to the entrance of Arctic sound we passed many columnar precipices of clinkstone. Towards the bottom of the bay the rocks gave place to alluvial soils, but from Point Wollaston to our present encampment, the coast is lined with basaltic cliffs which have a columnar form and are very difficult of access. These cliffs lie in ranges parallel to the shore and the deer that we killed were feeding in small marshy grass plots that lay in the vallies betwixt them. The mosquitoes continue numerous in these spots.

Only a few fragments of sea weed have been seen since we embarked on the arctic sea which all belong to the *Fucus ceranoides* (Wahl.) or *Fucus dislichus* (Trem.) Today another was found probably the *F. subaliforus* Wahl. but it could not be exactly determined from the want of fructification – *Floridae* (Lam.) Amongst the phenogamous plants collected during the last few days are – *Serratula alpina?* (or *salicifolia?*)[58] *Tussilago frigida* (Wahl.)[59] *Parnassia* _____?[60] *Erysimum* _____[61] *Juncus* _____?[62] *Stellaria* _____ (*crassifolia?*)[63] and *Pulmonaria maritima.*[64]

Friday Augt 3^d 1821

The gale of wind continuing all the morning of the 2^d prevented us from embarking before 10 p.m. Augt 2^d. We then paddled round the southern end of the island and continued our course to the eastward. Much doubt at this time prevailed as to the land on the right being the main shore or merely a chain of islands. The latter opinion was strengthened by the broken appearance of the land and the extensive view we had up an inlet [Brown Sound] whose mouth we passed, and we were in some apprehension of being led away from the main shore and perhaps after passing through a group of islands of coming to a traverse greater than we durst venture upon in our bark canoes. On the other hand the continuous appearance of the land on the north side of the channel and its trending to the southward excited a belief that we were entering a deep sound [Bathurst Inlet]. In this state of doubt we landed often and endeavoured from the summits of the highest hills adjoining the shore to ascertain the true nature of the coast but in vain and we continued paddling through the channel

58 A thistle-like plant, clearly *Saussurea angustifolia* (John Hudson, pers. comm.).
59 Sweet Coltsfoot, *Petasites frigidus*.
60 Grass of Parnassus.
61 Treacle Mustard.
62 Bog Rush, exact species not known.
63 Chickweed or Stitchwort, *Stellaria humifusa*.
64 Sea Lungwort, *Mertensia maritima* or *Lithospermum maritimum*.

all night, against a fresh breeze of wind, which at half past four increased to a violent gale and compelled us to land. The gale diminished a short time after noon and permitted us to re-embark and continue our voyage until four p.m. when it returned again with its former violence, and finally obliged us to encamp. From the want of drift wood to make a fire we had fasted all day and were under the necessity in the evening of serving out pemmican, which was done with much reluctance, as we had some fresh deer's meat remaining. The rocks which we had an opportunity of examining during today's voyage consisted of light-red sandstone and blueish grey slate clay upon which there were frequently imposed cliffs of basalt & amygdaloid or trap tuff. Strata in general dipping to the westward. The inlet when viewed from a high hill adjoining to our encampment exhibits so many arms, that the course we ought to pursue is more uncertain than ever. Course SE¾S 24 miles.

Courses per compass SE 1½ miles, EbS 2¼ miles, E½N 6 miles, E½S 5 miles. 67°20′12″ North (Obs.).

EbS¾S 7½ miles. Longitude 108°38′00″ (Chr.).

SE¾S, 4 miles. Encampment a little to the northward of a remarkable cliff. 67°10′30″ North (R), 108°36′10″ West (R).

Daily direct course corrected SE¾S 24 miles.

"The inlet when viewed from a high hill adjoining to our encampment ..."

Saturday Aug.ᵗ 4 1821

Embarked at half past 3 a.m. and paddled the whole day through channels from 2 to 5 or 6 miles wide all tending to the Southward. In the course of the days voyage, we ascertained, that the land which we have had on our right hand, since yesterday morning, consists of several large islands, but the land on our

"... paddled the whole day through channels 2 to 6 miles wide ..." The southernmost arm of Bathurst Inlet sketched from the Western highlands.

left preserved its unbroken appearance and at 8 p.m. when we encamped, we were still uncertain whether it was the eastern side of a deep sound, or merely a large island. It differs remarkably from the main shore in being very rugged, rocky and sterile, whereas the outline of the main is even, and its hills are covered with a comparatively good sward of grass and exhibit little naked rock. We have seen no drift timber for two days but the shores are covered with small pieces of willows which would seem to indicate our neighbourhood to the mouth of a river.[65]

65 The mouth of the Burnside River (Richardson's Anatessy River) is hidden by Quadyuk and Wignick Islands and Point Elliott. Richardson was incorrect in giving the name of Burnside to the Wolf or Amagok River.

The shallows we have passed today are covered with shoals of a small fish probably spawning. It belongs to the genus *Salmo*? and is termed by the Eskimaux Angmaggouk (Augustus). Capelin.[66] [2½-page description]

The individual here described was a male, ready to spawn and six inches long to the insertion of the caudal fin. The angmaggouck frequents the coast of Hudson's bay to the northward of Churchill and is delicate eating.

In the evening we shot a female deer, small and very lean.

Course and distance sbE½E 33 miles.

Courses per compass se¾42 7¾ miles, sebs 2½ miles, se¾4s 8 miles. Northern end of Youngs Island [Young Point],[67] 66°50′30″ North (R), 108°30′00″ West (R).

se¾4E 9 miles. Southern end of Youngs Island. 66°42′45″ North (R), 108°20′30″ West (R).

Ebs½s 5½ miles. Mouth of Burnside river [Amagok River] which flows from the southward. 66°38′15″ North (R), 108°15′20″ West (R).

Encampment on a Sandy point, Augt 4 1821, 66°38′30″ North (R), 108°14′10″ West (R).

Direct daily course corrected sbE½E, 33 miles.

Sunday Augt 5th 1821 Bathurst Inlet

Embarked at 4 a.m. and after paddling until 8, had the mortification to discover, that we had reached the bottom of an inlet into which a broad but shallow and unnavigable river [Western River] flows. We were somewhat consoled, however, for the loss of time in exploring this inlet, by the success of Junius in killing a musk ox, the first we have seen on the coast. The present state of our stock of provisions, rendered this an invaluable acquisition, and the river fortunately furnished us with a sufficient quantity of decayed willows to cook it.

About 7 in the evening, in returning along the eastern shore of the inlet, a brown Bear was seen marching slowly along the beach, and a party being instantly landed, it was killed. It proved to be a very fat female. [1-page description]

Encamped in the evening on the shores of a sandy bay and set the nets. The Bear proved excellent eating superior to anything we have tasted on the coast. It was highly relished by the voyageurs, who delight in any thing that is fat. Collected specimens today of the *Tofielda palustris*[68] and *Pisum maritimum*[69] & of a *Phaca* (floribus caeruleis). *Oxytropis* (Persoon) caerulae affinis.[70]

---

66 Capelin, *Mallotus villosus* (see Appendix c).
67 What Richardson considered to be Young's Island was a two-pronged projecting peninsula with a northern (Young Point) and southern point. Two small lakes and Fishing Creek occupy the low land to the west of this peninsula.
68 *Tofieldia pusilla*.
69 Vetchling or Wild Pea, *Lathyrus japonicus*.
70 Loco-weed, probably *Oxytropis arctica*.

The nets produced a Salmon trout, some round fish see p. 49,[71] some Cotti p. 123, angmaggouck p. 145, several herrings and two kinds of pleuronectes of which the descriptions follow – Clupea _____?[72] [1½-page description of Pacific Herring] Pleuronectes Rhombus.[73] [¾-page description of Arctic Flounder]

Course and distance sebe 5 miles.

Courses per compass, e½s 12 miles. Mouth of Back's River [Western River], 66°29′42″ North (r), 107°54′00″ West (r). se extremity of Bathurst's Inlet.

w¾n 7 miles. Encampment on ne side of Bathurst Inlet. Augt 5. 66°36′00″ North (r), 108°03′00″ West (r). Caught Herrings, Flounders, &c.

Direct daily course corrected sebe 5 miles.

"Encamped in the evening on the shores of a sandy bay ..."

Monday August 6th 1821 Bathurst Inlet

We were detained in the encampment by stormy weather until 5 p.m. when we embarked and paddled along the northern shore of the inlet, the weather still continuing foggy, but the wind moderate. Observing a she-Bear, with three

71 These page numbers refer correctly to page numbers in Richardson's journal.

72 Pacific Herring, *Clupea harengus pallasi*.
73 Arctic Flounder, *Liopsetta glacialis*.

Bear Creek Falls, near site of encampment of 6 August

young ones on the beach, a party was landed to attack them, but being approached without due caution, they took the alarm and scaled a precipitous rocky hill, with a rapidity that baffled all pursuit. At 8 o clock the fog changing into rain, we encamped.

The berries of the *Arbutus uliginosus* growing here, are scarcely shaped yet, whereas at the same season last year on the banks of the Yellow knife river they were perfectly ripe. The cloud berries (*Rubus chamaemorus*)[74] are becoming red. The *Arbutus vitis idaea* is only in blossom and the berries of the *Empetrum nigrum* are still green.

Many seals were seen today.

Course per compass w¾N 8 miles. Encampment on the NE side of the Inlet, Augt 6th, 66°42′35″ North (R), 108°13′15″ West (R).

Direct daily course corrected NW¼N 8 miles.

Tuesday August 7th 1821 Bathurst Inlet

Foggy and Rainy weather the whole day. Employed paddling out of the sound. Encamped at 5 p.m. [Manning Point] nearly opposite the spot from whence we started on the morning of the 4th having come today 22 miles on a NNW course. There is a beautiful conglomerate rock here, the basis a greyish-red sandstone, the imbedded pieces white quartz, about an inch in diameter and in general quadrangular. Large portions of the sandstone exist in the neighbourhood, which contain no imbedded minerals.

Some portions of the *Fucus digitatus*[75] were picked up on the beach and a sea conferva.[76]

74 Sometimes called Baked-Apple.
75 Brown algae of genus *Fucus*, modern species
     not determined.
76 Green algae.

Courses per compass w¾n 11 miles. Tinney's Cove.

nw¾n 8 miles, nwbn 2½ miles, n½w 6¾ miles. Encampment Augt 7th & 8th 67°04'00" North (ʀ), 108°27'00" West (ʀ). Red sandstone, conglomerate rock. Direct daily course corrected nnw 22 miles.

Manning Point, site of encampment of 7–8 August

Wednesday Augt 8th 1821 Bathurst Inlet

Remained on shore, wind-bound all day. Fog, rain and wind without intermission. The fresh meat being consumed, a little pemmican was served out in the evening.

Thursday Augt 9th 1821

Much wind and rain during the night – and a heavy sea running in the morning. A little more moderate about 7 a.m. when we embarked and after paddling for 3 or 4 miles round a point turned into an arm of the inlet which had an easterly direction and ran for some hours, before a fresh breeze, followed by a heavy sea. Put ashore at 11 a.m. to breakfast and with much regret made another inroad on our stock of provision which is now reduced to two bags of pemmican and a small bundle of dried meat. The men begin to apprehend the approach of absolute want, and we have for some days had to listen to their gloomy forebodings of the deer entirely quitting the coast in a few days.

Mr Franklin having ascertained from the summit of a hill, that it was fruitless to proceed farther in this direction in search of a passage out of the inlet, we were about to embark with the intention of returning, when a large bear was discovered on the opposite shore. We instantly crossed [to Bear Island] and had the good fortune to kill it. It proved to be a female and very fat. Its stomach contained the remains of a seal, several lemmings (ground hog of Hearne)[77] and a large quantity of the roots of different species of *Phaca* and *Hedysarum* which are common on the shores and which resemblance in appearance and taste the common liquorice-root. There was also a small quantity of grass intermixed with these substances. The shores here are barren and rocky consisting of light red and greyish sandstone with superimposed cliffs of greenstone and basalt. In the evening we found a single log of driftwood. It was pine and sufficiently large to enable us to cook the bear which had a slight fishy taste but was deemed very palatable. Encamped at 9 p.m. having come 14 miles on a North course.

Courses per compass. NW¾W 5¾ miles, round Elliots Island[78]

EbN¾N 7¾ miles, on the north side of Bear Island, 67°04'50" North (R), 108°13'28" West (R). East side of Gordon's bay as seen from Bear Island, 107°57'30" West (R).

WNW 8½ miles, NW½W 6 miles. Encampment Augt 9th a little to the southward of Fowlers bay, 67°18'14" North (R), 108°26'44" West (R).

Direct daily course corrected North 14 miles.

Friday August 10th 1821

Embarking at half past 4 a.m. we continued our voyage out of the Inlet, the paddles aided at times by a light breeze of wind.

At noon cloudy weather with slight showers. After halting for some time to breakfast we re-embarked and paddled along the shore contending with the wind which was now contrary, and had freshened into a strong breeze. In the afternoon we saw a female bear on the shore followed by a cub of this year, both of which were killed by the hunters, neither of them very fat. [6 lines description]

Long. obs. here 108°52'30" W. Var^n 41°09'40" E.

Encamped at the entrance of the Inlet at 6 p.m. The wind having become too strong, to admit of our proceeding any further. Driftwood very scanty and no rein deer.

Course and Distance NbW 23½ miles.

---

77 Arctic Ground Squirrel, close to ground-hog size.

78 Probably the peninsula northeast of Manning Point.

Courses per compass. NW½W 11 miles. Along Rideout Island which lies across the entrance of Fowlers bay. Bottom of Fowlers bay, 108°15′00″ West (R).

NNW¾W 5½ miles. The long. per chr. at this spot was 108°52′30″ Chr. supposed to be too much to the eastward & no[r]t[h]ward 67°40′00″ North (R), 108°39′50″ West (R). Variation 41°09′40″ East.

WbN½N 6½ miles. Barry's Island in the offing.

WbN½N 1½ miles. Encampment near Point Evrette which forms the eastern side of the entrance of Bathurst Inlet. 67°41′16″ North (R), 108°41′10″ West (R).

Direct daily course corrected NbW 23½ miles

Saturday Augt 11th 1821

Embarked at 5 a.m. and paddled round Point Evrette [Everitt] which forms the east side of the entrance to Bathursts inlet: our progress much impeded by a heavy swell. Landed to breakfast – and killed three small deer. Strata at this spot consisting of gneiss and syenite contained imbedded chrystals of hornblende, some of them a foot long. They were hexagonal and very generally contaminated with scales of mica. Latit. obs. 67°45′44″ N. Re-embarked at noon and continued our voyage along the coast which is protected by a continuous chain of islands from one to eight or ten miles distant. Encamped at 8 p.m. on a spot near the northern end of Buchan's bay which had been visited a month or 6 weeks ago by a small party of Eskimaux the remains of some eggs containing young ones lying beside some half burnt fire wood. Strata here horizontal, composed of fine grained light red sandstone. Evening fine but cold.

Course and distance NbE¾E 18¾ miles.

Courses per compass, NW 2 miles. Point Evrette. Bathurst Inlet runs about 76 miles SE from Point Evrette. In coasting this Inlet we sailed 174 geogr miles or 201 statute miles. 67°43′00″ North (R), 108°42′30″ West (R).

North 3¼ miles. 67°45′44″ North (Obs.) 108°36′36″ West (R).

NNW 4¼ miles, N¾W 4½ miles, NEbN 3 miles. Fisher's Islands running across Buchans bay. A stream of water falls into the bottom of the [Epin? – illegible].

W¼S 4¼ miles. North point of Buchans bay, 67°56′40″ North (R), 108°28′14″ West (R).

NbW½W 2½ miles. Encampment Augt 11th a little north of Buchans bay, 67°59′00″ North (R), 108°24′30″ West (R).

Direct daily course corrected NbE¾E 18¾ miles.

Sunday August 12th 1821

Frost during the night. Paddled all the morning against a head wind, which at noon became so strong that we could proceed no further. Lat. obs. 68°01′ N. Saw several deer but the hunters were unable to approach them. Strata here red sandstone whose debris formed a shelving and utterly barren shore. View to seaward still bounded by islands [Cockburn Islands] distant from eight to ten miles. Course ENE distance 5½ miles.

Courses per compass, NWbW 1½ miles, NNW 3 miles. Cape Croker, southern entrance to Melville Sound, 68°03′27″ North (R), 108°24′14″ West (R).

EbN½N 5 miles. Encampment in Melville sound Augt 12th, 68°01′20″ North Obs. 108°12′00″ West (R).

Direct daily course corrected ENE, 5½ miles.

Monday August 13th 1821 Melville Sound

Being unable to find any drift wood last night we went supperless to bed. Embarked at sun rise and being occassionally favoured with a fresh westerly breeze we ran 18 miles to the eastward by 10 a.m. when we landed in Hope's bay to breakfast. We found here a considerable quantity of small willows such as are brought down by the rivers that we have hitherto seen and hence we judged that a river discharges itself into the bottom of this bay. In the course of the morning we passed the embouchure of a pretty large stream and saw the vestiges of an Eskimaux encampment not above a month old. Lat. obs. at noon 68°6′40″ N.

Re-embarking and running before a fresh breeze[79] we found ourselves in an extensive bay from which no outlet could at first be perceived but the one by which we entered. After some search however we found a winding shallow passage running to the NW which we followed for a short time and then encamped. The shores of this (Warrender's) Bay are low and clayey and the country for many miles level and much intersected with pieces of water, but we had not leisure to ascertain whether they were branches of the bay or fresh water lakes. Near our encampment we found an Eskimaux winter sledge, raised upon four stones with some snow shovels and other trifling articles – and what was more interesting a small piece of whalebone. A paddle was also found, which Augustus on examination declared to be made after the fashion of the White-goose Eskimaux a tribe with whom his countrymen had had some trading interviews on the shores of Island Lake. Some white geese were seen this evening, and some young grey ones[80] were caught on the beech being unable to fly. Two deer were

79 Across Melville Sound.
80 Greater White-fronted Goose, *Anser albifrons*; Richardson in Swainson and Richardson,

Birds, said that he did not encounter Canada Geese on the shores of the Arctic Ocean. Young Snow Geese are also grey in colour.

also seen but our hunters did not succeed in killing them. Long. obs. in the afternoon. [no entry]

Course and distance NNE¾E 23¾ miles.

Courses per compass NNE 11 miles, NE¼E 7 miles. This observation was made in Hopes bay at the entrance of an inlet running SE, 68°06′10″ North (Obs.), 107°26′56″ West (R).

NW¼N 5½ miles. Cape seperating Warrender & Hope bays. Longitude of eastern side of Warrender's bay, 107°16′20″ West (R), the most easterly

Cliffs of greenstone and basalt. Each stone monument atop these cliffs is an inuksuk, placed there by Inuit ("Eskimaux") long before Richardson and Franklin paddled by

part of the coast attained by the Expedition the difference of Long. betwixt this and Richardson's River the most westing part of the coast visited is 8°36′10″

NWbW 9 miles, W½S 2¾ miles. Encampment at the entrance of Eskimaux cove Augt 13, 68°21′40″ North (R), 107°38′10″ West (R).

Direct daily course corrected NNE¾E, 23¾ miles.

Tuesday August 14th 1821 Melville Sound

Paddled the whole day along the northern shores of Melville sound. They are flat and invisible from the opposite side of the sound, otherwise a short traverse might have saved us some days of time. The few eminences that are on this side were mistaken for islands when seen from the opposite shore. These eminences are for the most part cliffs of greenstone and basalt which are not above 100 feet high. The subjacent strata are of white sandstone. The rocks are mostly confined to the capes and shores, the soil inland being flat, clayey and barren. Many ducks were seen today, mostly belonging to the species termed by the voyageurs from their cry, Caccawees.[81] We also saw some grey geese and swans.[82] Drift timber is extremely scarce on this part of the coast. Most of the headlands displayed traces of visits from the Eskimaux, none of them recent. Weather in the morning windy, calm and fine in the afternoon. Encamped in Parry's bay. Course and distance wbs¾s 23 miles.

Courses per compass. sw½s 1½ miles, sebs 3½ miles, ne 3 miles. Outlet of Eskimaux cove.

sbe 3½ miles. Point Hay. 68°15'20" North (r), 107°41'28" West (r).

sw½w 6 miles, South ½ mile. Eastern point of Parry's bay. Hurd's Islands lie across its mouth.

sw½w 5½ miles, sw¾s 6½ miles, ssw 2 miles. Encampment in Parry's bay Augt 14th, 68°13'55" North (r), 108°38'10" West (r).

Daily course corrected wbs¾s, 23 miles.

Wednesday August 15th 1821 Melville Sound

Fresh breezes and clear weather. In paddling round Parry's bay several deer were observed, but owing to the open[n]ess of the country, the hunters could not approach them. They killed however two swans, that were moulting, and saw several cranes[83] and many grey geese. The Caccawees are moulting at present and assemble together in immense flocks. In the evening we were exposed to much inconvenience and considerable danger from a heavy rolling sea, the canoes receiving many severe blows and shipping a considerable quantity of water – which induced us to encamp at 5 p.m. opposite to the Cape (Croker) we passed on the morning of the 11th[84] – the channel between being from ten to twelve miles wide.

The fears of our voyageurs have now entirely mastered their prudence and they are not restrained by the presence of their officers from giving loose to a free and sufficiently rude expression of their feelings. They have now so often canvassed the dangers of our journey from the coast, that they despair of ever seeing home again, and the broken state of the weather and coldness of the nights, together with the smallness of our stock of provision cause them to deem any attempt to proceed farther as little short of madness. Indeed they have of late assumed the privilege of thinking for their Commanding officer, and that they may compell him to put a period to the voyage, the Interpreters have expressed their intentions of killing no more deer, nay from the want of success that has attended their hunting excursions we have reason to believe that they have actually begun to put their scheme in execution. The danger they were

81 Oldsquaw, *Clangula hyemalis*.
82 Tundra Swan, *Olor columbianus*.

83 Sandhill Crane, *Grus canadensis*.
84 In fact, 12 August.

exposed to this afternoon, has added fuel to the flame and soon after we encamped the Steersmen made a report to Mr Franklin that twelve timbers were broken in the first canoe and that the other was so shattered that they were in daily dread of the body dropping from the gunwales. This conduct of our crew is not mentioned as influencing Mr Franklin's determination, for it had been long evident to the officers that the time spent in exploring what has been since named Accession Gulph with its extensive branches, Arctic and Melville sounds and Bathurst Inlet had precluded every hope of getting round to Repulse bay, and that in order to insure a fair prospect of a safe journey across the barren grounds, our voyage along the coast must speedily terminate – but we were all desirous of finding the shore trending to the eastward again before we left it. We had so frequently mistaken the mainland for chains of islands that doubts were excited in our minds of the distant land we had seen between the mouth of the Coppermine River and Cape Barrow being actually islands and we feared that it might prove to be the northern shore of one great gulph.

To calm the minds of the Voyageurs Mr Franklin communicated to them in the evening his intentions of proceeding only until he ascertained the coast trending away to the eastward again, at the same time limiting the advance to four days. This information was received gladly and we hoped that the industry of the hunters being once more excited we should be able to add to our stock of provision now reduced to a bag and a half of pemmican – or not quite two days consumption. Lat. of enc^t. by dead reckoning 68°7′ N Long. obs. pr. chr. 109°10′28″ w. Course and distance s¼E 7¾ m.

SE½E 2½ miles, EbN½N 3½ miles, EbN 4½ miles. Point Beechy, north Point of Melville sound, distant from Cape Croker 4¾ miles. Melville sound is 30 miles wide from East to west and 20 miles from North to south. In coasting it we sailed 87¼ geogr. miles or 100¾ statute miles.

swbs 7½ miles. Encampment on a flat beach August 15th, 68°06′15″ North (R), 108°36′15″ West (R).

Direct daily course corrected s¼E, 7¾ miles.

Thursday August 16th 1821

Weather in the morning fine, afterwards foggy. Started at 5 a.m. ran to the westward for ten miles and landed on a point under a basaltic cliff to breakfast. Reembarking we rounded the point and entered a deep bay which ran to the northward. Cliffs of trap rocks with intervening low beaches which were below the horizon at the distance of a few miles produced here as in other instances the semblance of a range of islands and induced us to coast the bay in search of a passage. We landed on its northern shore and found traces of an old encampment. Leaving it we passed through another small bay and rounding Cape Flinders found a low gravelly coast running away to the NNE the sea in the offing unusually clear of islands. Being assailed by a heavy thunder storm we put ashore and encamped at 8 p.m.

The shore here is so flat that it is difficult to approach it even in a canoe – one deer was seen today but the hunters did not get near it. The coast is

"The shore is so flat ..."

every where extremely barren, the rocks are for the most part a kind of slate clay much impregnated with quartz, having a greyish blue colour and disposed in layers in general horizontal but not infrequently concentric forming globular concretions – which were insensibly blended into the surrounding mass. The basaltic cliffs were almost always distinctly columnar and often imposed on the Slate-clay. The general aspect of the country was flat – the rocks being confined to the islands and promontories.

Course and distance NWbW 21½ miles.

Courses per compass SWbS 3 miles, SWbW 6½ miles. Slate clay point, 68°06′46″ North (R), 109°01′13″ West (R). Cockburn's group of islands lie to the Southward of this point.

WbN 4½ miles. Across Rileys & Walkers bays.

NW½N 3 miles. Western point of Beluga bay, 68°13′27″ North (R), 109°07′24″ West (R).

SSE 4½ miles, WbS 1 mile, WbS½S 6½ miles, Cape Flinders. Cook's island lies WSW from this point.

NNW¼W 6 miles. Encampment Aug. 16. 17. 18. 19. 20. 21st, 68°18′50″

North (Obs.), 109°25′00″ West (R). Variation 44°15′16″ East. Magn. dip 89°22′25″
Direct daily course corrected NWbbW[85] 21½ miles.

Friday August 17th 1821

Stormy weather. Thermometer 41°. Unable to embark from the high sea. Several
hunting parties went out, but although they saw several deer the flatness of the
country prevented them from approaching them. They obtained however, a few
unfledged geese. A handful of pemmican was served out to each man.

Lat. obs. 68°18′50″ N. Long. 110°05′15″ W. Varⁿ 44°15′16″ E. Dip
89°22′25″

Point Turnagain, "The most distant land we saw ..."

Saturday Augt 18th 1821

Strong WNW winds. Much sea. The^r 38°. Mr Franklin, Mr Back and myself went
about 10 miles along the coast which continued flat and kept the same direction
that it has at the encampment, namely NNE. The most distant land we saw had

85 NWbW, eliminating the meaningless extra "b."

the same bearing and made like two islands, the shore on their insides apparently trending more to the eastward so that it is probable that we have reached the pitch of the Cape which is only about 15 miles to the northward of Cape Barrow. This then is the limit of our voyage along the coast, which has occupied us nearly a month, but in which we have traced the open sea only five degrees and a half to the eastward of the mouth of the Coppermine River. The longitude assigned to Repulse bay is 87° so that we have come little more than a fifth part of the distance from thence to the Coppermine River, in a straight line, but if the length of our voyage round the indented coast of Accession Gulph is considered we have sailed upwards of 550 miles, very little less than the estimated direct distance between the above mentioned places.

"The hunters found the burrows of a number of White foxes …"

Large flocks of White geese flying to the southward. The hunters found the burrows of a number of White foxes[86] today and killed one of these animals which proved excellent eating esteemed by us as equal to young geese and far superior to the lean deer that we have had on the coast. Augustus killed a deer in the afternoon but the men who went to bring it, returned without being able to find it. There is plenty of drift wood on this part of the coast; indeed except in the inlets, we have always found enough to make one or two fires, for the purpose of cooking.

Course per compass NNW¼W 15 miles. Point Turnagain, 68°32′45″ North (R), 109°09′57″ West (R), distant in a direct line from the mouth of the Coppermine River _____ miles geog. or _____ statute miles on a _____ course true. The difference of Long. is 6°26′52″. The distance actually sailed 555¼ geog. or 641½ st.

Direct daily course corrected N19E, 15 miles.

86 Arctic Fox, *Alopex lagopus.*

Sunday August 19th 1821

Much rain in the night with heavy gales of wind. Stormy and heavy weather all day. Thermometer 33°. High surf on the beach. Two men went with Junius for their guide to bring the deer. Junius returned with a part of the meat, but owing to the thickness of the atmosphere the other two went astray. Read Prayers.

Monday August 20th 1821

Much wind in the night, ground covered with snow in the morning. Hazy weather 32°. Considerable anxiety prevailing respecting Belanger and Michel, the two men who strayed yesterday, the rest were sent out to look for them today. The search was successful and they all returned in the evening. The stragglers were much fatigued and had suffered severely from the cold, one of them having his thighs frozen, and what under our present circumstances was still more grievous, they had thrown away all the meat during the night. Made another scanty meal on pemmican.

Tuesday August 21st 1821

Strong winds but dry weather. The.r 33°. Hard frost during the night. The snow still remains on the ground and the small pools are covered with ice. The sea continued very turbulent all day. Our last bag of pemmican is now half done.

Wednesday August 22d 1821

The wind became more moderate during the night and the surf diminishing with equal rapidity we were enabled to embark at 6 a.m. It was Mr Franklin's intention to have returned by the Coppermine River and Bear Lake where it was hoped the Hook's party had made caches of provision, but in addition to the hazard we should incur by so long a voyage in the open sea, when we had reason to believe that the weather was finally broken up for the season, the want of provision was an inducement to him to change his plan. We had found during our advance that the country to the westward of Cape Barrow was inadequate to supply our wants, and it seemed probable that it would be still more unproductive now. Under these circumstances it was deemed most advisable, to proceed at once to the bottom of Arctic Sound where we had found the animals more abundant than in any other place, and strike from thence across the Barren grounds to Point

Lake, keeping on the banks of Hoods river as long as we could without being led too far from the direct track. Our men cheered by the prospect of returning, embarked with the utmost alacrity and paddling with unusual vigour carried us across Riley's and Walker's bays a distance of 20 miles before noon, when we landed to breakfast on Slate-clay point, the same spot where we breakfasted on the 16th. In the afternoon the wind freshened too much to permit us to continue the voyage, and the whole party went a hunting but had no success and the pemmican being reduced too low to admit of two meals a day we went supperless to bed. Cold weather with thick fogs and strong winds during the night. Course SE¾S 14½ miles.

Courses per compass, SSE¼E 6 miles, EbN 6½ miles, East 8½ miles. Slate clay point. Encamp^t Augt 22 & breakfasting place Augt 16th 68°06'46" North (R), 109°01'13" West (R).

Direct daily course corrected SE¾S 14½ miles.

Thursday August 23^d 1821

Embarked at 2 a.m. and steering for Point Evrette, we made without the least remonstrance from the men, a traverse of twenty five miles running all the time before a strong wind and a heavy sea. The privation of food under which our voyageurs were at present labouring, absorbed every other terror, otherwise the most powerful eloquence would not have induced them to attempt such a traverse. Towards noon being now on a high rocky lee shore on which a heavy surf was beating. The wind being on the beam the canoes drifted fast to leeward and in rounding a point the recoil of the sea from the rocks was so great that they were with difficulty preserved from foundering. Some idea may be formed of the height of the waves when it is stated that the mast head of the other canoe was often hid from our view although it was sailing within hail of us. We looked in vain for a sheltered bay to land in, but at length being unable to weather a point we were obliged to put ashore on the open beach which fortunately was sandy at this spot. The debarkation was effected with great dexterity and fortunately without further injury than the splitting of the head of the second canoe.[87]

Encamped on Point Evrette, near where we breakfasted on the morning of the 11th. Rocks here mica slate and gneiss, their strata dipping to the NE at a large angle with the horizon. The whole party went a hunting but saw no animals, and a moiety of the small remainder of the pemmican was distributed for supper. Cold disagre[e]able weather with snow showers in the afternoon. Ther. 42°. Calm and fine during the night.

Course per compass ESE 22¾ miles. Encamp^d Augt 23^d, 67°46'12"

87 This scene was depicted by Back's drawing reproduced opposite page 394 in Franklin, *Journey*, 1823.

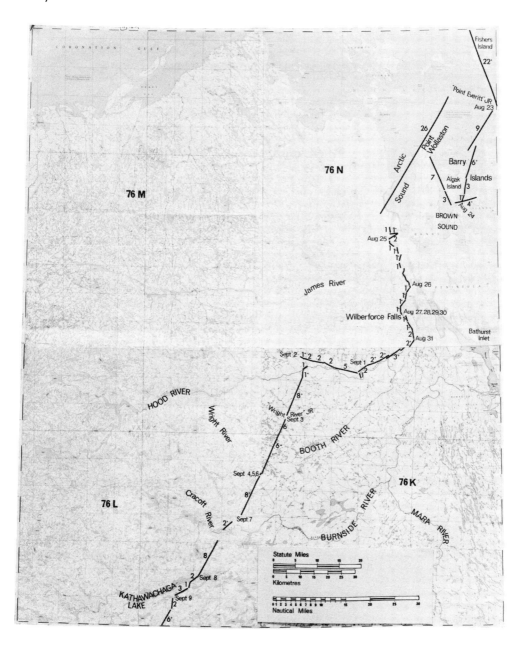

Map 6   *23 August–10 September 1821*

North (R), 108°36'12" West (R). Gneiss and Syenite with large chrystals of horn-blende.

Direct daily course corrected SSE 22¾ miles.

Friday August 24th 1821

Fine morning. Embarked at 3 a.m. and paddled across the entrance of Bathurst Inlet to Barry's Isles on one of which, we landed a party to hunt a deer that was seen grazing in a meadow. After an absence of three or four hours they returned with three female deer which although very lean were highly acceptable. A number of other deer were seen, all females followed by their young. And they observed also on the banks of a small river which flowed into a lake in the centre of the island recent tracks of the Musk ox. This seasonable supply of provision induced us to halt and breakfast. We recommenced our voyage a little after noon and paddling along Musk-ox island [one of the Barry Islands] found ourselves in the evening at the bottom of a narrow sound which was seperated from another piece of water by a gravelly bank only a few yards wide. The canoes were carried across and being put into the water again we entered Bathurst Inlet through a small strait and encamped. The wind which had been SE all day and strong, changing suddenly at this time to West brought on some heavy showers of rain. Musk-ox island is composed of trap rocks, mostly basalt, columnar and forming cliffs from 50 to 150 feet high, superimposed on horizontal strata of various coloured clay stone. On the northern end of the island there is a red amygdaloi-dal rock which contains many beautiful pebbles and some small beds of jasper. The greatest part of the pebbles are formed of concentric layers of calcedony with drusy cavities, but some of them approach to nearly pure carnelian. One of the deer which was killed today bore marks on the legs of the bites of a wolf. Weather cold to the sensations, especially when sitting inactive in a canoe. Course SSW 21¾ miles.

Courses per compass, SbE 9 miles. An amygdaloidal rock at this point contains beautiful agates.

SSE 6½ miles, SEbS 3 miles, SbE½E 1½ miles. Encampment on Barry's Island Augt 24, 67°26'05" North (R), 108°58'00" West (R).

Direct daily course corrected, SSW 21¾ miles.

Saturday August 25th 1821

Embarked at 5 a.m. and running before a fresh breeze soon arrived at the Island [Algak Island] on which we were detained on the 2d and 3d of August – and contrary to what we experienced when here before now found great plenty of deer, the most of them females followed by their young of this year, but there were also a few males of two or three years of age. A hunting party succeeded in killing two. Reembarking we carried the fair wind to the entrance of arctic sound, when a fortunate change in its direction enabled us to steer directly for the mouth of the River which we entered at 7 p.m. and at 9 arrived at the rapid and encamped. Our canadians may be said to have in general shewed considerable courage in bearing the dangers of the sea, magnified to them by their novelty, but they could not restrain their expressions of joy on quitting it. The consideration that the most painful and certainly the most hazardous part of the journey was to come, did not depress their spirits at all. Warm & fine weather.

Courses per compass, swbw½w 4¾ miles. Point of an Island. 67°27'10" North (R), 109°09'37" West (R).

WNW 3 miles. Encampment of Augt 1 on same island

WNW 7 miles, s¾E 26 miles. Mouth of Hood's River, 67°21'50" North (R), 109°42'00" West (R). The distance actually sailed on the Arctic sea from the mouth of the Coppermine river to this place including the return from Point Turnagain is 659¾ geographical [555¼ advances and 104½ return] or 764⅓ statute miles.

SE 1 mile, NE 1¾ miles, SSW 2 miles. First fall of Hood's river July 31st and Aug 25th, 67°19'23" North (Obs.), 109°44'30"[88] West (Obs.). Variation 41°43'32" E. 88°54'50" Dip.

Direct daily course corrected wbs¼s, 19½ miles.

Sunday August 26th 1821

Having planted the English Ensign on the summit of a hill to attract the attention of any parties of Eskimaux that might pass this way and deposited some iron work at the foot of it for their use we proceeded 6 or 7 miles farther up the river and encamped at a cascade 12 or 14 feet high – which is produced by a ridge of clay stone crossing the river. The river is from one to two hundred yards wide here, and is bounded by high and steep banks of alluvial clay which reposes on floetz rocks, mostly a kind of indurated clay stone but sometimes that kind of red amygdaloid which exists in such abundance on this coast. A little below the fall, Hood's river is joined by a stream [James River] nearly half its own size. Bear and deer tracks were numerous on the banks of the river when we were here before, but there is not a single recent one to be seen now. The mosquitoes are not quite gone. We enjoyed a delightful repast this evening upon the berries of the *Vaccinium uliginosum*, *Arbutus alpina* and *Empetrum nigrum*. Although none of

88 After correction of 40 minutes for difference
in chronometer readings between the two
visits to Hood River.

them were fully ripe yet they appeared delicious to us, who had been so long confined to animal diet. The berries of the two latter plants were particularly fine, having a juiciness and size which they want in more southern climates. The nets were set below the fall. Credit, the steersman of one of the canoes, having gone a hunting in the evening killed a small deer. Course and distance today SBE½E 5¾ miles.

Courses per compass, SE ½ mile, EBN 1 mile, SE 1¼ miles, SSE 1¼ miles, SEBE 1 mile, SE ¼ mile, SSE ¾ mile, East ½ mile, SEBE ¾ mile. Confluence of James' branch.

East ½ mile, SEBE ½ mile. Slept at the 2ᵈ fall, Augᵗ 26, 67°13'35" North (R), 109°40'00" West (R).

Direct daily course corrected SBE½E 5¾ miles.

Wilberforce Falls of the Hood River

Monday August 27ᵗʰ 1821

Sent for the deer and took up the nets in which there were ten attihawmegh and Trout. Made a further deposit of iron work here and proceeded up the river. The shoals and rapids were so frequent in this part of the river that we walked along the banks the whole day, and the crews laboured hard in carrying the canoes thus lightened over the shoals or dragging them up the rapids, yet our whole journey in a direct line was only about 7 miles. In the evening we encamped at the lower end of a narrow chasm through which the river flows for upwards of a mile. The walls of this chasm are upwards of two hundred feet high, quite perpendicular and in some places only a few yards apart. The river precipitates itself into it, over a rock, forming two magnificent and picturesque falls close to each other [Wilberforce Falls]. The upper fall is about 60 feet high and the lower one at least one hundred, but it appeared considerably greater, for the narrowness of the chasm into which it fell prevented us from seeing its bottom and we could merely see the top of the spray far beneath our feet. The lower fall is divided into two by an isolated column of rock which rises about 40 feet above it. The whole descent of the river at this place probably exceeds 250 feet. The rock is a very fine sandstone, or perhaps it might be termed by a mineralogist compact felspar. It has a smooth surface and a light red colour. The river being surveyed from the summit of a hill, appeared so rapid and shallow that it was deemed useless to attempt proceeding any further in the large canoes. It was therefore determined that we should construct two smaller ones out of their materials. Weather very fine the heat being even oppressive. Much tormented by sandflies and mosquitoes. Junius killed a rein deer and a musk ox.

Course and distance swbs 6¾ miles.

Courses per compass, sEbE ½ mile, South 1 mile. 67°12′14″ North (Obs.), 109°43′11″ West (R).

sEbs 1¼ miles, South 1½ miles, sE¼s 1¼ miles, sEbE½E ½ mile.

Enc^t below Wilberforce falls, 67°07′04″ North (Obs.), 109°48′15″ West (Obs.) Augt 27–28–29 to build canoes. Variation 40°37′42″ East.

Direct daily course corrected swbs, 6¾ miles.

Tuesday August 28th 1821 Hood's River

Weather warm and fine. Employed about the canoes. Lat. obs. 67°07′04″ N. Long. 109°48′10″ w. Var^n 40°37′42″ E.

Wednesday August 29th 1821 Hood's River

Employed as yesterday. Credit and Junius went a hunting and killed two musk oxen. They saw some large bands of these animals, which are rutting at present. No deer seen. Many white wolves – and great numbers of Hamsters.[89] Immense

---

89 The Common Hamster in Europe can be 12
   inches long and has a bushy tail. Richardson
   here refers to the Arctic Ground Squirrel.

flocks of white and grey geese passed today going to the south-east. Much rain in the evening and during the night.

Thursday August 30th 1821

Weather remarkably fine. Mosquitoes occassionally seen and still strong enough to bite. The canoes were completed in the evening.

Friday August 31st 1821 Hood's River

Weather warm and fine. The men's loads consisting of ammunition, clothing, bedding, cooking utensils, nets, hatchets, ice chisels, astronomical instruments and the two canoes, being arranged and distributed by lot, we breakfasted and set out at 11 a.m. Notwithstanding the men were very heavily laden, the party advanced at the rate of a mile an hour including rests. A little before 6 p.m. a large band of musk oxen appearing on the left [south] bank of the river, two hunters were sent across, whilst we encamped having come upwards of 5 miles on a SE course by compass. One small buffalo [Musk ox] was killed, but the men were too much loaded to carry more than a few pounds of it away.

The alluvial soil which towards the mouth of the river spreads into plains covered with grass and willows is now giving place to a more barren and hilly tract on which the most abundant plants are the *Cetraria cucullata* and *Cornicularia ochrileuca*. Some plants of a species of *Dufourea* and the *Potentilla fruticosa* were observed today.

Courses per compass, SEbE 1¼ miles, EbS½S 1½ miles, SE½E 2 miles, S½W ¼ mile. Enc^t Augt 31, 67°02′16″ North (R), 109°45′05″ West (R).

Direct daily course corrected SbE, 5 miles.

6

STARVATION ON THE BARRENS

September 1st 1821 Saturday

Heavy rain in the night. The tent was blown down near midnight by a squall and our beds wet. Towards the morning a fall of snow took place. Ther at 5 a.m. 34°. Wind NW per compass. Set out soon after six o clock and walked slowly along the banks of the river, the canoes proving a cause of delay through the difficulty of carrying them in a high wind. They sustained much damage from the falls of those that carried them. Day cold, with slight snow showers at intervals. The from 34° to 36°. In the afternoon a heavy fall of snow took place the wind changing at the same time to the SW. Encamped at half past five and sent for a musk ox and rein deer which were killed by Pierez and Augustus. The face of the country is broken by hills of moderate elevation, in character like those to the southward of Fort Enterprise, but the ground is more plentifully strewed with loose stones. Walking over such a country is necessarily painful, but it is particularly so to men with heavy burdens on their backs, whose feet are protected only by soft moose-skin shoes. Course swbw Distance 10¾ miles.

Courses per compass, s¼w 2¾ miles, sbw¾w 3½ miles, sbw 2½ miles, ssw½w 2½ miles, Enc' Sept' 1st, 66°55′35″ North (R), 110°10′09″ West (R).

Direct daily course corrected swbw 10¾ miles.

Sunday September 2d 1821 Hood's River

Thermometer at sun rise 31°. Wind NW fresh. The snow disappeared before the sun in the course of the morning and the weather became fine. Soon after setting out we passed the mouth of a large stream [Sellwood River] which joins the river from the eastward. Saw a herd of 20 muskoxen, also a rein deer on the opposite bank of the river. At 10 a.m. we halted to prepare breakfast – and resumed our journey again at one p.m. Lat. obs. 66°53′35″ N. Encamped at half past 5. Afternoon remarkably fine. The^r at 6 p.m. 50°. We walked this day about 13 miles but unfortunately we were led by following the river away to the westward a long way from our route. Long. observed about a mile from the Encampment 110°40′ W. The hills here are lower and more round backed than those we crossed yesterday and exhibit but little naked rock being covered with a pretty thick coat of vegetables principally consisting of the arborescent lichens and the *Arbutus alpina*. The *Vaccinium uliginosum* attains a considerable size, in the sheltered vallies amongst these hills. The hunters killed a musk ox in the evening. Course West. Distance 11½ miles.

"... *a rein deer on the opposite bank of the river*"

Courses per compass, s¾w 2 miles, SEbE 1 mile, swbw 5 miles. 66°53′35″ North (Obs.) 110°26′40″ (Chr.).
wbs 2 miles, swbw 2 miles. 66°55′13″ North (R), 110°40′12″ West (Chr.).
wsw 2 miles, wsw 1 mile. Slept Septr 2^d 66°55′30″ North (R), 110°44′50″ West (R).
Direct daily course corrected West 11½ miles.

Wednesday[1] Septr 3^d 1821 Barren grounds

Sent for the musk ox. Set out at half past five a.m. and after walking about a mile, along the banks of the river, and finding that it continued to lead us away from the direct route, crossed in the canoes and turning to the SE per compass marched two miles, and halted to breakfast. The hills here, were round backed and perfectly even in their outline, no rocks being visible except some small cliffs of basalt which contained imbedded white crystals. We made a fire of moss and

1 Monday.

the *Andromeda polifolia*; neither willows nor dwarf birches being found except on the banks of the river. Resuming our march after breakfast we ascended completely from the valley of the river and entered a level and very barren country, varied only by small lakes and marshes. The ground was covered with rolled stones, of gneiss, greenstone or basalt. There was very little rock exposed but gneiss was observed in one or two places. There were many old tracks of the rein deer in the clayey soil and some more recent ones of the musk ox. Encamped at 6 p.m. on the banks of a small river flowing to the eastward. Evening fine.

Course ssw distance 10¾ miles.

Courses per compass, sbw 1¼ miles. Distance Hood River was traced – 51¾ or 60 statute miles.

sEbs 1¼ miles, sbE½E 8½ miles. Enc^d at Wright's River Sept 3^d, 66°45′35″ North (R), 110°53′16″ West (R).

Direct daily course corrected ssw 10¾ miles.

Tuesday September 4th 1821 Barren grounds

Morning very fine, towards noon quite warm. Set out at 6 a.m. and walked over a perfectly level country, interspersed with small lakes, which communicated with each other by streams running in various directions. Ground stony and swampy. Many large flocks of white geese were feeding on the borders of the lakes but the ground was too even to admit of the hunters approaching them. Halted to breakfast at half past ten, and making a fire with the *Cornicularia ochrileuca* cooked the remainder of the buffalo meat. No berry-bearing shrubs here, the surface of the earth being thinly covered in the moister places with a few grasses, and on the dryer spots with the above mentioned lichen.

Continuing our journey in the afternoon we saw several large male deer, seemingly on a march to the southward to rejoin the females. Two of them were wounded by our hunters but escaped from us. We encamped at 7 p.m. having come 12½ miles on s22°w course. The country to the southward is now more broken several conical eminences shewing themselves. Evening warm but dark and cloudy. A small bit of pemmican was distributed to each of the party being our whole stock. This with the addition of a little arrow root formed a very scanty supper.

Courses per compass, sbE½E 6 miles. 66°40′42″ North (Obs.)

sbE½E 6½ miles. Slept Septr 4th 5th & 6th, 66°34′18″ North (R), 111°04′38″ West (R). Snow fell 2 feet deep.

Direct daily course corrected s22w, 12½ miles.

Wednesday September 5th 1821 Barren grounds

We were detained in our encampment all day by a heavy and continuous rain, which about 5 p.m. on a severe gale springing up from the NW changed into snow. As we had nothing to eat, the whole party kept in bed, but suffered much during the night from cold and from the snow drifting into the tents.

Thursday September 6th 1821

Heavy storm of wind and snow. Suffered much from the cold but more from hunger. Ther. 20°.

Friday September 7th 1821

In the morning it cleared up a little, but the wind still blew fresh, and the weather was extremely cold. It became necessary however to set out, although we were in a very unfit condition for starting, the ground covered a foot deep with snow, and our garments stiffened by the frost the tents having proved a very insufficient shelter from the rain; and we had no means of making a fire – the moss at all times difficult to kindle being now covered with ice and snow. A considerable time was consumed in packing up the frozen tents and bedclothes the wind blowing so keen that no one could keep his hands long out of his mittens. Just as we were about to commence our march Mr Franklin from exhaustion and sudden exposure to the cold wind was seized with a fainting fit. Upon eating a small bit of portable soup, however, he recovered so far as to be able to move on. After a short but cheerless march, those who carried the canoes having been repeatedly blown down by the violence of the wind, one of them was so much broken as to be rendered utterly unserviceable. This was a serious misfortune to us as the remaining canoe having through mistake been made too small, it was doubtful whether it would be sufficient to carry us across a river. Indeed we had found it necessary in crossing Hood's River to lash the two canoes together. To turn the accident however to the best account we made a fire of the bark and timbers of the broken vessel and cooked the remainder of the portable soup and arrow root. This served to allay the pangs of hunger for a time, but was considered by the voyageurs as a poor substitute for 8 pounds of solid animal food, their customary daily allowance.

Indeed, after three days fasting, there was not one of them that would have been satisfied with less than twenty pounds of deers' meat at a meal. In the afternoon we walked over a more broken country, consisting of low gravelly hills, covered with large stones, and small marshy meadows. A few partridges were killed and having encamped and dug a few willows from under the snow, cooked our slender meal, amounting to half a partridge each man. Course and distance s22°w 8½ miles.

Course per compass sbE½E 8½ miles. Slept Septr 7th, 66°26'10" North (R), 111°12'35" West (R).

Direct daily course corrected s22w, 8½ miles.

Saturday September 8th 1821

We set out at half past five and after walking about two miles came to a small river [Cracroft River] flowing to the westward which had a very rapid current and a rocky channel. We found much difficulty in crossing this, the canoe being of no use, not only from the rockyness of the channel but also from its requiring gumming, an operation which we could not perform, from the want of wood and the frostyness of the weather. After following the course of the river for some distance, however, we effected a passage by means of a range of large rocks, that crossed a rapid.

As the current was strong and the rocks were in general covered with water to the depth of two or three feet, the men were exposed to much hazard in carrying their heavy burdens across, and several of them actually slipped into the stream but were immediately rescued by the others. Junius went farther up the river in search of a better crossing place and did not rejoin us again today.

As several of the party were drenched from head to foot, and we were all wet to the middle, our clothes became stiff with the frost, and we walked with much pain for the remainder of the afternoon. We had no breakfast, but having killed a few partridges, we encamped at 4 p.m. and supped upon them and a little Tripe de roche (various lichens of the genus *Gyrophora*.)[2] This, although scanty for men endued with appetites, such as the daily fatigue we underwent created in us, proved a cheerful meal and was received with thankfulness. Credit, Pierez, Adam and Augustus who had gone ahead to hunt, did not rejoin us tonight, nor did Junius.

Course ssw½w Distance 10¼ miles.

Courses per compass, sbw 2½ miles. Cracroft River, 66°24'34" North (R), 111°17'25" West (R).

sbE 8 miles. Slept Septr 8th, 66°15'30" North (R), 111°22'27" West (R).

Direct daily course corrected ssw½w, 10¼ miles.

---

2 The four species *G. proboscidea*, *G. hyperborea*, *G. pensylvanica*, and *G. Muhlenbergii*, "were found in greater or less abundance in all rocky places throughout the journey. We used them all four as articles of food, but not having the means of extracting the bitter principle from them, they proved noxious to several of the party, producing severe bowel complaints." Richardson, "Botanical Appendix," p. 759. Modern Latin names for these four lichens are given in chap. 1, notes 31–4. They "cover the surfaces of most of the larger stones" Richardson explained on 1 October 1820.

Sunday September 9, 1821

Thermometer 17°. Set out at 6 a.m. our march much impeded by the deepness of the snow, which rendered it necessary for the man who beat the track, to be frequently relieved. After walking about two miles we overtook the absent hunters, by the side of a lake, and halted to await the arrival of Junius whom they had not seen. In the mean time we gathered a little Tripe de roche and breakfasted upon it and two or three partridges that were killed in the morning.

"… we gathered a little Tripe de roche and breakfasted upon it"

Observed the tracks of two deer on the borders of the lake. Junius arrived in the afternoon and informed us that he had seen a large herd of Musk oxen, on the banks of the little river we crossed yesterday, and had wounded one of them but it escaped. He brought about 4 lbs. of meat the remains of an ox that had been devoured by the wolves. During the halt, it was ascertained that we would have to cross a rapid stream 150 yards wide by which the waters of the lake were discharged, and a small clump of willows being found the canoe was gummed for the purpose. This place was judged to be the Congecathewchaga of Hearne [Kathawachaga Lake], a conjecture which has been since verified by information from the Indians. The river is the Ana-tessy or Cree River[3] and is supposed to fall into Bathurst's Inlet, but although the Indians have visited its mouth, their descriptions were not sufficient to identify it with any of the rivers, whose mouths we had seen. The small canoe being put into the water was found to be

3 It was here the Burnside River, but only 10 miles west of where its tributary, the Cree River, joins it from the south-south-east. Although the Indians had no maps, they had an incredibly good understanding of geography, and were able to convey this to Richardson.

extremely ticklish, but it was managed with much dexterity by Pierez and Adam who ferried one passenger over at a time, causing him to lie flat in the bottom of the canoe. As the canoe was leaky, this was by no means a pleasant posture, but there was no alternative. The transport of the whole party was effected by 5 o clock and we walked about two miles farther and encamped. The evening although frosty turned out very fine. Two young alpine hares were killed near the encampment, and together with the small piece of meat brought in by Junius, shared amongst the party. We found no tripe de roche here. The country has now become decidedly hilly and appears from the shape of the hills and a few patches of exposed rock to belong to the gneiss formation. Course and distance sw 5¾ miles.

Courses per compass, sbw 2 miles. 66°13′51″ North (Obs.), 111°26′15″ West (Chr.) Congecathewachaga

SSE½E 1 mile. SSW 3 miles. Anatessy [a small unnamed stream], 66°10′56″ North (R), 111°32′13″ North (R) Slept. Septr 9th.

Direct daily course corrected sw, 5¾ miles.

Monday September 10th 1821 Barren grounds

Wind northerly, thick foggy weather. The^r 18°. Very cold.

In the course of our march this morning we passed many small lakes and the ground becoming higher and more hilly, as we receded from the river, was covered to a much greater depth with snow. This rendered walking not only extremely laborious but also hazardous in the highest degree for the sides of the hills, as is usual throughout the barren grounds, abounding in accumulations of large angular stones, it often happened that the men fell into the interstices with their loads on their backs, being deceived by the smooth appearance of the drifted snow. If any one had broken a limb here, his fate would have been melancholy indeed, we could neither have remained with him, nor carried him on with us. Our men were somewhat cheered by observing on the sandy summit of a hill from whence the snow had been blown, the summer track of a man. Several deer tracks were also seen in the snow. About noon the weather cleared up a little, and to our great joy, we saw a band of musk oxen grazing in a valley before us. The party instantly halted and all the hunters we could muster amongst us were sent out. They approached the animals from to leeward with extreme caution, no less than two hours being consumed before they got within gun shot. In the mean time we beheld their proceedings from the top of a hill with extreme anxiety but at length they opened their fire and we had the satisfaction of se[e]ing one of the largest cows in the herd, fall to the ground. Another one that was wounded escaped with the rest of the herd which fled instantly. This success infused spirit into our starving party. To skin and cut up the animal was the work of a moment. The contents of its stomach were devoured upon the spot, and the raw intestines which were next attacked were pronounced by the most delicate amongst us to be excellent. The tops of a few willows peeping through the snow in the bottom of the valley, they were grubbed up the tents pitched and the supper cooked and devoured with avidity. This was the 6th day since we had a good meal. The tripe de roche even when we had enough only serving to allay the pangs of hunger for a short time. Course and distance s23°w. 8¼ miles.

Average temperature for 10 days about 24°5 Fa[h]renheit

"… we saw a band of musk oxen …"

Courses per compass sEbs 2 miles, sbE 6½ miles. Slept Septr 10th & 11th, on Peacock Hills, 66°03′12″ North (R), 111°40′18″ West (R)
Direct daily course corrected s23w, 8¼ miles.

Tuesday September 11th 1821 Barren grounds

Thermometer 20°. Cloudy weather. Strong southerly gales. Remained in the encampment all day. Much incommoded in the tents by the drift snow.

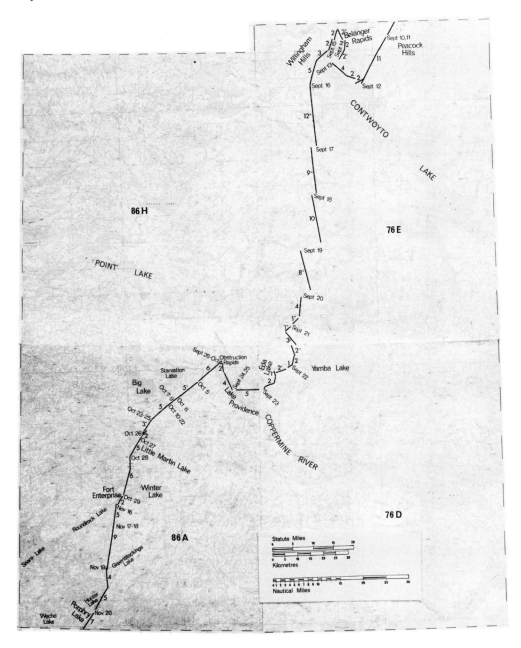

Map 7   *10 September–21 November 1821*

Wednesday September 12th 1821

Strong southerly gale with much snow. Notwithstanding the difficulty of carrying the canoes was nearly as great as yesterday the men tired of remaining in the tents intreated us to set out, which we did at 7 a.m. and marched until 6 p.m. through very deep snow. The^r during the day about 32°. The whole party complained more of faintness and fatigue today than they had ever done before. Their strength seems to have been impaired by the recent supply of animal food.

"... found ourselves at the border of a large lake (Contwoy-to or Rum Lake) ..."

Course and distance ssw½w 11 miles.
Course per compass, sbE 11 miles. Slept Septr 12th, 65°53'30" North (R), 111°52'58" West (R).
Direct daily course corrected ssw½w, 11 miles.

Thursday September 13th 1821 Barren grounds

Commenced our journey in the morning in thick hazy weather and after an hours march, found ourselves on the borders of a large lake (Contwoy-to or Rum Lake) which appearing to spread out to a great extent to SE we coasted it all day to the westward to look for a crossing place. This lake being bounded by steep and lofty hills, the march, today, was very fatiguing and the party straggled much –

and when we encamped Credit was missing, nor did he come in during the night. The musk-ox meat being all consumed we supped on Tripe de roche.

Course and distance N73W 6¾ miles.

Courses per compass, sbw½w 2 miles, wsw 2 miles, West 4 miles.

Slept Septr 13, 65°55'32" North (R), 112°09'10" West (R).

Direct daily course corrected N73W, 6¾ miles.

Friday September 14th 1821

The officers being assembled round a small fire of willows this morning, before starting, Pierrot [Pierre St Germain][4] presented each of us with a small piece of meat that he had saved from his allowance. It was received with great thankfulness and such an act of self denial and kindness, being totally unexpected in a Canadian, filled our eyes with tears. The lake appearing to terminate, at the distance of a few miles, in a river we directed our course thither, and during our march we met Credit who communicated the joyful intelligence of his having killed two deer in the morning. We instantly halted and having shared the deer that was nearest to us, prepared breakfast. Lat. observed 65°57'43" N.

After breakfast the other deer was sent for and we went down to the river [Burnside River], which was about 200 yards wide, and flowed with great velocity through a broken rocky channel. The canoe being put into the water, an attempt was made to cross at the head of a rapid, where the current was rather smoother than elsewhere. Mr Franklin, Pierez and Belanger embarked first, but they proved too great a load for the canoe, particularly as there was a fresh breeze blowing at the time, which rendered it more difficult to manage. In consequence of these circumstances, conjoined with the unskilfulness of Belanger, who was unaccustomed to a small canoe, they got involved in the rapid and upset in the middle of it. They kept hold of the canoe, however, until they touched a rock where the water did not reach higher than their middles. Notwithstanding the strength of the current, they kept their footing, here, until Pierez, with great dexterity, emptied the water out of the canoe, replaced Mr. Franklin in it, and finally embarked himself. Belanger was left standing in a very perilous situation on the rock, but the other two, were also in considerable hazard, for the canoe had been much damaged and actually sank before the traverse was completed. This time however it was in shallow water; they

---

4 Pierre St Germain, the interpreter, was presumably a native of the Northwest, and not a French-Canadian voyageur. He was the most successful hunter by far, occasionally helped by Adam, the other interpreter, and by Augustus and Junius, the two Eskimos.

Credit was the only voyageur who had much success in hunting: Credit shot a caribou on 31 July and again on 26 August, a muskox on 29 August 1821, and two caribou on 14 September.

reached a small rocky island and having again emptied out the water re-embarked and reached the other side in safety. In the mean time Belanger was suffering extremely, immersed to his middle in a strong current where temperature was very little above the freezing point, and the upper part of his body covered with wet clothes and exposed to a strong breeze not much above zero. He called piteously for relief and Pierez on his return endeavoured to embark him, but in vain. Pierez himself was now rendered incapable of further exertion by the cold, but having brought the canoe to the shore, Adam attempted to embark Belanger but found it impossible, from his situation in the middle of the rapid, and there was a deep channel betwixt him and either shore. An attempt was next made to carry out a line to him made of the slings of the mens loads. This also failed, the current acting so strongly upon it, as to prevent the canoe

"... at the head of a rapid ..."

from steering, and it was finally broken and carried down the stream. At length when Belanger's strength seemed almost exhausted, the canoe reached him, with a small cord belonging to one of the nets and he was dragged perfectly senseless through the rapid. He was instantly stripped and being rolled up in blankets, two men undressed themselves and went to bed with him – but it was some hours before he recovered his warmth and sensation. By this disastrous accident Mr Franklin's portfolio, containing his journal, and astronomical and meteorological observations, was carried down the stream and lost. The most of the party and almost all the baggage were transported across, in the course of the afternoon although the canoe filled with water at every traverse.

Course and distance N19°E 4¼ miles.
Courses per compass Nbw 2¼ miles. 65°57'43" North (Obs.).

NWbN 2 miles, Belanger's Rapid at the discharge of Contwoy-to or Rum Lake, 65°59′41″ North (R), 112°5′55″ West (R), so named by the Indians as being the spot where Hearne distributed his keg of Rum. Encamped here. Canoe upset & Capt F. lost all his journals.

Direct daily course corrected N19E, 4¼ miles.

Saturday September 15th 1821 Rum Lake

Cold northerly wind but fine weather. Long. of rapid observed 112°23′06″ w. The rest of the party were brought across this morning and Belanger had recovered so as to be able to walk so that we were enabled to resume our march after breakfast. Soon after leaving the encampment, a herd of deer were seen and after a long chase and considerable expence of ammunition one of them was killed by Pierrot [St Germain]. After this we marched about 3 miles along the lake and encamped amidst a range of rocky hills [Willingham Mountains]. Temp^r at 6 p.m. 30°.

Course and distance N81°w. 1¾ miles.

Courses per compass, WNW 2½ miles, amongst the Willingham mountains.

SSE 2 miles. Encampment Septr 15, 65°59′53″ North (R), 112°10′13″ West (R).

Direct daily course corrected N81°w, 1¾ miles.

Sunday September 16th 1821 Barren grounds

Wind north, cloudy weather with slight snow showers. Ther^r 25°.

Set out at 7 a.m. and marched until noon when we stopped to breakfast. Our route lead us along the lake, over steep craggy mountains and across deep ravines. We observed many summer deer roads, and some recent tracks. Some marks that had been put up last summer by the Indians were also noticed. Indeed we have since learnt that this is a regular deer pass and on that account annually frequented by the Red knives and that the Lake is named Contwoy-to or Rum Lake being the place where Hearne distributed his rum amongst the Indians. We slept opposite to the hill on which we encamped on the night of the 13th.

Course and distance s26w 10¼ miles.

Courses per compass, SSE 2½ miles, sbw 3 miles. Crossed some small lakes on the ice.

SSE 5 miles, Encamp^t Septr 16, 65°50′54″ North (R), 112°20′55″ West (R)

Direct daily course corrected s26w, 10¼ miles.

Monday September 17th 1821 Barren grounds

Started at 7 a.m and after walking hard all day put up at 4 p.m. The country was tolerably level but intersected by a few ravines and strewed with large stones. Some deer were seen in the morning but the hunters failed in killing them and in the afternoon we fell into the track of a large herd which had passed the day before but did not overtake them. In consequence of this want of success we had no breakfast and but a scanty supper, but we allayed the pangs of hunger by eating pieces of singed hides. A little Tripe de roche was also obtained. These would have satisfied us in ordinary times, but we were now exhausted by slender fare, and travel, and our appetites had become enormous. Ther^r from 25° to 28°.

Course and distance s9°E 12½ miles.

Course per compass SE 12½ miles. Passed several small lakes.
Encamp^t Septr 17, 65°38′24″ North, 112°16′10″ West (R).

Direct daily course corrected s9E, 12½ miles.

Tuesday September 18th 1821 Barren grounds

Wind south. Weather hazy and foggy. The^r 28°. Thaw in the afternoon. We walked today over a level marshy and gravelly country. All the small lakes frozen. Snow deep. One deer was seen, but the hunters could not approach it. Supped on Tripe de roche. Course and distance s9°E 9½ miles.

Course per compass, SE 9½ miles. Passed through small lakes & encamped near another. Enc^t Septr 18, 65°29′01″ North (R), 112°12′34″ West (R).

Direct daily course corrected s9E, 9½ miles.

Wednesday September 19th 1821 Barren grounds

Heavy snow all night. Slight thaw in the day. Made an uncomfortable march and put up at 3 p.m. Men faint from hunger. Country, as yesterday, level, but full of small lakes and intersected by ravines. Soil gravelly and interspersed with large stones. No tripe de roche. Ther at 6 p.m. 30°. Snow.

Course and Distance s11°E 10 miles.

Course per compass, SE¼E 10 miles. Enc^t Septr 19, 65°19′12″ North (R), 112°08′00″ West (R).

Direct daily course corrected s11E, 10 miles.

Thursday September 20th 1821 Barren grounds

By our reckoning, we should have seen Point Lake today, but after a miserable march of eight or nine miles it seemed to fly from us. Men dispirited and exhausted. Supped on Tripe de roche. Hard frost during the night. Snow towards the morning. Course and distance s14°E 8½ miles.

Course per compass, SE½E 8½ miles. Enc^t on the border of a small lake Septr 20th, 65°10'57" North (R), 112°03'06" West (R).

Direct daily course corrected s14E, 8½ miles.

Friday September 21st 1821

Wind sw. Thick fog. Hard frost. Set out in the morning. The men much dispirited at the absence of tracks of deer or of any other animal. The weather became milder towards noon and Mr Franklin obtained an observation in Lat. 65°07'06" N. by which we learnt that we had kept to the eastward of the proper course, to that part of the lake, to which we wished to go, and had come six or seven miles to the southward of it. In consequence of which we altered our direction to wsw and after walking for about 1½ mile put up to allow the party which had straggled in consequence of the change of the course to collect. Nothing to eat. A gloom spread over every countenance. Course and distance s15°w 5¼ miles.

Course per compass, SE¾s 4 miles. 65°7'06" North (Obs).

sbw 1¾ miles. Enc^t Septr 21, 65°5'54" North (R), 112°6'03" West (R).

Direct daily course corrected s15w, 5¼ miles.

Saturday September 22^d 1821

Started at 7 a.m. and after walking about 2 miles wsw came upon a large lake,[5] which led us a long way to the eastward. The Longitude per chr. was obs. to be 112°01' w. We encamped on the borders of the lake,[6] supped on Tripe de roche and derived some consolation from the circumstance of finding some dwarf pines and willows larger than usual. The track of a single deer was also seen. Course and distance s13°E 8 miles.

Courses per compass, s½w 1¾ miles, Ebs 3½ miles, sEbE½E 2¼ miles. Fell upon a large lake supposed to be Point Lake,[7] 65°00'34" North (R), 111°59'48" West (Chr.).

5 An unnamed lake, elevation 1396 ft, immediately north of Eda Lake.

6 Now the tip of the eastern arm of Eda Lake

proper, elevation 1360 ft, and only about two miles west of Yamba Lake.

7 As above.

SSE½E 2 miles. Enc^t Septr 22^d, 64°58′12″ North (R), 112°2′44″ (R).
Direct daily course corrected S13°E, 8 miles.

"… some dwarf pines [white spruce] larger than usual"

Sunday September 23^d 1821

Mr Back and the Ind Interpreters Pierez and Adam were sent on before, to hunt
and to await our arrival at the river. Soon after we started, the men found some
pieces of the skin and a few bones of a deer that had been devoured by the
wolves in the spring. They halted and lighted a fire, and rendering the bones
friable by burning, devoured them with avidity. They also eat several of their old
shoes. Thaw in the afternoon. Walked until dark, fording in the course of the
day two arms of the lake. The canoe was broken today[8] and left behind, notwithstanding every remonstrance. The men had become desperate and were perfectly
regardless of the commands of their officers. Rain during the night. Course and
distance S39°W 6¾ miles.

Courses per compass, SSW½W 1 mile. Forded a shallow part of the

8 The remaining made-down canoe had been
broken on 19 September when the person
carrying it fell and was "rendered incapable
of repair" by another fall on 23 September.
Franklin, *Journey*, pp. 413, 417.

lake. ssw½w 2¼ miles, ebs½s 1¼ miles, sse½e 1½ miles. Passed many small lakes.

swbs 2 miles, sebs ½ mile. Snow thawing for the first time since the 5th Sept^r, Enc^t Septr 23^d, 64°53′18″ North (r), 112°10′44″ West (r).

Direct daily distance corrected s39°w, 6¾ miles.

September 24th 1821

Snow melting rapidly. Set out amidst a drizzling rain. The tracks of Mr Back and the hunters being traced with difficulty and becoming more and more obliterated as the day advanced the men became furious under the idea that they were deserted by the hunters, threw down their bundles and prepared to set out after them with their utmost speed. The persuasions of the officers however prevented them from putting this mad scheme into execution, but not until Belanger was dispatched with orders to Mr Back to halt until we came up – we walked about 6 miles to the westward when we overtook Mr Back and his party on the borders of a lake [Lake Providence]. The afternoon proving foggy we encamped in a valley where there were a number of pines 7 or 8 feet high. Obtained some Tripe de roche.

Course and distance West 5 miles.

Course per compass, sw¼w 5 miles. Enc^t on the borders of Lake Providence Septr 24th & 25, 64°53′18″ North (r), 112°22′00″ West (r). Killed 5 small deer.

Direct daily distance corrected West, 5 miles.

Tuesday September 25th 1821

Just as we were about to start a herd of deer was seen and the hunters going after them five small ones were killed. This was the 11th day without meat.[9] We encamped again to prepare breakfast and the men petitioning to be allowed to have one days rest, their request was granted – and they consumed upwards of a third of the meat before night. Weather very mild. Snow very nearly gone.

Wednesday September 26th 1821

We set out this morning, early, and after walking about three miles along the lake, came to the River, which flowed from it and which we at once recognized, from its size, to be the Coppermine River. Its course is to the northward and after

9 Franklin named the lake after this "bounty of Providence."

winding for about five miles, it terminates in another lake which we judged at the time to be Point Lake a conjecture which the Indians have since confirmed. The width of the river here is about 120 yards, its current is pretty swift, and there are two strong rapids in its course, but in a canoe we could have crossed it with ease and safety. The men were at first unwilling to believe that this was actually the Coppermine River, and so little confidence had they in our reckoning and so much had they bewildered themselves in the march that some of them asserted that it was the River on which we had built the small canoes (Hood's River) and others that it was the Bethee-tessy [Tree River] a river which rises from a lake to the northward of Rum lake and holds a course to the sea parallel to the Coppermine River. In short their despondency had arrived at its height and they all despaired of ever seeing Fort Enterprise again. The steady assurances of the officers however, that they were actually on the banks of the long looked for stream, and that the distance to Fort Enterprise did not exceed forty miles, at length convinced them, that the only obstacle to our progress was the difficulty of crossing the river. Then, they bitterly execrated their folly and impatience in breaking the canoe and the remainder of the day was spent in wandering slowly along the river, looking in vain for a fordable place and inventing schemes for crossing, no sooner devised than abandoned. We encamped in the evening at the head of Point Lake.

Course and distance Nbw¾w 6 miles.

Courses per compass, Nwbw½w 4 miles came to the Coppermine River. Nwbw 2 miles to obstruction rapid where the latitude was observed in 65°00', Long. D.R. 112°20' R.

Thursday September 27th 1821 Point Lake

It was determined that we should coast Point Lake, until we found wood large enough to make rafts, and Mr Back, Pierez Adam and Beauparlant were sent forward to hunt, with directions to halt for us, at the first place fit for crossing at.

The day was very mild and fine, and the snow totally disappeared under the influence of the sun. This rendered it necessary for Mr Franklin, to give strict orders for the party to keep together, and especially to the two Eskimaux not to leave us, for they had frequently strayed away in search of the remains of animals. The people, however, through despondency, had become careless and disobedient, they had ceased to dread punishment or hope for reward and it is a melancholy truth that gratitude for past favours or a sense of duty seldom influence the conduct of a Canadian voyageur. Although they beheld their officers suffering even in a greater degree than themselves, yet they considered the want of food as dissolving all ties between us, and they had not scrupled to steal from us [the officers] part of the meat which had been allotted to us, with strict impartiality. In consequence of this total want of discipline, much time was lost in halting and firing guns to call in the stragglers. Yet the labour of walking was so much reduced by the disappearance of the snow that we had advanced 6 or 8 miles along the lake before noon, exclusive of the loss of distance, in rounding its numerous bays. At length we came to an arm of the lake running away to the NE and apparently connected with the lake [Eda Lake] which we had coasted on the 22^d–23^d and 24th of the month. The idea of again rounding such an extensive piece of water and of travelling over so barren a country a second time, was dreadful to us, and we feared that other arms of the lake equally large might obstruct our path, and that the strength of the party would entirely fail long before we could reach the only part where we were certain of finding wood, distant in a direct line 25 miles. Indeed the strongest amongst us, was reduced to little more than the shadow of what he had been a month ago. While we halted to consider upon this subject, and to collect the party together, the carcase of a deer was discovered in the cleft of a rock, into which it had fallen in the spring. It was putrid, but it was not the less acceptable to us on that account, in our present circumstances, and a fire being kindled a large portion of it was devoured on the spot, thus affording an unexpected breakfast to the party, for in order to husband the small portion of meat we had remaining, we had agreed to make only one scanty meal a day. The men cheered by this unhoped for supply, were sanguine in the hope of being able to cross the stream on a raft of willows, although they had before declared such a project to be impracticable and unanimously entreated us to return back to the rapid a request which accorded with our own opinions and was accordingly acceded to – Credit and Junius however were missing and it was necessary to send to Mr Back and his party. Augustus being promised a reward undertook the task and we agreed to wait for him at the rapid. It was supposed that he could not fail meeting with the two stragglers, in his way to or from Mr Back, as it was likely that they would keep on the borders of the lake. He accordingly set out after Mr Back whilst we returned about a mile towards the rapid and encamped in a deep valley amongst some large willows. We supped on the remainder of the putrid deer and the men having gone to the spot where it was found, scraped together the contents of its intestines which were scattered on the rocks and added them to their meal. We also enjoyed the luxury today of eating a large quantity of excellent Blue berries and Cran-berries which were laid bare by the melting of the snow, but nothing could allay our inordinate appetites. The borders of the lake here, consisting of round backed hills of gneiss with intervening narrow vallies and precipices of syenite are similar in general aspect to the country about Fort Enterprise. The *Arbutus uva ursi* was seen here for the first time since we arrived on the sea-coast and the Indians report that it is not found to the north-ward or eastward of the Coppermine River.

Course and distance North 6 miles. Wind East, strong. Cold weather.

Friday September 28th 1821 Obstruction rapid

In the night time we heard Credit firing in answer to our signal muskets and he rejoined us in the morning but we got no intelligence of Junius. In the morning we had light southerly breezes with cloudy weather and setting off as usual, about an hour after day break, arrived at the rapid about 2 p.m. Eight deer were seen by Michel and Credit who loitered behind the rest of the party but they could not approach them. A great many shots were fired by those in the rear at partridges, but they missed or at least did not choose to add what they killed to the common stock. Some willows were cut down in the afternoon for the raft. Collected a little Tripe de roche and supped on it, and the moiety of the remainder of our deers meat.

Saturday September 29th 1821 Obstruction rapid

Strong SE winds with fog in the morning. More moderate in the evening. Temperature of the rapid 38°.

A raft was constructed today, of the largest willows that could be found, bound together in faggots, but as they were green it proved to be very little buoyant and was unable to support more than one man at a time. Even on this however it was hoped that the whole party might be transported across by hauling it from one side to the other provided a line could once be carried to the other bank. Several attempts were made by [Solomon] Bellanger the strongest and most adroit of the party to convey the raft across the stream, but they failed from the want of oars. A paddle, the only substitute for an oar we had, proving utterly inef[f]icient and the longest pole we could construct by tying the tent poles together, being too short to reach the bottom, at a short distance from the shore. The wind too, blowing from the opposite bank was a strong obstacle. The men suffering severely from the coldness of the water, in which they were necessarily immersed to their middles in their endeavours to aid Belanger, were about to give up the plan as hopeless when I proposed to swim across with a line and to haul the raft over. This scheme also failed. I had advanced but a little distance from the bank with a line round my middle when I lost the power of moving my arms through the cold.[10] I was then obliged to turn upon my back and had nearly reached the opposite shore in that position, when my legs also became powerless, and I sunk to the bottom. The men hauling upon the line however, I immediately came to the surface again and regaining my recollection, was enabled by keeping in my breath as much as possible, to remain above water until I was drawn ashore. Being then rolled up in a blanket and placed before a good

---

10 When Richardson "was about to step into the water, he put his foot on a dagger, which cut him to the bone; but this misfortune could not stop him from attempting the execution of his generous undertaking." Franklin, *Journey*, 1823, p. 425.

fire of willows I recovered tolerably in the course of the evening, but the fire being too hot, although it was regulated by my sensations at the time, the skin of the left side of my body, which was most exposed to the heat, was deprived of feeling, and it did not regain its proper tone, nor did that side become as strong as the other, for five months afterwards.

It may be worthy of remark, that I would have had little hesitation in any former period of my life, of plunging into water even below 38° F. but at this time I was reduced almost to skin and bone and like the rest of the party suffered from degrees of cold that would have been disregarded whilst in health and vigour. During the whole of our march we experienced that no quantity of clothing would keep us warm whilst we fasted, but on those occasions on which we were enabled to go to bed with full stomachs, we passed the night in a warm and comfortable manner. In the evening Augustus came in. He had walked a day and a half beyond the place from which we turned back but had neither seen Junius nor Mr Back. Of the former he had seen no traces, but he had followed the tracks of Mr Back's party for a considerable distance, until the hardness of the ground rendered them imperceptible. Junius was well equipped with ammunition, blankets, knives a kettle and other necessaries and it was the opinion of Augustus, that when he found he could not rejoin the party he would endeavour to gain the woods on the west end of Point lake and follow the river until he fell in with some of the parties of Eskimaux, who frequent its mouth. The Indians too, with whom we have since conversed upon this subject, are confident that he would be able to subsist himself during the winter. We consumed the last of our deer's meat this evening, at supper.

Sunday September 30th 1821 Obstruction rapid

Fresh south east breezes. The men went out today in search of dry willows and returned with 8 large faggots of which they made a raft, much more buoyant than the former, but the wind being still adverse they delayed attempting to cross until a more favourable opportunity. Pleased however with the appearance of their raft they collected some Tripe de roche and made a cheerful supper.

Monday October 1st 1821

Wind ssw dark, cloudy and cold weather – as unfavourable as before for crossing upon the raft. Mr Back and his party arrived this morning. They had traced the lake about 15 miles farther than we did and found it undoubtedly connected, as we had supposed, with the lake we fell upon, on the 22d of the month of September. Pierez now proposed to make a canoe of the fragments of painted canvas in which we wrapped up our bedding. His scheme appearing practicable a party was sent to our encampment of the 24th and 25th ultimo to collect pitch amongst the small pines that grew there, to pay over the seams of the canoe.

In the afternoon, we had a heavy fall of snow which continued all night. A small quantity of Tripe de roche was gathered and Credit who had been hunting brought in the antlers and back bone of a deer that had been killed in the summer. The wolves and birds of prey had picked them clean, but there still remained a quantity of the spinal marrow which they had not been able to extract. This although putrid, was esteemed a valuable prize, and the spine being divided into portions was distributed equally amongst the different messes. After eating the marrow, which was so acrid as to excoriate the lips, we rendered the bones friable in the fire, and devoured them likewise.

Tuesday October 2ᵈ 1821 Obstruction rapid

A heavy fall of snow, which lasted all the night, has covered the ground to the depth of a foot and a half. The party which went for gum, returned without having found any. They had visited the spot where the deer were killed, in the hope of finding some of their dung, but it was all gone. Pierez commenced the canoe today, but the bad weather and the lowness of his spirits, make him very slow in his operations.

The people have again become extremely despondent, a settled gloom hangs on every countenance, and they refused to pick Tripe de roche, choosing rather to go entirely without eating than to make any exertion. Augustus went to fish at the rapid, but a large trout having carried away his bait, we had nothing to replace it with.

Strong breezes with heavy snow all day.

Wednesday October 3ᵈ 1821 Obstruction Rapid

Strong winds with snow all the forenoon. In the morning Mʳ Franklin endeavoured to go to Pieresh's tent, about ½ a mile from our encampment but after an absence of three hours, he returned without having reached it, his strength not being equal to the labour of wading through the deep snow. A little Tripe de roche was gathered today. This weed produces occassionally such distressing bowel complaints, that several of the men wont eat it, and amongst others Mʳ Hood, who is unable to take even a few spoonfuls, without suffering from severe gripings. The sensation of hunger is no longer felt by any of us, but we are scarcely able to converse upon any other subject than the pleasures of eating.

Thursday October 4 – 1821 Obstruction Rapid

Light northerly winds. Snow at times. The canoe being finished, it was brought to the encampment; and the whole party being assembled in anxious expectation on the beach, Perez Sᵗ Germain embarked, and to our great joy and admiration of his dexterity, succeeded in reaching the opposite shore, with a double line. The canoe was then drawn back again and another person transported across, and in this manner by drawing it backwards & forwards we were all conveyed over without any serious accident. By these frequent traverses the canoe was materially injured, and latterly generally filled, before reaching the shore so that all our bedclothes were wet and one of the men's blankets was carried down the stream nor was there a sufficiency of wood upon the side on which we now were, to make a fire sufficient to dry the wet articles. Mʳ Back with Perez [St Germain], Beauparlant and Bellanger *le gros* [Solomon Belanger], went forward to look for the Indians. The rest of the party encamped at the spot where the traverse was made.

"The tripe de roche *disagrees with this man ..."*

Friday October 5ᵗʰ 1821

Light westerly winds, cold & clear weather. We were all on foot by day-break this morning, but from the frozen state of our tents and bed clothes, it was long before the bundles could be made up, and as usual, the men lingered about the embers of a small fire they had kindled, so that we were late in starting. Our advance from the depths of the snow was slow, and about noon coming to a spot where there was some Tripe de roche we stopt to collect some and breakfasted. Resuming our march we followed the track of Mʳ Back's party being nearly sbw by compass and encamped early, all of us being much fatigued – particularly Credit who having today carried the men's tent, it being his turn to do so, was so exhausted, that when he reached the encampment he was unable to stand. The *tripe de roche* disagrees with this man and with Vaillant, in consequence of which they are amongst the greatest sufferers. Mr Hood also is distressed from the same cause. Every little scrap of shoe [moccasin] leather, is now highly prized, and after boiling is greedily devoured. Distance 6 miles.

Saturday October 6th 1821

Winds sw moderate. Very cold weather. Credit's load was reduced to little more than his personal baggage (his blanket, shoes & gun). We left the encampment at nine a.m. and pursued our route over a range of bleak hills. The wind having encreased to a strong gale in the course of the morning, became piercingly cold and the drift rendered it difficult for those in the rear to follow the track over the heights, whilst in the vallies, where it was sufficiently marked from the depth of the snow, the labour of walking was proportionably great. Those in advance, made as usual, occassional halts, yet being unable from the severity of the weather to remain long inactive, they were obliged to move on, before the rear could come up and the party of course straggled very much.

Towards noon I was informed, that Credit and Vaillant could advance no further, and having communicated this intelligence to Mr Franklin, he proposed to halt at the first convenient spot and light a fire, whilst I went back to visit them. I found Vaillant about a mile and a half in the rear, much exhausted with cold and fatigue. Having encouraged him to advance to the fire, after repeated solicitations, he made the attempt but fell down amongst the deep snow at every step. Leaving him in this situation, I went about half a mile farther back, to the spot where Credit was said to have halted, but did not see him and the track being nearly obliterated by the snowdrift it became unsafe for me to go on. On my return I repassed Vaillant who having moved only a few yards in my absence, had fallen down, was unable to rise and scarcely capable of replying to my questions. Being unable to afford him any effectual assistance I hastened on and found the party assembled round a small fire, and having related poor Vaillants condition Bellanger *le rouge* [Jean Baptiste Belanger] went back to aid him and bring up his burthen. As for Credit, we were informed by Semandrè who saw him last and who had brought on his gun, that he stopt a short distance behind Vaillant, but that his intention was to return to the encampment we left in the morning. When Bellanger came back with Vaillants load he told us that he found the poor man lying on his back, benumbed with cold and incapable of being roused. The stoutest men of the party were now earnestly solicited to bring him to the fire but they declared themselves unequal to the task, and, on the contrary fearing the decay of their own strength, they urged Mr Franklin to allow them to throw down their loads and to proceed to Fort Enterprise with their utmost speed. Mr Hood (who was very feeble) and I, now proposed to remain behind with a single attendant, at the first place where there was a sufficient quantity of fire wood, for ten days consumption. This would contribute towards the safety of the rest of the party, by relieving them from the burthen of a tent and several other articles and we might afford some aid to Credit should he unexpectedly come up. We hoped too, that the men being thus lightened would not attempt to desert Mr Franklin who was to lead them to the house, and to send us immediate relief, and we trusted that the ammunition which was to be deposited in our tent, would be a strong inducement to the Indians to venture across the barren grounds to our aid. Mr Franklin strongly combated our intentions, from a reluctance to leave us in so dangerous a situation, but our arguments at length prevailed and we communicated our resolution to the men, who were cheered by the slightest prospect of alleviation of their present miseries and promised with great appearance of earnestness, to return to us, upon the first supply of food. Our knowledge however of the voyageur character, prevented us from confiding in their promises, and unless Mr Franklin was fortunate enough to fall in with Indians, we had no hope whatever of human aid. Vaillants blanket being left in the track, without any hope however that he would ever be able to reach it, we moved on and after marching upwards of two miles without finding a favourable place for encamping, night compelled us to take shelter under the lee of a hill amongst a few willows, with which after many attempts we at length made a fire. It was not sufficient, however, to warm the whole party, much less to thaw our shoes, and no tripe de roche being gathered we had nothing to cook.

Course sbw by compass. Distance 5½ miles.

Sunday October 7th 1821

Cold & clear weather. Left the encampment about nine and a little before noon came to a pretty extensive thicket of small willows. Here Mr Hood, John Hepburn, and myself determined to remain, and our tent being pitched, Mr Franklin said prayers and took a very affectionate leave of us. His baggage consisting only of a single blanket, and the officers journals, added very little to the mens loads, which were now reduced to their personal clothing and a single tent. No tripe de roche today. Drank an infusion of the *Ledum palustre*.[11]

The melancholy circumstances attendant on the deaths of Mr Hood and Michel (who returned to us, on the 9th) and the other painful occurrences until the 29th of this month when after a most distressing journey Hepburn and myself reached the house, have been detailed in an account drawn up and transmitted home, I shall not therefore enter upon a subject so harrassing to my feelings here – but proceed at once to [Richardson's journal continues in chapter 8.]

11 "Labrador tea," "country tea," or "Indian tea."

7

DR RICHARDSON'S NARRATIVE REPORT

"The Account Drawn up and Transmitted Home"[1]

After Captain Franklin had bidden us farewell we remained seated by the fireside as long as the willows, the men had cut for us before they departed, lasted. We had no *tripe de roche* that day, but drank an infusion of the country tea-plant, which was grateful from its warmth, although it afforded no sustenance.[2] We then retired to bed, where we remained all the next day [October 8], as the weather was stormy, and the snow-drift so heavy, as to destroy every prospect of success in our endeavours to light a fire with the green and frozen willows, which were our only fuel. Through the extreme kindness and forethought of a lady,[3] the party, previous to leaving London, had been furnished with a small collection of religious books, of which we still retained two or three of the most portable, and they proved of incalculable benefit to us. We read portions of them to each other as we lay in bed, in addition to the morning and evening service, and found that they inspired us on each perusal with so strong a sense of the omnipresence of a beneficent God, that our situation, even in these wilds, appeared no longer destitute; and we conversed, not only with calmness, but with cheerfulness, detailing with unrestrained confidence the past events of our lives, and dwelling with hope on our future prospects. Had my poor friend been spared to revisit his native land, I should look back to this period with unalloyed delight.

1 This official report to the authorities in Great Britain was separate from and not included in Richardson's journal. We thus have no original, first-hand, unedited account for these days. However, it has been introduced here to provide continuity for the reader.

2 The leaves of *Ledum* contain 9.8 percent protein and some of this might be imparted to the tea.

3 Lady Lucy Barry, wife of the Hon. Col. Barry, of Newton-Barry. The books included Bickersteth's *Scripture Helps*, a Church of England prayer-book, and a series of meditations by Fenelon containing a prayer that Hood repeated often in his last days. McIlraith, *Richardson*, pp. 93, 100, 117–18.

On the morning of the 29th [October 9th], the weather, although still cold, was clear, and I went out in quest of *tripe de roche*, leaving Hepburn to cut willows for a fire, and Mr. Hood in bed. I had no success, as yesterday's snow drift was so frozen on the surface of the rocks that I could not collect any of the weed; but, on my return to the tent, I found that Michel, the Iroquois, had come with a note from Mr. Franklin, which stated, that this man, and Jean Baptiste Belanger being unable to proceed, were about to return to us, and that a mile beyond our present encampment there was a clump of pine trees, to which he recommended us to remove the tent. Michel informed us that he quitted Mr. Franklin's party yesterday morning, but, that having missed his way, he had passed the night on the snow a mile or two to the northward of us. Belanger, he said, being impatient, had left the fire about two hours earlier, and, as he had not arrived, he supposed he had gone astray. It will be seen in the sequel, that we had more than sufficient reason to doubt the truth of this story.

Michel now produced a hare and a partridge which he had killed in the morning. This unexpected supply of provision was received by us with a deep sense of gratitude to the Almighty for his goodness, and we looked upon Michel as the instrument he had chosen to preserve all our lives. He complained of cold, and Mr. Hood offered to share his buffalo robe with him at night; I gave him one of two shirts which I wore, whilst Hepburn, in the warmth of his heart, exclaimed, "How I shall love this man if I find that he does not tell lies like the others." Our meals being finished, we arranged that the greatest part of the things should be carried to the pines the next day; and, after reading the evening service, retired to bed full of hope.

October 10th

Early in the morning Hepburn, Michel, and myself, carried the ammunition, and most of the other heavy articles to the pines. Michel was our guide, and it did not occur to us at the time that his conducting us perfectly straight was incompatible with his story of having gone astray on his way to us. He now informed us that he had, on his way to the tent, left on the hill above the pines a gun and a forty-eight balls, which Perrault had given to him when with the rest of Mr. Franklin's party, he took leave of him. It will be seen, on a reference to Mr. Franklin's journal, that Perrault carried his gun and ammunition with him when they parted from Michel and Belanger. After we had made a fire, and drank a little of the country tea, Hepburn and I returned to the tent, where we arrived in the evening, much exhausted with our journey. Michel preferred sleeping where he was, and requested us to leave him the hatchet, which we did, after he had promised to come early in the morning to assist us in carrying the tent and bedding. Mr. Hood remained in bed all day. Seeing nothing of Belanger to-day, we gave him up for lost.

"... there was a clump of pine trees ..."

October 11th

After waiting until late in the morning for Michel, who did not come, Hepburn and I loaded ourselves with the bedding, and, accompanied by Mr. Hood, set out for the pines. Mr. Hood was much affected with dimness of sight, giddiness, and other symptoms of extreme debility, which caused us to move very slow, and to make frequent halts. On arriving at the pines, we were much alarmed to find that Michel was absent. We feared that he had lost his way in coming to us in the morning, although it was not easy to conjecture how that could have happened, as our footsteps of yesterday were very distinct. Hepburn went back for the tent, and returned with it after dusk, completely worn out with the fatigue of the day. Michel too arrived at the same time, and relieved our anxiety on his account. He reported that he had been in chase of some deer which passed near his sleeping-place in the morning, and although he did not come up with them, yet that he found a wolf which had been killed by the stroke of a deer's horn, and had brought a part of it. We implicitly believed this story then, but afterwards became convinced from circumstances, the detail of which may be spared, that it must have been a portion of the body of [J.B.] Belanger or Perrault. A question of moment here presents itself; namely, whether he actually murdered these men, or either of them, or whether he found the bodies on the snow. Captain Franklin, who is the best able to judge of this matter, from knowing their situation when he parted from them, suggested the former idea, and that both Belanger and Perrault had been sacrificed. When Perrault turned back, Captain Franklin watched him until he reached a small group of willows, which was immediately adjoining to the fire, and concealed it from view, and at this time the smoke of fresh fuel was distinctly visible. Captain Franklin conjectures, that Michel having already destroyed Belanger, completed his crime by Perrault's death, in order to screen himself from detection. Although this opinion is founded only on circumstances, and is unsupported by direct evidence, it has been judged proper to mention it, especially as the subsequent conduct of the man shewed that he was capable of committing such a deed. The circumstances are very strong. It is not easy to assign any other adequate motive for his concealing from us that Perrault had turned back, and his request overnight that we should leave him the hatchet; and his cumbering himself with it when he went out in the morning, unlike a hunter who makes use only of his knife when he kills a deer, seem to indicate that he took it for the purpose of cutting up something that he knew to be frozen. These opinions, however, are the result of subsequent consideration. We passed this night in the open air.

"... the smoke of fresh fuel ..."

October 12th

On the following morning the tent was pitched, and Michel went out early, refused my offer to accompany him, and remained out the whole day. He would not sleep in the tent at night, but chose to lie at the fire-side.

October 13th

On the 13th there was a heavy gale of wind, and we passed the day by the fire.

October 14th

About two, P.M., the gale abating, Michel set out as he said to hunt, but returned unexpectedly in a very short time. This conduct surprised us, and his contradictory and evasory answers to our questions excited some suspicions, but they did not turn towards the truth.

October 15th

In the course of this day Michel expressed much regret that he had stayed behind Mr. Franklin's party, and declared that he would set out for the house at once if he knew the way. We endeavoured to soothe him, and to raise his hopes of the Indians speedily coming to our relief, but without success. He refused to assist us in cutting wood, but about noon, after much solicitation, he set out to hunt. Hepburn gathered a kettle of *tripe de roche*, but froze his fingers. Both Hepburn and I fatigued ourselves much to-day in pursuing a flock of partridges from one part to another of the group of willows, in which the hut was situated, but we were too weak to be able to approach them with sufficient caution. In the evening Michel returned, having met with no success.

October 16th

Michel refused either to hunt or cut wood, spoke in a very surly manner, and threatened to leave us. Under these circumstances, Mr. Hood and I deemed it better to promise if he would hunt diligently for four days, that then we would give Hepburn a letter for Mr. Franklin, a compass, inform him what course to pursue, and let them proceed together to the fort. The non-arrival of the Indians to our relief, now led us to fear that some accident had happened to Mr. Franklin, and we placed no confidence in the exertions of the Canadians that accompanied him, but we had the fullest confidence in Hepburn's returning the moment he could obtain assistance.

October 17th

On the 17th I went to conduct Michel to where Vaillant's blanket was left, and after walking about three miles, pointed out the hills to him at a distance, and returned to the hut, having gathered a bagful of *tripe de roche* on the way. It was easier to gather this weed on a march than at the tent, for the exercise of walking produced a glow of heat, which enabled us to withstand for a time the cold to which we were exposed in scraping the frozen surface of the rocks. On the contrary, when we left the fire, to collect it in the neighbourhood of the hut, we became chilled at once, and were obliged to return very quickly.

Michel proposed to remain out all night, and to hunt next day on his way back.

October 18th

Michel returned in the afternoon of the 18th, having found the blanket, together with a bag containing two pistols, and some other things which had been left beside it. We had some *tripe de roche* in the evening, but Mr. Hood, from the constant griping it produced, was unable to eat more than one or two spoonfuls. He was now so weak as to be scarcely able to sit up at the fire-side, and complained that the least breeze of wind seemed to blow through his frame. He also suffered much from cold during the night. We lay close to each other, but the heat of the body was no longer sufficient to thaw the frozen rime formed by our breaths on the blankets that covered him.

At this period we avoided as much as possible conversing upon the hopelessness of our situation, and generally endeavoured to lead the conversation towards our future prospects in life. The fact is, that with the decay of our strength, our minds decayed, and we were no longer able to bear the contemplation of the horrors that surrounded us. Each of us, if I may be allowed to judge from my own case, excused himself from so doing by a desire of not shocking the feelings of the others, for we were sensible of one another's weakness of intellect though blind to our own. Yet we were calm and resigned to our fate, not a murmur escaped us, and we were punctual and fervent in our addresses to the Supreme Being.

October 19th

Michel refused to hunt, or even to assist in carrying a log of wood to the fire, which was too heavy for Hepburn's strength and mine. Mr. Hood endeavoured to point out to him the necessity and duty of exertion, and the cruelty of his quitting us without leaving something for our support; but the discourse far from producing any beneficial effect, seemed only to excite his anger, and amongst other expressions, he made use of the following remarkable one: "It is no use hunting, there are no animals, you had better kill and eat me." At length, however, he went out, but returned very soon, with a report that he had seen three deer, which he was unable to follow from having wet his foot in a small stream of water thinly covered with ice, and being consequently obliged to come to the fire. The day was rather mild and Hepburn and I gathered a large kettleful of *tripe de roche*; Michel slept in the tent this night.

Sunday, October 20th

In the morning we again urged Michel to go a hunting that he might if possible leave us some provision, to-morrow being the day appointed for his quitting us; but he shewed great unwillingness to go out, and lingered about the fire, under the pretence of cleaning his gun. After we had read the morning service I went about noon to gather some *tripe de roche*, leaving Mr. Hood sitting before the tent at the fire-side, arguing with Michel; Hepburn was employed cutting down a tree at a short distance from the tent, being desirous of accumulating a quantity of fire wood before he left us. A short time after I went out I heard the report of a gun, and about ten minutes afterwards Hepburn called to me in a voice of great alarm, to come directly. When I arrived, I found poor Hood lying lifeless at the fire-side, a ball having apparently entered his forehead. I was at first horror-struck with the idea, that in a fit of despondency he had hurried himself into the presence of his Almighty Judge, by an act of his own hand; but the conduct of Michel soon gave rise to other thoughts, and excited suspicions which were confirmed, when upon examining the body, I discovered that the shot had entered the back part of the head, and passed out at the forehead, and that the muzzle of the gun had been applied so close as to set fire to the night-cap behind. The gun, which was of the longest kind supplied to the Indians, could not have been placed in a position to inflict such a wound, except by a second person. Upon inquiring of Michel how it happened, he replied, that Mr. Hood had sent him into the tent for the short gun, and that during his absence the long gun had gone off, he did not know whether by accident or not. He held the short gun in his hand at the time he was speaking to me. Hepburn afterwards informed me that previous to the report of the gun Mr. Hood and Michel were speaking to each other in an elevated angry tone; that Mr. Hood being seated at the fire-side, was hid from him by intervening willows, but that on hearing the report he looked up, and saw Michel rising up from before the tent-door, or just behind where Mr. Hood was seated, and then going into the tent. Thinking that the gun had been discharged for the purpose of cleaning it, he did not go to the fire at first; and when Michel called to him that Mr. Hood was dead, a considerable time had elapsed. Although I dared not openly to evince any suspicion that I thought Michel guilty of the deed, yet he repeatedly protested that he was incapable of committing such an act, kept constantly on his guard, and carefully avoided leaving Hepburn and me together. He was evidently afraid of permitting us to converse in private, and whenever Hepburn spoke, he inquired if he accused him of the murder. It is to be remarked, that he understood English very imperfectly, yet sufficiently to render it unsafe for us to speak on the subject in his presence. We removed the body into a clump of willows behind the tent, and, returning to the fire, read the funeral service in addition to the evening prayers. The loss of a young officer, of such distinguished and varied talents and application, may be felt and duly appreciated by the eminent characters under whose command he had served; but the calmness with which he contemplated the probable termination of a life of uncommon promise; and the patience and fortitude with which he sustained, I may venture to say, unparalleled bodily sufferings, can only be known to the companions of his distresses. Owing to the effect that the *tripe de roche* invariably had, when he ventured to taste it, he undoubtedly suffered more than any of the survivors of the party. *Bickersteth's Scripture Help* was lying open beside the body, as if it had fallen from his hand, and it is probable that he was reading it at the instant of his death. We passed the night in the tent together without rest, every one being on his guard.

October 21st

Having determined on going to the Fort, we began to patch and prepare our clothes for the journey. We singed the hair off a part of the buffalo robe that belonged to Mr. Hood, and boiled and ate it. Michel tried to persuade me to go to the woods on the Copper-Mine River, and hunt for deer instead of going to the Fort. In the afternoon a flock of partridges coming near the tent, he killed several which he shared with us.

October 22nd

Thick snowy weather and a head wind prevented us from starting the following day.

October 23rd

The morning of the 23rd we set out, carrying with us the remainder of the singed robe. Hepburn and Michel had each a gun, and I carried a small pistol, which Hepburn had loaded for me. In the course of the march Michel alarmed us much by his gestures and conduct, was constantly muttering to himself, expressed an unwillingness to go to the Fort, and tried to persuade me to go to the southward to the woods, where he said he could maintain himself all the winter by killing deer. In consequence of this behaviour, and the expression of his countenance, I requested him to leave us and to go to the southward by himself. This proposal increased his ill-nature, he threw out some obscure hints of freeing himself from all restraint on the morrow; and I overheard him muttering threats against Hepburn, whom he openly accused of having told stories against him. He also, for the first time, assumed such a tone of superiority in addressing me, as evinced that he considered us to be completely in his power, and he gave vent to several expressions of hatred towards the white people, or as he termed us in the idiom of the voyagers, the French, some of whom, he said, had killed and eaten his uncle and two of his relations. In short, taking every circumstance of his conduct into consideration, I came to the conclusion, that he would attempt to destroy us on the first opportunity that offered, and that he had hitherto abstained from doing so from his ignorance of the way to the Fort, but that he would never suffer us to go thither in company with him. In the course of the day he had several times remarked that we were pursuing the same course that Mr. Franklin was doing when he left him, and that by keeping towards the setting sun he could find his way himself. Hepburn and I were not in a condition to resist even an open attack, nor could we by any device escape from him. Our united strength was far inferior to his, and, beside his gun, he was armed with two pistols, an Indian bayonet, and a knife. In the afternoon, coming to a rock on which there was some *tripe de roche*, he halted, and said he would gather it whilst we went on, and that he would soon overtake us. Hepburn and I were now left together for the first time since Mr. Hood's death, and he acquainted me with several material circumstances, which he had observed of Michel's behaviour, and which confirmed me in the opinion that there was no safety for us except in his death, and he offered to be the instrument of it. I determined, however, as I was thoroughly convinced of the necessity of such a dreadful act, to take the whole responsibility upon myself; and immediately upon Michel's coming up, I put an end to his life by shooting him through the head with a pistol. Had my own life alone been threatened, I would not have purchased it by such a measure; but I considered myself as intrusted also with the protection of Hepburn's, a man, who, by his humane attentions and devotedness, had so endeared himself to me, that I felt more anxiety for his safety than for my own. Michel had gathered no *tripe de roche*, and it was evident to us that he had halted for the purpose of putting his gun in order, with the intention of attacking us, perhaps, whilst we were in the act of encamping.

I have dwelt in the preceding part of the narrative upon many circumstances of Michel's conduct, not for the purpose of aggravating his crime, but to put the reader in possession of the reasons that influenced me in depriving a fellow-creature of life. Up to the period of his return to the tent, his conduct had been good and respectful to the officers, and in a conversation between Captain Franklin, Mr. Hood, and myself, at Obstruction Rapid, it had been proposed to give him a reward upon our arrival at a post. His principles, however, unsupported by a belief in the divine truths of Christianity, were unable to withstand the pressure of severe distress. His countrymen, the Iroquois, are generally Christians, but he was totally uninstructed and ignorant of the duties inculcated by Christianity; and from his long residence in the Indian country, seems to have imbibed, or retained, the rules of conduct which the southern Indians[4] prescribe to themselves.

October 24th & October 25th

On the two following days we had mild but thick snowy weather, and as the view was too limited to enable us to preserve a straight course, we remained encamped amongst a few willows and dwarf pines, about five miles from the tent. We found a species of *cornicularia*, a kind of lichen, that was good to eat when moistened and toasted over the fire; and we had a good many pieces of singed buffalo hide remaining.

October 26th

The weather being clear and extremely cold, we resumed our march, which was very painful from the depth of the snow, particularly on the margins of the small lakes that lay in our route. We frequently sunk under the load of our blankets, and were obliged to assist each other in getting up. After walking about three miles and a half, however, we were cheered by the sight of a large herd of rein-deer, and Hepburn went in pursuit of them; but his hand being unsteady through weakness he missed. He was so exhausted by this fruitless attempt that we were obliged to encamp upon the spot, although it was a very unfavourable one.

4 Cree Indians. The Chipewyan Indians were
  the "northern Indians."

October 27th

We had fine and clear, but cold, weather. We set out early, and, in crossing a hill, found a considerable quantity of *tripe de roche*. About noon we fell upon Little Marten Lake, having walked about two miles. The sight of a place that we knew inspired us with fresh vigour, and there being comparatively little snow on the ice, we advanced at a pace to which we had lately been unaccustomed. In the

"… a large herd of rein-deer …"

afternoon we crossed a recent track of a wolverene, which, from a parallel mark in the snow, appeared to have been dragging something. Hepburn traced it, and upon the borders of the lake found the spine of a deer, that it had dropped. It was clean picked, and, at least, one season old; but we extracted the spinal marrow from it, which, even in its frozen state, was so acrid as to excoriate the lips. We encamped within sight of the Dog-rib Rock, and from the coldness of the night and the want of fuel, rested very ill.

October 28th

We rose at day-break, but from the want of the small fire, that we usually made in the mornings to warm our fingers, a very long time was spent in making up our bundles. This task fell to Hepburn's share, as I suffered so much from the cold as to be unable to take my hands out of my mittens. We kept a straight course for the Dog-rib Rock, but, owing to the depth of the snow in the valleys we had to cross, did not reach it until late in the afternoon. We would have encamped, but did not like to pass a second night without fire; and though scarcely able to drag our limbs after us, we pushed on to a clump of pines, about a mile to the southward of the rock, and arrived at them in the dusk of the evening. During the last few hundred yards of our march, our track lay over some large stones, amongst which I fell down upwards of twenty times, and became at length so exhausted that I was unable to stand. If Hepburn had not exerted himself far beyond his strength, and speedily made the encampment and kindled a fire, I must have perished on the spot. This night we had plenty of dry wood.

October 29th

We had clear and fine weather. We set out at sunrise, and hurried on in our anxiety to reach the house, but our progress was much impeded by the great depth of the snow in the valleys. Although every spot of ground over which we travelled to-day had been repeatedly trodden by us, yet we got bewildered in a small lake. We took it for Marten Lake[5] which was three times its size, and fancied that we saw the rapid and the grounds about the fort, although they were still far distant. Our disappointment when this illusion was dispelled, by our reaching the end of the lake, so operated on our feeble minds as to exhaust our strength, and we decided upon encamping; but upon ascending a small eminence to look for a clump of wood, we caught a glimpse of the Big-Stone, a well known rock upon the summit of a hill opposite to the Fort, and determined upon proceeding. In the evening we saw several large herds of rein-deer, but

"... a glimpse of the Big-Stone ..."

5 A peculiar error to have been perpetuated in many editions. Obviously Richardson meant to say Winter Lake, not Marten Lake. They had already spent 27 October traversing the length of Little Marten Lake.

Hepburn, who used to be considered a good marksman, was now unable to hold the gun straight, and although he got near them all his efforts proved fruitless. In passing through a small clump of pines we saw a flock of partridges, and he succeeded in killing one after firing several shots. We came in sight of the fort at dusk.

8

RESCUE AND RECOVERY

[RICHARDSON'S JOURNAL RESUMES]

Monday October 29th 1821

When we entered Fort Enterprise, in the dusk of the evening, and had the melancholy satisfaction of embracing Mr Franklin. No language that I can use, being adequate to convey a just idea of the wretchedness of the abode, in which we found our commanding officer, I shall not make the attempt, but merely mention, that the greatest part of the house had been pulled down for firewood, and that the only entire chamber which was left, was open to all the rigour of the season, the windows being but partially closed by a few loose boards. Peltier, Semandrè and Adam were Mr Franklin's only companions, the others having left him to go in search of the Indians on the 21st instant. Of these Peltier alone was able to bring in firewood, Semandrè was scarcely able to stir from the fire side, and Adam was confined to bed. The noise that we made on entering the house, was first heard by Peltier and he rushed to the door in expectation of seeing the wished for Indians, but turned away in despair on beholding our ghastly countenances. He recovered however, in a short time, sufficiently to welcome us to this abode of misery, but the disappointment had evidently given him a great shock. The hollow and sepulchral sound of their voices, produced nearly as great horror in us, as our emaciated appearance did on them and I could not help requesting them more than once to assume a more cheerful tone. The partridge that Hepburn had killed was divided amongst the party and in return they supplied us with singed hide. Our spirits rose during this meal and we endeavoured to cheer them with the prospect of Hepburns being able to kill a deer and thus providing for their subsistence until the arrival of the Indians. Having finished supper and read the evening service we retired to bed in hopes that to morrow the chase might prove fortunate.

Tuesday October 30th 1821 Fort Enterprise

Wind Easterly; fresh breezes. Dark, cloudy and cold weather.

Food for the starving, old caribou skin and warble-fly larvae

Hepburn and I went out to hunt Rein deer in the morning, but the cold soon compelled me to return. Hepburn persisted until late in the evening, but had no success although he fired frequently. Mr Franklin employed himself in raising deer skins, from under the snow and dragging them into the house but his weakness was so great that he brought in only two or three in the course of the day although the distance he had to drag them did not exceed 20 or 30 yards.

Of these skins (which had been used during the preceding winter, as beds by the Indians, and were thrown away when they left the Fort in the spring) there are about 26 collected but many of them are rotten and most of them very thin. Those that contain the larvae of the oestrus are most prized by us, and eagerly sought after.[1] Peltier and Samandrè were very weak today and dispirited. They were unable to cut firewood. Adam being much distressed with oedematous swellings, I made several scarifications in his scrotum abdomen and legs[2] and a large quantity of water flowing out he obtained some ease. We supped on singed skins, and the soup of a few pounded bones.

---

1 The larva of the warble-fly, *Oedemagena tar-andi* is a high-protein source of nourishment, as explained in the Commentary.

2 Franklin omitted mention of the abdomen and scrotum as sites of the small incisions that allowed the fluid to drain.

Wednesday October 31st 1821

Fresh northerly wind – very cold. Hepburn went again in pursuit of deer, and I endeavoured to kill some partridges but we were equally unsuccessful as yesterday. In our present weak state, the cold incapacitates us from holding the gun straight, and we are utterly unable to run. Adam is rather easier but Peltier and Semandrè are much weaker and complain of a soreness in the throat which prevents them from eating the skin or bones. They have been accustomed to eat large quantities of salt, a barrel of that article having been left in the house. Semandrè is affected with cramp in his fingers.

Thursday November 1st 1821

A fine, clear and mild day. Hepburn went a hunting but his efforts were attended with their usual want of success, and as his strength is sinking rapidly we have advised him to desist. I obtained a little Tripe de roche but Peltier and Semandrè were unable to eat from the soreness of the throat. Peltier became quite speechless towards the evening and died during the night. Semandrè whose strength throughout the day appeared to be greater, as if terrified at the fate of his companion, grew very low and lived only until the morning.

Friday November 2d 1821

Extremely cold weather. The fate of our companions rendered us very melancholy. Hepburn and I were occupied all the day in bringing in wood from the storehouse, but the mud between the logs was so hard frozen, that the labour of seperating them exceeded our strength, and we were completely exhausted by bringing in wood, which sufficed to keep the fire in only half the day.

Saturday November 3d 1821

Cloudy sky. Very cold weather. Hepburns limbs began to swell today and his strength as well as mine is declining with extreme rapidity. Our stock of bones was exhausted by a small quantity of soup we made in the evening. This soup was so acrid as to excoriate the mouth but is grateful perhaps from its pungency. It does not appear, however, to contribute much to the support of our strength and the deer skins are so thin, and covered with so dense a coat of hair, that the labour of sing[e]ing them prevents us from eating as much as we would otherwise do.

Sunday November 4th 1821

Calm and comparatively mild weather. Sky cloudy. We gathered some Tripe de roche today. The incisions in Adam's legs have been renewed, and they discharge a considerable quantity of water but he is extremely weak and dispirited. Eat some singed skin.

Monday November 5th 1821

Light breezes with dark cloudy weather and some snow – more mild to the feelings. Hepburn and myself are more weak, the limbs of the former much swelled. Mr Franklin and Adam are in the same condition as yesterday. The latter in general keeps his bed but sometimes surprises us with getting up, and walking with an unexpected appearance of strength. Whenever he reflects upon his situation, however, his accustomed depression of spirits returns, and with it his usual debility. Collected some Country Tea, and had it with the skins for supper.

Tuesday November 6th 1821

Clear and very cold weather. Adam extremely low and refuses to eat. The rest in the same state as yesterday.

Wednesday November 7th 1821

Hepburn and I went as usual in the morning to the storehouse, to cut wood leaving Mr F. & Adam remaining in bed until we could collect sufficient to make a fire. Whilst we were engaged in this occupation, we heard the report of a musket, and soon after a great shout, and on looking out beheld a party of Indians on the river. I ran in with the joyful intelligence to Mr Franklin, who immediately returned thanks to the Almighty for his goodness – but poor Adam was so low that he could scarcely comprehend the news.

   The Indians, three in number, The Rat, Crooked-foot and Boudelkell, belonged to Akaicho's band and had been sent by Mr Back with dried meat and fat. We devoured with great eagerness the food they presented us with and in their desire to satisfy us they incautiously permitted us to eat as much as we could; in consequence of which, with the exception of Adam, we all suffered dreadfully from distention of the abdomen, and had no rest during the night. In addition to this Hepburn's legs and mine swelled very much. Adam being unable to feed himself, was more judiciously treated, and suffered less. The Indians were dispatched to our relief on the 5th ins^t the day after Mr Back reached

Akaicho's encampment. Boudelkell, the youngest of the three, after resting about an hour with us, returned to carry intelligence of our being alive, and send further supplies whilst the other two remained to take care of us. The ease with which these two kind creatures seperated the logs of the store-house, carried them in, and made a fire, was a matter of the utmost astonishment to us, and we could scarcely by any effort of reasoning, efface from our minds the idea that they possessed a supernatural degree of strength.

Thursday November 8th 1821 Fort Enterprise

Cold stormy weather. Mr Franklin and I suffered much to day from distention. Hepburn is getting better and Adam recovers his strength with amazing rapidity. The Indians today cleared the room of part of the filth which had accumulated in it, through our inability to remove it. In addition to the good fires the Indians keep up, our plentiful cheer enables us to resist the cold, infinitely better than before, and it is difficult for us to believe otherwise, than that the season has become milder, instead of growing more severe as the winter advances.

Friday November 9th 1821

Fine weather. Crooked-foot caught four fine trout in Winter Lake today, which were very much prized by us, as Mr F. and I have taken a dislike to meat, in consequence of our sufferings from repletion. Adam and Hepburn are getting better, but Mr F. & I are scarcely able to move.

Saturday November 10th 1821

Moderate and fine weather. M^r F & I spent a restless night from distention. Adam & John [Hepburn] recover fast and the latter is now able to assist in bringing in wood, which he does when the Indians are out fishing or hunting. The Indians brought in a fish and a hare today, but they restrict us at our meals, lest our provision should be consumed before a supply arrives. This restriction is favourable to the recovery of our health, and is necessary, from the little government we are able to exercise at present over our appetites.

Sunday November 11th 1821

Cold stormy weather. One trout & five partridges were taken by the Indians today. A small portion only of the dried meat they brought with them remains, scarcely sufficient for one days consumption. Mr Franklin and I are still much distressed, by disorders of the stomach. My limbs also continue to be greatly swelled.

Monday November 12th Fort Enterprise

The last of the dried meat was expended for breakfast, this morning, but the Rat brought in a hare upon which we supped. The fishery failed today and Crooked-foot with the superstition usual to these Indians, refuses to try it again, alledging that his good luck had departed from him. The Indians looked out with great anxiety today for the arrival of further supplies from Akaicho and their disappointment, when the night closed in without their appearance, was much greater than ours.

Tuesday November 13th 1821

Stormy weather with constant snow. The Indians were quite despondent today at the non-arrival of the expected supply and in consequence would neither go a hunting or fishing. They frequently expressed their fears of some misfortune having befallen Boudelkell, and in the evening they went off suddenly, without acquainting us with their intention, having previously given to each of us a handful of pounded meat that they had reserved. Their departure surprised us and at first gave rise to a suspicion of their having deserted us without the intention of returning, especially as Adam's explanations were very unsatisfactory. By dint of interrogation however, we learnt that he was privy to their intentions, and that they had gone off with the design of marching, night and day, until they reached Akaicho's encampment; that they might send aid to us. As we had endeavoured to combat their apprehensions of Boudelkell having met with an accident, they perhaps apprehended that we would oppose their determination, and therefore concealed it. The entrails of the fish, which had been thrown aside, were collected and eaten with some singed skin.

Wednesday November 14th 1821 Fort Enterprise

Remarkably fine weather. The view down Winter River as beheld from the house, at all times beautiful, was uncommonly so today. Adam whose expectations of the Indians arriving had been raised by the fineness of the weather became very despondent, as the evening approached without their fulfillment, and refused to eat of the singed skin of which the rest partook.

Thursday November 15th 1821

The night was stormy and towards the morning a heavy fall of snow took place. Adam was more low spirited than ever but the rest were full of hope and endeavoured to cheer his spirits – and to persuade him to preserve his strength by eating hide. About 11 a.m. when we were sing[e]ing some of the skin for breakfast, Hepburn who had gone out for wood came in with the information of a party of Indians being upon the river. The room was instantly swept and in compliance with the prejudices of the Indians every scrap of skin carefully removed out of sight, for these simple people imagine that burning deer-skin renders them unsuccessful in hunting.

   We then went out and received them at the door. They proved to be Crookedfoot, Thoveeyorre and the Fop, with the wives of the two latter dragging provisions. They were accompanied by Benoit one of our own men. We again suffered from repletion, but less than before, as we were more cautious. Adam recovered his spirits on the arrival of the Indians, and arose from his bed with an appearance of strength and activity that surprised us all. As it is of consequence to get amongst the Rein-deer, before our present supply of provision fails, we made preparation for quitting Fort Enterprise to morrow.

Friday November 16th 1821

This morning after breakfast the whole party left the house. The day was fine. Our feelings on quitting the Fort where we had formerly enjoyed much comfort if not happiness and latterly experienced a degree of misery scarcely to be paralleled, may be more easily conceived than described. It was a species of joy tempered with regret and elevated by a deep sense of gratitude to the Supreme Being that pervaded all our minds. The Indians treated us with the utmost tenderness, gave us their snow shoes and walked without themselves, keeping by our sides that they might lift us when we fell. We descended Winter River and about noon had crossed the head of Round Rock Lake, about three miles distant from the house, where we encamped, as I was unable to go any further. Indeed the swellings of my limbs rendered me by the much the weakest of the party. The Indians cooked for us and fed us as if we had been children evincing a degree of humanity that would have done honour to the most civilized nation.

Saturday November 17th 1821

Stormy and very cold weather. Recommencing our journey about an hour after day break, we walked about 6 miles over the hills, exposed to all the violence of the wind, which brought with it much snow drift. The kindness of the Indians was conspicuous in this days march, as they halted frequently to chafe our hands or countenances when they were affected by the cold. Their instant care preserved Mr Franklin from being severely frost-bitten as several parts of his face became repeatedly white. We encamped at an early hour, in a small clump of wood, to wait for Adam, who being unable to withstand the force of the wind had as we afterwards learnt halted a short time after starting, and encamped along with Benoit who staid by him.

Wind sse extremely cold. Course sbw 5 miles.

Sunday November 18th 1821 Barren grounds

A considerable quantity of snow fell during the night. The wind changed to the northward in the morning but continued to blow as violently as yesterday. An Indian went to look for Adam and Benoit, and they reached our encampment in the afternoon but it was then too late to attempt crossing the track of barren land which lay in our route. The Indians took advantage of the delay to construct temporary snow shoes for themselves, as they had been much fatigued by walking through the deep snow without them. It was also arranged that we should make the best of our way to the Hunters Portage when[3] two deer had been put *en cache* whilst Adam who was unable to keep pace with us and Benoit came on at their leisure and that they might not run any risk of suffering from want, we gave them all our pounded meat and fat, trusting to the *cache* and the exertions of the hunters for our own support. Evening very cold.

Monday November 19th 1821 Barren grounds

Fine weather with moderate NW wind. In the course of the day, the wind became southerly, the weather continuing fine. We started early and walked more vigorously than we had hitherto done, making 9 miles good, on a sbw course, but we were much exhausted at night and would have encamped earlier had we found wood. It was dusk before we reached a proper spot.[4] Mr Franklin & John are now free from swellings of the limbs but I still suffer considerably from that complaint.

Tuesday November 20th 1821

Wind northerly moderate and cloudy. Towards noon, it veered to the southward. We left our encampment before day break and crossing three lakes and

---

3 Where, not when is meant.   4 At or near Greenstockings Lake.

several swamps arrived at the *cache* on Hunters portage[5] about 11 a.m. Here the womens sledges were loaded with the meat of the two deer, with the exception of some pieces which were left for Adam and Benoit. The remainder of the days march was extremely fatiguing both to us and to the poor women, from the depth of the snow. It was pretty late when we encamped on the borders of Porphyry Lake having come 10½ miles.

The Fop, who had been appropriately named from his fantastic behaviour and attention to dress, beat his wife, a girl about 16 years of age severely, before starting in the morning by the way of inducing her to encounter with more alacrity the labours of the day, which he foresaw would be great and repeated his treatment during the march, as often as she sank amongst the snow through fatigue. He accompanied his blows with the gestures and expressions which the Canadian voyageurs use when they beat their dogs. Such brutal conduct, although said to be common amongst the Chepewyans is rarely observed in a Red Knife. Thoveeyorre was attentive and even affectionate to his wife but the Fop had unfortunately taken lessons in the Voyageur school. We supped on fresh deer's meat, this night, and devoured an enormous quantity without any evil consequences resulting.

Wednesday November 21st 1821

Light NE winds and pleasant weather. Sky clouded. After a march of 7 miles we encamped on the borders of Rein-deer Lake. We saw some herds of deer in the course of the day and the hunters killed two, the greatest part of which they put *en cache* for Adam and Benoit as we had a considerable quantity of meat with us and there was besides a *cache* upon the adjoining lake. Night clear and cold. Aurora borealis visible.

Thursday November 22 1821

Cloudless sky, wind WNW clear and very cold. We began our march before dawn of day, and crossing Rein-deer Lake examined the *cache* but found the meat damaged by the water of the lake having flowed into the excavation in the ice, in which it was deposited. We next descended a part of the Yellow knife River and walking for some distance through Upper Carp Lake, put up on its borders, at sun set. In the course of the day we saw many herds of deer and were obliged to halt frequently whilst they went in pursuit of them in consequence of which our distance did not exceed 10 miles notwithstanding the length of time we were on foot. Our hunters were unsuccessful today, although they fired frequently.

5 The rapids north-north-east of Hunter Lake.

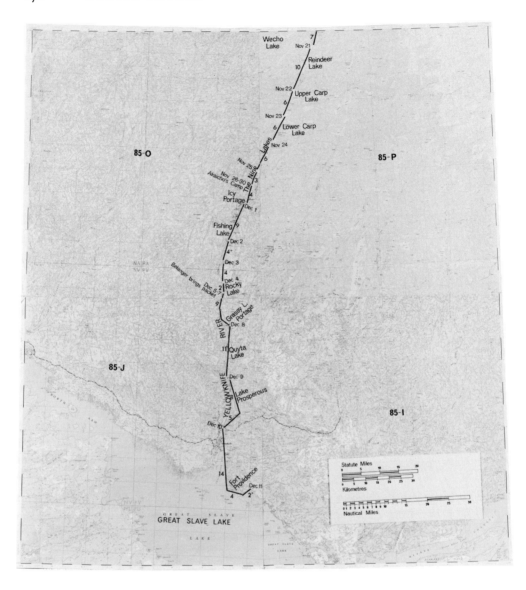

Map 8   *21 November–11 December 1821*

Night clear. A brilliant arch-form aurora crossing the Zenith from NW to SSE.

Friday November 23^d 1821

Wind light. Cold weather. In the course of the day the sky was frequently obscured by fogs which rendered the cold more disagre[e]able. Set out about nine, and were detained as usual by the hunting excursions of our Indian friends, which were more successful than yesterday, for Thoveeyorre killed a deer soon after we started. In the afternoon the Fop's gun burst and wounded him slightly on the wrist, upon which he instantly left us to go to Akaicho's lodge. His departure seemed to please his wife, and was productive of satisfaction to us, for his capricious treatment of the poor girl had rendered his company disagre[e]able. At 3 p.m. we arrived at the spot where Akaicho & his band were when our present companions left them, to come to us, and found two deer *en cache*. Here we encamped and the Indians judging that Akaicho was not far off cut up the greatest part of the meat with a hatchet for the purpose of getting at the marrow. Wind SW. Fresh and Cloudy.

Saturday November 24th 1821

Light SSW winds. Hoar frost in the morning. Day pleasant.

The women were lightly loaded today, as they took but little meat, from the expectation of reaching Akaicho's encampment in the evening in consequence of which we got on better than usual, and the Fop's wife being relieved from her tyrant, dragged her sledge more cheerfully. In the course of the morning we passed two encampments, neither of them very recent, and Thoveeyorre after inspecting them, signified to us that the Leader had gone much farther to the Southward than he expected, in consequence he supposed of the scarcity of deer. This rendered him very solicitous to kill a deer as it might be several days before we could overtake Akaicho if he were moving on – and he hunted the whole day with great perseverance, but without success. Towards the evening however, we fell in with a beaten track which had been formed within a few days and our hopes revived.

It was extremely pleasing to us, after so long an interval, to behold this vestige of the neighbourhood of society. We encamped on Lower Carp Lake.

Sunday November 25th 1821

Cloudy and warm weather. The whole of our provision was expended at breakfast, but as we confidently expected to reach Akaicho today this gave us little concern. After walking about six miles we came to several Indian lodges amongst which was that of the Parents of Akaicho's wife and of Tho[v]eeyorre our attentive hunter. These good old people welcomed us with the utmost kindness and entreated us to remain with them for the night which we did, whilst Thoveeyorre went on to the leader who was an encampment further off. The old woman shewed her stock of meat and desired us to take what we liked best, but after witnessing Hepburns awkward attempt at cookery arising from his weakness, she herself culled out the most delicate bits and cooking them expressed much satisfaction in seeing us eat. Many others of the Indians, also came to see us in the afternoon, and most of them presented us with meat, so that we were surrounded with more than we could consume in a week.

Monday November 26th 1821 Akaicho's Lodge

Fine weather. Northerly winds. After breakfast Mr F. and I took leave of our kind hosts (who indeed intended to move today themselves) and set out for Akaicho's Lodge at which we arrived after a march of three miles.[6] We were kindly received and hospitably entertained, the Leader himself shewing every personal attention in his power and every one in the encampment, expressing a high degree of sympathy with our sufferings, in their countenances. In the course of the day we were visited by every person of the band, either out of curiosity or kindness. John, who remained at our last nights encampment with the baggage, not arriving today we remained all night in Akaicho's lodge.

We learnt that Mr Back with Belanger and Perez St Germain had gone to Fort Providence and that previous to his departure he had left a letter in a *cache* of pounded meat, which we missed two days ago. As we supposed that this letter might acquaint us with his intentions, more fully than we could gather from the Indians, through our imperfect knowledge of their language – Augustus the Eskimaux whom we found here in perfect health and an Indian boy were dispatched to bring it.

The White-Capot [Annoethai-yazzeh] and Humpy, the two brothers of the Leader and several of our hunters with their families, were encamped here together with a number of old men and women amounting in all to [blank]

6 On or near the Nine Lakes, 63°25′ N.

Tuesday November 27ᵗʰ 1821 Akaicho's Lodge

Cold clear weather. Aurora brilliant during the night.

In the course of the day Hepburn arrived, having dragged our bedding from the last encampment himself, the two women having left him in the lurch, from a supposition that he was now strong enough to drag a sledge himself. He was however much fatigued. The kindness of the Indians enabled us to indulge very freely today, in fat meat for which we had a great longing, but it proved too strong for Mʳ F's powers of digestion and he suffered very much in consequence. I escaped this danger, through a degree of caution, produced by recollection of my late sufferings from indigestion.

Wednesday November 28ᵗʰ 1821

Strong sw winds. In the evening we left the Leaders lodge and slept in our encampment which Hepburn had prepared in the course of the day. Mʳ Franklin still suffers from a disordered stomach. The deer are pretty numerous in the neighbourhood of this place, but from the want of ammunition the Hunters kill but few.

Thursday November 29ᵗʰ 1821

Snow in the night. Morning warm & cloudy. Mʳ Franklin, who still suffers from his late surfeit, received some relief today from a mess of *Tripe de roche*, fish soup and blood prepared by Akaicho today.

Friday November 30ᵗʰ 1821

Mild cloudy weather. The deer moving to the southward, the Indians struck their tents and followed them. We remained behind in hopes that Mʳ Franklin would be more able to march to morrow.

Saturday December 1ˢᵗ 1821

Early in the morning Hepburn having put our bedding on a sledge followed the track of the Indians. Mʳ F. and I remained by the fire until sun rise when we set out, soon overtook him, and at nine arrived at the last nights encampment of the Indians whose fires were still burning. Although we had only come 4 miles, we were fatigued and determined upon remaining here. In the course of this morning's march we crossed two of the Nine Lakes and the Icy portage and descended the Yellow knife river for upwards of a mile. Adam, Benoit and Augustus joined us in the evening. Adam has recovered surprisingly. The Cyprès of the Canadians *Pinus Banksiana* grows to a tolerable size in this part of the country. Moose deer too, are occassionally found here.

Sunday December 2ᵈ 1821

Setting out at day break or about half past 8 a.m. we arrived at the last nights encampment of the Indians, on the Sandy Portage, and soon afterwards overtook them on Fishing Lake. We encamped along with them about 3 p.m. having come to day nine miles, and in the evening, were informed by the Leader, through the medium of Adam, that he intended to approach Fort Providence by slow marches. Adam has recovered so much that he is now the best walker of our party.

Monday December 3ᵈ 1821

Light SE winds. Clear weather. We set out at noon and followed the Indians, who had raised their camp about two hours earlier, and joined them at 3 p.m. as they were encamping at the Three Portage rapid. The distance walked to day was about 4½ miles. The time having passed, which the Indians had fixed for the arrival of men from Fort Providence, Akaicho and his old men begin, as usual, to account for it in their own melancholy way. As they cannot suppose that the whole party has miscarried in its way thither they begin to imagine that the Trading Companies are unwilling to assist us – and although we took much trouble in a long conference, and suggested many causes of detention, we could not efface the idea from their minds. As this impression might in time influence our supply of provisions, Mʳ Franklin to divert their attention for some days, proposed sending two Indian boys to the Fort with a letter, requesting that dogs might be sent to convey us down. We expect an answer in five days, and for so long the Indians have consented to suspend their inferences.

Tuesday December 4ᵗʰ 1821

Set out after the Indians about noon, but soon overtook them as they had halted to cut up and share a moose deer, that had been drowned in a rapid part of the river partially covered with ice. These detentions are very disagre[e]able to us, particularly in cold weather, and to avoid them we generally remain in our encampment an hour or two after the Indians. Today the weather was extremely unpleasant from cold low fogs, and we were all much fatigued at the hour of encamping, which was deferred until two hours after sun set, although the distance walked did not exceed 4 miles. The halts however much *we* disliked them, are turned to good account by the elderly men of the tribe, who make holes in the ice and put their lines in the water every opportunity – one of them shared the product of his fishery with us this evening. The young men, who were out hunting today, saw three moose deer but did not get near enough to fire. The Leader, however, discovered a Beaver Lodge which he proposes to work tomorrow.

Wednesday December 5th 1821

Fresh ssw winds. Weather warm & clear. Snow softening in the sun.

We made a short march of two miles today across a lake [Rocky Lake], and encamped early, to afford time for Akaicho to break up the Beaver Lodge. Mr F. and I went to witness his operations but after waiting patiently for upwards of an hour we came away without witnessing the capture of any of these industrious animals. A short time after we left them, however, they killed one and in the evening the Leader sent us a large portion of it for supper. It resembled roast pig very much in flavour & appearance, and was much relished by us.

Thursday December 6th 1821

We remained stationary today, the Indians having gone to resume their labours at the Beaver Lodge. Fresh breezes with occasional snow showers. In the afternoon Belanger and another Canadian arrived from Fort Providence with two trains of dogs, some spirits and tobacco for the Indians and a change of dress for ourselves. We learnt by letters from Mr Back that the two Rival Companies had united,[7] but that owing to some cause, which had not been explained to him, the goods intended as rewards to Akaicho and his band, which had been demanded from the NW Company in the spring, were not sent in. This was a grievous disappointment to us, as we had looked forward with pleasure to the time when we should be enabled to repay our kind entertainers for their tender sympathy and assistance in our distresses. We also learnt that Mr Wentzel and his party had arrived in safety, after suffering considerably from want of provisions, in his march along the Coppermine River, having on one occasion fasted 7 days.

7 Officially on 1 June 1821 the two companies began to function as one, but the draft agreement dated from 26 February and it was formally placed before the General Court of the Hudson's Bay Company on 26 March. E.E. Rich, *The History of the Hudson's Bay Company 1670–1870* (London 1959), II, p. 397.

Friday December 7th 1821

Strong southerly winds – mild weather. We received today a sufficiency of dried meat and tongues from the Indians, for our journey to Fort Providence, which we propose to commence to morrow. Hepburn & Augustus will accompany Capt. Franklin and myself with the two men who arrived last. Adam and Benoit are to remain with the Indians who will come to the Fort by easy marches. Our letters brought the gratifying intelligence of Capt Franklin's promotion[8] and of Capt Parry's successful voyage.[9] Changed my shirt today for the first time since quitting the sea coast on the 31st Augt 1821.

Saturday December 8th 1821

We took leave of the Indians at 10 a.m. and set out with two sledges, heavily laden with provisions, and bedding, drawn by the dogs and conducted by Belanger and the other Canadian. John and Augustus dragged a smaller sledge betwixt them, laden principally with their own bedding. We encamped at 3.30 p.m. on the Grassy Lake portage, having walked about 9 miles principally on the Yellowknife river – as the rapids were all open, our journey was rendered very fatiguing by necessity we were under of climbing the banks frequently, to avoid them, and particularly so to myself who from the bad construction of my snow shoes suffered severely from galled toes. Weather fine.

Sunday December 9th 1821

Night clear & cold with fresh northerly breezes. Morning cloudy & mild. Light airs. Began our march at 9 a.m., and after a pleasant walk of 11½ miles encamped. Our appetites and those of our attendants being enormous, the lading of the sledges has suffered a proportionate diminution, in consequence the load which was dragged by John and Augustus has been distributed betwixt the two dog sledges.

8 From lieutenant to commander, retroactive to 1 January 1821. Hood and Back were each promoted from midshipman to lieutenant, though Hood had been dead for 47 days before news of his promotion reached the party.

9 Since Parry had reached west to Melville Island at 113° in August 1820, there was an unexplored north-south gap of 400 miles, largely occupied by inhospitable Victoria Island.

Monday December 10th 1821

Breakfast reduced the provision so much, that Capt. Franklin and I were enabled to mount one of the sledges by turns, in consequence of which we got on much quicker. In the evening we met with 3 voyageurs belonging to Fort Providence, going for meat, and soon after arrived at a fishing house, situated at the embouchure of the Yellow knife river.[10] We found here Angelique Adam's wife with her children. The atmosphere of the small fishing hut was oppressively close, to us who had been so long accustomed to sleep in the open air and hence we enjoyed little rest during the night.

"... the embouchure of the Yellow knife river"

Tuesday December 11th 1821 Fort Providence

We set out at 9½ a.m. and made a rapid journey to Fort Providence the Fisherman having lent us an additional sledge drawn by three dogs, so that Capt Franklin & I had each of us a sledge. We arrived at Fort Providence at 2 p.m. and were kindly welcomed by Mr Weekes, the gentleman in charge of the post. We found here a few articles selected by Mr Back from the equipment intended for

10 Near present site of Yellowknife, administrative capital of the Northwest Territories.

our Canadians, as a temporary present to Akaicho and his band. Mr Back had gone over to Moose deer island for the purpose of forwarding these things.

Friday December 14th 1821

Akaicho with his whole band came to the Fort in the afternoon. He smoked his customary pipe, with Mr Weekes in the hall and learnt from him that our expected supplies had not come in. Afterwards in a conference with Capt F. he spoke of this circumstance as a disappointment indeed, sufficiently severe to himself, to whom his band looked up for the support of their interests, but without attaching any blame to us. "The world goes badly" he said, "all are poor. You are poor, the traders appear to be poor, I and my party are poor likewise, and since the goods have not come in we cannot have them." "I do not regret having supplied you with provisions, for a Red Knife can never permit a White man to suffer from want on his lands, without flying to his aid." "I trust however that we shall, as you say, receive what is due to us, next autumn, and at all events" he added in a tone of good humour "it is the first time that the White people have been indebted to the Red Knife Indians."

He then cheerfully received the small present we made to himself, and although we could give a few things to those only who had been most active in our service, the others who perhaps thought themselves equally deserving, did not murmur on being left out in the distribution. Akaicho afterwards expressed a strong desire that we would represent the character of his nation in a favourable light to our countrymen; and in the course of the desultory conversation which ensued he said, that "he had been always told by us to consider the traders in the same light as ourselves, and that for his part he looked upon both parties as equally respectable." This assurance made in the presence of Mr Weekes was particularly gratifying as it completely disproved the defence that had been set up respecting the reports that had been circulated amongst the Indians in the spring and which had proved so prejudicial to our interests, namely that they were circulated in retaliation for our endeavours to lower the Traders in the eyes of the Indians. After this such Indians as were indebted to the Company were paid for the provisions they had given us by deducting a corresponding sum from their debt. As the debts of Akaicho however and of his hunters had been effaced at the time of his engagement with us this mode could not be resorted to in his case. These things being adjusted through the moderation of the Indians with an unexpected facility we gave them a keg of mixed liquor (5 parts water) and they retired to spend the night in merriment.

Adam our Interpreter being unlikely to be employed by the United Companies, was desirous of associating with the Red Knives and leading an Indian life, and applied to Capt. F. for his discharge, which was granted to him.

Strong NW winds & cold weather.

Saturday December 15th 1821

Mr Weekes having provided Capt Franklin and me with a cariole each, we set out about 11 a.m. for Moose Deer Island. Our party consisted of Belanger who had charge of a sledge laden with the bedding and drawn by two dogs, our two cariole men, John, Benoit and Augustus. Previous to our departure we had another short conference with Akaicho who bid us farewell with a kindness of manner, rarely seen in an Indian. We felt a deep sense of humiliation at being compelled to quit men capable of such liberal sentiments and humane feelings, in the beggarly manner in which we did. The badness of Belanger's dogs & the roughness of the ice impeded our progress very much and at length compelled us to encamp early. We had a good fire made of drift wood, which lines the shores of the lake in great quantities.

Sunday December 16th 1821 Great Slave Lake

Cold weather. Encamped in the evening at the Gros Cap – having made another *short* journey from the same causes as yesterday.

Monday December 17th 1821

Strong sw gales. Made the traverse today from the Gros Cap to one of the most southerly of the Carrieboeuf islands where we encamped. Stormy weather during the night.

Tuesday December 18th 1821

Weather more moderate. We rose our encampment at dawn of day and commencing our journey, obtained a view of the southern shores of the lake by noon, and reaching Point au Pierre [Stony Island] by sunset took up our abode in one of the huts built for the convenience of the men employed fishing there. We found here Mr Andrews[11] of the H.B.C^o. with his family.

11 Probably George Peter Andries, usually called Andrews, who was engaged by Colin Robertson in Montreal in 1818, and sent north with two canoes for McKenzie's River in 1820, under charge of McVicar on arrival at Great Slave Lake. Rich, *Colin Robertson's Correspondence Book*, pp. 117–18.

Wednesday December 19th 1821

Two men with sledges having arrived in the evening, sent by M^r McVicar[12] who expected us about this time, we set off in the morning with a large train and arrived at Moose deer Island, about 1 p.m., where we were received with the utmost hospitality by M^r McVicar the chief trader to the H.B.C°. in this district.

"Moose deer Island" (now Mission Island), as seen from Fort Resolution

51¾	Length of Hoods river which we traced.
44¼	Distance between Hoods River and the Anatessy
34¾	To Contowoy-to or Rum Lake through which the Anatessy flows
90¼	Distance travelled between Anatessy & Coppermine Rivers
14	Along Point Lake & returning
24½	To Martin Lake ⎫
16	To Fort Enterprise ⎬ these are direct distances

276½   Distance travelled on the barren grounds between the sea and Fort Enterprise of 320¼ Statute miles.

12 Robert McVicar, chief trader of the Hudson's Bay Company at Fort Resolution, became a life-long friend and correspondent of Richardson's. McVicar billeted Franklin and Richardson for over five months until their departure on 27 May 1822 (HBCA, PAM, B181/a/4, Fort Resolution journal, 1822–3). On the Second Arctic Land Expedition, Richardson stayed with McVicar and his young Scottish wife from 28 September to 25 December 1826, and Franklin stayed with them from 26 March to 5 April 1827. Nevertheless, Richardson did not postpone his departure for Carlton because of Mrs McVicar's pregnancy, for she delivered a son on 26 January 1827, 'the first Scot that was ever born at Slave Lake,' without medical assistance (B181/a/7, Fort Resolution journal, 1826–7).

Summary of distances between June & October 1821

between Fort Enterprise & Point Lake	46¾ geog. miles	54½ st.
Dragged the canoes on Point Lake	54¼	62½
Water travelling in Coppermine River	187¼	217
From mouth of Coppermine R. to Cape Turnagain	555¼	641½
From Cape Turnagain to Hoods River	104½	123
Traced Hoods River	51¾	60
From Hood's River to Fort Enterprise	224¾	260¾
	1224½	1418½
From Fort Enterprise to Fort Providence the first post at which we arrived	157½	276
From Fort Providence across Slave Lake to Moose Deer Island our Winter Quarters	81	
	1463	1694½

"The Yellow knife River"

Commentary

Richardson's journal is a primary source which gives us new information and new insights, and corrects some errors made by Franklin in his published account. For example, it tells more than Franklin's of the early forebodings of the voyageurs, about caribou shot at and missed (25 June and 4 September), about how tired the men were (on 25 June and 4 September), and about the premature use of pounded meat intended for the sea voyage (28 June, 1 and 3 July).

Richardson's account is shorter and easier to read, written in a more direct style, able to create an immediate impression of the situation. Speaking of hungry voyageurs and their ravenous appetites (19 July 1821), for example, Franklin had written: "These thoughtless people would, at any time, incur the hazard of absolute starvation, at a future period, for the present gratification of their appetites..."[1] In contrast, there is Richardson's colourful statement of 20 July: "...it is of no use to talk to a Canadian voyageur of going on short allowance. They prefer running the risk of going entirely without hereafter, that they may have a present belly full."

MacLeod and Glover have described Franklin's prose style as "turgid."[2] Even Traill, whose enthusiasm for Franklin bordered on adulation, spoke of him as "the most regular and laborious of chroniclers."[3] Franklin himself recognized what he called the "defective style" of his writing, and explained it by saying that he had had little time to devote to this skill, having led "a life of constant employment in [his] profession from a very early age."[4] In contrast, Richardson gives evidence at every turn of an education and store of knowledge that Franklin lacked. He had a talent for spontaneous and lively composition, well shown in his unedited letters published in McIlraith's biography.

The important new material in Richardson's journal includes accounts for fifty days not detailed by Franklin:

30 April–7 May 1821: Richardson's visit to Akaicho's camp allows us to pinpoint its location. His natural history notes include what is apparently the second record of the incredibly early nesting of the Gray Jay in late winter.[5]

4–20 June 1821: Richardson's advance party with fifteen voyageurs and seven Indians proceed to Point Lake. We are given details of the first nest of the Eskimo Curlew ever found.

28–30 August 1821: The canoes were made down into smaller craft, easier to carry, and three muskoxen and a caribou were killed.

10–12 November 1821: We learn that the survivors at Fort Enterprise ate one trout, one unidentified fish, two hares, five ptarmigan, and some fish entrails.

17–25 and 27–30 November and 1–3, 5, and 9–10 December 1821: We learn with what patience and compassion Akaicho and his Indians guided the surviving explorers back to Fort Providence. We learn locations of three of the winter camps of Akaicho's nomadic Copper Indian tribe.

Moreover, there are "snippets" throughout Richardson's journal which Franklin did not include: for example, Richardson's entire entry for 20 May dealing with weather and signs of spring.

Franklin, however, occasionally included interesting information that was not entered in Richardson's daily journal. An excellent example is Franklin's use of George Back's observation of the first robin at Fort Enterprise on 14 May 1821, with the appropriate note, "This bird is considered by the natives as the infallible precursor of warm weather." Similarly, on the night of 13–14 July, Franklin reported how Richardson during the first night watch, and Wentzel during the second watch on the hill above camp on the Coppermine, each saw nine white wolves close by. Neither Richardson's journal nor Richardson's *Fauna Boreali-Americana* mentioned the sighting of this large group of wolves, but Back's journal had the following notation for 13 July: "... in the evening we saw a number of White Wolves – on the summit of a steep hill close to us – they remained some time looking at us – and having satisfied their curiosity – ran away." It should be mentioned that Richardson's Zoological Appendix to Parry's *Second Voyage* recorded Parry's sighting of thirteen wolves on the ice near Winter Island in February 1822.[6] By no means could Richardson include all bird and plant observations in his daily entries – a notable omission was his climb to a Gyrfalcon nest on a lofty precipice at Point Lake in mid-June, the account of which appeared instead in *Fauna Boreali-Americana* and is reproduced in Appendix A.

There are discrepancies between the accounts of Richardson and Franklin, all of which should probably be resolved in favour of the primary source, Richardson's journal. These discrepancies, many involving dates, include the following (the published Franklin statement is given first and Richardson's second, with Back's version added in square brackets on three occasions):

10 or 12 December 1820 for the date of Akaicho's departure;

30 December 1820 or 8 January 1821 for the arrival of two of Akaicho's Indians;

27 or 25 January for the arrival of Augustus and Junius;

5 or 4 March for the arrival of the men from Fort Providence, who carried 40 pounds of tobacco or 40 pounds of ball;

St Germain left on 22 April and returned on the third day, or returned on 22 April; mergansers, gulls, and loons were first seen on 9 May, or the first merganser was recorded on 9 May, two gulls on 10 May, and two loons on 11 May [or two gulls and some "ducks" on 10 May and two loons on 12 May]; the expedition started at "an early hour" or "about noon" on 25 June [or 11.30 A.M.];

on 15 August they killed two swans, several cranes, and many geese, or they killed two swans and saw several cranes and geese [or they killed some swans and geese];

on 15 August they had three or less than two days' supply of pemmican left; on the return trip from the Coppermine, Wentzel and his party of Indians and four voyageurs were eleven or seven days without meat.

Similarly, Franklin's published arrival dates for Canada Geese do not correspond with Richardson's, as shown in the following table:

	Franklin	Richardson
Cumberland House	12 April	8–12 April
Fort Chipewyan	25 April	20 April
Fort Resolution	1 May	6 May
Fort Enterprise	12–14 May	20 May [21 May in Richardson's day entry]

Richardson's journal allows belated correction of two uncharacteristic errors in Franklin's published journal. On the night of 9–10 August 1821 the party did *not* paddle all night following their entry into Sir J.A. Gordon's Bay; they paddled until 8:30 PM (Back) or 8:40 PM (Richardson) on 9 August, not "forty minutes after eight A.M." as Franklin's journal says. The column of rock at Wilberforce Falls described on 27 August was an "isolated" column, not an "insulated" column as appears in Franklin. Both of these errors were perpetuated in the two-volume 1824 edition of Franklin's journal.

Some discrepancies of course are too trivial to be of concern. For example, after a traverse of heavy sea on 15 August, Franklin reported that fifteen of one canoe's seventy-three ribs were broken, while Back says fourteen and Richardson, twelve.

Richardson omits several personal experiences of hardships. He does not tell us, as Back does, of how, accompanied by Augustus, he spent much of the night of 28–29 June hiking back five miles to the previous encampment to retrieve his packet, which one of the voyageurs had inadvertently left behind. Only Franklin and Back record how Richardson, as he began his attempt to carry a rope across the Coppermine, stepped on a submerged Indian dagger and cut his foot to the bone.

A medical historian will find that Richardson demonstrates the breadth of knowledge and interest of a generalist medical doctor of those times; a physiologist interested in man's capacity to work under stress with inadequate food will find that an estimate of the party's daily food consumption is now possible; a naturalist, that Richardson tells where driftwood was found, the kinds of fish caught, the species of flower in bloom, and the number of caribou seen; an ornithologist, that Richardson provides notes on eighteen species of birds not mentioned in Sabine's Appendix v to Franklin's 1823 account, including the first description of the Yellow-billed Loon and the first record of the nesting of the Eskimo Curlew, with additional notes on another thirty-seven species of birds; a geologist will obtain an understanding of terminology then in current use (Appendix f); a geographer or cartographer will find that Richardson's courses and distances, up to thirty-three in a day's travel, allow more accurate pinpointing of some (but not all) campsites and observation sites; a climatologist, detailed information about weather and winds in the 1820s; an anthropologist, that Richardson's journal is more sympathetic to the plight of the Indians and voyageurs and gives St Germain the credit he deserves; a historian, that Richardson's journal offers a fresh perspective on Franklin's leadership, demonstrating that Franklin's reputation depended more on the quality of the men under his command than on his own abilities. Richardson also provides occasional details about landscape, geology, weather, Indians, and voyageurs that were not included by Franklin.

MEDICAL

As the medical officer for the expedition, Richardson might reasonably have expected to suture wounds, lance boils, and set fractures, but he tells us of no disorders of this type during the first Franklin expedition. Strangely, it is Back's journal of 2 September 1821 that mentions one voyageur suffering from a swollen knee with a boil. It was fortunate that no fractures occurred as they stumbled over rocks, carrying their heavy loads across the Barren Lands. As the surgeon observes (10 September 1821): "If anyone had broken a limb here, his fate would have been melancholy indeed, we could neither have remained with him, nor carried him on with us."

Robert Hood tells us of an operation performed by Richardson in the winter of 1819–20: "The guns trafficked with the Indians by the Companies, are of a very bad quality, and occasion accidents every year. A poor man whose hand had been dreadfully shattered by the bursting of his gun, the year before our arrival, was brought down from Carlton House to Dr. Richardson, who amputated it above the wrist and restored the use of his arm. He bore the operation with an unchanging countenance, and afterwards manifested much gratitude."[7]

Richardson's important description of the unusual prevalence of iodine-deficient goitre at Fort Edmonton has been quoted by many subsequent authorities. Dr Richardson did indeed examine "several of the individuals afflicted with it," but he examined them at Fort Carlton or at Cumberland House, not at Edmonton, as at least one historian has suggested.[8] Goitre affected chiefly the halfbreed women at Edmonton, who drank river water, Richardson reported. It was less common among those who left the fort for periods, and it could be "cured" by a visit to the seacoast at York Factory or by ingestion of burnt sponge. Richardson was told that a single year's residence at Edmonton was sufficient to cause goitre, and that the children of such women were sometimes cretins. The inhabitants of Rocky Mountain House, upstream from Edmonton, were said to be affected even more severely.[9] Richardson's is a remarkably perceptive and correct account of iodine-deficient thyroid enlargement, almost unknown at sea level but common in mountainous areas before the advent of iodized salt. Indeed, the first results of treatment of goitre with iodine were reported on 25 July 1820, after Richardson had left Europe.[10] Medical theory at the time suggested that goitre might be caused by drinking snow-water, since goitre was endemic in sub-alpine districts. Richardson points out that those North American Indians who drank much snow-water but rarely drank river water were free from disease, thus refuting this theory. He adds: "I could not learn whether it was necessary that both parents should have goitres, to produce cretin children; indeed the want of chastity in the half-breed women would be a bar to the deduction of any inference on this head."[11]

Richardson was the first medical doctor in the northwest to record the extreme susceptibility of the Indians, especially children, to the white men's diseases, whooping cough and measles.[12] One of these children actually died in January 1820 at the gates of the North West Company fort at Cumberland House.

We know from Franklin's account of six other medical episodes not mentioned in Richardson's journal: the preparation of a sweating-house for sick Indians;[13] the successful treatment by Richardson of an Indian boy in pain during the ascent of the Yellowknife on 3 August 1820;[14] the discharge of Emanuel Connoyer because of biliary colic (gallstones);[15] the treatment on 16 May of a minor Copper Indian chief for snowblindness by Richardson, using the surface application of drops of laudanum;[16] the consultation by "The Hook," an invalid for several years, who on 7 July received medicine.[17]

Richardson with great medical interest reported Wentzel's story of the Chipewyan Indian man who had raised his infant after his wife died in childbirth, feeding the infant meat broth (perhaps one of the earliest records of meat-base formula), and suckling it successfully at his breast.[18] Macleod and Glover may not be justified in claiming that Richardson was a gullible victim of a Wentzel hoax.[19] We now know that males as well as females have the hormone prolactin and can produce milk (inappropriate galactorrhea or inappropriate lactation are the technical terms). In some parts of Africa it is common for grandmothers, up to fifty years of age, to put their grandchild to the breast.[20] There are a few well-documented cases of men successfully nursing infants, including that of a negro male wet nurse who was displayed before a medical class in Maryland in 1827; milk from the male breast is nourishing.[21]

Dr Richardson's reputation preceded his arrival at Fort Providence. Hood says in his journal that the Indians believed this "medicine chief" had the power to "prevent any person from dying."[22] It is less plausible that they believed, as Franklin put it, that Dr Richardson "was able to restore the dead to life."[23] In striking contrast to the experience of the Indians in other winters in this harsh climate, however, not a single Indian died while Dr Richardson lived among them during the winter of 1820–1.[24] When Richardson's advance party left the fort on 4 June 1821, a Copper Indian, Akaiyazza or Little-foot, who was ill, hurried after him to receive medical attention. In exactly one week, time or faith or the ministrations of the doctor had affected a cure of whatever ailed him. In contrast, on 23 November 1821 another Copper Indian named The Fop, when his gun exploded and "wounded him slightly on the wrist," did not stay for care from the weakened doctor but hurried on alone to Akaicho's camp.

Both Franklin and Richardson tell (1 December 1820) of the rodent ulcer, a type of skin cancer, on the face of the wife of Cascathry. They describe (25 June 1821) the severe chafing of the inside of the men's thighs while pulling heavy loads on the ice of Point Lake. Richardson adds that the chafing produced marked reddening of the skin, and that it was a recurrence of a problem first encountered during similar travel north from Fort Enterprise to Point Lake. Richardson and Franklin tell us how one voyageur froze his thighs near Point Turnagain on 20 August 1821. It is noteworthy that no one lost a foot, toe, or fingertip from frostbite, thus offering good evidence of the adequacy of moccasins and fur mittens in extreme cold.

Richardson sometimes provides details that Franklin does not: for example, his entry for 17 July 1821 describes the intricate tattooing patterns on an old Eskimo woman's face. Franklin spares his readers the gory and intimate details of the incisions to relieve Adam, the interpreter, on 30 October 1821. He simply says that "The Doctor having scarified the swelled parts of Adam's body, a large quantity of water poured out," while Richardson is more specific: "I made several scarifications in his scrotum, abdomen and legs and a large quantity of water flowing out he obtained some ease." Adam, as well as Franklin, Peltier, and Semandrè, had been eating "large quantities of salt, a barrel of that article having been left in the house," and with severe protein deficiency, this excess salt ingestion probably contributed to fluid retention (edema). Franklin and Richardson both tell how the starving men had sores in their mouths from eating acrid soup, made from the bones of the previous winter's camp.

The fragility of the doctor-patient relationship was evident from two events at Fort Enterprise. On 5 January 1821 Richardson gave medicine to old Cascathry for his ailing wife. As he watched Cascathry wrap the drug with extraordinary care, Richardson could not help smiling. As medication was supposed to be a serious business, and this smile aroused the suspicions of the old Indian and in turn destroyed his wife's confidence, the medicine failed to produce the customary and desired effect. Richardson describes (17 June 1821) how an old Copper Indian, the father of Thoveeyorre and Petit Chasseur, suffered from acute urinary obstruction. After the doctor administered a drug, probably paregoric, the old man passed a large stone in his urine. Too honest to take full credit for the man's relief, Richardson spoiled the scenario by telling the old Indian that there might well be a second stone yet to come. The Copper Indian medicine man then took over management of the case with a frenzied and exhausting night of chanting in a conjuring house. The old man survived his ordeal, for he and his wife, together with Akaicho's wife's parents, served Richardson selected tender morsels of meat when he arrived at the outpost Indian camp five months later.

Richardson's biographer, Dr Robert E. Johnson, a physiologist, notes that Richardson's "clinical descriptions are classics for protein-calorie malnutrition in working men under cold stress. The progression through the stages emaciation, famine oedema, asthenia, decubitus ulcer, dementia, and finally cardiovascular collapse and death is well described."[25]

Richardson superintended the treatment of Solomon Belanger's severe hypothermia after prolonged immersion in the frigid waters of the Burnside River on 14 September. Belanger was instantly stripped of his wet clothing and then rolled up in blankets in close contact with the naked bodies of two of his fellow voyageurs, "reminding one of a Linnaean recipe."[26]

Richardson gives us a good clinical description of his own experience on 29 September 1821 with severe hypothermia, while malnourished. He begins by telling us how he "would have had little hesitation in any former period of my life, of plunging into water even below 38° F." Yet on 29 September 1821 when he tried to carry a line across the Coppermine River at Obstruction Rapid, having already lost much of his insulating body fat, he was in difficulty. First he lost the use of his arms. He tried to complete the swim on his back and almost succeeded, but then his legs also became powerless. The voyageurs dragged Richardson back to their side of the river, pulling on the line round his middle. They rolled him in a blanket placed before a good fire of willows. Richardson's journal describes his experience of warming up: "The fire being too hot, although it was regulated by my sensations at the time, the skin of the left side of my body which was most exposed to the heat, was deprived of feeling, and it did not regain its proper tone, nor did that side become as strong as the other, for five months afterwards." Later, when he wrote a letter to his wife from Fort Resolution in April 1822, Richardson tells how he experienced detached sensations similar to those of others who have been rescued during the very moment of death: "… as the waves closed over me, and I was losing the sight of the light of day, as I thought for ever, your happiness and that of my mother was my principal concern, and the last moments of recollection were spent in breathing a prayer for the temporal and eternal welfare of two so deservedly dear to me."[27]

In a letter to Hood's father on 29 October 1822, Dr Richardson gave a description of his reactions to starvation: "Our sufferings were never acute during the march, the sensation of hunger ceased after the third day of privation, and with the decay of strength, the love of life also decayed. We could calmly contemplate the approach of death, and our feelings were excited only by the idea of the grief of our relatives."[28]

Richardson describes how Régiste Vaillant fell exhausted in the snow on 6 October 1821, unable to rise and scarcely able to speak, shortly before freezing to death. Richardson himself almost suffered the same fate. On 28 October he became exhausted in the attempt to reach a clump of spruce trees about a mile from Dogrib Rock, only a day's walk north of Fort Enterprise. It was dusk, and the last few hundred yards, he tells us, "lay over some large stones, amongst which I fell down upwards of twenty times, and became at length so exhausted that I was unable to stand. If Hepburn had not exerted himself far beyond his strength, and speedily made the encampment and kindled a fire, I must have perished on the spot." Previously, Richardson had written of "Hepburn," but after this experience had brought them together, he usually spoke of him as "John."

Richardson describes how Joseph Peltier and François Semandrè suffered slow, lingering deaths from malnutrition in the buildings of Fort Enterprise and finally passed away on 1 and 2 November. Concerning the effect of malnutrition on ability to withstand cold, Richardson adds (29 September 1821): "During the whole of our march we experienced that no quantity of clothing would keep us warm whilst we fasted, but on those occasions on which we were enabled to go to bed with full stomachs, we passed the night in a warm and comfortable manner." The day after the Indians had brought food to the starving men at Fort Enterprise on 7 November, Richardson remarks that food "enables us to resist the cold, infinitely better than before, and it is difficult for us to believe otherwise, than that the season has become milder, instead of growing more severe as the winter advances."

Speaking of extreme cold, Richardson provides new information on how the Indians, assisting Franklin and Richardson in their southward trek from Fort Enterprise towards Akaicho's camp on 17 November 1821, helped them prevent frostbite. They "halted frequently to chafe our hands or countenances when they were affected by the cold. Their instant care preserved Mr. Franklin from being severely frost-bitten as several parts of his face became repeatedly white."

Richardson also mentions (9 November) the effects of a sudden indulgence in food following a long period of starvation. These "sufferings from repletion" consisted mainly of abdominal distention. Franklin (8 November) more delicately spoke of "indigestion," but in a footnote remarked that the first bowel movements were painful, an experience that had been shared by Samuel Hearne under similar circumstances.[29] These "disorders of the stomach" continued for at least five days, and caused the Indians to restrict the amount of meat they allotted, an action that Dr Richardson on 10 November was ready to approve: "This restriction is favourable to the recovery of our health, and is necessary, from the little government we are able to exercise at present over our appetites." Lake trout caused less discomfort than did meat.

No symptoms of scurvy appeared, even though the naval officers no longer had naval rations of lemon or lime juice. They ate fresh meat with a low but adequate Vitamin C content,[30] occasionally supplemented by berries rich in ascorbic acid. There is also a slight antiscorbutic property in "Indian tea," *Ledum*, as claimed by McGregor in 1828 and confirmed by Brown in 1954.[31] Scurvy was unknown among natives and those white men who followed a native diet of fresh meat and berries.[32]

When they left Fort Enterprise, Richardson was the weakest of the four survivors at the fort, still suffering from swollen feet and ankles, the result of nutritional edema. On 19 November, after four days' travel with adequate food, such swelling had disappeared from Franklin and Hepburn, but persisted with Richardson. Even less able to keep up, Adam lagged behind, attended by Benoit. Adam, however, soon showed the generally recognized, but poorly documented, Indian powers of rapid recuperation after famine. From having been edematous and so weak that he could not feed himself on 7 November, he had "recovered surprisingly," so that by 2 December he was "the best walker" in the party. Richardson recuperated more slowly during the journey but this ordeal did not seem to impair his later health. He was vigorous beyond his seventy-seventh year, outliving two of his three wives.

FOOD CONSUMPTION

During the winter of 1820–1 Akaicho's Copper Indians took good care of the explorers. By 5 November 1820 the fishery had taken in about 3000 pounds of whitefish.[33] Caribou were so numerous that Franklin on 10 October saw over two thousand of them in a short morning's walk near the fort.[34] Wentzel wrote to the Hon. Roderick McKenzie on 26 March 1821: "Six hunters of the Red Knife or Copper Indians have been found sufficient to supply us with the means of subsistance. Indeed it was scarcely possible for people to want where the Reindeers are in thousands and not difficult to approach; so little skill in hunting does it require that any man who can level a fire arm would live with little trouble or care."[35] This picture became less rosy as belts were tightened during the last ten days of April 1821, when the caribou were less available.

Richardson's journal, which fills in many gaps in Franklin's account, allows for the first time a fair estimate of the food consumed by the expedition after leaving Fort Enterprise. The year-round average gross weight of an adult female caribou, 27 months or older, is 180 pounds and of an adult male, 58 months or older, 251 pounds, increasing to 323 pounds in autumn. Caribou calves, usually born in mid-June, achieve 40 pounds weight by 2 months; females reach 92 pounds and males 103 pounds by 5 months.[36] The average live weight of caribou of all ages is 188 pounds, with 100 pounds of meat fit for human consumption.[37]

The dressed or carcase weight is, as in domestic cattle, 50 per cent or slightly more of the total weight, and 15 to 20 per cent of this weight is bone.[38] To compensate for the bone, edible portions of the intestines and head would increase the caloric value available. However, men on the move could not stop to boil heads, feet, and other parts; under normal conditions they did not eat the hides. On this basis, I have allowed 100 pounds of edible meat from a caribou of unstated age, 125 pounds from an adult male, and 60 pounds from a yearling or a small or very lean caribou.

Dr Peter Flood of the Western College of Veterinary Medicine, Saskatoon, has provided me with unpublished raw data for 213 muskoxen killed on Banks Island. Average gross weights for 39 yearling females were 233 pounds; for 50 yearling males, 269 pounds; for 80 subadult and adult females, 413 pounds; for 44 subadult and adult males, 545 pounds. Choice commercial cuts for public sale yielded 100,000 pounds of meat from the muskoxen kill, just over 100 pounds per animal. Franklin's statement on 4 July that the largest of eight had a gross weight of 300 pounds has caused me to allow 185 pounds of meat for a large muskox, 150 pounds of meat from a muskox of undetermined age and sex, 120 pounds from a lean or small adult, and 100 pounds each for lean young on 4 July.

A typical grizzly bear weighs 500 to 600 pounds, but the expedition seems not to have utilized bear meat to its full extent. Although a fat female grizzly was killed on 5 August, together with a muskox, the meat was all consumed by 7 August, suggesting that twenty men ate less than 200 pounds of grizzly meat. Similarly, after killing a large grizzly on 9 August, a not very fat grizzly and her cub on 10 August, and three caribou on 11 August, the men had to dip into their pemmican stores on 14 August. I have therefore allowed only 200 pounds of meat for an adult grizzly, and 10 pounds for an arctic hare, 5 pounds for an arctic fox, 5 pounds for a young goose, 10 pounds for a whistling swan, and 1 pound for a ptarmigan. Unfortunately, there are few clues as to the number of pounds of fish consumed.

It has been generally accepted that the first Franklin expedition was too large a group to "live off the land" during their period of exploration. Nevertheless, between Fort Enterprise and the sea the party of twenty-six, plus assorted Indian hunters, had to dip into their provisions of dried meat on only four of forty-seven days. During the same period they saved or collected eight days' new supply of dried meat, so they were in a positive balance until they reached the ocean. The women with Richardson's advance party prepared about 200 pounds of dried meat at Point Lake. The men prepared another unspecified amount along the Coppermine on 5 July, and purchased about 320 pounds of dried meat from The Hook and another party of Indians.

During the ocean exploration by canoe, they fared less well, having to take full rations of dried meat from their stores on twelve of twenty-seven days through 16 August. Full rations were considered to be eight pounds of fresh meat, four pounds of dried meat, or two pounds of pemmican per man per day.[39] Stefansson recommended either six pounds of fresh lean meat and one pound of fat, or two pounds of pemmican per day.[40] The Franklin expedition men preferred caribou to other meat, and it seems that an average caribou, with 100 pounds of meat, though falling a little below their expectations, was adequate to keep the twenty men reasonably satisfied for one day. When they had dried meat or pemmican (the differentiation was not always made), the men expected four pounds each per day, as Richardson tells us on 15 August. In contrast, Franklin that day estimated that one-and-a-half bags of pemmican would last for three days, a ration of two pounds per man per day. Calculations of consumption based on four pounds of meat per man per day on those days when fresh meat was not available (15, 28, 30 June, 20, 22, 25–9 July, 3, 7, 8, 12, 14, 16 August) and allowing for lessened rations after this (17, 21–3 August, 4 September) show it to be Richardson's figure that fits almost perfectly with our knowledge of the expedition's meat supply and consumption (Tables 2 and 3).

TABLE 2   Pemmican, fat, and dried meat available

4 June, prepared by Richardson's party	160 lb pemmican
	400 lb fat
	80 lb dried meat
14 June, prepared by Franklin's party	80 lb dried meat
21 June, prepared by Richardson's party	200 lb dried meat
5 July, prepared by Expedition party	±200 lb dried meat
7 July, purchased from The Hook	160 lb dried meat
9 July, purchased from old Indians	70 lb dried meat
Total	±1350 lb

It is much more difficult to give an estimate of caloric value consumed, since the caloric total available from fresh meat varies greatly with its fat content, from 500 to 1500 kilocalories [kcal] per pound.[41] Pemmican contains about 2800 kcal per pound, 63 per cent of these in the form of fat.[42] A gram of fat yields 9.3 calories, whereas a gram of protein or a gram of carbohydrate yields only 4.1 calories. Weight for weight, fat meat is more valuable than lean meat, not only because of its higher caloric value, but because of its greater palatability and its higher satiety value. Hunger reappears three hours after lean meat but five hours after fat meat is ingested.[43]

How much food did the Franklin expedition need to consume to maintain a balance with energy expenditure? Such estimates can only be approximate, but a man paddling a heavily laden canoe might easily expend 5 kcal per minute or 3000 kcal in a ten-hour day. Hiking with a heavy load expends 8 or 9 kcal per minute, 5000 kcal per day.[44] Three pounds of meat with a good admixture of fat could supply the daily requirement of 5000 kcal.

Every year, most of the caribou have moved south from the coast by early August. It is no wonder that hunger became a problem, especially from 15 through 25 August. At Point Turnagain on 19 August the explorers ate part of a caribou, then had little if anything to eat on 20 August. On 21 August they were each served "a handful" of pemmican, probably about half a pound, and now had only forty pounds of pemmican left. On 22 August they had a breakfast of approximately half the normal ration, probably a pound of pemmican each, but went supperless to bed. On 23 August they ate half of what remained, perhaps half a pound of pemmican each, just one-eighth of their previous ration. From 24 August through 2 September they were well supplied with game, obtaining three muskoxen and one caribou more (Richardson) or four muskoxen and one caribou more (Back) than mentioned in Franklin's journal. The transient period of hunger was described in a letter written by Richardson to his wife in April 1822: "... we launched our bark canoes on an icy sea, and commenced our voyage with only fourteen days' provisions. This scanty stock, however, with the addition of a few deer which we killed, and with some little fastings, lasted until the 25th of August, when its total consumption and the broken state of the weather compelled us to quit the sea and attempt to cross the Barren Grounds. We did tolerably well, living on the casual products of the chase, until September 4, when we were surprised by the premature appearance of winter ..."[45]

At Hood River, from 26 August to 2 September, the men were well fed as they killed six muskoxen, one of them small, and three caribou: about 1200 pounds of meat, 7.5 pounds per man per day. Some of the muskox meat was left behind, too heavy to carry. For the rest of September and October, everyone starved most of the time. The voyageurs, each carrying heavy loads of 90 pounds – tents, nets, two made-down canoes, instruments – were now continually in severe caloric deficit.

The expedition obtained no game during the first four days of the overland trek. They ate their last pemmican, perhaps half a pound for each man, on 4 September and their last portable soup and arrowroot on 7 September, the day they shot ten ptarmigan. During the next two days, three ptarmigan, two arctic hares, and four pounds from a muskox carcass were barely enough to allay their hunger pangs, supplemented by their first *tripe de roche*, a soup made from lichens whose caloric value cannot be substantial, although some lichens contain up to 2.4 per cent fat.[46] A large muskox cow on 10 September provided perhaps 300 pounds of meat. On 14 September after three more gameless days they killed two caribou, and promptly ate one for breakfast. The meat intake over the twelve days to Belanger Rapids thus averaged 1.8 pounds per man per day, about one-quarter of their need.

A single caribou on 15 September and five on 25 September completed the intake of fresh meat, apart from a few ptarmigan. The men also consumed some singed hides, a putrid caribou carcass, and the bones and antlers of two caribou. On 27 September they had blueberries and cranberries. Between Belanger Rapids and the eventual crossing of the Coppermine on 4 October, they averaged only about 1.6 pounds of fresh meat per man per day (Table 3).

TABLE 3 Food consumption during arctic exploration

Dates	Number men	Travel	Place	Number of days			Dried meat (lbs)	Pounds consumed					Fresh game man/day
				Total	no game killed	ate dried meat		Caribou	Muskox	Other	Fish	Total fresh game	
4–11 June (R)	19	foot	Ft Enterprise/Point Lake	8	2	0	0	1060	0	0	0	1060	7.0
12–21 June (R)	3	camp	Point Lake	10	5	0	0	485	0	0	0	485	16.2
14–21 June (F)	23	foot	Ft Enterprise/Point Lake	8	4	1	80	600	0	0	0	600	3.3
22–29 June	26	foot	Point Lake	8	4	1	80	820	0	0	20	840	4.0
30 June–12 July	26	canoe	Coppermine River	13	3	1	80	500	3365	75	40	3980	11.8
13–20 July	26	camp	Bloody Falls	8	2	1	80	0	180	0	400	580	2.8
21–31 July	20	canoe	Arctic Ocean	11	6	6	480	405	0	10	30	445	2.0
1–16 Aug.	20	canoe	Bathurst Inlet	16	8	6	480	580	185	700	0	1465	4.6
17–25 Aug.	20	canoe	Arctic Ocean	9	4	4	50	440	0	5	0	445	2.5
26 Aug.–2 Sept.	20	camp	Hood River	8	2	0	0	100	1045	0	20	1165	7.3
3–14 Sept.	20	foot	Barren Lands	12	6	1	10	200	185	40	0	425	1.8
15 Sept.–4 Oct.	20	foot	Barren Lands	20	14	0	0	630	0	10	0	640	1.6
Total				131*	60	21	1340	5820	4960	840	510	12130	4.6

Note: All figures are estimates. Fish consumption is the most difficult to estimate.
*8 days overlap between two parties Franklin (F) and Richardson (R) on 14–21 June.

Thereafter nine of the eleven voyageurs died of starvation, accelerated by exposure. The survivors ate an occasional hare and ptarmigan, moccasins, and hides. For liquids they had *tripe de roche* and "country tea." Richardson and Hepburn no doubt owed their survival to eating Hood's buffalo robe and some human flesh. Franklin and his group, joined much later by Richardson and Hepburn, would have perished had there not been a great many edible caribou skins left at Fort Enterprise from the previous winter. These skins were not, however, sufficient to prevent severe protein deficiency (hypoproteinemia) that caused their tissues to swell with edema.

Perhaps one of the most interesting new understandings gained from Richardson's journal concerns the nutritive value of moccasins and caribou-skin blankets. Franklin speaks of eating "roasted leather" and Richardson gives a little more detail (5 October): "Every little scrap of shoe leather is now highly prized, and after boiling is greedily devoured." It may be difficult for many readers to appreciate how any sustenance or satisfaction could be gained from shoe leather until they realize that in the 1820s in the wilds of the far northwest, all leather was untanned and untreated. Because proteins had not been denatured and hardened, moccasins retained considerable food value, though Stefansson thinks the men may have reduced the nutritious potential through overcooking.[47] It was not uncommon for the Indians to eat their moccasins and their robes in time of famine.[48]

To what extent did food determine survival in the three different parties? The "advance group" of Back, St Germain, Solomon Belanger, and Beauparlant had the highest survival ratio of the three groups, even though their food supply seemed precarious; they lost only Beauparlant. In the "rearward group" which lagged behind after the crossing of the Coppermine, Credit and Vaillant were the first to perish, followed by J.B. Belanger, Perrault, and Fontano. Hood and Michel were shot. Richardson and Hepburn, the only survivors, were sustained in part by eating Hood's buffalo robe and some human flesh until they could reach Fort Enterprise and partake of caribou skins. In the "middle group," Franklin, Augustus, Adam, and Benoit survived only because of the gigantic, somewhat scattered refuse heap of sleeping robes and bones left by whites and Indians alike from the previous winter's camp. In this instance, fortunately, Franklin had not been too fastidious. A leader with a penchant for orderliness or cleanliness might have burned the piles of animal skins and carcasses before breaking camp in June 1821, and thus would have sealed his doom. Nourishment from such skins was, however, inadequate to save Peltier and Semandrè, the two of the middle group who died of starvation.

On 30 October after twenty-six caribou skins, used as bedding by the Indians the previous winter, had been dug up from beneath the snow, Richardson tells us: "Those that contain the larvae of the oestrus are most prized by us, and eagerly sought after." For desperate, starving men, these succulent high protein morsels were welcome, and no doubt contributed greatly to their survival – but

Franklin did not mention this important detail, which might have turned the stomachs of squeamish readers.

Oestrus larvae develop from eggs laid in the fine, woolly hairs of the underdown of the caribou coat by the warble fly or botfly, *Oedemagena tarandi*, a yellowish-orange bee-like insect. The newly hatched larvae measure 1 mm or less, the second instar is 7 to 10 mm, and the third instar is ovate and robust.[49] Their growth continues through the winter. These are the prize edible items in a caribou skin, expressed between two thumbnails. By Indian custom, these warbles "are always eaten raw and alive, out of the skin; and are said, by those who like them, to be as fine as gooseberries."[50]

NATURAL HISTORY

Richardson was hired because of his special expertise in natural history. His journal allows us to assess, with greater accuracy than before, his strengths and weaknesses in specific sciences. His attention in the journal to small details of history, ornithology, and geography allows us to understand better the conditions that he found and therefore the changes that have taken place in wildlife distribution and abundance over 160 years.

Richardson accorded a high priority to geology and meteorology since, together with botany, they were indicators of the future economic prospects of a new land. He had a good grasp of the geologic principles known at the time, as we know from Back's notes of Richardson's lectures given to the officers of the second Franklin expedition at Great Bear Lake in 1825–6[51] and from Richardson's long, rambling "Geognostical Observations."[52]

Frequent, accurate Latin lists of plants in his daily journal confirm that Richardson was already a remarkably competent botanist, able to identify a prodigious number of known species in a totally new region. He himself wrote the detailed descriptions, all in Latin, of many other plants which he recognized as new and hitherto undescribed species.[53]

Richardson's exemplary list of lichens at Fort Enterprise further illustrates the extraordinary scholarship of the man. He relied on Acharius's *Lichenographia Universalis*, written totally in Latin, for identification. Although many of the lichen species have since been reclassified into different genera, most remain readily recognizable[54] and after 160 years allow Richardson to be given full credit for the description of two new species. (See John W. Thomson's comments in Appendix E, and footnotes 28 to 64, inclusive, in chapter 1.)

Richardson was also a competent ichthyologist and mammalogist, entirely familiar with the principles of scientific classification, such as the number of rays in each fin in fish and the complex dental formulas of mammals. He made long, detailed descriptions of sixteen species of fish in his journal; these were largely reproduced in his Appendix VI to Franklin's *Journey* (1823) and in *Fauna Boreali-Americana*, III: *Fish*. Mammalogy and ichthyology were both related to the procurement of meat for food. More important, the fur trade was then of central economic importance in the Northwest. Beaver skins were a measure of trade, a form of currency.

Ornithology was less important economically, although some of the larger species of birds were used for food. Bird identification was at the time incredibly difficult. Although Richardson was not yet skilled in the science, nothing can excuse what was later done with his bird and mammal specimens. Collected by Richardson and Hood at Cumberland House in 1819–20, and by Richardson at Carlton House from 10–26 May 1820, these specimens were sent to York Factory with the Hudson's Bay Company men. When the twelve species of mammals and "above forty species of birds" reached England, they were given by the Earl of Bathurst, secretary for war and the colonies, to Joseph Sabine, the inspector-general of taxes and an honorary secretary of the Horticultural Society, who had a large collection of British birds. Bathurst requested that Sabine "prepare a scientific description of the different specimens, and communicate the same to the Linnaean Society," and then place the specimens in the British Museum.[55] Bathurst had no business requesting one scientist to prepare for publication the work of another, before the latter had even returned from the expedition.

On 15 January 1822 Sabine presented a review of the "marmots" of North America and a description of three new species before the Linnean Society of London. The three new species of ground squirrel he named *Arctomys Franklinii*, the Grey American Marmot; *Arctomys Richardsonii*, the Tawny American Marmot; and *Arctomys Hoodii*, the Striped American Marmot. These accounts were in press when an irate Captain Franklin returned. He forced Sabine to append the following note in proof: "October 29, 1822, Captain Franklin, who returned in the present month, whilst the preceding pages were printing, having intimated his desire that an account of the subjects of Natural History collected by him during his expedition should accompany the narrative which he is preparing for the press, the descriptions of the collections alluded to at the commencement of this paper will form a part of that publication."[56] This explanation shows how Joseph Sabine, who had already invested much time and effort in studying Richardson's specimens, came to prepare Appendix v, the Zoological Appendix, and to receive credit for description of new forms, including a new race of magpie.[57]

Many of Richardson's journal descriptions and specimens obtained after June 1820 were either not shared with or not used by Joseph Sabine. The Arctic Ground Squirrel, and a lemming, both new species, did not appear in Sabine's Zoological Appendix. Similarly, eighteen species of birds recorded by Richardson were totally omitted and additional specimens of another thirty-seven species were overlooked. Richardson politely tells how the Stilt Sandpiper, or what he called the "Slender-shanks Sandpiper," had been overlooked by Sabine: "Specimens were brought home in spirits; but, probably from being too much injured were not noticed by Mr. Sabine with the other birds, in the Appendix to Sir John Franklin's narrative of his first journey." In the same book Richardson tells of an albino phalarope which he had collected at York Factory in 1819 on the outward journey to Cumberland House. "I put the bird into spirits, and sent it, along with a considerable number of other specimens, to England by a ship which was then on the point of sailing. They reached London, but I never could trace what became of any of them afterwards."[58] The rocks and plants collected along the Coppermine reached England safely and were later described by Richardson himself. They were carried at least as far as Great Slave Lake by Wentzel, Parent, Forcier, Dumas, and Gagné.[59]

The long account in Richardson's journal of how the Indians hunted caribou before the advent of guns and ammunition was "lifted" and quoted almost verbatim by Franklin.[60] When Richardson produced his first volume of *Fauna Boreali-Americana*, he reprinted from Franklin an entire page of what were originally his own observations of the caribou, but with the traditional deference shown a superior officer he simply noted: "Captain Franklin observes that ..."[61]

Richardson's journal allows correction of some errors in the second volume of *Fauna Boreali-Americana* and adds some useful information. For example, the Eskimo Curlew specimen and first-ever nest at Point Lake date from 1821, not 1822.[62] The undated Belted Kingfisher specimen is now known to have been collected on 28 May 1822, on the Slave River halfway between Great Slave Lake and Lake Athabasca.[63] The "clerical error" in Sabine's appendix stating that the Snowshoe or American Hare did not occur north of Fort Carlton rather than north of Fort Enterprise was noted by Richardson in 1829.[64]

The first naturalist to visit any new part of the world tries to sort the species observed there into three categories: species already known in Europe or elsewhere, simple varieties or subspecies, and entirely new species. Once such species are well known and all their characteristic features illustrated in books these decisions may look deceptively simple, but it was not an easy task at the time. Richardson had an incredibly advanced perception of varieties that interbred freely, and thus he forfeited priority for some forms that later proved to be new species, by lumping them together with similar forms and thereby losing the opportunity to bestow a new Latin name.

For a naturalist, Richardson's experiences on this expedition were sometimes heart-breaking. He found and preserved new species, carried them "for many days through the snow," only to leave them behind, unsung and undescribed, everyone's "strength being completely exhausted."[65] As he said: "... the disasters attending our return across the Barren Grounds from the sea-coast, caused us to leave behind the whole collection made during the summer of 1821, with the exception of a few plants collected during the descent of the Copper-Mine River, which were intrusted to Mr. Wentzel's care when he left us. The part of the collection, which is lost, contained some plants, which I deemed to be new or curious."[66] Since Richardson did not mention this grave disappointment in his daily journal, he may not have jettisoned "the specimens of plants and minerals" all at once as Franklin said on 21 September, or left them with the books and instruments abandoned as Franklin recounted on 13 September, or as Back noted with "every article that could possibly be dispensed with" on 16 September. My suspicion is that Richardson may have first left the rocks, then the bird skins, and finally the precious new species of plants, as yet undescribed.

GEOGRAPHY AND MAPPING

One of the treasures of Richardson's journal is his provision of twenty-two pages of courses and distances for the entire journey from Fort Enterprise, down the Coppermine River, along the arctic coast, and south overland to Obstruction Rapids. There are listings of as many as thirty-three changes of direction in a single day (6 July). These entries were all in nautical miles of 6080 ft, whereas Franklin's published accounts made correct conversions into statute miles of 5280 ft. Hood and Back made the initial calculations, which included the daily courses for the 14–20 June trip to Point Lake made by Franklin, Back, and Hood, and excluded the itinerary of Richardson's advance party of 5 to 9 June. Evidently all were later copied by Richardson from the journals of Robert Hood and George Back, for they were placed after his narrative but before most of his descriptions of birds, mammals, and fish. For the reader's convenience, these courses and distances have been moved forward and placed at the end of each day's narrative.

The entries allow us a greater appreciation of the Franklin expedition maps which were remarkably accurate, considering that they were made under arduous conditions and checked by formal readings of latitude only every one to three days, with longitude readings dependent entirely on the accuracy of the chronometers. Richardson's "courses and distances" also provide an explanation for the occasional inaccuracies in Franklin's maps.

On occasion we can now pinpoint exact locations that were previously only conjectured. Such matters are still of interest; a surprising number of people have visited parts of the Arctic and tried to determine just where Franklin's party camped on a particular night. My wife and I were part of such a group that spent the last two days of July and the first eight days of August at Bathurst Inlet in 1979, the very days of the Franklin expedition visit there 158 years earlier. Like them, we became cold and wet in retracing the path of their canoes and beaching at their campsites in similar weather. Only after more than 100 years, with the advent of new maps made from aerial photographs, have there been maps of the area more accurate than Franklin's.[67]

With Richardson's detailed notes, it is evident that subsequent surveyors, cartographers, and members of government-appointed committees on geographical names have at times erred in ascribing Franklin's names to geographic features. Franklin's "Sandstone Rapids" were twelve miles upstream from the location on present maps; "Inman's Harbour" was three miles west of the deeper inlet that now carries this name; "Snug Harbour" was a wider bay centred four miles west of the smaller bay so named on present maps; "Point Everitt" was three miles north and west of the present point; "Wright's River," a small stream running from west to east, was crossed six miles east of a different south-north river now carrying this name. Some of these names have been on official maps for so many years that it might prove awkward to change them back again, but it is nevertheless interesting for geographers and arctic buffs to know exactly where Franklin and his men were, and exactly which features were named by Franklin, who as leader was the one with this prerogative.

All the officer's entries are based on a compass of 32 points, each of 11¼ degrees on a modern 360-degree compass. Using the first consecutive points west of north as an example, Nbw (north by west) is 11¼ degrees west of north and NNW is 22½ degrees west of north. Each of the 11¼° segments can be divided into halves or quarters, so that Nbw¼w is one-quarter of the way between Nbw and NNW, or 14 degrees west of north, adding one-quarter of the next 11¼ degrees to the original 11¼ degrees at Nbw. A designation was thereby available for roughly every three degrees. Each "leg" of the day's journey had a "course" listed in terms of this direct compass reading for a given distance.

Only at the end of the day was the composite sum of the day's bearings on the magnetic compass then corrected for the number of degrees of magnetic declination (variation), the difference between true north and magnetic north, to

Compass bearings as used in the 1820s

give an overall course and distance for the entire day, corrected in terms of true north. A summary of these findings forms the "corrected course and distance" in Table 4. The magnetic declinations change appreciably over relatively short distances, sometimes introducing an error of 5 or even 10 degrees which might or might not be corrected when next the officers had a chance to make a formal calculation of the declination, often only one every day or two.

TABLE 4   Corrected daily courses and distances

Date	Franklin's Journal	Richardson's table	Back's Journal	Houston's plot
1820				
Sept. 9		NbE 13¾		N 11° E 13
10		N 2° E 10		N 2° E 10
11		N 4° W 14		N 4° W 19
12				N 40° E 8
13		S 13° E 12½		S 13° E 12½
14		S 26° W 11¼		S 26° W 11¼
15		S 9° E 19		S 9° E 21
1821				
Apr. 30	Ft Enterprise	S 55° W 15½	Ft Enterprise	S 55° W 15½
May 1	,,	S 44° W 24½	,,	S 44° W 24½
2	,,	S 54° E 3	,,	S 54° E 3
June 4	Ft Enterprise		Ft Enterprise	N 21° E 11½
5	,,		,,	N 20° W 8½
6	,,		,,	N 6° W 11
7	,,		,,	N 11° E 7½
8	,,		,,	N 20° E 5
9	,,		,,	N 2° W 5
10	,,		,,	N 11° W 4
MAP 2				
June 25	6	NW 5½	NW 5½	N 45° W 5½
26	4	W¼N 6	W¼N 5¾	N 84° W 9
27	8½	NW½W 10½	NW½W 10½	N 51° W 11
28	6	NNW¾W 5¾	NNW¼W 5¾	N 30° W 6¼
29	12¾	NWbW 11	WNW½W 11	N 62° W 11
30	6	N¼E 5¼	N¼E 5½	N 10° E 6
July 1		NE 4	NE 4	N 52° E 6½
2		NW¾W 5	NW½W 5	N 47° W 7
(3)				
MAP 3				
July 4	24½	N½E 21	N 21	N 2° E 23
(5)				
6	50	NWbN 42¾	NW¼N 42¾	N 30° W 41
7		NWbW 8	NWbW 8	N 58° W 10½
8	25	NWbW½W 21¾	WNW¼W 21¼	N 65° W 21½
9		NbE 9	NbE 9	N 23° E 9
(10)				
11		NbE 9½	NbE 9½	N 2° W 11
12		NbE½E 13½	NbE½E 13½	N 45° E 14
(13)				
14	14	NbE½E 12	NbE½E 12	N 11° E 11

TABLE 4   (*continued*)

Date	Franklin's Journal	Richardson's table	Back's Journal	Houston's plot
15		NbE 8¾	NbE 8¾	N 24° E 10
(16, 17)				
18	9	NE¼N 8	NE¼E 9½	N 50° E 9
(19, 20)				
21	37	EbS½S 37	EbS½S 37	S 79° E 28
MAP 4				
July 22		E½S 38½	E½S 38½	E 37½
23–24	31	ENE 31	ENE 31	N 75° E 39
25	28	E 28¼	E 28¼	E 16
(26)				
MAP 5				
27	1½	E½N 3¼	E½N 3½	N 80° E 3
(28)				
29–30	SE¾S 41	SE¾S 41½	SE¾S 41½	S 36° E 39½
31		W 4½	W 4½	W 2
Aug. 1–2	NE 16½	NE 16¼	NE 16¼	N 40° E 16
3	SE¾S 24	SE¾S 24	SE¾S 24	S 36° E 31
Aug. 4	SbE½E 33	SbE½E 33	SbE½E 33	S 9° E 35
5		SEbE 5	EbS 5½	S 60° E 3½
6		NW¼N 8	NW¾N 7¼	N 25° W 7
7	NNW 23	NNW 22	NbW½W 23	N 10° W 24½
(8)				
9	inlet 13	N 14	N 15¼	N 17
10	24	NbW 23½	NNW 22	N 12° W 25
11	18¾	NbE¾E 18¾	NbE¾E 19	N 9° E 20
12	NEbE 6	ENE 5½	ENE 5½	N 70° E 4½
13	NbE½E 23	NNE¾E 23¾	NNE½E 23¾	N 47° E 27
14	24	WbS¾S 23	WbS¾S 23	S 78° W 25
15	S¼E 9¼	S¼E 7¾	S¼E 9¼	S 2° W 8
16		NWbW 21½	NWbW 24½	N 56° W 25½
(17)				
18	NNE 11	N 19° E 15	NNE 10	N 19° E 10
(19, 20, 21)				
22	20	SE¾S 14½	SE¾S 14¾	S 30° E 17
MAP 6				
23		SSE 22¾	SSE 22¾	S 26° E 26
24	18	SSW 21¾	SSW 21¾	S 18° W 19
25		WbS¼S 19½	WbS¼S 19½	S 65° W 16½
26	6	SbE½E 5¾	SbE½E 6	S 28° E 10
27	7	SWbS 6¾	SSW½W 4¾	S 17° W 6
(28, 29, 30)				
31		SbE 5	SbE 4¾	S 25° E 5½
Sept. 1	11	SWbW 10¾	SWbW 10¾	S 66° W 10¾
2		W 11½	W 11½	W 12
3	10¾	SSW 10¾	SSW 10¾	S 22° W 11½
4	12½	S 22° W 12½	SSW 12	S 22° W 12½
(5, 6)				
7		S 22° W 8½	SSW 8½	S 22° W 8½
8	10¼	SSW½W 10¼	SSW½W 10¼	S 31° W 13
9	SW 5¾	SW 5¾	SW 5¾	S 50° W 6
10		S 23° W 8¼	SSW 8¼	S 23° W 9
(11)				

TABLE 4   *(concluded)*

Date	Franklin's Journal	Richardson's table	Back's Journal	Houston's plot
MAP 7				
Sept. 12	11	SSW½W 11	SSW½W 11	S 29° W 11
13	6½	N 73° W 6¾	WNW½W 6½	N 60° W 7½
14		N 19° E 4¼	NbE¾E 4¼	N 19° E 4¼
15		N 81° W 1¾	W¾N 1¾	N 88° W 2½
16	10¾	S 26° W 10¼	SSW½W 10¼	S 26° W 10¼
17	12½	S 9° E 12½	S¾E 12½	S 5° W 14
18		S 9° E 9½	S¾E 9½	S 5° W 11
19	10	S 11° E 10	SbE 10	S 5° W 11
20		S 14° E 8½	SbE½E 8½	S 5° W 10
21	5¼	S 15° W 5¼	SbW½W 5¼	S 30° W 8
22	8	S 13° E 8	SbE¼E 8	S 10° E 7
23		S 39° W 6¾	SW½S 6¾	S 52° W 8
24		W 5	W 5	W 7
(25)				
26	along lake 3		NbE½E 9½	N 45° W 6
27	at rapids		E½N 10	at rapids
28	,,	at rapids	NW½W 3	,,
29	,,	,,	[SE½E] 4	,,
30	,,	,,	back to rapid	,,

NOTE: Richardson's table almost certainly represents the calculations of Robert Hood, later copied into Richardson's journal. All distances are in nautical miles of 6080 feet. All courses are a summary of all the "legs" of that day, corrected for magnetic variation (declination). On the return trek across the Barren Grounds (3–26 September 1821), the explorers did not stop to make calculations of the variation and hence their corrected course was 10° too far east.

As an example, the magnetic declination at Fort Enterprise was determined by Franklin, Back, and Hood to be 37° east. One must then move 37 degrees in a clockwise direction from the compass reading to obtain a reading related to true north as opposed to magnetic north. With a compass bearing of NW (45° west of north), and a magnetic declination of 37° east, the true bearing is 45 minus 37 or 8° west of north. When I used this 37° correction and plotted Franklin's seven-day trek from Fort Enterprise to the south shore of Point Lake, where Richardson's advance party was waiting, I found the distance correct but the final position nearly four miles too far west. However, at Point Lake the magnetic declination was then 43° east. Using the mean of 37° and 43°, a re-plotting reached the very point where they camped.

Using Franklin's figures for magnetic declination (owing to the moving magnetic poles, these figures are quite different today), and the individual courses and distances recorded in Richardson's journal, I have plotted the route followed by the expedition with black tape on modern 1:250,000 maps. On the map, numerals beside each "leg" indicate nautical miles, except that no numeral is given for any fraction under one mile. A dot beside a numeral indicates an omitted fraction; for example, 5˙ could represent 5¼, 5½, or 5¾ miles. In spite of inherent errors in bearings as explained, for many days the readings fit almost exactly for both direction and distance (maps 2 to 8), thus attesting to the meticulous accuracy of Robert Hood and George Back. In order to obtain such accuracy, the officer in charge of these sightings had a full-time job "keeping bearings." He could not paddle the canoe. He was handicapped by the restricted view available from a low canoe, virtually at water level. The method used was that described by Bourne in 1567, who "made his way down the River Thames using a mariner's compass as his only instrument. With the compass he got the direction of every reach of the river and fixed his position at the end of the reach by taking bearings on two objects already fixed by a triangulation of the area."[68]

Franklin, in somewhat greater detail, describes how Hood surveyed the Hayes River in the fall of 1819 on the first inland leg of their journey: "The survey of the river was made by taking the bearings of every point with a pocket compass, estimating the distances, and making a connected eye-sketch of the whole. This part of the survey was allotted to Messrs. Back and Hood conjointly: Mr. Hood also protracted the route every evening on a ruled map, after the courses and distances had been corrected by observations for latitude and longitude, taken by myself as often as the weather would allow."[69]

Such plottings were complicated enough on the well-known, regularly travelled Hayes River in 1819. The problems were far greater for explorers in the summer of 1821, as the first white men to trek over stony, snow-covered hills, march along the rough ice of Point Lake, descend the turbulent Coppermine River, and finally make their way in birchbark canoes between ice floes along the arctic coast. In clear weather and fog, and sometimes in the waning light of the midnight sun, they made their way. Often they detoured around an island or a point, but they would still make for a fixed landmark which bore an exact directional reading from the previous point. No matter how their canoes were blown by the wind, their "fixes" on specific landmarks ahead, behind, and to the sides allowed them a remarkably accurate assessment of the distance as well as the direction of every single change of course, although the distance actually travelled around bends and islands was usually greater than this straight-line distance.

Plottings based on these courses and distances were called "Dead Reckoning," commonly abbreviated to "R," more rarely to "D.R." Latitude and longitude calculations by this method were quite tentative. They were checked every day or so by readings of latitude with a sextant, abbreviated as "Obs." Large-scale modern maps demonstrate that the sextant observations were usually correct within one minute of latitude or roughly within an accuracy of one mile. A few readings of latitude appear to have been up to two or even three minutes in error, perhaps in some circumstances because of misleading diffraction of light rays.

Longitude was determined by timepieces or chronometers, abbreviated "Chr." Reliance could be placed on what appeared to be the most accurate of the officers' chronometers, or upon a mean of the readings of four chronometers. Unlike the latitude readings, longitude readings were subject to moderate error, even though the Admiralty had supplied the best chronometers available. Buffeted by heavy winds, subject to changing temperatures and humidity, and at times even immersed in water, these timepieces performed with amazing accuracy. If one slowed or gained four minutes, as it might well do in the course of a month or year, that meant an error of one degree (sixty minutes) of longitude. At the latitude of Fort Enterprise this meant an error of thirty miles and at the latitude of Point Turnagain, an error of twenty-six miles. At Fort Enterprise the reading was only two minutes of longitude or roughly one statute mile in error. This calculation was achieved by taking the mean of the result of the difficult and somewhat inexact lunar observations and the chronometer readings.

There was, then, a gradual exaggeration in the longitude above what is known to be true on modern maps, as during the summer of 1821 the chronometers lost time until they were a few minutes slow. This exaggeration of longitude increased from an error of eight minutes of longitude along the upper reaches of the Coppermine, to thirty minutes at the mouth of the Coppermine, to forty-eight minutes at the mouth of Hood River on 31 July.

When the expedition returned to the mouth of the Hood River on 25 August, the chronometers were giving a reading of forty minutes of longitude farther west than they had on 31 July; they had slowed by about two minutes and forty seconds in twenty-six days. Franklin therefore subtracted forty minutes of longitude for his August readings; had he also subtracted forty minutes for July, his longitude at the mouth of the Hood River would have been almost exactly correct. As it is, he placed Cape Flinders and Point Turnagain about twenty miles too far west.

For many days, the black tape plottings fit almost perfectly on the modern map. However, a few of the larger discrepancies explain disproportions on Franklin's published map. Some of these may have resulted from simple copying errors by Richardson – on 25 August the first "leg" clearly should have been 1¾ nautical miles, not 4¾, and the fourth leg sixteen not twenty-six miles. Three "legs" of 2½, 4, and 1 nautical miles, traversed while facing great peril on Rocknest Lake on 1 July, are missing, with the result that Rocknest Lake appears abnormally small on Franklin's map. The tenth entry for 6 July had no mileage beside the course. Similarly, the single "leg" of under eight miles on 9 August into Gordon's Bay is clearly an error since Franklin stated a penetration of thirteen miles and since this extra distance was essential to show Bear Island in its proper shape and location on Franklin's map.

Most often distances were underestimated and show on the map as small gaps between the individual black tapes, but on 7 and 8 September there were gaps of two miles each on either side of the Cracroft River. On other days the presence of parallel tapes indicate that distances were overestimated; moderate overlap discrepancies are evident on 28–30 July near Detention Harbour, as well as on 10 June, 6, 8 and 18 July, 13 August, and 1 and 2 September.

On large bodies of water, the drift vector could not be calculated as winds blew the canoes from their course. This caused a seven-mile southward drift during 29 July, explains two slightly smaller displacements within Melville

Sound on 13 and 14 August, and may explain the ten-degree error in bearings between Wollaston Point and the mouth of the Hood River. Melville Sound as a result was somewhat distorted on Franklin's map, which also shows a noticeable widening and shortening of Arctic Sound.

To make such accurate maps, and to avoid overlooking any possible entry to the long-sought-for Northwest Passage to the orient, the explorers had to go to the mouth of every bay and inlet, greatly lengthening their journey. Towards the end they became less thorough, and completely overlooked Elu Inlet, which extends another thirty miles east beyond Warrender's Bay. Even with this omission, their exploration of Bathurst Inlet and Melville Sound required 460 statute miles of circumnavigation, though the distance across its mouth from Cape Barrow to Cape Flinders is only thirty-seven miles, and that from Point Wollaston to Point Everitt is only nineteen miles.

Finally, it should be appreciated that [François] Beaulieu ("Boileau" at times to both Franklin and Richardson), "a half-breed who had been brought up amongst the Dog-ribbed and Copper Indians" and who had descended the Coppermine "a considerable way," had in March 1820 at Fort Chipewyan already drawn a rough map of the area for Franklin. Together with an old Chipewyan Indian named Black Meat, who had himself visited the arctic shores, these two had been able to indicate the approximate direction and distances required to reach Contwoyto Lake and the mouths of the Coppermine and Anatessy [Burnside] rivers. In their exploration of the arctic coastline, the officers consequently kept watching for a river mouth answering the description of the mouth of the Anatessy. We now appreciate that the mouth of the Burnside was hidden from them by Quadyuk Island and Elliott Point, and this explains why they first contemplated the Hood River and then the Western River as a possible Anatessy; had they found and recognized the mouth of the Burnside they might possibly have chosen this river as their return route as far as Contwoyto Lake.

By pushing on around countless bays and inlets as far as Point Turnagain, Franklin has made his achievements look much better in historical perspective than if he had been more prudent and stopped at the bottom of Bathurst Inlet. Perhaps it was a sailor's "sixth sense" or just sheer luck, but he did achieve a point where the arctic coast trended east in a fairly regular fashion. This achievement reflects in large part the dogged determination of Franklin, although, as Neatby says, he "could have turned back from the coast only at the cost of professional ruin. It would have implied a censure on those who had planned the expedition, and would have wasted the money and effort that had already been expended ... In a single summer he had laid down nearly six hundred miles of a coast which had cost Hearne and Mackenzie much labour even to approach, and had acquired a first-hand knowledge of conditions which permitted the rest of the Arctic shoreline to be mapped with comparative cheapness and ease. He had put a roof on the map of Canada, and given a definite shape to the North American continent."[70]

CLIMATOLOGY

Franklin and his officers provided the first careful records of temperature and wind conditions in the northern interior of North America, demonstrating a much colder climate than experienced at the same latitude in Europe. Furthermore, they documented the unseasonably early onset of winter in 1821, a fact that made the trek across the Barren Lands more difficult than it might have been another year.

It seems that unseasonable cold was fated to conspire against Franklin. In October 1820 at Fort Enterprise "there had been very little snow on the ground, and we were surrounded by vast herds of rein-deer ... Winter River was then open." In October 1821 "there were but few recent tracks of these animals, and the snow was upwards of two feet deep ... Winter River ... was frozen two feet thick."[71] G.C. Jacoby's unpublished tree-ring studies from the Coppermine Mountains confirm that Franklin encountered a major dip in temperatures in 1821.[72]

TRIBULATIONS AND RESCUE

The scientific achievements of the expedition appear even more remarkable when viewed in relation to the hardships endured, the near-starvation, and the incredible risks taken on long traverses of ocean in fragile birchbark canoes, overloaded and becoming increasingly damaged. Richardson's journal gives an added appreciation of these difficulties, as well as a better sense of the strengths and weaknesses of the officers, voyageurs, Eskimos, and interpreters under Franklin's command, especially of one of the interpreters, Pierre St Germain. Richardson's comments make it easier to understand why Akaicho and his Indians failed to arrange provisions at Fort Enterprise, nearly causing all to perish. The question of cannibalism, and Wentzel's accusations that Michel was murdered by Richardson, deserve comment. These events are based on such complex relationships that the reader may benefit from a recapitulation and correlation of the entries of Franklin, Richardson, and Back.

When the expedition set out from the mouth of the Coppermine to explore the ocean, the voyageurs were understandably apprehensive about travelling along ice-packed shores in two frail, overloaded birchbark canoes. Their worst fears were almost realized on 26 July, when one of the canoes was squeezed between two ice floes and narrowly escaped being destroyed. By 15 August twelve of the structural timbers were broken in one canoe and the other canoe was so shattered that the men were in daily dread that the birchbark would drop from the gunwales.

It is no wonder that the voyageurs were on the verge of open rebellion. Richardson that day reported what Franklin did not: "The fears of our voyageurs have now entirely mastered their prudence and they are not restrained by the presence of their officers from giving loose to a free and sufficiently rude expression of their feelings. They have now so often canvassed the dangers of our journey from the coast, that they despair of ever seeing home again, and the broken state of the weather and coldness of the nights, together with the smallness of our stock of provision cause them to deem any attempt to proceed farther as little short of madness." Subsequent events proved that madness it truly was. Neither did Franklin quote the following observation from Richardson's journal entry for that same day: "… in order to insure a fair prospect of a safe journey across the barren grounds, our voyage along the coast must speedily terminate …" Franklin promised that day to proceed only until he ascertained the coast trending away to the eastward, or for four more days, whichever occurred first. But he did not keep his promise.

The first eastward trending of the coast at Point Turnagain was determined on 18 August. Franklin felt he had at last achieved a minimum objective. Yet five miserable and wasted days were spent on the inhospitable Kent Peninsula. The return trip, which did not begin until 2 AM on 23 August, was too late. They had tarried far too long. With evident signs of impending winter, these desperate men made a daring traverse of twenty-five miles of ocean before a raging north wind, in canoes that were literally falling apart. The waves were so high that sight of the mast of the adjacent canoe was intermittently hidden. Not surprisingly, they split the head of one canoe while beaching it. Richardson paid tribute in his entry of 25 August 1821 to those intrepid men who "… shewed considerable courage in bearing the dangers of the sea, magnified to them by their novelty." As they left the ocean, to begin their long, gruelling, 320-mile hike overland, Richardson added: "The consideration that the most painful and certainly the most hazardous part of the journey was to come, did not depress their spirits at all."

The men were "very heavily laden" on the overland trek from the mouth of the Hood River. Even before they had to contend with snow, they could average only a mile an hour. They could carry only a small fraction of their fresh muskoxen meat, and they had not had time to prepare the more portable pemmican. They ate their last pemmican on 4 September and their last portable soup and arrowroot on 7 September, using the bark and timbers of one canoe for fuel.

The officers knew the correct course to set for Fort Enterprise, and were able to calculate its approximate distance – but they had no way of knowing what lay in their path. They crossed the Hood River on 3 September with two canoes lashed together; they forded the Cracroft River on slippery rocks on 8 September; they crossed the Burnside River in the remaining made-down canoe on 9 September; they crossed the Burnside again at Belanger Rapids on 14 September, losing Franklin's journal when the canoe upset.

They might possibly have saved two days had they stayed on the north and west sides of Kathawachaga Lake, but as it was they did not meet any insuperable obstacle until they arrived on 26 September, three days after leaving the last canoe behind, at the raging, icy waters of the Coppermine. Here at Obstruction Rapids everything went wrong. The unfortunate and demoralizing eight-day delay broke their spirits. Richardson tells us that the men then "bitterly execrated their folly and impatience in breaking the canoe and the remainder of the day was spent in wandering slowly along the river, looking in vain for a fordable place and inventing schemes for crossing, no sooner devised than abandoned." It is no wonder that by 27 September the voyageurs, "through despondency, had become careless and disobedient. They had ceased to dread punishment or hope for reward."

There were two heroic but premature and poorly managed attempts to cross the river on 29 September. First St Germain tried to paddle a raft of insufficiently buoyant green willows against a wind blowing from the opposite bank. Next Richardson attempted to swim across, carrying a line. A more buoyant raft was prepared the next day but never used. Perhaps they should have waited for a favourable wind. Perhaps the men who went back to the campsites of 24 and 25 September in a vain search for pitch could have brought several bundles of the six- or seven-foot spruce poles that were available there. Perhaps it would have been worthwhile to go back to where the remnants of the last canoe had been abandoned on 23 September. Back and St Germain instead spent 27 to 30 September in a fruitless search for wood along the shores of Point Lake.

A cockleshell craft of painted canvas was finally completed by St Germain on 4 October but it was too late. Junius had wandered away, never to return. Although the nineteen remaining men all survived the crossing of Obstruction Rapids on 4 October, they were so chilled, hungry, and weak that the days of many were numbered. At this point, on the basis of strength, they divided into three groups.

George Back was delegated by Franklin to lead the advance group to contact Akaicho and his hunters. Back took the strongest men, Pierre St Germain, Solomon Belanger, and Gabriel Beauparlant, and in five days hiked the forty-two statute miles from the Coppermine River crossing to the deserted buildings at Fort Enterprise. Akaicho's help was desperately needed, but he was not waiting there with provisions as both Franklin and Hood had been promised. Akaicho simply did not believe that the "crazy white men" would reappear alive.[73]

Richardson's journal is much more specific than Franklin's concerning the range of the nomadic Indians' movements when following the caribou. The locations, given by Richardson for six of Akaicho's 1820–1 campsites, help us to understand why the rescue at Fort Enterprise the following winter was so long delayed. In the winter of 1820–1, Akaicho's camp on 23 October had been somewhere just south of Winter Lake; on 8 January it was near Reindeer Lake, about forty statute miles south-southwest of Fort Enterprise; on 12 February it was southwest of Fort Enterprise; on 28 March, at a lake only twelve miles from the fort; on 29 April, south of the midpart of Snare Lake; on 2 May Akaicho was south of the Ghost River, at exactly 64° north latitude, about forty-five miles southwest of Fort Enterprise. From the known sites of the previous winter, Back might therefore have looked first for Akaicho's tribe within the triangle bounded by

Winter, Snare, and Reindeer lakes, even though these Indians were known to follow caribou widely over thousands of square miles and to move south to trade at Fort Providence after freeze-up. Indeed, St Germain said he had been told by Akaicho to look for him first along Roundrock Lake.

After stopping two days at Fort Enterprise to make mittens and snowshoes, Back's party of four set out on the morning of 11 October, only hours before Franklin's middle group arrived at the fort. That night Back was forced to camp only three miles from the fort at the head of Roundrock Lake, to warm up St Germain who had fallen through the ice. In the following days Back's weakening party progressed only a few miles along the lake. On 14 October Back sent Solomon Belanger back to Fort Enterprise for further instructions from Franklin. Belanger in turn fell through the ice of the rapids and took four days to recuperate in the fort. He returned on 18 October with Franklin's instructions for Back to proceed at once to Reindeer Lake. In the meantime, Back and St Germain barely kept alive by finding four caribou heads, though unfortunately not in time to save Beauparlant, who froze to death beside the lake on 16 October. St Germain and Belanger resolutely refused to move on, victims of the counterproductive vicious cycle of decreased strength and interest brought on by famine. Back tells us that he and the two men remained within ten miles of Fort Enterprise until they recouped some strength after finding another twelve caribou heads and half a caribou carcass. Finally, on 30 October they set out, camping that night at the head of Roundrock Lake within three miles of the fort, which they did not visit. During the next four days these surviving members of the "advance group" walked south, covering about ten miles a day, until they stumbled upon recent footprints which led them to Akaicho's camp on Upper Carp Lake.

We must now return to the tragic chronicle of the remaining two groups who were still travelling together when the stronger men of the advance group forged on ahead after the crossing of Obstruction Rapids on 4 October. Two days later, on 6 October, Credit and Vaillant, weakened by diarrhea, fell behind and perished. On 7 October Hood was too weak to go on, so Richardson and Hepburn volunteered to stay behind with him while Franklin's middle group of Augustus, Jean Baptiste Adam, Joseph Benoit, Joseph Peltier, and François Semandrè plodded on to Fort Enterprise. All were of course counting on help from Akaicho's Indians, who were expected to rescue them in less than a week, within two or three days of Back's arrival at Fort Enterprise. Jean Baptiste Belanger, Ignace Perrault, Vincenza Fontano, and Michel Teroahauté carried on with Franklin until 8 October, but then turned back towards the tent of Richardson and Hood. On 9 October only Michel, the Iroquois Indian who was alone among the voyageurs in using his first name rather than his surname, arrived at the tent. Thereupon hangs a tale of cannibalism and accusations of murder.

When Michel on 11 October brought welcome meat to Richardson, Hood, and Hepburn, it had an unfamiliar taste. Michel said it was wolf meat, from an animal killed when gored by the horns of a caribou – a somewhat implausible story. Hood, steadily weaker, was near death. Michel became moody, with long absences from the others. On October 20 Hood's suffering was ended by a bullet through the back of his head, evidently fired by Michel who was alone with him at the time. Two days later Richardson and Hepburn were left alone to discuss the incident and form an opinion as to Michel's guilt. Richardson then shot Michel through the head. Of the rearward group of nine, only Richardson and Hepburn survived.

Meanwhile, after nine days' rest at Fort Enterprise, the three strongest men of the middle group, Franklin, Joseph Benoit, and Augustus, started south on 20 October to seek Akaicho. Franklin wore the caribou-skin clothing of Joseph Peltier and François Semandrè, who with Jean Baptiste Adam were too weak to travel. Like Back, they camped at the head of Roundrock Lake, where Franklin from weakness was forced to return to the fort. There he rejoined Adam, Peltier, and Semandrè in the cold and cheerless buildings of Fort Enterprise, portions of which they tore apart for firewood. The four made a pathetic group, growing weaker day by day, their only food the refuse from the previous winter's camp.

On 29 October the four were joined at the fort by Richardson and Hepburn, the only survivors of the rearward group. The augmented group was once again reduced to four with the deaths from starvation of Peltier and Semandrè during the night of 1–2 November.

Back tells us that Augustus and Benoit meanwhile carried on slowly for two weeks, made an unfortunate detour to the east, killed four caribou, rested five days, and finally reached Akaicho's camp on the morning of 3 November. St Germain joined them late that evening, and Back and Belanger at 3.30 PM the next day. Although Back was the last of the four to arrive and to inform Akaicho of the desperate situation at Fort Enterprise, it was no doubt his appearance and his exhortations that galvanized the Indians into mounting a rescue party. The day before, when Augustus and Benoit, and then St Germain had arrived, the fatalistic Indians, knowing that those in the fort were even weaker, probably had given up Franklin and Richardson for dead.

Nevertheless, at Fort Enterprise, Franklin, Richardson, and their remaining two companions were still awaiting rescue. On 7 November Franklin heard a musket shot and a shout and feared that a part of the building, in being torn apart for fuel, had fallen on Richardson or Hepburn. Mercifully it was the first rescue party of three Indians, Crooked-foot, The Rat, and Boudelkell, who had travelled about forty-eight nautical or fifty-five statute miles in two-and-a-half days with meat for the dying men. Adam was so weak that he could scarcely speak and was unable to rise. Richardson later wrote to his wife that the Indians "wept on beholding the deplorable condition to which we were reduced."[74]

The second and more heavily laden Indian relief party of Thoveeyorre and The Fop, with their wives dragging the sledges and accompanied by Benoit, left the south end of Upper Carp Lake on 10 November. Their journey back to Fort

Enterprise took exactly five days. They picked up Crooked-foot, who had left Fort Enterprise on 13 November, one day's journey from the fort.

Strengthened by the meat brought to them on 7 and 15 November, Franklin, Richardson, Hepburn, and Adam left Fort Enterprise early on 16 November on their slow, halting journey south to Akaicho's camp. Richardson tells of the devoted care he and Franklin received from Crooked-foot, Thoveeyorre, and The Fop. The Indians cooked for them and fed them, lent them their snowshoes while doing without themselves, protected them from frostbite, and helped them up when they fell. "They nursed and fed us with the same tenderness they would have bestowed on their own infants," said Richardson in a letter home.[75] He was still very weak.

Franklin and Richardson reached the outpost camp occupied by the parents of Akaicho's wife and of Thoveeyorre on 25 November. Akaicho's camp by then was a few miles farther south along the Nine Lakes, three nautical miles north of Icy Portage, for he had already moved four times since leaving Upper Carp Lake on the slow trek towards Fort Providence. When Franklin and Richardson arrived the next day at Akaicho's camp, the officers were given the most delicate bits of meat, carefully selected by the old women, and they were visited by many Indians, each of whom presented them with meat. They were soon offered more than they could have consumed in a week. Franklin again developed gastrointestinal symptoms from this surfeit of food and to cure him Akaicho himself brewed up a soup of blood, fish, and lichens. More compassionate care could not have been given.

Another true measure of Akaicho's character was his philosophic and cheerful manner on arrival at Fort Providence, when he learned that the goods promised him as payment and reward had not arrived. His stoicism was coupled with an admirable sense of humour; Akaicho, on 14 December 1821, thinking that most Indians were in perennial debt to the fur companies, noted that at least this was "the first time that the White people have been indebted to the Red Knife Indians."

In truth, Franklin, Richardson, and Hepburn owed much more than money and goods to Akaicho – they owed their lives to him and his people. All three Englishmen were within a few days of death when food was finally brought them at Fort Enterprise on 7 November. In all, four of the five Englishmen on the expedition lived. In startling contrast, only two of the eleven voyageurs survived. Under the circumstances, one might have expected the two survivors, Joseph Benoit and Solomon Belanger, to refuse to leave Fort Providence until they were rested and had gained weight, perhaps never again to make a long trek. Amazingly, Joseph Benoit trekked back to Fort Enterprise with the Indians from Akaicho's camp, taking two trains of meat for the men, and then helped the survivors back to Fort Providence. Solomon Belanger was one of two messengers who on 6 December brought fresh clothing and the packet of mail telling of the promotions of the officers, when they were yet six days' march north of Fort Providence. Indeed, the eleven voyageurs remain the unsung heroes of this important expedition.

The lack of food at Fort Enterprise on the return of the survivors requires some explanation. Franklin had depended on Akaicho having provisions for them at the fort as promised. Yet Akaicho had told Wentzel that the Indians "had not the least hopes of ever seeing one person return from the Expedition," and thus prepared nothing:

> ... the party of Indians, on whom I had placed the utmost confidence and dependance, was Humpy and the White Capot Guide, with their sons, and several of the discharged hunters from the Expedition. This party was well-disposed, and readily promised to collect provisions for the possible return of the Expedition, provided they could get a supply of ammunition from Fort Providence; for when I came up with them [Wentzel left the mouth of the Coppermine on 19 July, travelled 11 days without meat, and arrived at Akaicho's camp sometime in September] they were actually starving, and converting old axes into ball, having no other substitute – this was unlucky. Yet they were well inclined, and I expected to find means at Fort Providence to send them a supply, in which I was, however, disappointed, for I found that establishment quite destitute of necessaries; and then shortly after I had left them, they had the misfortune of losing three of their hunters, who were drowned in Martin Lake: this accident was, of all others, the most fatal that could have happened – a truth which no one, who has the least knowledge of the Indian character, will deny; and as they were nearly connected by relationship to the Leader, Humpy, and White Capot Guide, the three leading men of this part of the Copper Indian Tribe, it had the effect of unhinging (if I may use the expression) the minds of all these families, and finally destroying all the fond hopes I had so sanguinely conceived of their assisting the Expedition, should it come back by the Annadessé River, of which they were not certain.[76]

In a letter to Hood's father, Richardson told a similar story in less detail: "The grievous disappointment we experienced in not finding the supply of provision at Fort Enterprise, solemnly promised to us by the Indians, arose partly from the natural fickleness of that people, which renders them expert in finding reasons for changing an arrangement however important, but principally from two of their hunters having been drowned by the oversetting of a canoe. As usual on such an occasion, the rest threw away their clothing, broke their guns, and thus by their mode of expressing their grief curtailed themselves of the means of procuring their food."[77]

PIERRE ST GERMAIN

More than any other man, Pierre St Germain deserves credit for the survival of the four Englishmen. Richardson's journal and Robert McVicar's unpublished Fort Resolution journals for 1819–20 and 1820–1 shed considerable light on the character of this hunter and interpreter.

St Germain, part French and part Indian ("Half Gentry" in George Simpson's[78] and "half-breed" in George Back's terms), had worked under McVicar at the Hudson's Bay Company post at Fort Resolution in 1819–20. St Germain's employers recognized his ability but also his independent ways. Colin Robertson, superintendent of the Athabasca department, in his 1819 instructions to McVicar described St Germain as "an intelligent young man"[79] and on 5 June 1820 wrote: "I have given up an excellent Chippeyan interpreter, St. Germain."[80] McVicar considered him indispensable, mentioning how he could travel without either a blanket or provisions, but also noted his liking for alcohol, especially when "for his pleasure" St Germain delayed his departure from Fort Wedderburn (opposite Fort Chipewyan on Lake Athabasca) until after the new year's celebrations of 1820: "his long stay shews a complete contempt for the interests of the concern." Later, McVicar wrote of "that scoundrel's machinations … a dangerous man."[81] George Simpson, the new HBC governor, on 26 January 1821 wrote "St. Germain is out of a bad nest."[82]

Soon after arriving at Fort Resolution on 24 July 1820, Franklin "visited the Hudson's Bay Company post on the same island, and engaged Pierre St. Germain, an interpreter for the Copper Indians."[83] In fact, Franklin's letter written at Fort Wedderburn on 20 June was delivered to McVicar at Fort Resolution on 1 July 1820, and in turn enclosed a letter from Colin Robertson dated 5 June: "Being given to understand that Pierrish St. Germent has expressed a wish to join the Expedition under the command of Lieut. Franklin and others – and as I consider St. Germent particularly calculated for rendering much service to these Gentlemen, not only from his knowledge of the Country but the Languages and habits of the Natives, I therefore give him full permission to enter into a new Engagement with the above party."[84]

McVicar's journal entry of 2 July noted that "St. Germent has joined the service of the Expedition and has taken up his quarters in the N. Wt. Fort."[85] St Germain was then receiving what McVicar considered "exorbitant" wages of £100 per year, but Franklin to obtain his services was forced to offer St Germain £150 (3000 Halifax livres) per year, two-and-a-half times the amount he offered a voyageur.[86] Richardson considered St Germain one of the most reliable men on the expedition, one who had the most influence with the Indians. St Germain was intelligent, determined, and, when reasonably fed, indefatigable. He made the preliminary trip to Point Lake with Back and Hood, 29 August–10 September 1820. During the winter of 1820–1 he made the trip from Fort Enterprise to Fort Resolution, bringing back the two Eskimos, Augustus and Junius.

St Germain was also somewhat of a troublemaker, and he thereby gained the enmity of both Franklin and Back. As early as 23 March 1821 St Germain expressed his concern about the dangers involved in the proposed arctic explorations and shared his views with Akaicho's Indians. Because of this indiscretion, Franklin that day described him as "an artful man," and said he was "perfectly satisfied of his baseness."[87] Franklin suspected the Indian hunters and St Germain were lessening their efforts in the hope of preventing the expedition from even making a start, and threatened to "convey him to England for trial if the Expedition should be stopped through his fault."[88] At the mouth of the Coppermine on 19 July, Adam and St Germain "made many urgent requests to be allowed to return with Mr. Wentzel." Franklin denied them, because the two interpreters had already proved to be the party's only skilled hunters. To prevent their "plan for eloping" they were in fact conscripted: "... lest they should leave us by stealth, their motions were strictly watched ... the rest of the men knowing that their own safety would have been compromised had they succeeded, kept a watchful eye over them."[89]

Throughout the entire arctic journey St Germain was by far the most successful hunter. Strong, resourceful, practical, a man of great stamina, his dexterity was evident in crossing the Burnside in a made-down canoe on 9 September, in ferrying Franklin across Belanger Rapids on 14 September, and in manipulating the little makeshift canvas craft across Obstruction Rapids on 4 October. One can sense the varying degrees of Richardson's affection for St Germain as he calls him in turn: Pierre, Pierez, Perez, and Pieresh; he used the affectionate diminutive Pierrot after St Germain had been particularly helpful. However, Richardson's use of "Pierrot" confused Franklin greatly and caused him twice in the published journal to ascribe actions to Perrault that in Richardson's daily journal are credited to St Germain. One of these was the sharing of an extra portion of meat with the officers on 14 September, an act of generosity singled out for special mention in Louis Melzack's introduction to the recent reprint of Franklin's journal.[90] The second was the crucial killing of a fine caribou on 15 September, when they were starving.

Franklin was helpless during St Germain's four-day absence, searching unsuccessfully for wood with which to make a raft. St Germain alone had the experience and the ability to improvise, that allowed him single-handedly to make the fragments of "painted canvas" [Richardson] or "oil-cloth" [Back] into a cockleshell that finally transported everyone across Obstruction Rapids on 4 October.

Pierre St Germain was an indispensable man, without whom Franklin, Richardson, Back, and Hepburn would have perished. It was a close call indeed. Without St Germain, we would have had no surviving officers, no published journals, and no books of natural history observations.

CANNIBALISM AND MURDER CHARGES

One cannot avoid the conclusion that on at least one occasion (11 October) Richardson, Hepburn, and Michel ate human flesh. Richardson's "The account drawn up and transmitted home," as edited by Franklin and as reproduced in this book, admits this fact and also alludes to "circumstances, the detail of which may be spared," that could be construed as an admission that he has not told the whole story. Most probably Richardson wished to avoid giving offence to his sensitive readers. In the 1820s, much more so than today, it was believed preferable to die rather than to survive by eating the flesh of a dead comrade. Dr John Rae, thirty-three years after this event, mentioned evidence suggesting cannibalism among the dying men of the third Franklin expedition, and was not forgiven for his breach of decorum.[91]

We shall never know whether Michel killed one or more of his three comrades, or simply cut up their flesh after they had died of fatigue, starvation, and exposure, and we shall never know whether Richardson ate the flesh of one of the voyageurs knowingly or unknowingly. But eat it he did. Without doubt Michel kept up his strength by eating human flesh, and this may explain his mysterious absences from Richardson's tent.

What then was the source of the rumours of cannibalism that circulated among the Copper Indians, rumours which Wentzel referred to in a letter of 1 March 1824?[92] Not one of the weakest voyageurs who stayed back with Richardson's rearward party survived to give a first-hand report. Hepburn was the only witness and he may well have been asked to say nothing. Later, as a garrulous sixty-two-year-old who accompanied the French expedition under Joseph René Bellot in the search for the missing third Franklin expedition, Hepburn certainly talked a lot about the first Franklin expedition and in particular about Lieutenant Hood fathering the baby born to Greenstockings. Apparently, however, he did not play up the story of Michel and cannibalism.[93]

As a forthright man, Richardson would later have given Franklin a full report at Fort Enterprise, and his story might have been overheard by Adam and later relayed to others. However, the mere fact of the survival of four of five Englishmen, and the disappearance of nine of eleven voyageurs, would alone have been sufficient to start such rumours, even without well-founded basis in fact.

An unpublished letter preserved within the Fort Resolution journal of 1826–7 tells more of Franklin's experience with the widespread transmission of rumours throughout the fur countries during his first expedition:

> There is no country where rumours spread so rapidly and generally so unlike the original reports as in this, and there is no point on which I am more guarded, and should wish my friends to be likewise than the spreading of

reports whether favourable or unfavourable respecting the present Expedition ... I hope therefore that they will repress all rumours which may come to them by any other channel – for if they once get circulated either by Indians, women, or the voyageurs, they will undoubtedly spread and perhaps reach England and cause unnecessary pain to our relations and friends. That this is not an unnecessary caution we have been taught by the experience of our last voyage, when it was reported and believed at Fort Wedderburn that the Expedition was enclosed by the Esquimaux on an Island, at the time we were at Fort Enterprise, and had not been within 200 miles of that tribe ...[94]

Wentzel said of the four officers "that they acted on some occasions imprudently, injudiciously and showed in one particular instance an unpardonable want of conduct," and in the letter of 1 March 1824 he told how Lieutenant Back, when he stopped at Fort Chipewyan en route to England, had told him that "there had been dissensions among themselves" and had said, "to tell the truth, Wentzel, things have taken place which must not be known."[95] Wentzel had already speculated in an earlier letter (10 April 1823) that "it is doubtful whether, from the distant scene of their transactions, an authentic account of their operations will ever meet the public eye in England."[96]

Wentzel was particularly hard on Richardson, for whom he reserved the accusation of "unpardonable want of conduct." He had acquired a great dislike for the doctor; he appeared to believe that Richardson was responsible for the murder of Michel and "richly merited to be punished."[97] His accusations are indeed disturbing and have been given credence by Richard Glover.[98]

The analysis of Stefansson is pertinent:

It seems clear from the evidence that Michel killed one or more of the men he was suspected of killing; that important or chief in the motive for killing was that he was going to eat them; that his mysterious absences and his futile caribou hunts were visits to the places where he could eat human flesh; and that he had the hatchet with him for this purpose – north of Slave Lake at this time of year the frosts are hard and meat cannot be sliced with a knife.

The murder of Hood was no doubt chiefly so that the party would not have to stay in camp and nurse him but would be free to move ahead towards the Fort. As Richardson states, it was pretty clearly Michel's purpose to kill him and Hepburn and to arrive at the Fort as a sole survivor, free to explain how and why the others had dropped behind or died.[99]

Richardson, then, would have killed Michel in self-defence, reasonably certain that Michel had killed Hood and perhaps one or more fellow voyageurs. Unfortunately for later historians, he did not transcribe into his journal the entries for these contentious three weeks, 8–29 October. Instead he wrote only the confidential letter to the Admiralty and it, like the remainder of

Franklin's narrative, was most certainly modified for public perusal. Several searches of Admiralty records, one at the request of Robert E. Johnson, have failed to locate Richardson's original report. I feel, however, that the published version may be reasonably close to the truth; it is undoubtedly more dependable than rumours and second- or even third-hand reports transmitted across hundreds of miles. Richardson, after all, was a man with a life-long reputation for integrity and compassion.

RICHARDSON'S ACHIEVEMENTS

Though much attention has been focused on Franklin as the leader of the expedition, Richardson decidedly outdistanced Franklin in his qualities of mind and in the contributions these enabled him to make to science. Yet Richardson was not the kind of man to push himself into the limelight or to demand personal recognition. It was a mark of his "freedom from pretension"[100] and of his generosity of spirit that he should commend his leader for the support always accorded him. Mr Franklin, he said, gave him "every assistance in collecting specimens that was in his power to give; his sympathy encouraged me, and his claims which, as commanding officer, he might have to the reputation of whatever was done by one of his subordinates, he honourably and cheerfully ceded to him who did the work, in my case as in others. So that contributions were made to science, no personal interests were allowed to interfere."[101]

This book abundantly illustrates the character and variety of Richardson's attainments during the first Arctic Land Expedition. Owing to more favourable circumstances, Richardson's achievements were even more noteworthy during the second Arctic Land Expedition, for this time the two fur-trading companies were now amalgamated under the name of the Hudson's Bay Company and could offer excellent support; most of the crew were disciplined naval men; they travelled in larger, stronger boats of mahogany and ash, and they were able to use the eminently navigable Mackenzie River.

Richardson's great proficiency as a surveyor became evident from his completion of two major tasks. During the last three weeks of August 1825 he mapped by canoe about 450 miles of the northern shoreline of Great Bear Lake, the fourth largest lake in North America. Between 10 and 23 April 1826 he mapped by ice sled the southern shoreline as far as an unnamed island, now known as Richardson Island, in the bottom of McTavish Arm. Indeed, all five arms of this giant lake were given names of fur company men by Richardson. In the summer of 1826 Richardson and Franklin parted near the mouth of the Mackenzie. Franklin's party went west and mapped only 374 miles of ocean shoreline; because of fog, they failed by 160 miles to meet the sledge party sent to meet them from Beechey's ship *Blossom* at Cape Barrow. Meanwhile, Richardson's party mapped 863 miles of new coastline between the mouths of the Mackenzie and the Coppermine, covering 1980 statute miles in only seventy-one days.

Richardson's natural history contributions, aided by assistant natural-ist Thomas Drummond, were also of special importance on this second expedition. The seven new species of birds that he collected (Trumpeter Swan, White-tailed Ptarmigan, Forster's Tern, Black-backed Woodpecker, Olive-sided Flycatcher, Clay-colored Sparrow, and Smith's Longspur)[102] have retained their priority of recognition to this day, as have subspecies of the Canada Goose, Hairy Woodpecker, Swainson's Thrush, Varied Thrush, Loggerhead Shrike, Rosy Finch, and Rufous-sided Towhee.[103] Allan R. Phillips, the foremost authority on Empidonax flycatchers, feels that Richardson's specimen of the Least Flycatcher also deserves priority.[104] In addition, vernacular names such as Swainson's Hawk,[105] Richardson's Merlin,[106] Richardson's Owl,[107] and Richardson's Wood Pewee[108] were given by later authorities to specimens first collected by Richardson. Proportionately similar contributions were made to mammalogy, ichthyology, and botany, and to a lesser extent, entomology, as is evident in the four volumes of *Fauna Boreali-Americana* and in Hooker's *Flora Boreali-Americana*.

On the second expedition, Richardson had his most interesting surgical patient. Finan McDonald had been travelling downstream on the North Saskatchewan with fur traders Edward Ermatinger and John Rowand and the famous botanist David Douglas, who was on his way back to England from the Pacific. When they stopped on 2 June, somewhere between the mouths of the Battle River and Eagle Creek, Finan McDonald was badly gored by a wounded buffalo bull. Ermatinger described the accident: "The first blow ... gored the most fleshy part of the thigh nearly to the bone ... his whole side is bruised black and blue and some of his ribs appear to be broken."[103] Richardson added that McDonald "had the presence of mind to seize the animal by the long hair on its forehead as it struck him on the side with its horn, and being a remarkably tall and powerful man, a struggle ensued, which continued until his wrist was severely sprained, and his arm was rendered powerless; he then fell, and after receiving two or three blows became senseless. Shortly afterwards he was found by his companions lying bathed in blood."[110] Douglas bound up McDonald's wounds and gave him a stiff dose of twenty-five drops of laudanum, which procured sleep.[111] The party carried McDonald to the boat and they drifted down-river all night in the hopes of finding Dr Richardson at Carlton, but the journal entry there for 5 June states that "Mr. Finan McDonald proceded on to Cumberland House with one Boat & 5 Men for the purpose of getting Doctor Richardson assistance who is at Cumberland House."[112] The Cumberland House journal entry of 8 June in turn states "Ten boats arrived today ... McDonald ... has been much bruised by a wounded bull in the plains. So much so that he must be carried in and out of the boats. After we had him carried in a room Dr. Richardson attended him."[113] Richardson later reported that McDonald "recovered from the immediate effects of the injuries he received, but died a few months afterwards."[114] This report of death proved to be erroneous, for McDonald lived to become a captain in the militia in Glengarry County, Upper Canada.[115]

After his years of major exploration were over, Richardson continued to make important contributions to science. For example, he was a key member of the Strickland Committee which composed the authoritative and lasting "Series of Propositions for Rendering the Nomenclature of Zoology Uniform and Permanent," known since as the "Rules of the British Association" or as "The Stricklandian Code."[116] Paul Farber observes that the Strickland report, "clear, practical and simple," was quickly accepted and "established the law of priority." Further, this "reform of nomenclature gave zoology, and ornithology in particular, a common language ... and removed much unnecessary confusion."[117]

From a historical perspective, we can now understand that Richardson's naturalist years coincided happily and exactly with what Lynn Barber has termed the "Heyday of Natural History (1820–1870)," when "natural theology made the study of natural history not only respectable, but almost a pious duty" and "the purpose of studying Nature was to approach a closer knowledge of God."[118] To catalogue all of God's creation, classification became the "central and defining task."[119] In this cataloguing, Richardson played a major role, in the 1820s as a field naturalist, and thereafter as a classifier of specimens brought by others from remote regions.

Richardson thus experienced first-hand the "Age of Revolution" as defined by Eric J. Hobsbawm, who considers that 1830 marked a "turning-point in ... the history of industrialization and urbanization ... in the history of human migrations ... in the arts and of ideology."[120] Farber adds that the year 1830 was not only Hobsbawm's social turning-point, but also marked the end of the "heroic age" of exploration and the emergence of separate disciplines (not yet professions) such as ornithology from the general meld of natural history.[121] It was in the discipline of ichthyology that Richardson made his greatest contribution, describing forty-three still-accepted genera of fish[122] and well over two hundred new species of fish. For the eighth edition of the *Encyclopaedia Britannica*, Richardson wrote a 128-page article on ichthyology, a 21-page article on polar regions, and a 6-page biography of John Franklin.

In his medical vocation, Richardson became the chief medical officer of Haslar Hospital, then the largest hospital in the world and the largest brick building in the British empire. He raised the quality of nursing care in the navy, improved the treatment of mental disease in sailors, and introduced general anaesthesia into naval surgery.[123] He helped a young surgeon at Haslar, Thomas Henry Huxley, to get his first appointment as a zoologist.

A member of the prestigious Arctic Council, Richardson in 1848 led a strenuous, well-organized searching expedition for his old chief, John Franklin, whose ill-fated third expedition had not been heard from for three years. In the fastest boat and canoe travel on record, Richardson and Dr John Rae left Montreal on 19 April and spent August searching the familiar coastline between the mouths of the Mackenzie and the Coppermine. Although nearing his sixty-first birthday,

Richardson kept up to the younger men on the fifteen-day overland march back to Great Bear Lake.[124]

Richardson was knighted in 1846, made Companion of the Bath in 1850, received the royal medal of the Royal Society of London in 1856, and the degree of LLD from Trinity College, Dublin, in 1857. His acceptance speech on receipt of the medal is indicative of his modesty:

> ... I had to travel over a country reaching from the great American lakes to the islands of the Arctic Sea, and embracing more than the fourth of the distance from the equator to the pole, which had never before been visited by a professional naturalist. I perceived at once the magnitude of the field, and comprehended at a glance that it was far beyond my grasp. The only previous training I had was the little natural science that I had learnt at my northern Alma Mater as a collateral branch of my medical education, but I thought that I could at least record what I saw; and I determined so to do as intelligently as I could and without exaggeration, hoping in this way to furnish facts on which the leaders of science might reason, and thus promote the progress of Natural History to the extent of my limited ability. This was the rule I followed during the eight years that I passed in those countries actually engaged in the several expeditions.[125]

No less a man than Charles Darwin praised his thoroughness when he said, "Respect good describers like Richardson."[126]

Dr David Alexander Stewart, before the combined annual meetings of the British and Canadian Medical Associations in Winnipeg in 1930, paid one of the finest tributes to Richardson: "... men of our Northland should have a special interest in one who traversed it in three laborious expeditions, lived nearly eight years in it, and a lifetime in working over its natural history. Plants of Northern Canada named by and for Richardson would make a garden of respectable size, and animals named by and for him a considerable zoo ... He had in his life many of the conventional honours, and some special marks of distinction as well. His was perhaps a life of industry more than a life of genius, but it was a full, good life, and in many ways even a great life. It is not every day that we meet in one person – surgeon, physician, sailor, soldier, administrator, explorer, naturalist, author, and scholar, who has been eminent in some roles and commendable in all."[127]

Appendix A

After a century and a half of omission and oversight, a complete list of birds described by Richardson during the first Arctic Land Expedition is presented herewith. Richardson identified, collected, and described many more birds than has been evident from a perusal of Joseph Sabine's "Zoological Appendix v" in Franklin, *Journey*.

Five important points must be kept in mind:

1. Specimens attributed to "Franklin" or "the Expedition" were collected by John Richardson and his assistant, Robert Hood.

2. Most bird or mammal specimens in Sabine's account were included in a small shipment from York Factory in 1819, and a second, larger shipment from Cumberland House in June 1820. Many of these specimens were collected at Cumberland House and a few were obtained during Richardson's side-trip to Carlton House in May 1820.

3. Because of the jealousy and antipathy between Richardson and Joseph Sabine, the man who was unfairly given the former's collection to prepare for publication, few of the bird descriptions in Richardson's journal and only a portion of the corresponding specimens were seen by Sabine.

4. Most waterfowl species expected in the area, including a few erroneous entries, were simply listed by Sabine without further commentary, since no specimens had been provided for these species in his simple list.

5. The geographic term "Hudson's Bay" is by no means restricted to the bay itself, but includes all of the Hudson's Bay Territories, or Rupert's Land, to the Rocky Mountains.[1] The inhabitants of this vast area were sometimes called "Hudsonians," and new Latin names applied to a magpie from Cumberland House, 400 miles inland, and to a skunk from Carlton House, 600 miles inland, were, respectively, *hudsonia* and *hudsonica*.

Bird species are presented in the order of the *Sixth American Ornitholog-*

ists' Union Check-List of North American Birds. Species for which there is additional information not given by Sabine are indicated by an asterisk (*); those completely omitted by Sabine, by a dagger (†); and species credited as being new species for fifty years or more, previously undescribed, by a double dagger (‡).

When available, quotations from Sabine's Appendix are given first (Sabine, "Appendix"), followed by species mentioned in Hood's journal or painted by Hood (Houston, ed., *To the Arctic by Canoe*). Accounts from the narrative portion of Richardson's journal are given with the date of entry and (JR) while those from the last half of his journal, devoted to natural history descriptions from Fort Resolution and York Factory after his narrative had ceased, are given with his journal page numbers and (JR).

In spite of Richardson's self-effacing generosity in allowing William Swainson's name to be placed ahead of his on the title page of *Fauna Boreali-Americana*, II: *The Birds*, all useful information of current interest in the book is by Richardson; quotations from his entries are credited as (Richardson, *Birds*).[2] Quotations from his Zoological Appendix to Parry's *Second Voyage* are credited as (Richardson, "Appendix"),[3] and from *Fauna Boreali-Americana*, I: *The Mammals* as (Richardson, *Mammals*). Full citations of sources will be found in the Bibliography.

Red-throated Loon, *Gavia stellata* (Pontoppidan)
"This species, though spread over the whole Arctic Regions, is particularly abundant in Hudson's Bay, and in the lakes in the interior" (Sabine, "Appendix," p. 703).

†Arctic Loon, *Gavia arctica* (Linnaeus)
Painted at Fort Enterprise by Robert Hood in the spring of 1821, plate 23 (Houston, ed., *To the Arctic by Canoe*). "... common on the shores of Hudson's Bay ... rarely seen in the interior [correct for southern areas such as Carlton House and Cumberland House] (Richardson, *Birds*, p. 475). The first loons returned to Fort Enterprise on 11 May 1821 (JR, p. 51), but the species represented is not known.

*Common Loon, *Gavia immer* (Brünnich)
"It is found in the northern countries of both worlds, breeding and living on the sides of lakes, and going southwards in severe weather" (Sabine, "Appendix," p. 703). Painted by Robert Hood at Cumberland House, 1819–20, one of two of Hood's bird paintings that have not yet been published. Specimen "killed in July 1822 on the English River [Churchill River in late June] differing from it [The Yellow-billed Loon] only in having a black bill and the white spots on the body more distinct and regular ... The Indians make neat and strong bags of the skins of this bird, for holding their smoking materials. Fire steel &c. Their cry is melancholly sometimes resembling the howling of a wolf at other times strongly imitating the cry of a man in distress. They are caught in the fishing nets in

considerable numbers at some stations in the spring and autumn but their flesh is coarse" (JR, p. 316).

‡Yellow-billed Loon, *Gavia adamsii* (Gray)

"Colymbus _____? Copper-Indian, Palkyeh. Esk. Kuglooliek. The head and neck have a shining black colour with some strong green reflexions about the middle of the neck there is on each side a white spot, streaked longitudinally with black and there is one similar but smaller spot on the throat, a little behind the lower jaw. The feathers on the anterior part of the back are black, each with two small spots of white. These spots, arranged in transverse rows, increase in size towards the middle of the back and over the roots of the wings the white predominates. The tail and tail coverts have an uniform dirty brown colour, with a few scattered white specks towards the sides. The primary wing feathers are brownish black; the second is the longest, but the first is very little shorter. The secondaries are thinly speckled with white. The belly, vent feathers and under surface of the tail are pure white; but the sides of the bird under the wings are spotted black and white like the back, the white spots, however, being smaller, more distant and better defined. The under surface of the wing exhibits various shades of dirty brownish-white.

"The bill strong and awl-shaped but flattened on the sides or compressed is 4½ inches long, and has a dirty yellowish white colour. The two mandibles are applied to each other in a straight line, and the margin of the under one is received by a groove of the upper one. The ridge of the upper mandible is obtuse and straight, and a slight oblique groove proceeds from the anterior end of the nostrils which are slits about 5 lines in length. The short feathers which cover the base of the bill terminate in a point above the middle of the nostrils. The lower jaw is arched or boat-shaped inferiorly being nearly straight from its base to the termination of the symphysis and from thence slanting upwards or accuminated to form the point. The accuminated part is about one third of the whole length of the mandible.

"The legs (tarsi) are compressed and scaly. The three anterior toes are joined by webs which extend to the extremities of the nails. The nails themselves are thin, convex and obtuse, resembling those of the human hand but having a more oblong form and unequal sides. The outer toe is longest and has five articulations. The next has only four, but its bones are longer; and the one next the thumb is still shorter having only three phalanxes. It is furnished with a scaly membranous margin which is lined inferiorly by a continuation of the web. The thumb is about one inch long and is terminated by a pointed hooked nail. Its inner margin has a small scaly appendix. The length of this bird from the tip of the bill to the extremity of the tail is two feet eight inches. The tail scarcely exceeds one inch. Its envergure [wing-span] is about 4 feet. The first and second primary wing feathers are about 9 inches long" (JR, 1 November 1820, pp. 23–5).

The Yellow-billed Loon was unrecognized until August 1859, when its description was published by G.R. Gray,[4] from a specimen from "Russian America through Behring's Straits," eight years before Alaska was purchased by the United States.

Pied-billed Grebe, *Podilymbus podiceps* (Linnaeus)
"The specimen ... is supposed to be that of a male" (Sabine, "Appendix," p. 693). Richardson collected a specimen at Great Slave Lake in May 1822 (Richardson, *Birds*, p. 412).

*Horned Grebe, *Podiceps auritus* (Linnaeus)
"... it breeds in the countries round Hudson's Bay, and retires southward for the winter" (Sabine, "Appendix," p. 693). Specimen at Great Slave Lake 22 May 1822 (JR, pp. 317–8; Richardson, *Birds*, pp. 411–2).

*Red-necked Grebe, *Podiceps grisegena* (Boddaert)
"... the writer of these memoranda had received specimens of it from Hudson's Bay, before the specimen sent home by Captain Franklin was put into his hands" (Sabine, "Appendix," p. 692). Painted at Cumberland House by Hood in May 1820, plate 16. Specimen 1 ft. 11 in. long. Cree name *sekepe*: (Houston, ed., *To the Arctic by Canoe*). Richardson collected an adult specimen at Great Slave Lake in May 1822, but listed it as "not common" (Richardson, *Birds*, pp. xxxi, 411).

American Bittern, *Botaurus lentiginosus* (Rackett)
"... found in Hudson's Bay, and the adjoining countries ... breeds in swamps" (Sabine, "Appendix," p. 686).

*Tundra Swan, *Olor columbianus* (Ord)
Listed by Sabine, but identified incorrectly as the Whooper Swan of Europe. Richardson tells of killing two moulting swans for food in Melville Sound on 15 August 1821 (JR, p. 158). Under the heading of "Bewick's Swan" [the Whistling Swan of North America and the Bewick's Swan of Europe are now considered conspecific], he says: "This Swan breeds on the sea coast within the Arctic circle, and is seen in the interior of the fur countries on its passage only" (Richardson, *Birds*, p. 465).

Bean Goose, *Anser fabalis* (Latham)
This European species was listed by Sabine, probably in error.

Greater White-fronted Goose, *Anser albifrons* (Scopoli)
Listed by Sabine, who had no specimen. Hood painted a White-fronted Goose, probably at Fort Enterprise early in 1821, but it is one of his two bird paintings that have not yet been published. Recorded in Melville Sound on 13–14 August 1821,

when the explorers caught some young grey geese unable to fly; the meat made a welcome addition to their rapidly diminishing food supply. Large flocks of grey geese flew over the mouth of Hood River on 29 August 1821 (JR, p. 169). Called the Laughing Goose: "The Indians imitate its call by patting the mouth with their hand, while they repeat the syllable *wah*. The resemblance of this note to the laugh of a man has given the trivial name to the species" (Richardson, *Birds*, p. 466).

*Snow Goose, *Chen caerulescens* (Linnaeus)
Listed by Sabine, who had no specimen. Painted by Hood at Fort Enterprise in May 1821, plate 23 (Houston, ed., *To the Arctic by Canoe*). Richardson tells of several snow geese being shot on 12 September 1820, between Fort Enterprise and Point Lake. One was shot on 22 May 1821. Some white geese were seen on 13 August in Melville Sound, large flocks were flying south near Point Turnagain on 18 August, immense flocks were flying southeast over the mouth of Hood River on 29 August, and large flocks were feeding on the borders of lakes near Wright's River on 4 September 1821 (JR, pp. 10, 57, 157, 161, 169, 172). Another male was killed at Fort Enterprise on 1 June 1821. It "breeds in the barren grounds of Arctic America, in great numbers. The eggs, of a yellowish-white colour, and regularly ovate form, are a little larger than those of the Eider Duck ... feeds on rushes, insects, and in autumn on berries, particularly those of the *empetrum nigrum*. When well fed it is a very excellent bird, far superior to the Canada Goose in juiciness and flavour" (Richardson, *Birds*, p. 467).

Brant, *Branta bernicla* (Linnaeus)
Listed by Sabine. "... breeds in numbers on the coasts and islands of Hudson's Bay and the Arctic Sea, and is rarely seen in the interior" (Richardson, *Birds*, p. 469).

Barnacle Goose, *Branta leucopsis* (Bechstein)
This European species was listed by Sabine, probably in error.

*Canada Goose, *Branta canadensis* (Linnaeus)
Listed by Sabine. No specimen was brought home by the first Franklin expedition, since this species, called "Le cravant" by the voyageurs, was so well known. Specimen painted by Hood at Fort Enterprise in May 1821, plate 23 (Houston, ed., *To the Arctic by Canoe*).

"One goose, which, when fat, weighs about nine pounds, is the daily ration for one of the Company's servants during the season, and is reckoned equivalent to two snow geese, or three ducks, or eight pounds of buffalo and moose meat, or two pounds of pemmican, or a pint of maize and four ounces of suet. About three weeks after their first appearance, the Canada geese disperse in pairs throughout the country, between the 50th and 67th parallels, to breed, retiring at the same time from the shores of Hudson's Bay. They are seldom or never seen on the coasts of the Arctic Sea. In July, after the young birds are hatched, the parents moult, and vast numbers are killed in the rivers and small lakes when they are unable to fly. When chased by a canoe and obliged to dive frequently, they soon become fatigued and make for the shore with the intention of hiding themselves, but as they are not fleet, they fall an easy prey to their pursuers" (Richardson, *Birds*, pp. 468–9).

"A goose seen today" (JR, 21 May 1821, p. 54).

"… specimen killed at Fort Enterprise May 22 1821 … another killed at Fort Providence, Slave Lake, May 17th 1822 …" (JR, p. 293).

"The arrival of these birds from the southward marking the return of spring is an event of great importance to the natives in many parts of the country as it affords them a supply of food at a season when the moose hunting is impeded by the floods produced by the melting snow. They precede the Laughing and White Geese in the spring and also begin earlier in the autumn to retire to the south again, their routes at these seasons being somewhat different, for they halt at many places in the spring which do not afford them equally good pasture in the autumn hence they either take a different route or fly so high as not to be seen.

"The times of their arrival depending on the earliness of the spring varies of course in different years but may be stated in general as follows –
At Cumberland House from the 8th to 12th of April
Athabasca Lake about the 20th April
Slave Lake about the 6th May
Fort Enterprise about the 20th ditto" (JR, York Factory, July 1822, p. 293).

Wood Duck, *Aix sponsa* (Linnaeus)
"… it appears by a drawing made by Lieutenant Hood, at Cumberland-House, in May, 1820, to have been a visitor so far northward at that period" (Sabine, "Appendix," p. 702). Painted at Cumberland House, plate 16 (Houston, ed., *To the Arctic by Canoe*). Richardson killed another male at Cumberland House in June 1827.

*Green-winged Teal, *Anas crecca* Linnaeus
Specimen sent back by Richardson (Sabine, "Appendix," p. 697). Arrived at the rapids near Fort Enterprise on 17 May 1821 and a male specimen was collected the next day. Its crop was filled with insects (JR, 18 May 1821, p. 52).

*Mallard, *Anas platyrhynchos* Linnaeus
Specimen sent back by Richardson (Sabine, "Appendix," p. 697). A male was painted by Hood at Cumberland House in May 1820, plate 16 (Houston, ed., *To the Arctic by Canoe*). Richardson describes a male specimen from Slave Lake, 10 May 1822: "The speculum is of a dark shining colour which reflects deep green, blue or purple with considerable intensity when moved in the light …" (JR, pp. 299–300).

*Northern Pintail, *Anas acuta* Linnaeus
Specimen of the Pintail or Sea Pheasant sent back by Richardson (Sabine, "Appendix," p. 697). A male was painted by Hood at Cumberland House in May 1820, plate 15 (Houston, ed., *To the Arctic by Canoe*). It arrived at Fort Enterprise on 22 May 1821, "the most common duck that has arrived" (JR, pp. 55–6).

Blue-winged Teal, *Anas discors* Linnaeus
"Two specimens, both males … killed at Carlton-House, and there called the Shoe-string Duck" (Sabine, "Appendix," p. 701). A male was painted at Cumberland House, May 1820, plate 16 (Houston, ed., *To the Arctic by Canoe*).

*Northern Shoveler, *Anas clypeata* Linnaeus
Specimen sent back by Richardson (Sabine, "Appendix," p. 697). A male was painted by Hood at Cumberland House May 1820, plate 15 (Houston, ed., *To the Arctic by Canoe*). Richardson describes a dried specimen from York Factory in July or August 1822 (JR, pp. 309–10).

Gadwall, *Anas strepera* Linnaeus
Listed by Sabine.

*American Wigeon, *Anas americana* Gmelin
"The specimen received was of a male in the autumnal change" (Sabine, "Appendix," p. 700). Another specimen was collected at Fort Resolution, Great Slave Lake, on 21 May 1822 (JR, pp. 303–4).

*Canvasback, *Aythya valisineria* (Wilson)
"A male specimen … was received. It is represented by the American epicures as being much superior in flavour to any other known duck" (Sabine, "Appendix," p. 699). Painted by Hood at Cumberland House in May 1820, plate 15 (Houston, ed., *To the Arctic by Canoe*). A specimen of the Red-headed Duck or Smoking Duck, collected at Fort Moose Deer Island, Great Slave Lake, on 12 May 1822, with a 2-page description, was the other red-headed duck species, a Canvasback (JR, pp. 301–2).

Redhead, *Aythya americana* (Eyton)
Specimen sent back by Richardson (Sabine, "Appendix," p. 697).

Tufted Duck, *Aythya fuligula* (Linnaeus)
Listed by Sabine, although it is only a rare, casual visitor to North America.

Lesser Scaup, *Aythya affinis* (Eyton)
The two North American species of scaup duck were not recognized as different species until 1838, but Sabine listed a scaup specimen sent back by Richardson.

Hood's almost unrecognizable painting from Cumberland House in May 1820 appears to be this species, plate 15 (Houston, ed., *To the Arctic by Canoe*).

Common Eider, *Somateria mollissima* (Linnaeus)
Listed by Sabine.

King Eider, *Somateria spectabilis* (Linnaeus)
Listed by Sabine.

Labrador Duck, *Camptorhynchus labradorius* (Gmelin)
Listed by Sabine as "described and figured by Wilson" ("Appendix," p. 698).

*Harlequin Duck, *Histrionicus histrionicus* (Linnaeus)
Listed by Sabine, who had no specimen. Richardson includes a 3-page description of a dried specimen which was killed near York Factory, July or August 1822 (JR, pp. 306–8).

*Oldsquaw, *Clangula hyemalis* (Linnaeus)
Listed by Sabine. Many were seen in Melville Sound, "termed by the voyageurs from their cry, Caccawees ... The Caccawees are moulting at present and assemble together in immense flocks" (JR, 14–15 August 1821, pp. 157–8). Painted by Hood at Fort Enterprise in the spring of 1821, plate 23 (Houston, ed., *To the Arctic by Canoe*).

Black Scoter, *Melanitta nigra* (Linnaeus)
Listed by Sabine (no locality). Painted by Hood at Fort Enterprise in the spring of 1821, plate 23 (Houston, ed., *To the Arctic by Canoe*).

*Surf Scoter, *Melanitta perspicillata* (Linnaeus)
"The specimen received is that of a male" (Sabine, "Appendix," p. 699). Richardson gave a 1¼–page description of a skinned specimen from York Factory, July 1822 (JR, pp. 296–7).

*White-winged Scoter, *Melanitta fusca* (Linnaeus)
Specimen sent back by Richardson (Sabine, "Appendix," p. 697). Richardson includes a 2-page description of a skinned specimen from York Factory, 20 July 1822 (JR, pp. 294–5).

Common Goldeneye, *Bucephala clangula* (Linnaeus)
Listed by Sabine.

*Bufflehead, *Bucephala albeola* (Linnaeus)
"Specimens of a male and female were received" (Sabine, "Appendix," p. 701).

Male painted by Hood at Cumberland House in May 1820. Cree name, *wappanowsheep* or Conjuring Duck, plate 15 (Houston, ed., *To the Arctic by Canoe*). Richardson gives a 2-page description of a dried specimen obtained at York Factory, July or August 1822 (JR, pp. 311–12).

Hooded Merganser, *Lophodytes cucullatus* (Linnaeus)
"A specimen of a female of this species was brought home by the Expedition" (Sabine, "Appendix," p. 702).

*Red-breasted Merganser, *Mergus serrator* Linnaeus
"Specimens of two male birds were received" (Sabine, "Appendix," p. 702). Painted by Hood at Cumberland House, May 1820, plate 15 (Houston, ed., *To the Arctic by Canoe*). Mergansers, most probably this species, were first seen at Fort Enterprise on 9 May 1821 (JR, p. 48). Dried specimen obtained at York Factory by Richardson in 1822 (JR, pp. 324–5). The plumage description was definitely that of a male Red-breasted Merganser, though the stated length of 28½ inches must have been an error or a measurement of a stretched skin.

Ruddy Duck, *Oxyura jamaicensis* (Gmelin)
"The specimen received was that of a male, and is peculiarly valuable and interesting because it not only confirms the species as introduced by Wilson, but ascertains its summer habitation to be in the northern parts of America" (Sabine, "Appendix," p. 700). Painted by Hood at Cumberland House in May 1820, plate 15 (Houston, ed., *To the Arctic by Canoe*).

Northern Harrier, *Circus cyaneus* (Linnaeus)
Specimen mentioned (Sabine, "Appendix," p. 671). A specimen was collected by Richardson at York Factory on 23 August 1822, not 1821 as erroneously stated (Richardson, *Birds*, p. 64).

*Northern Goshawk, *Accipiter gentilis* (Linnaeus)
"The specimen received was that of a male in perfectly mature plumage" (Sabine, "Appendix," p. 670). An immature or female bird was killed near Fort Enterprise in September 1820. "It is said to remain in the country all the winter and to prey on the White Patridge" (JR, 11 May 1821, p. 51). Richardson gives a 2-page description of an immature specimen he killed at York Factory on 14 August 1822 (JR, pp. 332–3). This bird was also described in Richardson, *Birds*, p. 43.

Red-tailed Hawk, *Buteo jamaicensis* (Gmelin)
Sabine described a probable female, 23 inches long, but gave no locality (Sabine, "Appendix," p. 670).

†Rough-legged Hawk, *Buteo lagopus* (Pontoppidan)
Two hawks were killed near the Ghost River, 45 miles southwest of Fort Enterprise, "in the act of building their nest ... The tail is nearly square. The legs are feathered ... It is about the size of a sparrow hawk [*Accipiter nisus* of England], preys on partridges and quits this country in the winter." (JR, 3 May 1821, pp. 43–4).

†Merlin, *Falco columbarius* Linnaeus
Richardson collected a specimen at York Factory on 4 September 1822 (Richardson, *Birds*, p. 36).

†Gyrfalcon, *Falco rusticolus* Linnaeus
A nesting pair was encountered by Richardson at Point Lake: "In the middle of June, 1821, a pair of these birds attacked me as I was climbing in the vicinity of their nest, which was built on a lofty precipice on the borders of Point Lake, in latitude 65½°. They flew in circles, uttering loud and harsh screams, and alternately stooping with such velocity, that their motion through the air produced a loud rushing noise; they struck their claws within an inch or two of my head. I endeavoured, by keeping the barrel of my gun close to my cheek, and suddenly elevating its muzzle when they were in the act of striking, to ascertain whether they had the power of instantaneously changing the direction of their rapid course, and found that they invariably rose above the obstacle with the quickness of thought, showing equal acuteness of vision and power of motion ... the Jerfalcon ... is well calculated, from the whiteness of its plumage, for traversing a snowy waste, without alarming the birds on which it preys. As the Ptarmigan partially migrate southwards in the winter, some of the Jerfalcons follow them; but, from the young birds being much more common, about latitude 57°, than the mature ones, the latter probably keep nearer to their breeding-places in the more northern, rocky, barren ground districts all the year" (Richardson, *Birds*, p. 28). Recent research, over 150 years later, has finally confirmed Richardson's brilliant hypothesis, predicting year-round residence of the breeding pair.

*Spruce Grouse, *Dendragapus canadensis* (Linnaeus)
"Specimens both of a male and female bird were received in good condition" (Sabine, "Appendix," p. 683). Specimen collected south of the Ghost River, 45 miles southwest of Fort Enterprise on 4 May 1821 (JR, p. 44).

*Willow Ptarmigan, *Lagopus lagopus* (Linnaeus)
"The remarkable property which Grouse, that become white in winter, possess, of doubling each feather, is well known to naturalists; from the base of the shaft of all the feathers which cover the bodies of the birds, there proceeds, on the under side, a small, but perfect feather, of a downy softness, which is no doubt a provision of nature to protect them from the inclemency of the winter to which they are exposed. The White Grouse, of the countries round Hudson's Bay, are

inhabitants of the plains, where bushes of willows abound, on the buds of which they support themselves; from this circumstance they have acquired the appellation of Willow Grouse" (Sabine, "Appendix," p. 681). Painted at Cumberland House in the winter of 1819–20. They arrived there on 15 November 1819 and were considered the infallible harbingers of severe weather; plate 14 (Houston, ed., *To the Arctic by Canoe*). A specimen was collected near Fort Enterprise on 14 April 1821, but it was also mentioned as a winter resident on 1 November 1820 (JR, pp. 47, 200). Ptarmigan of both species contributed to the survival of the stragglers on their trek across the Barren Grounds, with daily success in shooting them on 7–9 September 1821, and more sporadic success later (JR, pp. 174–6).

*Rock Ptarmigan, *Lagopus mutus* (Montin)
"The specimen now under notice, which was obtained in the neighbourhood of York Factory, proves that the Ptarmigan is a native of that part of America" (Sabine, "Appendix," p. 682). Richardson mentioned that this smaller of the two species frequented the Barren Grounds in summer, but went towards the south in winter (JR, p. 47).

Ruffed Grouse, *Bonasa umbellus* (Linnaeus)
"Specimens of a male and female were sent from Cumberland-House, where they were killed, in November, 1819" (Sabine, "Appendix," p. 679).

Sharp-tailed Grouse, *Tympanuchus phasianellus* (Linnaeus)
"... common in the neighbourhood of the Hudson's Bay settlements, where it is called the Pheasant, or Sharp-tailed Grouse." Winter specimens were sent back from Cumberland House and summer specimens from York Factory (Sabine, "Appendix," p. 680). Painted at Cumberland House in early 1820, plate 13 (Houston, ed., *To the Arctic by Canoe*).

Sora, *Porzana carolina* (Linnaeus)
"... from the end of August to the end of September, afford easy amusement to the sportsman, and a plentiful supply to the epicure: being very fat at that season, they are particularly esteemed at table. A single specimen, apparently of a male, was received" (Sabine, "Appendix," p. 690).

American Coot, *Fulica americana* Gmelin
Sabine received one specimen from Richardson, probably from Carlton House or Cumberland House ("Appendix," p. 690). Richardson found the coot no higher than 55° latitude and did not see it near Hudson's Bay on either of the two expeditions (Richardson, *Birds*, p. 404).

*Sandhill Crane, *Grus canadensis* (Linnaeus)
"The specimen sent home is probably of a male, its size exceeding that which is

mentioned by authors: it is upwards of four feet in length." (Sabine, "Appendix," p. 685). This would be the larger subspecies, *Grus canadensis tabida*, and must have come from south of the Saskatchewan River. Richardson's specimen from the southern side of Great Slave Lake on 15 May 1822 was smaller and had a length of 39 inches but he was unable to prepare this specimen. [The dimensions given in Richardson, *Birds*, p. 373, were *not* the Slave Lake bird.] Several cranes were seen in Melville Sound on 15 August 1821 (JR, pp. 158, 314).

†Whooping Crane, *Grus americana* (Linnaeus)
Not mentioned by Sabine, although Richardson gave more than half a page of description of a specimen, without date or locality (JR, p. 263). Richardson killed another specimen near Carlton on 7 May 1827 with these notes: "This stately bird frequents every part of the fur-countries, though not in such numbers as the Brown Crane. It migrates in flocks, performing its journeys in the night, and at such an altitude, that its passage is known only by the peculiarly shrill screams which it utters ... It rises with difficulty from the ground, flying low for a time, and affording a fair mark to the sportsman; but, if not entirely disabled by the shot, fights with great determination, and can inflict very severe wounds with its formidable bill. We have known instances of the wounded bird putting the fowler to flight, and fairly driving him off the field. When fat its flesh is well-tasted, though inferior to that of the Brown Crane. Its eggs are nearly as big as those of the Swan, and of a bluish-white colour, with patches of brown. The wing-bone of this bird is converted by the natives into a kind of flute" (Richardson, *Birds*, p. 372).

*Black-bellied Plover, *Pluvialis squatarola* (Linnaeus)
"The specimen of this species is in the varied state which the mature birds exhibit in the progress of change from the winter dress to that of the breeding season" (Sabine, "Appendix," p. 684). Richardson killed one at York Factory, for which the date of 14 August 1822 is given in Richardson, *Birds*, p. 370.

*Lesser Golden-Plover, *Pluvialis dominica* (Müller)
"A specimen, in winter plumage, is in the collection" (Sabine, "Appendix," p. 683). A specimen collected by Richardson on 29 May 1821 at Fort Enterprise (JR, p. 61), allows correction of the erroneous 29 May 1822 date given in Richardson, *Birds*, p. 369. It was not the specimen described by Sabine.

*Semipalmated Plover, *Charadrius semipalmatus* Bonaparte
"... specimens received" (Sabine, "Appendix," p. 684). Specimen taken on the Hayes River near York Factory on 26 July 1822, with a description reproduced in Richardson, *Birds*, p. 367.

Killdeer, *Charadrius vociferus* Linnaeus
The Noisy Plover "is known to the Americans as the Kildeer, from the note which

it utters incessantly, when disturbed" (Sabine, "Appendix," p. 683). "This Plover arrives on the Saskatchewan plains about the 20th of April; and at that season frequents the gardens and cultivated fields of the trading-posts with the utmost familiarity, in search of food" (Richardson, *Birds*, p. 368).

Greater Yellowlegs, *Tringa melanoleuca* (Gmelin)
A specimen of the "Tell-tale Godwit" was "received in a very perfect state: it measured sixteen inches in length; the bill is two inches and a quarter long…" (Sabine, "Appendix," p. 687). The two species of Yellowlegs were encountered at York Factory and on the trip up the Hayes River on 23 September 1819. Near Limestone Point on the north shore of Lake Winnipeg on 8 October 1819 these "spotted snipes" and golden plovers "afforded us much sport and some excellent meals" (Houston, ed., *To the Arctic by Canoe*, p. 37).

*Lesser Yellowlegs, *Tringa flavipes* (Gmelin)
"… specimen … in its perfect summer dress" (Sabine, "Appendix," p. 688). The specimen collected by Richardson at York Factory on 29 July 1822 had a wing span of 18½ inches and a bill of 1½ inches (JR, p. 274–5).

†Eskimo Curlew, *Numenius borealis* (Forster)
Although at least four specimens of this then-common species were collected during the first Franklin expedition and the first-ever nest was discovered, this species was omitted by Sabine. The first specimen collected was painted by Hood at Fort Enterprise in the spring of 1821, plate 23 (Houston, ed., *To the Arctic by Canoe*). Richardson's advance party on the south shore of Point Lake collected a specimen with a 2-inch beak on 13 June 1821 and found a nest on the ground with "three eggs of a pyriform shape, and siskin-green colour, clouded with a few large irregular spots of bright umber-brown" (JR, p. 72). Two more specimens were killed at York Factory by Richardson on 14 August 1822, and a combined description made, giving bill length as 2 inches (JR, p. 326–7).

*Hudsonian Godwit, *Limosa haemastica* (Linnaeus)
"Two specimens were received, one of which was a young bird, and the other mature, in plumage intermediate between its winter and breeding state" (Sabine, "Appendix," p. 689). Richardson devoted 4 pages to descriptions of two specimens (JR, pp. 266–72). The first was killed on 22 July 1822 on the muddy shore at York Factory, and the second on 30 July 1822 on the sea coast at York Factory, with a wing span of 24 inches.

Marbled Godwit, *Limosa fedoa* (Linnaeus)
"The specimen is of a male, killed at Carlton-House on the 20th of May" (Sabine, "Appendix," p. 689).

Ruddy Turnstone, *Arenaria interpres* (Linnaeus)
"A specimen, obtained in the neighbourhood of York Factory, was received" (Sabine, "Appendix," p. 684).

?Semipalmated Sandpiper, *Calidris pusilla* (Linnaeus)
*Least Sandpiper, *Calidris minutilla* (Vieillot)
"Several specimens were taken by the travellers at different parts of the journey in the summer season" (Sabine, "Appendix," p. 686). There was at the time total confusion between the Least Sandpiper and the Semipalmated Sandpiper. Sabine gave Wilson's Latin name for the Semipalmated under his discussion of the "Little Sandpiper." Richardson collected two small sandpipers at York Factory on 21 July 1822, and preserved them in alcohol. His combined description of the two specimens mentions the wax yellow legs of the Least Sandpiper and the short web between the two outer toes of the Semipalmated Sandpiper, under the title of "Pigmy Sandpiper" (Richardson, *Birds*, p. 385; JR, pp. 282–3).

†Purple Sandpiper, *Calidris maritima* (Brünnich)
A specimen was collected by Richardson at York Factory on 29 July 1822 (JR, pp. 284–5). It was a male, killed before moulting (Richardson, *Birds*, p. 382).

*Dunlin, *Calidris alpina* (Linnaeus)
"The specimens of this bird are in the summer plumage" (Sabine, "Appendix," p. 686). A specimen described by Richardson from Fort Moose Deer Island on Great Slave Lake on 23 May 1822 may be this species, though the bill is too short (JR, p. 278).

†Stilt Sandpiper, *Calidris himantopus* (Bonaparte)
It is unfortunate that Sabine did not describe Richardson's "several specimens" which were "brought home in spirits; but, probably from being too much injured, were not noted by Mr. Sabine with the other birds." Because Sabine passed up the opportunity to describe and name this as a new species, the priority was grasped by Charles Lucien Bonaparte, who in 1826 named it *Tringa himantopus*. When *Fauna Boreali-Americana*, II: *The Birds* appeared in 1831, Richardson placed his York Factory specimen, collected on 29 July 1822 (JR, p. 270), tentatively under Bonaparte's name of *T. himantopus*, even though in his July 1822 journal description Richardson had given it the new scientific name of *Tringa hemipalma Douglassii*. Another Stilt Sandpiper collected on the Saskatchewan River in June 1827 during the second Arctic Land Expedition, was tentatively proposed as a new species, Douglas's Sandpiper, illustrated by Swainson's plate 66 (Richardson, *Birds*, p. 380).

*Short-billed Dowitcher, *Limnodromus griseus* (Gmelin)
"Two specimens, probably in perfect summer plumage, were sent home," one 12 inches and another 11 inches in length; the largest had a bill 2¼ inches long. "It is

in high estimation for the table, and is eagerly sought after by sportsmen" (Sabine, "Appendix," pp. 687–8). Richardson collected a specimen at York Factory on 26 July 1822 and provided a 2-page description (JR, p. 268). The bill was "2 inches 2 lines long," each line being a twelfth of an inch, so was smaller than Sabine's largest specimen.

†Common Snipe, *Gallinago gallinago* (Linnaeus)
Richardson killed a specimen in a swamp near Fort Resolution on the southern shore of Great Slave Lake on 15 May 1822. At the time the ground was still covered with snow, and ice on the lake was still solid. Richardson gave the Cree name as *pethay pa casew* (JR, p. 265).

‡Wilson's Phalarope, *Phalaropus tricolor* (Vieillot)
"This exquisitely beautiful bird, it is believed, has never before been described, or come under observation. It was received in the collection despatched from Cumberland House, in the spring of the year 1820" (Sabine, "Appendix," p. 691). Sabine named this new species of phalarope *Phalaropus wilsoni* for the Scottish ornithologist, Alexander Wilson:[5] "... in affixing his name to an American bird it is proposed to record the renown amongst naturalists, which that quarter of the world has acquired by his labours in Ornithology ... The specimen has much the appearance of being in its breeding dress" Sabine gave no indication that he knew that it is the female phalarope that has the bright plumage. Richardson in *Birds*, pp. 405–6, mentioned that his bright-plumaged phalarope collected on the Saskatchewan River on 21 June 1827 was indeed a female, and to my knowledge was the first scientist to make this observation. The new name, Wilson's Phalarope, has persisted to the present day, but the Latin name of *wilsoni* lasted only until 1886, when the priority of Vieillot's 1819 description in a French publication was appreciated.

†Red-necked Phalarope, *Phalaropus lobatus* (Linnaeus)
Not formally listed by Sabine, although he mentioned ("Appendix," p. 690) that "Dr. Richardson ... also saw the other known species ... the Grey Phalarope, but did not preserve a skin of it." Richardson gives a 2-page description of a phalarope, killed on the mud banks at York Factory on 20 July 1822, describing well the distinctive reddish-brown stripe on the neck. He took another specimen in fall plumage, without distinctive identifying features, on 28 August 1822 (JR, p. 280–1, and Richardson, *Birds*, p. 407).

Red Phalarope, *Phalaropus fulicaria* (Linnaeus)
"A specimen of this bird was brought home by Dr. Richardson" (Sabine, "Appendix," p. 690).

Parasitic Jaeger, *Stercorarius parasiticus* (Linnaeus)
"Specimens in mature plumage, and with the under parts white, were brought home by the Expedition" (Sabine, "Appendix," p. 697).

Franklin's Gull, *Larus pipixcan* Wagler
Sabine ("Appendix," pp. 695–6) told of a specimen sent back by Richardson, most likely from Cumberland House or Carlton House, and described the differences in size and colour of primaries from the Laughing Gull. He did not, however, give it a new Latin name. This was left to Richardson, who described a 6 June 1827 specimen from the Saskatchewan River as a new species, *Larus Franklinii*, Franklin's Rosy Gull (Richardson, *Birds*, pp. 424–5 and plate 71). The species is still known as Franklin's Gull, and the Latin name was used for 90 years until the priority of Wagler's description in May 1831 was recognized and the Latin name was changed to *Larus pipixcan*. Late in 1830 Swainson and Richardson, *Birds*, was already in proof. Richardson loaned his proofsheets to Professor Robert Jameson, who copied the description of *Larus Franklinii* in his European edition of Wilson's *American Ornithology* which appeared on 1 August 1831. The publication of *Birds* was delayed more than a year until February 1832 by co-author William Swainson's ill-advised attempts to force birds into a preconceived artificial classification. This delay robbed the Saskatchewan River of a type locality more than once.

Little Gull, *Larus minutus* Pallas
"The specimen received, exactly accords with M. Temminck's description of the young bird of the first year" (Sabine, "Appendix," p. 696). Ornithologists have felt the lack of a locality description more acutely for this species than any other, but by far the best possibility is that it was collected on the Saskatchewan River, as were at least three-quarters of all bird and mammal specimens reported by Sabine. Sabine had access to all specimens collected at Cumberland House and Carlton House before June 1820, but to very few of the bird and mammal specimens collected thereafter. As further confirmation, Richardson in his introductory table in 1831 listed the Little Gull as "Rare spring and autumn visitor" on the Saskatchewan (Richardson, *Birds*, p. xxxi).

†Mew Gull, *Larus canus* Linnaeus
A specimen collected at Fort Enterprise on 22 May 1821 had a yellow bill and feet, scarlet cere, and inside of mouth deep reddish orange, with a length of 16 inches and wing-span of 40 inches (JR, p. 57). A later specimen from the second expedition, collected at Great Bear Lake on 23 May 1826, was named by Richardson as *Larus brachyrhynchus*, the type specimen for what is now *Larus canus brachyrhynchus*.

Herring Gull, *Larus argentatus* Pontoppidan
"The specimen now under consideration, as well as others which have been received from Hudson's Bay, have the primaries marked as commonly described" (Sabine "Appendix," p. 695).

*Black-legged Kittiwake, *Rissa tridactyla* (Linnaeus)
"The specimen received is of an immature bird" (Sabine, "Appendix," p. 695). [An immature specimen, killed on the sea shore at York Factory on 14 August 1822, only 13 inches long, with pale flesh-red legs, was called *Larus tridactylus* by Richardson (JR, p. 330), but W. Earl Godfrey suggests it may have been an immature Bonaparte's Gull, *Larus philadelphia*.]

*Arctic Tern, *Sterna paradisaea* Pontoppidan
"... a specimen sent home by Captain Franklin" (Sabine, "Appendix," p. 694). Richardson described a tern killed along the Coppermine River, about 66°30' north latitude on 5 July 1821 (JR, p. 95). A second tern, which he called *Sterna arctica*, also impossible to differentiate from the Common Tern from his description alone, was taken at York Factory on 28 August 1822 (JR, p. 286).

Black Tern, *Chlidonias niger* (Linnaeus)
"The specimen received is in perfect summer plumage" (Sabine, "Appendix," p. 694).

Passenger Pigeon, *Ectopistes migratorius* (Linnaeus)
"... they come, however, to the countries near Hudson's Bay, and sometimes remain there late in the season. It seems likely that, as population and cultivation extend westward, the countless multitudes of these birds, which darken the air for hours and miles together in their flight, will be reduced; their visitations must be ruinous to agricultural districts, and consequently incompatible with civilization" (Sabine, p. 679). The specimen was probably from Cumberland House, where Thomas Drummond was to find them nesting in the summer of 1825.

*Northern Hawk-Owl, *Surnia ulula* (Linnaeus)
"This bird is the only one of the genus received from the Expedition" (Sabine, "Appendix," p. 671). Specimen obtained north of Great Slave Lake, between Fort Enterprise and Fort Providence, in late October 1820. "This owl builds its nest in trees, and preys on mice. It frequents also the neighbourhood of Churchill and is named by the Eskimaux *oodnohaeoot*. Copper Indian, *Theechazza*. Chevechette, Cuvier Reg. An. p. 331" (JR, pp. 26–7).

†Short-eared Owl, *Asio flammeus* (Pontoppidan)
Richardson describes one killed on the Slave River, about latitude 60° on 28 May 1822, as "too much injured to form a specimen," and another at York Factory on 20 August 1822, as "hunts in the day time" (JR, p. 322).

*Belted Kingfisher, *Ceryle alcyon* (Linnaeus)
"Our specimen is that of a male" (Sabine, "Appendix," p. 678). Richardson

devotes over one page to a description of a specimen killed in Slave River on 28 May 1822, about latitude 60°. He notes: "These birds fish from the trees that overhang the rivers and are accustomed to fly familiarly before the canoes from one overhanging stump to another uttering a shrill cry" (JR, 320–1, the measurements suggest a different specimen from that described by Sabine).

Yellow-bellied Sapsucker, *Sphyrapicus varius* (Linnaeus)
"The specimens received were those of a male and a female" (Sabine, "Appendix," p. 677).

Hairy Woodpecker, *Picoides villosus* (Linnaeus)
"Our specimen is that of a male bird" (Sabine, "Appendix," p. 677). Richardson on 4 May 1821 mentions that "The small black woodpecker with four toes is common in woods about the encampment" of Akaicho's Indians 45 miles southwest of Fort Enterprise. This is slightly farther north than the ranges mapped by Godfrey for both the Hairy and Downy Woodpeckers (JR, p. 45).

†Black-backed Woodpecker, *Picoides arcticus* (Swainson)
Painted by Hood at Cumberland House early in 1820, plate 13 (Houston, ed., *To the Arctic by Canoe*). A species new to science, it was not given an official Latin name until Thomas Drummond collected a specimen at the headwaters of the Athabasca River near the present site of Jasper in the Rocky Mountains in 1825 or 1826. Illustrated, plate 57 (Richardson, *Birds*, p. 313).

Northern Flicker, *Colaptes auratus* (Linnaeus)
"The specimen is that of a female" (Sabine, "Appendix," p. 676).

Purple Martin, *Progne subis* (Linnaeus)
"They arrive in Hudson's Bay in the end of May, and leave it in August, but come sooner and retire later in the more southern districts. The male, of which alone a specimen was received, is an uniform glossy black" (Sabine, "Appendix," p. 678).

Tree Swallow, *Tachycineta bicolor* (Vieillot)
The specimen was killed at Cumberland House (Sabine, "Appendix," p. 679).

Gray Jay, *Perisoreus canadensis* (Linnaeus)
"In Canada, these birds are abundant, and well known, being of familiar manners, approaching the habitations of men, and attending the hunters, to whom they are troublesome, in taking the baits from their traps. They are named by the natives Whiskey-Jonish which has been changed by the English into Whiskey-Jack" (Sabine, "Appendix," p. 672). Noted as numerous in winter as in summer.

Blue Jay, *Cyanocitta cristata* (Linnaeus)
"A well-known bird inhabiting all parts of North America" (Sabine, "Appendix,"
p. 672).

‡Black-billed Magpie, *Pica pica hudsonia* (Sabine)
"A new and hitherto undescribed species. The writer of this notice was acquainted with its existence previous to the departure of the Expedition, having been some time before in possession of a specimen from Hudson's Bay. It has no doubt been confounded with the Common Magpie (Corvus Pica), to which it bears much resemblance ... The Hudson's Bay Magpie is of less size in all its parts than the Common Magpie, except in its tail, which exceeds that of its congener in length; but the most remarkable and obvious difference is, in a loose tuft of greyish and white feathers on the back ... Two specimens were received, both killed on the 10th of November 1819, at Cumberland House, being caught in traps; they were male and female, but there is no difference in the sexes, except that one rather exceeds the other in length, the one marked as female, being the largest" (Sabine, "Appendix," p. 671–2). One of these magpies was painted by Hood in January 1820, plate 14 (Houston, ed., *To the Arctic by Canoe*). Cumberland House is now the type locality for the North American subspecies of the Black-billed Magpie, based on these specimens.

*Common Raven, *Corvus corax* Linnaeus
"A single fine specimen is in the collection" (Sabine, "Appendix," p. 671). In a letter home from Cumberland House, dated 6 March 1820, Richardson says: "The screams of a famished raven or the crash of a lofty pine, rending through the intenseness of the frost, are the only sounds that invade the solemn silence."[6] Equally at Fort Enterprise, "there remain for our winter companions, only, the Raven, Cinereous crow and Ptarmigan" (JR, 1 November 1820, p. 23). "Some ravens" were seen when Franklin's party was encamped near the mouth of Wentzel's River on 24 July 1821 (JR, p. 135). One of two species "which we recognized as being equally numerous at their breeding-places in winter as in summer; and they pair and begin to lay eggs in the month of March, – nearly three months earlier than any other bird in those quarters. ... The experienced native, when he sees from afar a flock of Ravens wheeling in small circles, knows that a party of his countrymen, well provided with venison, are encamped on the spot, or that a band of wolves are preying upon the carcass of some of the larger quadrupeds; and pushes on briskly in the certain prospect of having his wants supplied" (Richardson, *Birds*, pp. xvii–xviii, 290).

†Black-capped Chickadee, *Parus atricapillus* Linnaeus
Painted by Hood at Cumberland House early in 1820, plate 13 (Houston, ed., *To the Arctic by Canoe*).

†Boreal Chickadee, *Parus hudsonicus* Forster
Not mentioned in Richardson, *Birds*. Richardson on 4 May 1821 says: "... there is another small bird called by the voyageurs Messange which is also said to winter here but I did not obtain specimens ..." (JR, p. 45).

American Robin, *Turdus migratorius* Linnaeus
"The specimen received is not so brilliant as that figured by Wilson, and is probably therefore that of a female" (Sabine, "Appendix," p. 674). Painted by Hood at Cumberland House, plate 14 (Houston, ed., *To the Arctic by Canoe*).

Northern Shrike, *Lanius excubitor* Linnaeus
Sabine received a specimen that was sent home by Richardson ("Appendix," p. 674).

Yellow Warbler, *Dendroica petechia* (Linnaeus)
A specimen was sent to Sabine ("Appendix," pp. 674–5).

Rose-breasted Grosbeak, *Pheucticus ludovicianus* (Linnaeus)
"The specimen received is that of a young male" (Sabine, "Appendix," pp. 675–6). "A specimen of this brilliant bird was obtained near the Saskatchewan on Sir John Franklin's first Expedition ..." (Richardson, *Birds*, p. 271).

*Snow Bunting, *Plectrophenax nivalis* (Linnaeus)
"Two specimens in their winter plumage were received (Sabine, "Appendix," p. 675). Painted by Hood at Cumberland House in early 1820, plate 13 (Houston, *To the Arctic by Canoe*). A specimen came on board the Hudson's Bay ship, *Prince of Wales*, near East Main and eight days out of York Factory on 15 September 1822, the final bird entry in Richardson's journal (JR, p. 337–8), added when he and Back were returning to England. Richardson said it was "Common throughout the land", since he had recorded it in flocks at Fort Enterprise on 9 October 1820, and listed it as an occasional visitor there on 1 November. The first small birds to hatch, mentioned on 15 June 1821 at Point Lake, were probably Snow Buntings, and more Snow Buntings were seen on 24 July along the Arctic Ocean near the mouth of Wentzel's River (JR, pp. 17, 23, 74, 135).

Red-winged Blackbird, *Agelaius phoeniceus* (Linnaeus)
"The specimen received is that of a male" (Sabine, "Appendix," p. 673).

Western Meadowlark, *Sturnella neglecta* Audubon
"Two specimens were received, apparently male and female" (Sabine, "Appendix," p. 674). Not until 1844 did Audubon distinguish the Western Meadowlark from the Eastern Meadowlark.

†Yellow-headed Blackbird, *Xanthocephalus xanthocephalus* (Bonaparte)
"I procured specimens in the spring of the same year [1820], and despatched them to England along with many other objects of natural history; but they were irrecoverably lost after their arrival in London; and were not, therefore described by Mr. Sabine in the narrative of Sir John Franklin's first Journey" (Richardson, *Birds*, p. 281). Had these been described and given a Latin name, Saskatchewan would have had the priority for the type specimen and type locality. Painted by Hood at Cumberland House in early 1820, plate 13 (Houston, ed., *To the Arctic by Canoe*). The recognized type specimen was that collected in May 1820 by the expedition of Major Stephen H. Long in what is now Nebraska. Long's Rocky Mountain Expedition, with Thomas Say as zoologist, was sent to ascertain the nature of the western borders of the Louisiana Purchase, acquired from France in 1803. Their specimen was described by Charles Lucien Bonaparte in two publications in 1825 and 1826.

Common Grackle, *Quiscalus quiscula* (Linnaeus)
"The specimen received, which is that of a male, exhibits beautifully the glossy splendour of its dark plumage" (Sabine, "Appendix," p. 673).

Brown-headed Cowbird, *Molothrus ater* (Boddaert)
"A male specimen alone was received … The great peculiarity of this bird, first brought into notice by Wilson, is that, like the Common Cuckoo, it deposits its eggs in the nests of other and smaller birds, who hatch, feed, and rear the obtruded offspring of the interloper" (Sabine, "Appendix," p. 676).

Northern Oriole, *Icterus galbula* (Linnaeus)
"A male specimen of this pretty and interesting species was taken" (Sabine, "Appendix," p. 673).

Pine Grosbeak, *Pinicola enucleator* (Linnaeus)
"A single specimen of a young bird was received" (Sabine, "Appendix," p. 675). An adult male was painted by Hood at Cumberland House in January 1820, plate 14 (Houston, ed., *To the Arctic by Canoe*).

†White-winged Crossbill, *Loxia leucoptera* Gmelin
An adult and a young bird were painted by Hood at Cumberland House early in 1820, plate 13 (Houston, *To the Arctic by Canoe*).

†Hoary Redpoll, *Carduelis hornemanni* (Holböll)
Neither species of redpoll was listed by Sabine. Robert Hood painted a pale, white-rumped redpoll at Cumberland House early in 1820, obviously a Hoary Redpoll, plate 13 (Houston, ed., *To the Arctic by Canoe*). This was 23 years before C.

Holboell described a Greenland specimen as a new species separate from the Common Redpoll.

†Evening Grosbeak, *Coccothraustes vespertinus* (Cooper)
A female, which he called "Grey Grosbeak," and a male "Yellow Grosbeak" were painted by Hood at Cumberland House in January 1820, plate 14 (Houston, ed., *To the Arctic by Canoe*), representing the first authentic record of this species anywhere. It was first named by W. Cooper in 1825, from a specimen shot 7 April 1823 by an Indian boy with a bow and arrow at Sault Ste Marie, Michigan. Had Sabine described and named the birds that Hood painted, Cumberland House would have been the type locality.

Appendix B

Of different mammals listed by Sabine, 33 appear to have been reported only from the Saskatchewan River, with 24 definitely or probably from Cumberland House and 9 from Carlton House. One species was from Hudson Bay (polar bear), 4 from the Arctic Ocean (barren-ground grizzly, arctic fox, lemming, and muskox), and 5 from Fort Enterprise (ermine, white wolf, meadow vole, arctic hare, and barren-ground caribou). Of the 18 forms represented by specimens, all were from the Saskatchewan River. Sabine was supplied by Richardson with the description copied from his journal of the meadow vole at Fort Enterprise, probably on special request, since Sabine seems not to have had access to any of Richardson's specimens after June 1820.

For an explanation of the symbols and reference abbreviations used in Appendix B, see the introductory note to Appendix A. Mammals are presented in the order used by Banfield in *The Mammals of Canada*.

Snowshoe Hare, *Lepus americanus* Erxleben.
Specimen, Cumberland House, spring of 1820 (Sabine, "Appendix," p. 665). Painted by Robert Hood at Cumberland House, April 1820, plate 6 (Houston, ed., *To the Arctic by Canoe*). "The American Hare … has numerous enemies, such as wolves, foxes, wolverenes, martins, ermines, snowy owls, and various hawks; but the Canada lynx is the animal which perhaps most exclusively feeds upon it. It has been remarked that lynxes are numerous only where there are plenty of hares in the neighbourhood. At some periods a sort of epidemic has destroyed vast numbers of hares in particular districts, and they have not recruited again until after the lapse of several years, during which the lynxes were likewise scarce" (Richardson, *Mammals*, p. 218).

*Arctic Hare, *Lepus arcticus* Ross
"Dr. Richardson observed that the Polar Hare is never seen in woods, it frequents the Barren Grounds, living chiefly on the berries of the *Arbutus Alpina*, and the bark of the Dwarf Birch" (Sabine, "Appendix," p. 664). Described by Richardson, 20 April 1821 (JR, pp. 37–9). "… none of those obtained by Captain Franklin's party in the neighbourhood of Fort Enterprise exceeded … 9 lbs" (Richardson, "Appendix," p. 323).

†White-tailed Jack Rabbit, *Lepus townsendii* Bachman. Richardson called it the Prairie Hare.
"It frequents the open plains … but it does not resort to the thick woods like the American hare. It possesses great speed" (Richardson, *Mammals*, p. 225).

Woodchuck, *Marmota monax* (Linnaeus)
"A hunter's skin only of this animal was received" (Sabine, "Appendix," p. 662).

‡Richardson's Ground Squirrel, *Spermophilus richardsonii* (Sabine)
Sabine named it *Arctomys Richardsonii*, the Tawny American Marmot, from a first specimen collected by Richardson at Carlton House in May 1820 ("Appendix," p. 662). "The specific name is a tribute to the merits of Dr. John Richardson, who went out with the Expedition as a Naturalist, and to whose attention and care we are indebted for these additions to our zoological knowledge" (Sabine, "Marmots of North America," p. 30).

‡Arctic Ground Squirrel, *Spermophilus parryii* (Richardson)
Not mentioned by Sabine. Described by Richardson on 13 June 1821 (JR, pp. 72–3). Named *Arctomys Parryii*, Parry's Marmot, by Richardson who described Parry's specimen from Melville Peninsula in the appendix to Parry's *Second Voyage* (1825), four years before he published *Mammals*. "At Point Lake in lat. 65°, their pouches were observed about the middle of June to be filled with the berries of the *Arbutus alpina*, and *Vaccinium vitis idaea*, which were just then laid bare by the melting of the snowy covering, under which they had lain all the winter. In the end of July, on the shores of the Arctic Sea, their pouches contained the seeds of a *polygonum*" (Richardson, "Appendix," p. 319). "It abounds in the neighbourhood of Fort Enterprise, near the southern verge of the barren grounds, in latitude 65° … The Esquimaux name of the animal *seek-seek* is an attempt to express this sound" (Richardson, *Mammals*, p. 158).

‡Thirteen-lined Ground Squirrel, *Spermophilus tridecemlineatus* (Mitchell)
Named *Arctomys Hoodii*, the Striped American Marmot by Sabine and called the Leopard-Marmot by Richardson. "In the name of this beautiful little animal, I am desirous of recording the zeal of Lieutenant Robert Hood. His application to the various matters of science which have offered themselves to the notice of the

travellers well deserves to be thus recorded. His beautiful drawings and skilful delineations of the route of the Expedition, which were received at the same time with the specimens now described, are most satisfactory proofs of his ability" (Sabine, "Marmots of North America," 1822, p. 31). "It was observed living ... in the level country round Carlton-House. When the specific name of Hoodii was attached to this animal, the untimely fate of the deserving individual, in compliment to whom it was named, was unknown in England: it may be, therefore, permitted now to observe on the part of Natural History, that his many careful and accurate drawings of subjects connected therewith, bear ample testimony to the loss which that science, in common with his country and his immediate profession, have sustained by the premature termination of his life" (Sabine, "Appendix," p. 663). "... the most beautiful of the marmots ... Its burrows are interspersed among those of the *A. Richardsonii*, but may be distinguished by their smaller entrances and more perpendicular direction. Some of them will admit a stick to be thrust straight down to the depth of four or five feet" (Richardson, *Mammals*, p. 177).

‡Franklin's Ground Squirrel, *Spermophilus franklinii* (Sabine)
Called Grey American Marmot by Sabine, and Franklin's Marmot by Richardson. "... was obtained in the neighbourhood of Cumberland-House" (Sabine, "Appendix," p. 662). "The name is given in compliment to the intrepid and spirited Commander of the Expedition, to which, from his perseverance in the arduous enterprise intrusted to his conduct, so much of interest is attached" (Sabine, "Marmots of North America," p. 28).

American Red Squirrel, *Tamiasciurus hudsonicus* (Erxleben)
"*Sciurus Hudsonius*, Hudson's Bay Squirrel: its native country is solely that in the vicinity, and westward of, Hudson's Bay. Two specimens were received, a male and female, which had been caught at Cumberland-House, in October, 1819" (Sabine, "Appendix," p. 663).

American Beaver, *Castor canadensis* Kuhl
"Beavers are found to the northward as far as the wooded countries extend, but there were none in the Barren Grounds to the eastward of the Copper-Mine River. The import of Beaver skins last year by the Hudson's Bay Company, amounted to sixty thousand" (Sabine, "Appendix," p. 659). "Indians of note have generally one or two feasts in a season, wherein a roasted Beaver is the prime dish ... It resembles pork in its flavour ... Gangs of Iroquois were also introduced into the fur countries to the north some years ago; and by setting traps, which destroyed indiscriminately Beaver of all sizes, they almost extirpated the species from the hunting grounds ... In the year 1743, the imports of beaver-skins into the ports of London and Rochelle, amounted to upwards of 150,000 ... In 1827, the importation of beaver-skins into London, from more than four times the extent of fur country

than that which was occupied in 1743, did not much exceed 50,000" (Richardson, *Mammals*, pp. 106–8).

Deer Mouse, *Peromyscus maniculatus* (Wagner)
"American Field-Mouse: No sooner is a fur-post established than this little animal becomes an inmate of the dwelling-houses ... [it] has a habit of making hoards of grain or little pieces of fat ... these hoards are not formed in the animal's retreats, but generally in a shoe left at the bedside, the pocket of a coat, a nightcap, a bag hung against the wall, or some similar place ... The quantity laid up in a single night nearly equalling the bulk of a mouse" (Richardson, *Mammals*, p. 142).

‡Brown Lemming, *Lemmus sibiricus trimucronatus* (Richardson)
This new form was first described by Richardson as the Five-fingered American Lemming from a specimen killed by George Back at Point Lake on 26 June 1821. "It was a female and had six young in the womb, fully formed but destitute of hair" (Richardson, "Appendix," pp. 309–12).

†Collared Lemming, *Dicrostonyx torquatus* (Pallas)
Specimen from Point Lake 27 June 1821 (JR, pp. 81–3). In 1900, when C. Hart Merriam described a new subspecies from the tundra west of Hudson's Bay, he named it *Dicrostonyx torquatus richardsoni* in honour of Dr John Richardson.[1]

Muskrat, *Ondatra zibethicus* (Linnaeus)
"... abundantly found almost during the whole journey ... very nearly 150,000 of the skins were imported last year by the Hudson's Bay Company, and even more are annually killed and carried into Canada." A white or albino muskrat "was killed near Cumberland-House, and presented by Mr. Holmes, chief of that station, to the travellers" (Sabine, "Appendix," pp. 659–60).

*Meadow Vole, *Microtus pennsylvanicus* (Ord)
"... abundant in the settlements round Hudson's Bay. It shows a strong inclination to domesticate itself, by frequenting the houses." Sabine provided the full description from Richardson's journal of 20 April 1821 of a specimen he collected at Fort Enterprise which was sent home but "not found among the collection" (Sabine, "Appendix," p. 660). Specimen from Fort Enterprise 20 April 1821 (JR, pp. 39–41). "It seeks shelter in the barns and out-houses" (Richardson, *Mammals*, p. 124).

Meadow Jumping Mouse, *Zapus hudsonius* (Zimmermann)
"Labrador Mouse: ... a specimen sent home from Cumberland House" (Sabine, "Appendix," p. 661).

American Porcupine, *Erethizon dorsatum* (Linnaeus)
"Canada Porcupine: ... it is not, however, of frequent occurrence, which may be partly caused by its increasing slowly by breeding, (for they are said to produce only a single young one at a birth), and partly by the facility with which they are discovered and taken by the Indians; for their flesh being esteemed a delicacy, they are eagerly sought after" (Sabine, "Appendix," p. 664). "... brings forth two young ones in April or May. Its flesh, which tastes like flabby pork, is relished by the Indians, but is soon nauseated by Europeans" (Richardson, *Mammals*, pp. 214–15).

Coyote, *Canis latrans* Say
"Dr. Richardson mentions ... not uncommon in the plains" (Sabine, "Appendix," p. 654). "The Prairie Wolf: its skins have always formed part of the Hudson Bay Company's importations, under the name of Cased Wolves* (*The skins are not split open like the large Wolf skins, but stripped off and inverted or cased, like the skin of a fox or rabbit.) ... It inhabits the plains of the Missouri and Saskatchewan ... these animals start from the earth in great numbers on hearing the report of a gun, and gather around the hunter in expectation of getting the offal of the animal he has slaughtered. They hunt in packs, and are much more fleet than the Common Wolf ... next in speed [to] the Prong-horned Antelope" (Richardson, *Mammals*, pp. 73–4).

*Wolf, *Canis lupus* Linnaeus
"Grey Wolves are common in the neighbourhood of Cumberland-House, a magnificent specimen of one was caught in a trap during the residence of the Expedition at that place in January 1820 ... very satisfactory information was obtained ... of the readiness which Wolves shewed to have intercourse with domestic Dogs ... a Wolf entirely white ... killed at Fort Enterprise during the second winter ... Its length was four feet four inches, its height two feet ten inches, and the length of the tail was nineteen inches" (Sabine, "Appendix," p. 654).

"I had almost daily opportunities of observing the form and manners of the Wolves, but I saw none which had the gaunt appearance, the comparatively long jaw and tapering nose, the high ears, long legs, slender loins and narrow feet of the Pyrenean Wolf.

"... very common throughout the northern regions; their footmarks may be seen by the side of every stream, and a traveller can rarely pass a night in these wilds without hearing them howling around him ... During our residence at Cumberland House in 1820, a wolf, which had been prowling round the Fort, and was wounded by a musket-ball and driven off, returned after it became dark, whilst the blood was still flowing from its wound, and carried off a dog from amongst fifty others, that howled piteously, but had not courage to unite in an attack on their enemy" (Richardson, *Mammals*, pp. 60–72).

Richardson added that he "considered it unadvisable to designate the northern Wolf of America by a distinct specific appellation, lest I should unnecessarily add to the list of synonyms, which have already overburthened the science of Zoology," and therefore gave the Latin name, *Canis lupus griseus*, to the variety (subspecies) of grey wolf. On the basis of Richardson's specimen, Cumberland House is the type locality for the subspecies, *Canis lupus griseoalbus*. By restriction, Richardson's name of *Canis lupus occidentalis* is now given to wolves around Great Slave Lake and the Upper Mackenzie River (Fort Simpson). A specimen of the white wolf at Fort Enterprise was described and measured by Richardson in February 1821 (JR, p. 382), and painted by Hood in March, plate 12 (Houston, ed., *To the Arctic by Canoe*).

Arctic Fox, *Alopex lagopus* (Linnaeus)
"The Arctic Foxes were found breeding at Point Turnagain on the Arctic Sea" (Sabine, "Appendix," p. 658). "They breed on the sea coast, and chiefly within the Arctic circle, forming burrows in sandy spots, – not solitary, like the red fox, but in little villages, twenty or thirty burrows being constructed adjoining to each other. We saw one of these villages on Point Turnagain, in latitude 68½°. Towards the middle of winter they retire to the southward ... at Carlton House, in latitude 53°, only two were seen in forty years ... Its flesh ... particularly when young, is edible ... Captain Franklin's party agreed with Hearne, in comparing the flavour of a young Arctic fox to that of the American hare" (Richardson, *Mammals*, pp. 83–8).

Red Fox, *Vulpes vulpes* (Linnaeus)
Specimens of the red, cross, and silver colour phases were sent home to Sabine. "The fur of the Cross Fox is valuable, and some years ago it was worth four or five guineas a skin, whilst that of the Red Fox did not bring more than fifteen shillings." The Silver Fox "is more rare than the Cross Fox, a greater number than four or five being seldom taken in a season at any one post in the fur countries, though the hunters no sooner find out the haunts of one than they use every art to catch it, because its fur fetches six times the price of any other fur produced in North America (Richardson, *Mammals*, pp. 91–5).

Swift Fox, *Vulpes velox* (Say)
"Grizzled Fox: A hunter's specimen of this pretty quadruped was obtained at Carlton-House. It is common on the sandy plains between the north and south branches of the Saskatchewan. The skins of this species are imported by the Hudson's Bay Company, under the name of Kitt Foxes" (Sabine, "Appendix," p. 658). "I saw many hunter's skins. The Saskatchewan river is the northern limit of its range" (Richardson, *Mammals*, pp. 98–100).

American Black Bear, *Ursus americanus* Pallas
"The Hudson's Bay Company imported, in 1822, nearly 3000 skins of these animals" (Sabine, "Appendix," p. 648).

Grizzly Bear, *Ursus arctos* Linnaeus
"Hunter's skins were seen … inhabits the country at the foot of the Rocky Mountains" (Sabine, "Appendix," p. 649).

‡Barren-ground Grizzly, *Ursus arctos* Linnaeus
Encountered along the Coppermine River on 3 and 6 July; a lean male killed at Hood River on 1 August; a fat female killed in Bathurst Inlet on 5 August; a female killed on Bear Island on 9 August, and a female and cub of the year killed south of Point Everitt on 10 August (JR, pp. 93, 96, 140–1, 148–9, 154, 155).

"Barren-ground Bear: The barren lands … are frequented by a species of Bear, which differs from the American Black Bear in its greater size, profile, physiognomy, longer soles, and tail; and from the Grisly Bear also, in colour and the comparative smallness of its claws. Its greatest affinity is with the Brown Bear of Norway …

"Keskarrah, an old Indian … was seated at the door of his tent, pitched by a small stream not far from Fort Enterprise, when a large Bear came to the opposite bank, and remained for some time apparently surveying him. Keskarrah considering himself to be in great danger, and having no one to assist him but his aged wife, made a speech to the following effect: 'Oh Bear! I never did you any harm; I have always had the highest respect for you and your relations, and never killed any of them except through necessity. Go away, good Bear, and let me alone, and I promise not to molest you.' The Bear walked off; and the old man, fancying that he owed his safety to his eloquence, favoured us, on his arrival at the fort, with his speech at length" (Richardson, *Mammals*, p. 22).

Swainson in 1838[2] considered Richardson's specimen to be the first description of a new species, *Ursus richardsoni*, and Richardson's "Barren-ground Grizzly" was recognized as a full species for over 130 years, with the type locality near the mouth of Hood River, Arctic Sound. In 1974 Banfield "lumped" into a single species, *Ursus arctos*, all of the 77 supposed species and 10 subspecies of brown and grizzly bears that Merriam listed in 1914. Scientific nomenclature has thus come full circle, back to the name used by Linnaeus and Richardson.

Polar Bear, *Ursus maritimus* Phipps
"Was met with on the shores of Hudson's Bay" (Sabine, "Appendix," p. 648).

Raccoon, *Procyon lotor* (Linnaeus)
"… found as far north as Red River, in latitude 50°, from which quarter about one hundred skins are procured annually by the Hudson's Bay Company" (Richardson, *Mammals*, pp. 36–7).

American Marten, *Martes americana* (Turton)
"The Pine Marten is every where abundant in the pine forests. Numbers of the skins (in the last year near 90,000) are annually imported by the Hudson's Bay Company, the fur being held in much estimation" (Sabine, "Appendix," p. 651).

"... particularly abundant where the trees have been killed by fire, but are still standing ... very rare ... in the ... Barren lands ... A partridge's head, with the feathers, is the best bait for the log traps in which this animal is taken" (Richardson, *Mammals*, p. 51).

Fisher, *Martes pennanti* (Erxleben)
"Captain Franklin's specimen was killed at Cumberland-House, in November 1819, but the animal was seen at various places during the Expedition, even as far to the northward as the Great Slave Lake ... importation in the last year amounted to 1800" (Sabine, "Appendix," pp. 651–2). Painted by Hood at Cumberland House, April 1820, plate 7 (Houston, ed., *To the Arctic by Canoe*)."Wejack, the appellation under which Hearne mentions it, is a corruption of its Cree or Knisteneaux name, *otchoek* ... It is universally termed *Pekan* by the Canadian fur-hunters" (Richardson, *Mammals*, p. 53).

Ermine, *Mustela erminea* Linnaeus
"Stoat Ermine: It is known as the Stoat in the summer season ... In the vicinity of Hudson's bay and in the interior, the Ermine frequents the houses of the settlers in search of mice, which constitute its principal food (Sabine, "Appendix," pp. 652–3). The subspecies of the boreal forest was named *M.e. richardsonii* by Bonaparte in 1838. An ermine was painted by Hood within the buildings at Cumberland House in early 1820, plate 11 (Houston, ed., *To the Arctic by Canoe*).

American Mink, *Mustela vison* Schreber
"... a drawing of one was made by Lieutenant Hood [but is not extant] ... The number of skins of this species, imported by the Hudson's Bay Company in 1822, exceeded 4600" (Sabine, "Appendix," p. 652). "The Vison-Weasel: The fur of the Vison is of little value, and at many of the remote parts their skins are taken by the traders from the Indians merely to accommodate the latter, but are afterwards burnt, as they will not repay the expense of carriage. The fur, however, is very fine, although short, and is likely, in the revolutions of fashion, to become valuable again" (Richardson, *Mammals*, p. 49).

Wolverine, *Gulo gulo* (Linnaeus)
"Two specimens were sent home by the Expedition" (Sabine, "Appendix," p. 650). "It has great strength, and annoys the natives by destroying their hoards of provision, and demolishing their marten traps. It is so suspicious, that it will rarely enter a trap itself, but beginning behind, pulls it to pieces, scatters the logs of which it is built, and then carries off the bait (Richardson, *Mammals*, p. 43). Painted by Hood at Cumberland House, 2 February 1820, though not recognizable, plate 5 (Houston, ed., *To the Arctic by Canoe*).

American Badger, *Taxidea taxus* (Schreber)
"… specimen received … The animal is abundant in parts of the interior of North America, inhabiting holes in the earth … A few skins of it are annually imported from Hudson's Bay" (Sabine, "Appendix," pp. 649–50), "The sandy prairies, in the neighbourhood of Carlton-house … are perforated by innumerable Badger-holes, which are a great annoyance to horsemen, particularly when the ground is covered with snow … it passes the winter from the beginning of November to April in a torpid state … The strength of its fore-feet and claws is so great, that one which had insinuated only its head and shoulders into a hole, resisted the utmost efforts of two stout young men who endeavoured to drag it out by the hind legs and tail" (Richardson, *Mammals*, p. 39).

‡Striped Skunk, *Mephitis mephitis hudsonica* (Richardson)
"Two specimens were received from the Expedition, they were only seen in the first period of the journey" (Sabine, "Appendix," p. 653). "The Skunk … does not, I believe, extend to the north of latitude 56° or 57°. It exists in the rocky and woody parts of the country, but is still more frequent in the clumps of wood which skirt the sandy plains of the Saskatchewan … The Skunk passes its winter in a hole, seldom stirring abroad, and then only for a short distance (Richardson, *Mammals*, p. 55). The subspecies now recognized is based on Richardson's type specimen from Carlton, "the plains of the Saskatchewan," in the Hudson's Bay Territories.

River Otter, *Lontra canadensis* (Schreber)
"… the specimen supplied by Captain Franklin being quite perfect … the imports of last year from Hudson's Bay having amounted to 7300" (Sabine, "Appendix," p. 653). Painted by Hood at Cumberland House on 3 March 1820, plate 10 (Houston, ed., *To the Arctic by Canoe*). "In the winter season, it frequents rapids and falls, to have the advantage of open water; and when its usual haunts are frozen over, it will travel to a great distance through the snow, in search of a rapid that has resisted the severity of the weather" (Richardson, *Mammals*, p. 57).

Lynx, *Lynx lynx* (Linnaeus)
"A very fine specimen … was sent from Cumberland-House … The skins, which are imported from America, make a beautiful fur, and are in high estimation, near nine thousand being the amount imported last year by the Hudson's Bay Company … It preys chiefly on the common Hares (*Lepus Americanus*) of the country" (Sabine, "Appendix," p. 659). Painted by Hood at Cumberland House in April 1820, plate 6 (Houston, ed., *To the Arctic by Canoe*).

Bearded Seal, *Erignathus barbatus* (Erxleben)
Ringed Seal, *Phoca hispida* Schreber
Seals of one or both of these species were mentioned in Richardson's journal entries for 16, 17, 25, and 28 July, and 6 and 9 August (JR, pp. 80, 81, 90, 94, 104, 106).

Woodland Caribou, *Rangifer tarandus caribou* (Gmelin)
Listed by Sabine. "A few deer of this kind frequent the swamps near Cumberland-house in the winter, but it is extremely rare indeed for a stray individual to wander on that parallel so far to the westward as Carlton-house" (Richardson, *Mammals*, p. 250).

Barren-ground Caribou, *Rangifer tarandus groenlandicus* Linnaeus
Listed by Sabine. "When in condition, there is a layer of fat deposited on the back and rump of the males to the depth of two or three inches or more, immediately under the skin, which is termed *depouillè* by the Canadian voyagers; and as an article of Indian trade, it is often of more value than all the remainder of the carcass. The *depouillè* is thickest at the commencement of the rutting season; it then becomes of a red colour, and acquires a high flavour, and soon afterwards disappears. The females at that period are lean; but in the course of the winter they acquire a small *depouillè*, which is exhausted soon after they drop their young. The flesh of the caribou is very tender, and its flavour when in season is, in my opinion, superior to that of the finest English venison; but when the animal is lean it is very insipid, the difference being greater between well-fed and lean caribou than any one can conceive who has not had an opportunity of judging. The lean meat fills the stomach but never satisfies the appetite, and scarcely serves to recruit the strength when exhausted by labour" (Richardson, *Mammals*, pp. 243–4).

Mule Deer, *Odocoileus hemionus* (Rafinesque)
Listed by Sabine. "Their most northern range is the banks of the Saskatchewan, in about latitude 54°, and they do not come to the eastward of longitude 105° in that parallel" (Richardson, *Mammals*, p. 255).

White-tailed Deer, *Odocoileus virginianus* (Zimmermann)
Listed by Sabine. "This, like the preceding species, does not, on the east side of the Rocky Mountains, range further north than latitude 54°, nor is it found in that parallel to the eastward of the 105th degree of longitude" (Richardson, *Mammals*, p. 259).

Moose, *Alces alces* (Linnaeus)
Listed by Sabine. A doe moose was painted by Hood in the Pasquia Hills, 3 April 1820, plate 9 (Houston, ed., *To the Arctic by Canoe*). "The Moose Deer is said to derive its present English name from its Algonquin and Cree appelation of mongsoa or moosoa ... towards the Coppermine river, they are not found in a higher latitude than 65°, on account of the scarcity on the Barren Grounds of the aspen and willow, which constitute their food ... It has the sense of hearing in very great perfection, and is the most shy and wary of all the deer species; and on this account the art of moose-hunting is looked upon as the greatest of an Indian's

acquirements, particularly by the Crees, who take to themselves the credit of being able to instruct the hunters of every other tribe" (Richardson, *Mammals*, pp. 232–4).

Wapiti, *Cervus elaphus* Linnaeus
Listed by Sabine. "They are pretty numerous amongst the clumps of wood that skirt the plains of the Saskatchewan" (Richardson, *Mammals*, p. 251).

Pronghorn, *Antilocapra americana* (Ord)
"... resorts to the neighbourhood of Carlton-House, during the summer, to bring forth its young, and returns to the southward in the winter" (Sabine, "Appendix," p. 667). "They come every year to the neighbourhood of Carlton-house, when the snow has mostly gone; soon after their arrival the females drop their young, and they retire to the southwards again in the autumn as soon as the snow begins to fall. Almost every year a small herd linger on a piece of rising ground not far from Carlton-house, until the snow has become too deep on the plains to permit them to travel over them. Few or none of that herd, however, survive until the spring, as they are persecuted by the wolves during the whole winter" (Richardson, *Mammals*, p. 263).

American Bison, *Bison bison* (Linnaeus)
"... extremely numerous on the plains of the Sashatchawan" (Sabine, "Appendix," p. 668). A buffalo hunt was depicted in May 1820, plate 8, even though Hood had not watched such a hunt himself (Houston, ed., *To the Arctic by Canoe*).
        "Great Slave Lake, in latitude 60°, was at one time the northern boundary of their range; but of late years, according to the testimony of the natives, they have taken possession of the flat limestone district of Slave Point, on the north side of that lake, and have wandered to the vicinity of Great Marten Lake [Lac la Martre], in latitude 63° or 64° ... The flesh of a bison in good condition is very juicy and well flavoured, much resembling that of well-fed beef ... The hump of flesh covering the long spinous processes of the first dorsal vertebrae is much esteemed ... when salted and cut transversely it is almost as rich and tender as the tongue ... One bison cow in good condition furnishes dried meat and fat enough to make a bag of pemmican weighing 90 lbs" (Richardson, *Mammals*, pp. 279–83).

Muskox, *Ovibos moschatus* (Zimmermann)
"... they were not seen farther south than latitude 66° in the line of country examined by the Expedition" (Sabine, "Appendix," p. 668). "They were observed by Captain Franklin's party to rut in the end of August and beginning of September" (Richardson, "Appendix," p. 332).

Appendix C

FISH COLLECTED BY JOHN RICHARDSON DURING

THE FIRST FRANKLIN EXPEDITION

Richardson reported on all specimens collected as far as the mouth of the Coppermine River, and gave descriptions from his journal of those collected beyond that point. They are presented in the order used in Scott and Crossman's *Freshwater Fishes of Canada*, followed by four arctic marine species. Full citation of the references here abbreviated will be found in the Bibliography. Quotations from Richardson's "Notices of the Fishes," Appendix VI, are given first (Richardson, "Fishes"), followed by those from *Fauna Boreali-Americana, III: The Fish* (Richardson, *Fish*).

Arctic Lamprey, *Lampetra japonica* (Martens)
"... found in Great Slave Lake, adhering to an Inconnu (*salmo Mackenzii*) (Richardson, "Fishes," p. 705).

Lake Sturgeon, *Acipenser fulvescens* Rafinesque
"This fish, termed nameyoo by the Cree Indians, is caught in great abundance in the Saskatchawan, but is not known to exist in the more northerly rivers, that discharge their waters into the Arctic Sea. The sturgeon fishery at Cumberland House is most productive in the spring and summer, but some are caught occasionally in the winter" (Richardson, "Fishes," pp. 705–6). "The Saskatchewan sturgeon weighs from ten to twenty pounds, and rarely attains the weight of sixty" (Richardson, *Fish*, p. 280).

Arctic Char, *Salvelinus alpinus* (Linnaeus)
Specimen at Bloody Falls, 19 July 1821 (JR, p. 117). "This fish is inferior to the English salmon in size, its flesh is red, and it is taken in great abundance in the

months of July and August, in the Salmon Leap, at Bloody Fall, on the Copper-Mine River" (Richardson, "Fishes," p. 707). "Our party subsisted upon it for several days, but the Indians who then accompanied us, being unused to it, thought it unwholesome, and our Canadian voyagers were soon infected with the same apprehension" (Richardson, *Fish*, p. 167).[2]

Lake Trout, *Salvelinus namaycush* (Walbaum)

"We frequently observed trout weighing forty pounds, and were informed by the residents that fish of sixty pounds were not very uncommon in particular lakes. In Manito, or God's Lake, between Hill and Severn Rivers, they are reported to attain the enormous size of ninety pounds" (Richardson, "Fishes," p. 710). "When in good condition it yields much oil, and is very palling to the appetite if simply boiled, but roasting renders it a very pleasant article of diet. The Canadian voyageurs are fond of eating it raw, in a frozen state, after scorching it for a second or two over a quick fire, until the scales can be easily detached, but not continuing the application of the heat long enough to thaw the interior. The stomach when boiled is a favourite morsel with the same people" (Richardson, *Fish*, p. 180).

‡Cisco, *Coregonus artedii* Lesueur

"The Cree name of this fish ottonneebees, has been corrupted by the traders into tullibee. It is inferior to the attihhawmegh as an article of food … It is found in most of the lakes, and we caught a few in the sea at the mouth of the Copper-Mine River …" (Richardson, "Fishes," p. 711, based on JR, pp. 359–63).[3]

Lake Whitefish, *Coregonus clupeaformis* (Mitchill)

"The Cree name of this fish is attihhawmegh, which is corrupted into tittameg by the traders. The Canadian voyagers term it poisson blanc … The weight of an ordinary-sized fish is three pounds, but it is not uncommon to meet with individuals weighing eight pounds, and they have been known to reach even twenty pounds … We caught some fine attihhawmegh at the mouth of the Copper-Mine River, and in Bathurst's Inlet, and it abounds in every river and lake in the country. It forms a most delicious food, and at many posts it is the sole article of diet for years together, without producing satiety" (Richardson, "Fishes," pp. 710–11). Richardson has an extremely detailed, 6-page description of a specimen from Cumberland House (JR, pp. 353–8). [Northern specimens may have included what is now the Broad Whitefish, *Coregonus nasus*.] "Though it is a rich, fat fish, instead of producing satiety it becomes daily more agreeable to the palate; and I know, from experience, that though deprived of bread and vegetables, one may live wholly upon this fish for months, or even years, without tiring … The mode of cooking the Attihawmeg is generally by boiling. After the fish is cleaned, and the scales scraped off, it is cut into several pieces, which are put into a thin copper kettle, with water enough to cover them, and placed over a slow fire ... The Copper Indians strike the fish through holes cut in the ice, using a very ingenious fish-gig, constructed of rein-deer horns" (Richardson, *Fish*, pp. 195–8).

‡Round Whitefish, *Prosopium cylindraceum* (Pallas)
"This fish preys on small insects. It spawns in September. We found it in the small rivers about Fort Enterprise and in the Arctic Sea" (Richardson, "Fishes," p. 715, based on JR, p. 49).[4]

Inconnu, *Stenodus leucichthys* (Güldenstadt)
"This fish grows to the size of thirty or forty pounds, or upwards. Its flesh is white, and when in season agreeable; but it is rather soft, and proves palling when used as daily food ... The Indians report that it comes from the Arctic Sea ... Its most southerly *habitat* is at the Salt River, the cascades on Slave River preventing it from ascending higher" (Richardson, "Fishes," p. 709).[5]

‡Arctic Grayling, *Thymallus arcticus* (Pallas)
"In the autumn of 1820 we obtained many by angling in a rapid of Winter River, opposite to Fort Enterprise. The sport was excellent, for this grayling generally springs entirely out of the water when first struck with the hook, and tugs strongly at the line, requiring as much dexterity to land it safely as would secure a trout of six times the size" (Richardson, *Fish*, p. 191). Richardson considered this was a species new to science when he gave a description in his journal of 21 August 1820 (JR, pp. 2–5). He later named it Back's Grayling, *Salmo signifer*. "Signifer" referred both to its magnificent wing-like dorsal fin, but equally alluded to "the rank of my companion, Captain Back, then a midshipman, who took the first specimen that we saw with the artificial fly" (Richardson, *Fish*, p. 191).[6]

Goldeye, *Hiodon alosoides* (Rafinesque)
"This singular and beautiful fish ... is caught in nets at Cumberland-House in the spring, but not in sufficient quantity to be of importance in an economical point of view" (Richardson, "Fishes," p. 716). "... inhabits the lakes which communicate with the Saskatchewan, in the 53rd and 54th parallels of latitude, but does not approach nearer to Hudson's Bay than Lake Winipeg ... The Naccaysh is taken during the summer months only, and in small numbers, in the gill-nets set for other fish. It bites eagerly at an artificial fly or worm, but angling is seldom practised in the fur countries. Its flesh is white, resembling that of the perch in flavour, and excelling it in richness ... taken at Cumberland House, lat. 54° N., May, 1820" (Richardson, *Fish*, pp. 232–3, based on JR, pp. 364–7).[7]

Northern Pike, *Esox lucius* Linnaeus
"The pike abounds in every lake in the northern parts of America" (Richardson, "Fishes," p. 716.) "As it takes a bait set under the ice more readily than any other

fish of the same districts, it forms an important resource to the Indian hunter in the depth of winter, when the chase fails him. In the summer it is occasionally shot while basking in shallow waters, but except in very urgent cases, powder and ball are of too high value in the fur countries to be thus expended" (Richardson, *Fish*, p. 124, based on JR, pp. 378–81).

Longnose Sucker, *Catostomus catostomus* (Forster)
Richardson's description of the meethqua-maypeth in "Fishes," p. 720, occupied nearly two pages. "It makes a more gelatinous soup than any other of the northern fish, and is the best bait for trout or pike" (Richardson, *Fish*, p. 116, based on JR, pp. 350–2).

White Sucker, *Catostomus commersoni* (Lacépède)
"The namay-peeth is very abundant in the Saskatchawan" (Richardson, "Fishes," pp. 717–23). "It is a very soft watery fish, but devoid of any unpleasant flavour, and is considered to be one of the best in the country for making soup. Like its congeners it is singularly tenacious of life, and may be frozen and thawed again without being killed" (Richardson, *Fish*, p. 113, with description from JR, pp. 339–46).

Shorthead Redhorse, *Moxostoma macrolepidotum* (Lesueur)
"… the wawpawhawkeeshew is comparatively rare every where" (Richardson, "Fishes," pp. 721–3). "This handsome species was observed by us only in Pine-Island Lake, lat. 54°, long. 110° … specimens at Cumberland House, April, 1820" (Richardson, *Fish*, p. 118, based on JR, pp. 347–9).[8]

Channel Catfish, *Ictalurus punctatus* (Rafinesque)
"The nathemegh [mathemegh] is found sparingly in the lakes that flow into the Saskatachawan, and more abundantly in the lakes and rivers to the southward. It is much prized as a rich food" (Richardson, "Fishes," pp. 723–4).[9] "Its Cree appellation signifies 'ugly fish' … the head is very broad" (Richardson, *Fish*, pp. 135–6).

Burbot or Methy, *Lota lota* (Linnaeus)
"The burbot is found in every river and lake in the country … so little esteemed as food as to be eaten only in cases of necessity" (Richardson, "Fishes," p. 724). There is a 4-page description (JR, pp. 368–71). "specimen killed in Pine Island Lake, March 31, 1820 … filled with cray-fish to such a degree, that the form of their bodies was quite distorted … When well bruised and mixed with a little flour, the roe can be baked into very good biscuits, which are used in the fur countries as tea-bread" (Richardson, *Fish*, p. 249).

Ninespine Stickleback, *Pungitius pungitius* (Linnaeus)
"Specimens of them, which were put in spirits, were destroyed on their way home" (Richardson, "Fishes," p. 728). "In 1820, many sledge-loads were taken from a small pond in the vicinity of Cumberland-house for the purpose of feeding the dogs" (Richardson, *Fish*, p. 57).

Walleye, *Stizostedion vitreum* (Mitchill)
"Piccarel, or Dore, of the traders ... very abundant about Cumberland-House" (Richardson, "Fishes," pp. 725–6). "It is a well-flavoured, delicate fish, though, being too poor to please the palates of those who have been accustomed to feast upon the White-fish (*Coregonus albus*), Mathemeg (*Pimelodus borealis*), or Sturgeon, it is very often abandoned to the dogs, with whom, for the same reason, it is no favourite. Even an Epicurean ichthyophagist would relish it when fried; but from the scarcity of lard, butter or suet, this is not an usual mode of cooking in the fur-countries" (Richardson, *Fish*, pp. 14–15; his description was from JR, pp. 372–7).

Deepwater Sculpin, *Myoxocephalus quadricornis* (Linnaeus)
"... found abundantly in the Arctic Sea. Our Canadian voyagers gave it the name of Crapaud de Mer, which is very expressive, but has been already applied to a different fish (Richardson, "Fishes," pp. 726–7). "Numerous specimens of this fish were caught in a net set in the mouth ... of Tree River, near the Coppermine, lat. 67°12' North, July 23rd, 1821" (Richardson, *Fish*, p. 44, from JR, pp. 123–4).

Capelin, *Mallotus villosus* (Müller)
"This curious little fish termed by the Esquimaux angmaggoeuck was met with in Bathurst's Inlet, collected in large shoals on the shallows to spawn" (Richardson, "Fishes," p. 710, based on JR, 4 August 1821, pp. 145–8).[10] "... differs from the Newfoundland fish (of which through the kindness of M. Audubon, I possess a number of specimens preserved in spirits) in the appearance of the scales" (Richardson, *Fish*, pp. 187–90).

Pacific Herring, *Clupea harengus pallasi* Vallenciennes
"... description ... has been compared with the common herrings brought to the London market in January, and found to agree exactly" (Richardson, "Fishes," p. 716). "... taken in Bathurst's Inlet, August 5, 1821" (Richardson, *Fish*, p. 231), based on JR, pp. 150–1).

Starry Flounder, *Platichthys stellatus* (Pallas)
"... found at the mouths of the rivers in the Arctic Sea" (Richardson, "Fishes," p. 724). "taken July 16, 1821, off the Coppermine River, lat. 67½° N" (Richardson, *Fish*, p. 257, based on JR, pp. 119–20).

Arctic Flounder, *Liopsetta glacialis* (Pallas)
"Found in Bathurst's Inlet of the Arctic Sea" (Richardson, "Fishes," p. 724).
"Taken ... lat. 67°40′ N., 5th August, 1821" (Richardson, *Fish*, p. 259), based on JR, pp. 151–2).

Appendix D

PLANTS NAMED BY AND FOR JOHN RICHARDSON

Richardson's obituary notice in the *American Journal of Science*[1] observes that "The work by which his name is indelibly associated with American botany is his botanical appendix to Franklin's first overland journey, published in 1823, the most important essay of the time upon Arctic plants, and the precursor of Hooker's *Flora of British America*."[2] As David Alexander Stewart said: "Plants of Northern Canada named by and for Richardson would make a garden of respectable size."[3]

In the following list of plants of western and northern Canada, named by or for Richardson, the following notations are used:

†plants named by Richardson, and still recognized as species or varieties, using this name, by modern authorities.

*plants named by Richardson, with the name now listed only as a synonym by modern authorities.

‡plants named for Richardson by other botanists.

§plants recognized by former authorities, but now considered referable to another species.

The plants are presented in the order used by Porsild and Cody in *Vascular Plants of Continental Northwest Territories, Canada*. Full citations of main sources will be found in the Bibliography. "Richards." is the conventional botanical abbreviation for plants first named by Richardson (1787–1865). "Richards." means the plant is still classified within the same genus. "(Richards.)" indicates the plant is now classified within a different genus. Note that not all plants have an English common name.

‡*Potamogeton Richardsonii* (Benn.) Rydb. Richardson's Pondweed
Not listed from the first Franklin expedition. Found as *P. perfoliatus* as far north as Great Slave Lake during the second Franklin expedition.

‡*Festuca rubra* L. ssp. *Richardsonii* (Hook.) Hulten. Red Fescue (variety)
Not listed from the first Franklin expedition. Richardson found *Festuca rubra* from
Saskatchewan to Hudson's Bay on the second expedition.

‡*Muhlenbergia Richardsonis* (Trin.) Rydb. Mat Muhly
Named later. Occurs at Great Slave Lake and Great Bear lake.

‡*Stipa Richardsonii* Link. Richardson Needle Grass
Named later. Occurs in Saskatchewan and Alberta.

‡*Carex Richardsonii* R. Br. Richardson's Sedge
Named after the second expedition. Richardson brought specimens from Norway
House and Cumberland House.

†*Tofieldia coccinea* Richards. Richardson's False Asphodel
First described in Latin by Richardson in 1823 with specimens from the arctic coast,
which were "lost in crossing the Barren Grounds." Richardson nevertheless had
retained his Latin description, "taken from the live plant," and found that it
agreed with specimens in the Banksian Herbarium, brought from Unalaska by Mr
Nelson.

§*Anticlea chlorantha* (Richards.) Rydb. (*Zygadenus chloranthus* Richardson) a form of
White Camas, or Death-Camass
First described in Latin by Richardson in 1823 with specimens from the wooded
country between 54° and 64° north latitude. On the second expedition it was
found north to Great Bear Lake. Rydberg listed it in *Flora*. Porsild and Cody,
Vascular Plants, considered it referable to *Zygadenus elegans*.

†*Cypripedium passerinum* Richards. Northern Lady's-Slipper
First described by Richardson in the 1824 revision of Appendix VII to Franklin,
Journey. It was found in coniferous woods from the Saskatchewan north to
latitude 58°.

†*Habenaria obtusata* (Pursh) Richards. Small Northern Bog Orchid or Blunt-leaf
Orchis
This species was found along the Hayes River on the first Franklin expedition.
Formerly *Plantanthera obtusata*, Richardson placed it in its present genus.

*Salix desertorum Richards. A form of Short-capsuled Willow
Thought to be a new species when first described from the Barren Grounds in
1823. Now included with *S. brachycarpa* Nutt., but listed as a synonym by Scoggan,
Flora.

‡*Salix lanata* L. ssp. *Richardsonii* (Hook.) Skvortsov. Richardson's Willow
Described in Latin by Richardson as a new species from Fort Franklin on Great
Bear Lake, after the second expedition. Porsild and Cody, *Vascular Plants*,
considered it a subspecies of *S. lanata*.

*Salix rostrata Richards. A form of Long-beaked Willow
Described in Latin by Richardson as a new species in 1823. Scoggan, *Flora*, listed it
as a synonym for *S. bebbiana*.

†*Geocaulon lividum* (Richards.) Fern. Northern Comandra
Described in Latin by Richardson in 1823 as found in "shady mossy woods" north
to Great Slave Lake. In the second expedition he found it north to latitude 69° on
the Mackenzie River.

†*Stellaria laeta* Richards. A form of Chickweed or Stitchwort
Richardson first described this plant in Latin from the Barren Grounds in 1823.
During the second expedition he found it from Great Bear Lake to the shores of the
Arctic Ocean.

†*Stellaria stricta* Richards. A form of Long-stalked Stitchwort
This plant was first described by Richardson in the 1824 revision of Appendix VII
to Franklin, *Journey*, although in the 1823 edition he considered it merely a variety
of *S. palustris*. Porsild and Cody, *Vascular Plants*, listed it as a full species.
Richardson found it in wooded areas north to Great Bear Lake.

‡*Anemone Richardsonii* Hook. Yellow Anemone
First described by Hooker in the revision of Appendix VII to Franklin, *Journey*.
Found along the Hayes River and on the Barren Grounds during the first
expedition.

†*Ranunculus Purshii* Richards. Pursh's Buttercup or Yellow Water-Crowfoot
First described in Latin by Richardson in 1823 from wooded areas and from the
Barren Grounds. After the second expedition Richardson mentioned finding it
near lakes and marshes about Cumberland House and Great Slave Lake.

‡*Thalictrum sparsiflorum* Turcz var. *Richardsonii* (Gray) Boivin. Few-flowered
Meadow Rue
Richardson described slight differences from previously described *T. clavatum*, *T.
cornuti*, and *T. Anemonoides*. Found by Richardson only at Portage la Loche.

†*Arabis arenicola* (Richards.). Gel. A species of Rock Cress
Hooker, *Flora Boreali-Americana*, listed this plant as *Eutrema arenicola*, from

"Richardson's MSS." The habitat was given as "deep sand upon the shores of Arctic America."

†*Braya glabella* Richards.
First described in Latin by Richardson in 1823 from the Barren Grounds, especially on the Copper Mountains.

‡*Braya Richardsonii* (Rydb.) Fern.
In Hooker, *Flora Boreali-Americana*, Richardson lists a variety of B. *alpina* var. *americana* and lists another Braya that was similar to B. *pilosa*. One of these plants may be the basis for the new species described by Rydberg, *Flora*, and included in Porsild and Cody, *Vascular Plants*.

†*Cardamine digitata* Richards.
Described in Latin by Richardson in 1823 from the Barren Grounds. Porsild and Cody, *Vascular Plants*, listed *Cardamine Richardsonii* Hult. as a synonym.

†*Descurainia pinnata* (Walt.) Britt., var. *brachycarpa* (Richards.) Fern. Short-fruited Tansy Mustard
Described in Latin as a new species, *Sisymbrium brachycarpon*, by Richardson in 1823 from the wooded areas 54° to 64° latitude. Now considered only as a variety, not a full species.

‡*Descurainia Richardsonii* (Sweet) O.E. Schulz. Gray Tansy Mustard
Named in honour of Richardson by Sweet.

†*Lesquerella arenosa* (Richards.) Rybd. A variety of Sand Bladder-pod
First described in Latin by Richardson as *Vesicaria arenosa* in 1823 from the "sandy plains of the Saskatchewan." Hooker, *Flora Boreali-Americana*, was not convinced that it merited full species status, but thought it best described as a variety of *Vesicaria arctica*. Looman and Best, *Flora*, considered it only a variety, *Lesquerella ludoviciana* var. *arenosa*. Rydberg, *Flora*, recognized it as a full species.

‡*Boykinia Richardsonii* (Hook.) A. Gray. *Therofon Richardsonii* (Hook.) Ktze, is a synonym
First described by Hooker, *Flora Boreali-Americana*, as *Saxifraga Richardsonii* in 1840 based on specimens brought home by Richardson in 1827 from the "Arctic Sea-shore between the Mackenzie and Copper-mine Rivers."

‡*Heuchera Richardsonii* R. Br. Alumroot
A few of Richardson's specimens from the first Franklin expedition were given by Hooker to another eminent botanist, Robert Brown. Brown devoted a page to the

description of this new species at the end of Appendix vii to Franklin, *Journey*. Locality was given as "On the rocky banks of rivers from lat. 54° to 64° north."

†*Ribes hudsonianum* Richards. Northern Black Currant
First described by Richardson in the 1824 revision of Appendix vii to Franklin, *Journey*, although in the 1823 edition Richardson considered it as *Ribes nigrum*, the Black Currant of Europe. Richardson reported that the currants and gooseberries were grouped together by the Cree Indians under the name of *sappoom-meena*. The fruit was similar to that of *Ribes nigrum*, but the flowers were much smaller, whiter, with a shorter tube, and very downy, narrower segments. The berry the Crees named after the goose, *niske-min*, was a type of blueberry.

†*Dryas Drummondii* Richards. Yellow Mountain-avens
First described from "Richardson mss." by Hooker in *Botanical Magazine* t. 2972. In the 1823 edition Richardson considered it within *Dryas integrifolia*, which is the White Mountain-avens, the floral emblem of the Northwest Territories. Richardson found it on the first expedition in the woody country between latitude 54° and 64° north.

†*Potentilla concinna* Richards. Early Cinquefoil
First described by Richardson in 1823 from specimens collected at Carlton House in May 1820. Listed by Scoggan, *Flora*.

*Rubus triflorus Richards. Dewberry
First described by Richardson in the 1824 revision of Appendix vii to Franklin, *Journey*, although in the 1823 edition he considered it *Rubus saxatilis*, var. β. *Canadensis*. It is now classed as *Rubus pubescens* Raf. but Scoggan, *Flora*, gave *R. triflorus* as a synonym. The Cree Indians, Richardson said, called it *Athouscan*.

†*Astragalus aboriginum* Richards. Indian Milk-Vetch
First described by Richardson in Appendix vii to Franklin, *Journey*, as *Astragalus aboriginorum*. Recent texts (Looman and Best, *Flora*, Porsild and Cody, *Vascular Plants*) shortened the species' name by two letters, but Scoggan, *Flora*, used the original spelling in full. Richardson found it near Carlton in May 1820 and on the second expedition, as far north as Great Bear Lake. Richardson noted that the Cree Indians "gather its roots in the spring as an article of food."

‡*Astragalus Richardsonii* Sheldon. Richardson's Milk-Vetch
This species is closely related to *A. aboriginorum* and was described by Sheldon in honour of Richardson. It has a more restricted northern range in the Barren Grounds.

§*Geoprumnon succulentum* Richards. Succulent Ground Plum
Described by Richardson as a new species, *Astragalus succulentum*, collected on the "Hilly grounds of the Saskatchawan, especially about Carlton-house" in May

1820. Hooker, *Flora Boreali-Americana*, felt it was not distinct from *A. caryocarpus*. Rydberg, *Flora*, recognized it as a full species, *Geoprumnon succulentum*.

†*Hedysarum Mackenzii* Richards. Northern Hedysarum or Mackenzie's Liquorice-root
First described by Richardson in 1823 from the Barren Grounds as the liquorice plant described by Alexander Mackenzie.

‡*Geranium Richardsonii* Fisch. & Trautv. Wild White Geranium
Drummond collected plants considered to be *Geranium albiflorum* in valleys in the Rocky Mountains in 1826. Later these were recognized to represent a new species and were named in honour of Richardson, although he had not encountered the plant himself.

§*Vaccinium canadense* Kalm; *Cyanococcus canadensis* (Richards.) Rydb. Sour-top Blueberry or Velvet-leaf Blueberry
Described by Richardson as a new species in 1823, based on plants from the wooded areas between 54° and 64° latitude north, and on the second expedition, north to Great Bear Lake. Richardson noted that Kalm had already placed specimens in the Banksian Herbarium. Scoggan, *Flora*, placed this under *Vaccinium myrtilloides*, with the above two names as synonyms.

†*Gentiana propinqua* Richards. Felwort
First described by Richardson in 1823 from along the Hayes River, and on the second expedition from Cumberland House to Great Bear Lake.

‡*Gentiana Richardsonii* Porsild. Northern Fringed Gentian
A new species described in 1951 by the late A. Erling Porsild and named in honour of Richardson. Found near the Arctic Ocean.

†*Phlox Hoodii* Richards. Moss Phlox
First described and illustrated in 1823, with the following eulogy by Richardson in Appendix VII to Franklin, *Journey*, p. 733: "This beautiful species is a striking ornament to the plains in the neighbourhood of Carlton-House, forming large patches, which are conspicuous from a distance. The specific name is a small tribute to the memory of my lamented friend and companion, whose genius, had his life been spared, would have raised him to a conspicuous station in his profession, and rendered him an ornament to any science to which he might have chosen to direct his attention." It was collected on "Sandy plains, Carlton House Fort, and other places in lat. 54°'" in May 1820 and again in the spring of 1827.

‡*Phlox Richardsonii* Hook. Richardson's Phlox
First described from specimens collected by Richardson along the arctic coast in July and August 1826, on the second Franklin expedition. Hooker, *Flora*

Boreali-Americana, noted that the flowers are "of a brilliant lilac colour. It must be allowed that Dr. Richardson and Messrs. Drummond and Douglas, have been pre-eminently successful in discovering new and beautiful species of the genus Phlox in North America."

§*Pedicularis macrodonta* Richards. Purple Lousewort
First described as a new species, *Pedicularis macrodontis*, by Richardson in 1823, collected along the Hayes River. Hooker, *Flora Boreali-Americana*, considered it conspecific with *P. Wlassowiana*, but modern authors place it under *P. parviflora*. Scoggan, *Flora*, listed *macrodontis* as a synonym for *parviflora*.

‡*Artemesia Richardsoniana* Bess.
Named in honour of Richardson by Wilibald Swibert Joseph Gottlieb Besser (1784–1842). Besser named many species of North American Artemesias (Wormwoods) for famous botanists, including Chamisson, Douglas, Hooker, Lindley, Michaux, Nuttall, Prescott, and Tiles. Porsild and Cody, *Vascular Plants*, recognized it as a valid species from the arctic coast.

*Aster salicifolius Richards.
Porsild and Cody, *Vascular Plants*, gave the above as a synonym for *Aster Franklinianus* Rydb. Richardson listed *Aster salicifolius* from the wooded areas of lat. 54° to 64° north in Appendix VII to Franklin, *Journey*, but as a species already described by Carl Ludwig Willdenow. Hooker, *Flora Boreali-Americana*, considered this a synonym for *Aster laxifolius*.

†*Chrysanthemum integrifolium* Richards.
First described by Richardson in 1823 as from the Copper Mountains, the specimens carried back from the coast by W.F. Wentzel. On the second expedition he found it widely distributed on shores and islands in the Arctic.

†*Crepis nana* Richards. Dwarf Hawk's-beard
Mentioned in Richardson's journal, 21 July 1821, from the mouth of the Coppermine River, this specimen was carried south by Wentzel's party and was first described by Richardson in 1823.

‡*Hymenoxys Richardsonii* (Hook.) Cockerell. Colorado Rubberweed
This species was first collected by Richardson near Carlton House in the spring of 1827, and was named in his honour by Hooker, as *Picradenia Richardsonii*. Rydberg, *Flora*, listed it by the latter name, but Looman and Best, *Flora*, placed it under *Hymenoxys*.

*Senecio frigidus (Richards.) Less.
Described as a new species by Richardson in 1823 as *Cineraria frigida*; Hooker, *Flora*

Boreali-Americana, called it *Senecio frigidus*. Porsild and Cody, *Vascular Plants*, gave S. *frigidus* as a synonym for S. *atropurpureus* (Ledeb.) Fedtsch. Richardson had collected it in the Barren Grounds north of 64°.

†*Senecio eremophilus* Richards. Cut-leaved Ragwort
First described by Richardson in the revision of Appendix VII to Franklin, *Journey*. Hooker in 1840 listed the locality as "On the gravelly banks of Cedar Lake, lat. 54°". Presumably it was collected there during the return of the first expedition, on 30 June 1822.

†*Senecio lugens* Richards. Entire-leaved Groundsel
First described by Richardson in 1823 from plants collected on 15 July 1821. Porsild and Cody, *Vascular Plants*, told the story of the appropriateness of the Latin name: "The black tips of the involucral bracts inspired the specific name, from the Latin *lugeo* (to mourn), and refers to the massacre at Bloody Falls on the Coppermine River, of a group of unsuspecting Eskimo, by the Indian warriors who, in 1771 accompanied Samuel Hearne." Looman and Best, *Flora*, considered this plant as S. *integerrimus* Nutt. var. *lugens* Richards. (Boiv.).

†*Townsendia exscapa* (Richards.) Porter. Low Townsendia
Described by Richardson as a new species, *Aster exscapus*, in 1823; it was collected at Carlton House in May 1820. Hooker, *Flora Boreali-Americana*, placed it in a new genus which he named *Townsendia*. Listed by Scoggan, *Flora*.

‡*Cetraria Richardsonii* Hook.
This lichen was found "On the Barren Grounds generally in Rein-deer tracks. It was not found to the southward of Great Slave Lake" (Appendix VII, Franklin, *Journey*, p. 761). See also Appendix E below.

†*Dactylina arctica* (Richards.) Nyl.
Richardson deserves the credit for this new species, as discussed by John W. Thomson in Appendix E below.

Appendix E

JOHN RICHARDSON'S CONTRIBUTION TO

LICHENOLOGY: SOLUTION OF A 160-YEAR-OLD

PUZZLE

John W. Thomson

One of the puzzles in lichenology has been the relative contributions of John Richardson and William J. Hooker to the list of arctic lichens in the "Botanical Appendix" to Franklin's *Narrative of a Journey to the Shores of the Polar Sea in the Years 1819, 20, 21 and 22*. Among the 120 lichens listed are two species new to science, *Cetraria richardsonii* (Hooker, ms) and *Dufourea arctica*, the latter with no crediting of authorship. Both new species were beautifully illustrated in a fifth plate, beyond the four plates included in the list of illustrations, in the rare, revised edition which contains a more comprehensive botanical appendix, and which Hooker cites as "ed. 2."[1]

The difference in the crediting statements leaves open to interpretation whether only *Cetraria richardsonii* should be credited to Hooker and *Dufourea* (now *Dactylina*) *arctica* credited to Richardson as author of the botanical appendix, or whether both names should be credited to Hooker. In this connection one should consider two items. First, in the introduction to the botanical appendix, Richardson states "... and Professor Hooker by undertaking the examination of the Lichenes and Fungi, has stamped a value upon a portion of the catalogue, upon which it was peculiarly desirable to have the opinion and authority of an eminent cryptogamic botanist." One must immediately modify this crediting with a footnote to the fungi on page 776 of the second edition which states: "The fungi were determined by the acute mycologist, Dr. Grenville, author of the Scottish Cryptogamic Flora." It is important to note that Hooker "examined" both groups of plants but that Grenville "determined" (named) the fungi, and that no commitment is made as to who "determined" the lichens. Second, W.A. Leighton enumerated the lichens collected by Richardson during two Arctic Land expeditions.[2] Leighton cites a communication from Richardson which discusses the few lichens he collected on stones: "What I did bring home were obtained in 1822–23

[sic] near Fort Enterprise, and they are named by Sir William Hooker in the Botanical Appendix to Franklin's first journey, 4to edition, 1823."

Richardson's knowledge of flowering plants was considerable. But how extensive was his knowledge of lichens? The above quotation suggests that William Hooker was the final authority for the lichen names. Yet a nagging doubt persisted, principally caused by the difference in crediting of the two new species; this made it appear as if Richardson had actually prepared the paper himself and perhaps only submitted it to Hooker for critique and comments. The ascription to "Hooker, ms." as the authority for the name *Cetraria richardsonii* most obviously represents one of the gentlemanly conventions of the period in which the Franklin journal was published. The collector on an expedition always hoped to have species named after himself as a memorial. However, scientists frowned upon writing a paper describing new species and naming them after themselves. It was always necessary to submit a specimen to a trusted friend, who would then publish a description and name the new species after the collector. A splendid example of such behaviour was the submission by the famous Swedish botanist Carolus Linnaeus of a specimen of his favourite flower to Gronovius to be named *Linnaea borealis*. Thus his Lapland specimen became the basis for not just a new species but a new genus memorializing himself. In the case of Richardson, Hooker had not really published the new name *Cetraria richardsonii* but had only written it in a manuscript or letter, "Hooker, ms." Could Richardson, therefore, have written the Lichenes in the appendix and been responsible for the name of the other new species, *Dufourea arctica*? Did he have the necessary lichenological knowledge to have been the true author of that portion of the appendix?

The discovery of Richardson's journal with the entry of 1 October 1820 listing forty-two lichens which he observed in the environs of Fort Enterprise is strong substantiation for a remarkable knowledge of lichens, a knowledge comparable with leading lichenologists of his day. It must be remembered that in the 1820s lichens were mainly recognized by their gross structure. The use of spores and other microscopic characters was just beginning to be known nearer the middle of the century. It is obvious from the journal entry that Richardson had in the field with him at Fort Enterprise and was using the two books necessary for arctic lichen studies at that time. These were Erik Acharius's *Lichenographia Universalis* (1810) and Goran Wahlenberg's *Flora Lapponica* (1812). The Acharius *Synopsis Methodica Lichenum* (1814) was later substituted for the earlier *Lichenographia Universalis* in the writing of the appendix. The page references for each species leave no doubt. One of the most convincing to an arctic lichenologist is the entry for species 6 "*L [ecidea] albocaerulescens*? Ach. p. 189. in the fissures of rocks and on the shady sides of stones." *Lecidea albocaerulescens* does not occur in the Arctic and the correct page for that species in Acharius is 188, not 189. But in reading through the Latin text, one finds the discussion of that *Lecidea* includes discussion of a related species, unnamed, which has "crustae color ferruginosus vel ferrugineo-rufescens (cfr. Dicks. 1. c.) accidentalis est, nam cinerascens occurris." As I have worked in the field in the same general region of the arctic,[3] there is no doubt in my mind that Richardson did not make a mistake in the page number. He was utilizing the correct page for this lichen which Acharius placed in *Lecidea albocaerulescens* but which is now known as *Huilia flavocaerulescens* (Hornem) Hertel. The habitat of this lichen, which resembles *L. albocaerulescens* in the bluish powdery surface of its fruiting structure but has an orange thallus, is exactly as Richardson described it on shaded sides of stones, especially in boulder trains over flowing-but-hidden meltwaters and between such rocks and boulders.

Richardson's list is characteristic for the region. Only one well trained in lichenology could recognize these species in the field, particularly with the aid of the difficult Latin manuals which Richardson used.

Also impressive is his recognition of two species as new to science. Entry 31, a new species of *Cetraria* described as possibly belonging to near *C. odontella* and lying loose on the ground, is undoubtedly *Cetraria richardsonii*. The comparison of the species is astute. Entry 42, the *Dufourea*, is without doubt what was later described in the appendix as *Dufourea arctica*. It would be difficult for one not well versed in lichenology to take Acharius's and Wahlenberg's Latin texts and decide that what one had in hand was not in the books, and later to have that verified upon examination by Hooker.

With these points in mind we must conclude that the Lichenes text in the botanical appendix must have been contributed by Richardson and only checked by Hooker, who also made the drawings and provided the money for the printing of the extra plate 31. Richardson's deference to authority figures is revealed not only in his subservience to Hooker in the case of the lichens, but also in his contribution of appendices to the Franklin narrative. His desire to be commemorated in the name of the *Cetraria* lichen, which he had already realized in 1820 was a new species, led him to submit the lichens to Hooker for approval and for naming in accordance with the ethics of the day. It would seem only right to credit Richardson with the authorship of the *Dufourea arctica* (now *Dactylina arctica*), which modesty had led him to leave uncredited in the appendix, and that it should be *Dactylina arctica* (Richards). Nyl.

NOTE: In footnotes 28 to 64, inclusive, chapter 1, I have given the comparable name used today for each species. For absolutely certain confirmation one would of course have to have the exact specimens which Richardson had and would have to examine them with microscopic and microchemical techniques.

Appendix F

JOHN RICHARDSON'S GEOLOGICAL FIELD WORK

W.O. Kupsch

The basis for understanding the contribution made by John Richardson to geological knowledge of the northeastern part of what is now the District of Mackenzie, Northwest Territories, is the Journal kept by him on the journey from Fort Enterprise to Coronation Gulf and back. A second source is his "Geognostical Observations" in Franklin's *Narrative of a Journey*. Third, there is the map, or chart, accompanying Franklin's *Journey* on which the summary statements of geological observations are attributed to Richardson.[1] The Journal can be regarded as Richardson's field notebook; his "Geognostical Observations" and the chart are comparable to a geological report and an accompanying map.

THE FIELD NOTEBOOK

General remarks

Table 5 lists all 244 days on which Richardson made an entry, or "notice" as he called it, in his Journal; those that contain remarks pertaining to inanimate nature are emphasized in bold face. Of the 244 days, 58 days (24 per cent) have some observations on the geology or the landscape. If only the days of the journey from Fort Enterprise to the Arctic Ocean and back (4 June – 29 October 1821) are taken into consideration, it appears that 52 days (41 per cent) of the total 127 days have some record of geological interest. That only three geological observations were made after 10 September is understandable considering that hardships beset the party, that there are only a few outcrops along the route travelled, and that Richardson "travelled over this district when the ground was deeply covered with snow."[2]

Richardson's observations on inanimate nature can be divided into two broad categories: geological and physiographic. In the geological category belong

TABLE 5 Days of observations
Dates of some geological observations (bold face)

1820	
August	**21**, 22, 26, 29
September	6, 7, **9**, 10, **11**, **12**, 13, 14, 15, 16, 30
October	1, 6, 9, 18, 23, 26
November	1, 16, 23, 28
December	1, 12, 25
1821	
January	5, 8, 15, 17, 25
February	5, 12, 14
March	4, 12, 17, 23, 30, 31
April	4, 17, 20, 22, 27, 28, 30
May	1, 2, 3, **4**, 5, 6, 10, 18, 20, 21, 22, 23, 24, 25, 26, 27, 28, 29, 31
June	4, 5, **6**, 7, **8**, 9, 10, 11, 12, 13, 14, 15, 16, 17, 18, 19, 20, **21**, 22, 23, 24, **25**, 26, **27**, **28**, **29**, **30**
July	**1**, **2**, 3, **4**, 5, **6**, **7**, **8**, **9**, 10, **11**, **12**, 13, **14**, **15**, 16, 17, **18**, 19, 20, **21**, **22**, **23**, 24, **25**, 26, 27, **28**, 29, 30, **31**
August	1, **2**, **3**, 4, 5, **6**, 7, 8, **9**, 10, **11**, **12**, **13**, **14**, 15, **16**, 17, 18, 19, 20, 21, **22**, **23**, **24**, 25, **26**, **27**, 28, 29, 30, **31**
September	**1**, **2**, **3**, **4**, 5, 6, 7, 8, **9**, 10, 11, 12, 13, 14, 15, 16, **17**, 18, **19**, 20, 21, 22, 23, 24, 25, 26, **27**, 28, 29, 30
October	1, 2, 3, 4, 5, 6, 7, 29, 30, 31
November	1, 2, 3, 4, 5, 6, 7, 8, 9, 10, 11, 12, 13, 14, 15, 16, 17, 18, 19, 20, 21, 22, 23, 24, 25, 26, 27, 28, 29, 30
December	1, 2, 3, 4, 5, 6, 7, 8, 9, 10, 11, 14, 15, 16, 17, 18, 19

those on minerals, rocks, and stratigraphy. Physiographic descriptions deal with landscapes and landforms.

The entries in the Journal range from terse, one- or two-word names of rocks observed in the field to a one-page description of the landscape near Rocky Defile Rapid along the Coppermine River, or the only slightly shorter geological record of the Coppermine Mountains. Both the Journal and the "Geognostical Observations" are written in simple, straightforward language. Richardson's spelling is neither flawless nor consistent and his punctuation leaves much to be desired.[3] In a few places he reveals, by using expressions such as "beautiful" or "gloomy," some emotional appreciation of what he saw. Such sensitivities, though, are rare and confined to just one word. Richardson thus anticipated the recording style currently used by geologists which also (much to the detriment of the record according to some critics) excludes any intrusion of personal feeling.

Franklin had to rely on his "brother officers' journals" for the part of the journey from Fort Enterprise to the crossing at Belanger Rapids in September 1821, when he lost a portfolio containing his journals in a canoeing accident. Although only slightly, he did later embellish those previous terse notes.

Richardson's remarks for 1 July 1821, read: "The Coppermine river at this place is about 200 yards wide, 8 or ten feet deep, with a rocky bottom and strong current. Both banks are well wooded, but on the right side, at the distance of a few miles, there is a ridge of very barren hills, which the Indians report to be a continuation of the barren grounds."[4] Franklin, writing for a wide audience when romantic accounts of far away places were much *en vogue*, reworded the account: "The Copper-Mine River, at this point, is about two hundred yards wide, and ten feet deep, and flows very rapidly over a rocky bottom. The scenery of its banks is picturesque, the hills shelve to the waterside, and are well covered with wood, and the surface of the rocks is richly ornamented with lichens. The Indians say that the same kind of country prevails as far as Mackenzie's River in this parallel; but that the land to the eastward is perfectly barren."[5] In fact, the loss of notes was not confined to this one incident. Richardson lost his around 2–5 July and had to rely on memory: "unfortunately the notices respecting the strata have been lost, and we have only a general impression that a hornblendic gneiss, probably of the transition series, was abundant."[6] There is no indication as to how these notes were lost.

Minerals, rocks, and stratigraphy

A reader reasonably familiar with current geological nomenclature will have little difficulty in understanding Richardson's terms for minerals and rocks. Many of the names used by him are still in use today without much change in meaning. A few are obsolete and fewer still have a different meaning. Most are now much more rigorously defined, however, and as a general rule one should assume that Richardson used terms having a broad meaning that is not clearly delimited. Tables 6 and 7 have been compiled to assist the reader in understanding Richardson's usage of mineral and rock names and their present meaning.[7]

Richardson's descriptive strength clearly lies in the fields of geology now referred to as mineralogy and petrology. To him, however, there was no such distinction and, as for most of his contemporaries, "mineralogy" sufficed to refer both to the science dealing with minerals and the one concerned with aggregates of minerals – that is, rocks – in spite of the use of "petralogy" [sic] by John Pinkerton as early as 1811 in the title of his text on the *Science of Rocks*.[8] Richardson referred to his mentor Robert Jameson as a "distinguished mineralogist,"[9] which is a further indication that the term mineralogy was used to describe a much wider field of science than presently understood. Certainly Jameson was more than a specialist in minerals. He taught all aspects of geology that caught the attention of naturalists in the early nineteenth century.[10] Richardson acknowledged his debt to Jameson with the tribute that "His zeal for the promotion of science led him to take an early and deep interest in our proceedings, and his endeavours to serve us have been unwearied."[11] Jameson was a scientist, a geologist not limited to mineralogy, and Richardson followed in his footsteps. It should be kept in mind, therefore, that "mineralogist" in the beginning of the nineteenth century was an accolade for the naturalist interested in inanimate nature. Franklin named a group of islands in the southeastern part of Coronation Gulf after Jameson, "in honour of the distinguished Professor of Mineralogy at Edinburgh."[12] And Jameson himself

TABLE 6 Minerals mentioned by Richardson

Name	Definition/description	Remarks	Journal (day/month 1821)	Geognostical observations (page)
augite	Common Ca, Na, Mg, Fe, Al-silicate; black, greenish-black, or dark green			521, 536
calcareous spar	Common rock-forming mineral; $CaCO_3$. Commonly white, colourless, or occurs in pale shades of grey, yellow, or blue. The principal constituent of limestone	Now called calcite. The term spar (obsolete: spath) is loosely applied to any transparent or translucent, light-coloured crystalline mineral, commonly readily cleavable and somewhat lustrous, eg calc spar (calcite), fluor spar (fluorite), or feldspar	11/7	529
calc-spar				528
calcedony	Cryptocrystalline variety of quartz, translucent or semi-transparent, with an almost waxlike lustre and uniform tint; white, pale blue, grey, brown, or black. The material of most chert. Common as an aqueous deposit filling or lining cavities in rocks	Now spelled chalcedony. In the gem trade, the name refers specifically to the light blue-grey or "common" variety of chalcedony	24/8	532
carnelian	Variety of chalcedony. Translucent red or orange-red, pale to deep in shade, with iron impurities	Carnelian is used for seals and in the manufacture of signet rings	24/8	532
chiastolite	Opaque variety of andalusite with black carbonaceous impurities arranged in a regular manner so that a section normal to the longest axis of the crystal shows a black Maltese cross formed as a result of the pushing aside of impurities into definite areas as the crystal grew in metamorphosed shales	Chiastolite has long been used for amulets, charms, and other inexpensive novelty jewelry. Andalusite is brown, yellow, green, red, or grey: Al_2SiO_5. Occurs in thick, nearly square prisms in schists, gneisses, or hornfelses		536
copper glance	Dark lead-grey or black; Cu_2S. Metallic lustre; crystals or massive	Now called chalcocite, an important ore of Cu. A "glance" is a mineral with a resplendent lustre		529

TABLE 6 (continued)

Name	Definition/description	Remarks	Journal (day/month 1821)	Geognostical observations (page)
felspar	Group of rock-forming minerals of general formula M-Al-silicate where M is mainly K, Na, or Ca. The most widespread of any mineral group; in all kinds of rocks (eg schists, gneisses, granites) and as fissure minerals in clefts and druse minerals in cavities. White or nearly white or clear and translucent. No colour of their own but are commonly coloured (pink, flesh-colour, and green) by impurities such as iron	Still spelled so in Britain. North American and most European spelling is feldspar. Obsolete spelling: feldspath	9/7, 11/7, 27/8	521, 527, 528, 529, 530, 531, 536
feldspar			25/7	
flint	Massive, very hard, somewhat impure variety of chalcedony, commonly black or of various shades of grey, breaking with a conchoidal fracture, and striking fire with steel	Widely used synonym of chert (black chert). Identical with chert in texture and composition, despite the fact that the term "flint" has been in use since about 700 AD for "anything hard" and since 1000 AD for "a variety of stone" and it antedates "chert" by almost 1000 years. Flint has been described as having a denser texture, a more perfect (smooth) conchoidal or less splintery fracture, a smaller quartz content, and as having thin, translucent splinters or sharp cutting edges. The term is commonly used in southern England for one of the siliceous nodules occurring in the Cretaceous chalk beds	9/7	528
galena	Bluish-grey to lead-grey: PbS. Commonly contains included silver minerals. Common as disseminations in veins in limestone, dolomite, and sandstone. Shiny metallic lustre, exhibits highly perfect cubic cleavage, relatively soft, and very heavy	Galena is the most important ore of lead and one of the most important sources of silver	27/7, 28/7	531, 536

TABLE 6 (continued)

Name	Definition/description	Remarks	Journal (day/month 1821)	Geognostical observations (page)
green copper ore	See malachite		2/8	
copper green green ore				529, 531
gypsum	Widely distributed mineral: $CaSO_4 \cdot 2H_2O$. White or colourless when pure, but commonly tinted grey, red, yellow, blue, or brown. Soft. Commonest sulphate mineral and generally associated with halite	Especially in rocks of Permian and Triassic age gypsum forms thick, extensive beds interstratified with limestone, shale, and clay. Used in making plaster of Paris	11/7	536
hornblende	Commonest mineral of the amphibole group (Ca- and Na-bearing, hydrous, ferro-magnesian, and Ti-bearing minerals). Commonly black, dark green, or brown. In distinct elongated crystals or in columnar, fibrous, or granular forms. Primary constituent of many acidic and intermediate igneous rocks (granite, syenite); common metamorphic mineral in gneiss or schist	Hornblende is an old German name for any dark, prismatic crystal found with metallic ores but containing no valuable metal (the word "Blende" indicates a "deceiver")	11/8, 23/8	522, 523, 524, 525, 526, 529, 532
jasper	Dense, cryptocrystalline, opaque (to slightly translucent) variety of quartz associated with iron ores and containing iron-oxide impurities that cause various colours, characteristically red	Term is often applied to any red chalcedony	24/8	532
malachite	Bright green $Cu_2CO_3(OH)_2$; weathering product of native copper; the greening of copper roofs	Ore of copper and a common secondary mineral in the upper, oxidized, zones of copper veins. In masses with smooth mammillated or botryoidal surfaces. Commonly concentrically banded in different shades of colours. Used to make ornamental objects		529

TABLE 6 (continued)

Name	Definition/description	Remarks	Journal (day/month 1821)	Geognostical observations (page)
mica	Group of hydrous Al-silicates with low hardness, perfect basal cleavage, readily splitting into thin, tough, somewhat elastic laminae or plates with a resplendent lustre. Range from colourless, silvery-white, pale brown, or yellow to green or black	Prominent rock-forming constituents of igneous and metamorphic rocks. Commonly occur as flakes, scales, or shreds	11/8	522, 532, 535, 537
native copper	Reddish or salmon-pink native element Cu. Commonly dull and tarnished. Ductile and malleable. Commonly in dendritic clusters or mossy aggregates, in sheets, or in plates filling narrow cracks or fissures	Formerly an important ore of copper. The only metal that occurs native abundantly in large masses. Many uses, notably as the base metal in brass, bronze, and other alloys		528, 529, 531,
pistacite	Yellowish-green, pistachio-green, or blackish-green mineral: $Ca_2(Al, Fe)_3Si_3O_{12}(OH)$	Synonym of epidote, especially the pistachio-green variety rich in ferric iron		522, 528
potstone	Dark green or dark brown impure steatite or massive talc	Used in prehistoric times and by Eskimos to make cooking pots, vessels, and seal oil lamps. Steatite or soapstone is massive, fine-grained, fairly homogeneous, impure talc-rock. Talc is extremely soft, light green or grey hydrous Mg-silicate derived by alteration of other minerals in basic igneous rocks		536
prehnite	Pale green, yellowish-brown, or white hydrous, Ca, Al-silicate. Common in crystalline aggregates with a botryoidal or mammillary and radiating structure	Commonly associated with zeolites (white or colourless, hydrous Al-silicates analogous in composition to the feldspars, long been known to occur as well-formed crystals in cavities in basalt) in geodes, druses, fissures, or joints in altered igneous rocks		528, 529

TABLE 6 (continued)

Name	Definition/description	Remarks	Journal (day/month 1821)	Geognostical observations (page)
pyrites	Pyrite (the now common synonym of iron pyrites) is a common pale bronze or brass-yellow mineral: FeS_2. Commonly has small amounts of other metals	Magnetic pyrites (522) probably refers to a rock or ore having both pyrite (non-magnetic) and magnetite. Iron pyrites (523) is a common but now obsolete rendering of pyrite. Pyrite has brilliant metallic lustre and absence of cleavage. Has been mistaken for gold (fool's gold) which is softer and heavier. Commonly crystallizes in cubes (the faces of which are generally striated) but also in shapeless grains and masses. The most widespread and abundant of the sulphide minerals and occurs in all kinds of rocks, such as in nodules in sedimentary rocks and coal seams or as a common vein mineral. An important ore of sulphur, less so of iron. Is burned in making sulphur dioxide and acid. In places mined for the associated gold and copper		522, 523
quartz	Crystalline silica, an important rock-forming mineral: SiO_2. Next to feldspar, the commonest mineral	Derived from the provincial German Quarz	9/7, 7/8, 16/8	521, 522, 527, 528, 530, 532, 533, 536
rock crystal		Synonym of quartz crystal		529
salt	General term for naturally occurring NaCl	Synonyms are halite, common salt, rock salt		536
silica	Chemically resistant dioxide of silicon: SiO_2. Occurs in 5 crystalline forms (incl. quartz); in cryptocrystalline form (chalcedony); in amorphous and hydrated forms (opal); in less pure forms (eg sand, chert, flint); and combined in silicates as an essential constituent of many minerals			524

TABLE 6 (concluded)

Name	Definition/description	Remarks	Journal (day/month 1821)	Geognostical observations (page)
topaz	1/ White or lightly coloured mineral: $Al_2SiO_4(F, OH)_2$. Minor constituent in highly siliceous igneous rocks as translucent or transparent prismatic crystals and masses and as rounded waterworn pebbles. 2/ yellow quartz resembling topaz such as smoky-quartz turned yellow by heating (false topaz)			535
variegated copper ore	Synonym for bornite; a brittle, metallic looking mineral: Cu_5FeS_4. Reddish-brown, brown, or coppery-red on fresh fracture, but tarnishes rapidly to iridescent blue or purple	Other synonym: peacock ore, horse-flesh ore, purple copper ore. Valuable ore of copper		529
white crystals		Probably crystals of zeolite common in basalt in which their occurrence was noted by Richardson. See also prehnite	3/9	

TABLE 7 Rocks mentioned by Richardson

Rock name	Definition/description	Remarks	Journal (day/month 1821*)	Geognostical observations (page)
amygdaloid	Any igneous rock containing gas cavities or vesicles filled with secondary minerals such as calcite, quartz, chalcedony, or a zeolite	No longer used as a noun; modern usage only as an adjective	11/7, 3/8, 24/8, 26/8	528, 531, 532
amygdaloidal			11/7	533
basalt	General term for dark-coloured igneous rocks, commonly extrusive but locally intrusive (eg as dikes and sills) composed chiefly of calcic plagioclase and pyroxene	See also trap	21/7, 23/7, 24/7, 2/8, 3/8, 9/8, 14/8, 16/8, 24/8, 3/9	521, 530
chalk	Soft, pure, earthy, fine-textured, commonly white to light grey or buff limestone of marine origin	The best known and most widespread chalks are of Cretaceous age, such as those exposed in cliffs on both sides of the English Channel. Word derived from the Old English *cealc*, in turn from the Latin calx, lime		537
clay-stone clay stone claystone	1/ Indurated clay having texture and composition of shale but lacking its fine lamination or fissility 2/ Old English term for an argillaceous (clayey) limestone	Richardson appears to have used the term in the first sense and for shale (a term not used by him)	11/7 11/7, 24/8	528 528, 530, 531, 532
clay-slate clay slate Clay Slate	1/ Low-grade, essentially unreconstituted slate, as distinguished from more micaceous varieties; argillite (clay-rich rock) with a parting or slaty cleavage; weakly metamorphosed rock intermediate between shale and slate 2/ English term much used in the early 19th century for true slate	Richardson appears to make little distinction between what would now be called a shale (a term not used by him) and slate. See also slate and slate-clay	6/7 25/6, 28/6, 7/7	526, 535 523, 524, 525, 526, 536

TABLE 7 *(continued)*

Rock name	Definition/description	Remarks	Journal (day/month 1821*)	Geognostical observations (page)
clinkstone	Now called phonolite which in its broadest sense refers to any intrusive rock composed of alkali feldspar, dark minerals, and any feldspathoid (group of comparatively rare rock-forming minerals consisting of Al-silicates of Na, K, or Ca, and having too little silica to form feldspars)	Derived from the German Klingstein, an obsolete term for phonolite (from the Greek *phone*, "sound" for the alledgedly ringing sound produced by a phonolite when struck by a hammer). Appears to have been used by Richardson when he encountered a particularly hard basalt	2/8	530, 531
coal	Readily combustible rock containing more than 50% by weight and more than 70% by volume carbonaceous material formed by compaction and induration of variously altered plant remains similar to those in peat			536
conglomerate conglomerated	Coarse-grained sedimentary rock; consolidated equivalent of gravel	No longer used as an adjective; modern usage only as a noun. Puddingstone is a popular name applied chiefly in Great Britain to a conglomerate consisting of well-rounded pebbles with colours in such marked contrast with the abundant fine-grained matrix or cement that the rock suggests an old-fashioned plum pudding	7/8 11/7	523
flinty slate	Siliceous slate	Richardson probably used the term for a very hard variety of slate. The term "flint" was used in Great Britain in some parts of the country for "anything very hard"		528
freestone	Obsolete term for any stone (esp. a thick-bedded, even-textured, fine-grained sandstone) that breaks freely and can be dressed with equal ease in any direction without splitting or tending to split	The ease with which freestone can be shaped into blocks makes it a good building stone. The term was originally applied to limestone, and is still used for such rock. Richardson applied it to a red sandstone	12/7	

TABLE 7 (continued)

Rock name	Definition/description	Remarks	Journal (day/month 1821*)	Geognostical observations (page)
glance coal	Brittle, lustrous bituminous coal or lignite with conchoidal fracture; kind of jet [coal]	Synonym of pitch coal		536
gneiss	Foliated metamorphic rock, in which bands or lenticles of granular minerals alternate with bands or lenticles in which minerals having flaky or elongate prismatic habit predominate. Although a gneiss is commonly feldspar- and quartz-rich, the mineral composition is not an essential factor in its definition	Varieties of gneiss are distinguished by texture (eg Augen, German for eyes, or knotted gneiss), characteristic minerals (eg hornblende gneiss), or general composition and/or origin (eg granite gneiss)	21/8/1820, 12/9/1820, 1/5, 4/5, 6/6, 8/6, 27/6, 8/7, 28/7, 11/8, 23/8, 3/9, 9/9	521, 522, 523, 524, 525, 526, 532, 533, 534, 535, 536
granite	Plutonic rock in which quartz constitutes 10–50% of the felsic components and in which the alkali feldspar/total feldspar ratio is generally restricted to the range of 65–90%	Richardson made little distinction between granite and gneiss: "granite or gneiss rock" (28/7). In modern usage the term "granite" broadly applied refers to any holocrystalline, quartz-bearing plutonic rock	25/7, 28/7, 2/8	521, 522, 523, 524, 526, 530, 531, 532, 533, 535, 536
granitic gneiss				521
greenstone	Field term applied to any compact dark-green, altered, or metamorphosed basic igneous rock (eg basalt) that owes its colour to the presence of chlorite, actinolite, or epidote	To Richardson equivalent to basalt or trap	27/6, 11/7, 21/7, 9/8, 14/8, 3/9	522, 523, 524, 528, 530, 531, 532, 533, 536
green stone green-stone			6/7	523 521, 525
greenstone slate		Probably used by Richardson for a thin-bedded or fissile basaltic rock or a thin-bedded mafic green tuff and equivalent to his greenish-grey clay slate (25/6)		523

TABLE 7 (continued)

Rock name	Definition/description	Remarks	Journal (day/month 1821*)	Geognostical observations (page)
greywacke grey wacke	Old rock name variously defined but now generally applied to dark grey, firmly indurated, coarse-grained sandstone that consists of poorly sorted angular to subangular grains of quartz and feldspar, with a variety of dark rock and mineral fragments embedded in a compact clayey matrix having the general composition of slate and containing an abundance of fine-grained illite, sericite, and chloritic minerals. Greywackes are typically interbedded with marine shales and slates, and associated with submarine lava flows and bedded cherts	From the German *Grauwacke*, "grey-stone," probably so named because the original greywackes resembled partly weathered basaltic residues (Wackes). First recorded use by G.S.O. Lasius in 1789 who, in a description of the Harz Mountains, referred to "Grauewacke" as a German miner's term for barren country rock of certain ore veins, and who described the rock as a gray or dark quartz "breccia" with mica flakes and fragments of chert or sandstone in a clay matrix. The term "greywacke" or "grauwacke" was probably first used in English by Robert Jameson in his *Elements of Geognosy* (1808). As early as 1839 Sir Roderick Impey Murchison wrote that "… it has already been amply shown that this word should cease to be used in geological nomenclature, and … is mineralogically worthless"	21/6	523 536
hornstone	General term for a compact, tough, and siliceous rock having a splintery or subconchoidal fracture	Term has been used to describe flint or chert as well as hornfels and has also been confused with hornblende. It should be abandoned because it is doubtful that it can designate any readily identifiable material. From the context it appears that Richardson used the term to describe a "compact" (his term) fine-grained or lithographic (?) limestone		528

TABLE 7 (continued)

Rock name	Definition/description	Remarks	Journal (day/month 1821*)	Geognostical observations (page)
limestone	Sedimentary rock consisting chiefly of calcium formed by either organic or inorganic processes; many are highly fossiliferous and clearly represent ancient shell banks or coral reefs. Limestones include chalk and they effervesce freely with any common acid		9/7	527, 528
Lydian stone	Touchstone consisting of a compact, extremely fine-grained, velvet or grey-black variety of jasper	Derived from the Greek *Lydia*, an ancient country in Asia Minor. Touchstone is black, flinty stone, such as silicified shale or slate, or a variety of quartz allied to chert or jasper, the smoothed surface of which was formerly used to test the purity or fineness of alloys of gold and silver by comparing the streak left on the stone when rubbed by the metal with that made by an alloy of predetermined composition		536
marl	Old term loosely applied to a variety of materials, most of which are loose, earthy deposits consisting chiefly of an intimate mixture of clay and Ca-carbonate, formed under marine or, especially, freshwater conditions. Marl is commonly grey	From the French *marle*. Richardson appears to use the term for loose earthy deposits along the coast: clay or marl; the latter being grey, possibly calcareous		530, 531
mica slate mica-slate	Schist is a strongly foliated crystalline rock formed by metamorphism that can be readily split into thin flakes or slabs	Probably used by Richardson to describe a micaceous *schist* (a word not used by him)	23/8	523
muriatiferous clay	Clay yielding salt or another chloride but not in commercially valuable quantities			536

TABLE 7 *(continued)*

Rock name	Definition/description	Remarks	Journal (day/month 1821*)	Geognostical observations (page)
porphyry porphyritic gneiss	Igneous rock of any composition having conspicuous large crystals in a fine-grained groundmass	Term was first applied to a purple-red rock quarried in Egypt and characterized by large crystals of alkali-feldspar	9/7	537 522
protogine	Granitic rock, occurring in the Alps, that has gneissic structure, contains the minerals sericite, chlorite, epidote, and garnet, and shows evidence of a composite origin or crystallization (or partial recrystallization) under stress after consolidation	Alternate spelling is protogene. The term, dating from 1806, is obsolete		535
pummice	Excessively cellular, glassy lava	Obsolete spelling. Modern form is pumice. Richardson appears to have used the term for what now would be called scoriaceous (a coarsely vesicular) basalt, coarser than a pumiceous rock	23/7	
sandstone	Medium-grained sedimentary rock composed of abundant and rounded or angular fragments of sand size set in a fine-grained matrix of silt or clay and more or less firmly united by cementing material (commonly silica, iron oxide, or CaCO$_3$); consolidated equivalent of sand, intermediate in texture between conglomerate and shale		9/7, 11/7, 12/7, 14/7, 15/7, 3/8, 7/8, 9/8, 11/8 12/8, 14/8, 27/8	527, 528, 529, 530, 531, 532, 533, 534, 536, 537
sienite syenite	Group of plutonic rocks containing alkali-feldspar, a small amount of plagioclase, one or more dark minerals (especially hornblende) and quartz, if present, only as an accessory. With an increase in quartz it grades into granite	Sienite is an obsolete spelling. Its name is derived from Syene, Egypt. A.G. Werner in 1788 applied the name in its present meaning to rock at Plauenscher Grund, Dresden, Germany; the Egyptian rock is a granite containing much more quartz	27/6, 8/7 6/7, 9/7, 27/7, 31/7, 11/8, 23/8, 27/9	526, 533, 535

TABLE 7 (concluded)

Rock name	Definition/description	Remarks	Journal (day/month 1821*)	Geognostical observations (page)
slate	Compact, fine-grained, metamorphic rock formed from such rocks as shale and volcanic ash, which possess the property of fissility along planes independent of the original bedding (slaty cleavage) whereby they can be parted into plates		21/6, 9/7	533, 536
slate clay slate-clay slaty clay	Clay more or less transformed into slate	The term has been used specifically for a fire-clay in English coal measures. Richardson probably used the term as a synonym for shale (which he did not use)	15/7, 3/8, 16/8 16/8	531 533
Topaz rock	Topaz is a mineral: for a definition, see Table 6	An obsolete term used in 1796 by Kirwan, *Elem. Min.* (ed. 2) I, 368: "Topaz rock ... presents a compound of topaz, quartz, schorl, and lithomarge confusedly compacted together." lithomarge: a smooth, indurated variety of common kaolin (a clay mineral) schorl: 1/ term commonly applied to tourmaline, especially to the black, iron-rich, opaque variety 2/ obsolete term for any of several dark minerals other than tourmaline (eg hornblende)		535
trap	Any dark-coloured, fine-grained, shallow intrusive or extrusive rock, such as basalt	Derived from the Swedish *trappe*, "stair" or "step" in reference to the stairstep appearance created by the abrupt termination of successive flows	25/6, 1/7, 12/7, 23/7, 3/8, 16/8, 24/8	524, 527, 528, 529, 530, 531, 532, 533, 537
tuff	Compacted deposit of volcanic ash and dust that may or may not contain up to 50% sediments such as sand and clay		3/8	528, 531

NOTE: Unconsolidated materials such as clay, sand, and gravel of soils are not included, neither are accumulations of organic matter such as peat or marsh.
*All dates are 1821 except where indicated otherwise.

published a three-volume textbook entitled *System of Mineralogy* of which the third one was entitled *Elements of Geognosy*. Clearly, then, geognosy was subordinate to mineralogy. Geognosy was a term that developed out of mineralogy and in the eighteenth century was used for the science dealing with the origin, distribution, and sequence of minerals and rocks and thus comes close to the modern concept of "historical geology," or the narrower "stratigraphy." Richardson used "geognosy" in the title of his Appendix 1, "Geognostical Observations," to Franklin's *Journey* but he was also acquainted with the term geology which was not only to replace geognosy but to assume a much wider meaning that included mineralogy, petrology, stratigraphy, sedimentation, and the history of the earth. Rather than writing about "geognocists," Richardson refers to "geologists" – certainly a less awkward designation, but one that cut the ties between pupil and master.[13]

Stratigraphy as now understood is a branch of geology concerned with the order and relative position of stratified rocks such as sedimentary and volcanic rocks. The word was first used in 1865.[14] The middle and late eighteenth century saw the first attempts at the development of a relative time scale for the fossiliferous strata overlying the unfossiliferous crystalline igneous and metamorphic rocks that are now assigned to the Precambrian.

Table 8 shows the development of the geological time scale. Geologists in the late eighteenth and the first half of the nineteenth century divided the time elapsed since the Precambrian in units to which names were assigned, much as historians gave names such as Middle Ages or Renaissance. Only since the discovery of radioactivity and the determination of decay constants of radioactive elements in the first half of the twentieth century has it been possible to put accurate dates in years alongside the previously named relative time units. Such absolute dates are not shown in Table 8 as they are irrelevant to an understanding of Richardson's working method as a "stratigrapher": his attempts at putting a sequential order to the rocks he observed in the field. The standard against which Richardson calibrated his observations was the scale of Abraham Gottlob Werner,[18] which is shown in abbreviated form in Table 8 and in a more detailed manner below (with the oldest unit at the bottom, the youngest on top, as is the present convention for all time scales or stratigraphic columns):[19]

5 *Alluvial Period* with the formations sand, clay, pebbles, bituminous wood, aluminous earth, etc. The result of local conditions, almost contemporaneous with the Volcanic Period and extending into the present.

4 *Volcanic Period*, subdivided into true volcanic rocks (lava, ash, etc.) and pseudo-volcanic rocks (burnt clay, jasper, slag, etc.). The result of local conditions, almost contemporaneous with the Alluvial Period and extending into the present.

3 *Floetz Period* with the formations red sandstone, coal, old Floetz limestone, freestone, chalk, basalt, etc. Contains organic remains. Precipitates or deposits from a universal ocean extending into the present.

2 *Transition Period* with the formations clay-slate, greywacke, transition green-

TABLE 8 Development of the geological time scale[15]

LEHMANN 1756	ARDUINO 1760	WERNER 1790	RICHARDSON[16] 1823	LYELL 1833	PHILLIPS 1838	RICHARDSON[17] 1861	GENERAL USE (EUROPE) 1982
ALLUVIAL	ALLUVIAL	VOLCANICS	Loose blocks of stone	RECENT PERIOD	TERTIARY STRATA	DRIFT BEDS	QUATERNARY Desnoyers 1829 France
			Lake deposits, seashore deposits	NEWER PLIOCENE		ALLUVIAL	
	TERTIARY	ALLUVIAL AUFGESCHWÄMMTES or TERTIARY	ALLUVIAL DEPOSITS	OLDER PLIOCENE			
				MIOCENE		TERTIARY coal or lignite	TERTIARY Arduino 1760 Italy
				EOCENE			
SECONDARY	SECONDARY	STRATIFIED FLOETZ or SECONDARY	CHALK	CRETACEOUS	CRETACEOUS	CRETACEOUS	CRETACEOUS d'Omalius d'Halloy 1822 Belgium—France
			MOUNTAIN LIMESTONE	WEALDEN			
			NEW RED or VARIEGATED SANDSTONE with gypsum, salt and muriatiferous clay — TRAP and PORPHYRY ROCKS	OÖLITIC or JURA	OÖLITIC	LIASSIC BEDS	JURASSIC von Humboldt 1799 Switzerland
				LIAS			
			LIMESTONE	NEW RED SANDSTONE	RED SANDSTONE	TRIASSIC	TRIASSIC von Alberti 1834 Germany
							PERMIAN Murchison 1841 Russia
			COAL FORMATION	COAL MEASURES	CARBONIFEROUS	CARBONIFEROUS limestone series or coal measures; true coal fields	CARBONIFEROUS Kirwan 1799 England
				MOUNTAIN LIMESTONE			
		TRANSITION or ÜBERGANGSGEBIRGE	OLD RED SANDSTONE alternates in places with Transition rocks	OLD RED SANDSTONE		DEVONIAN or OLD RED SANDSTONE	DEVONIAN Murchison and Sedgwick 1839 England
			Clay-slate	GRAUWACKE and TRANSITION LIMESTONE	SILURIAN	SILURIAN	SILURIAN Murchison 1835 Wales
			Greywacke		GRAUWACKE		ORDOVICIAN Lapworth 1879 Britain
CRYSTALLINE or PRIMITIVE	PRIMITIVE or PRIMARY	PRIMITIVE or URGEBIRGE	Gneiss (most abundant), granite, mica-slate, clay-slate, and protogine (least abundant). Traversed by veins of feldspar, quartz and granite. Also galena and potstone.	PRIMARY PERIOD	Clay-slate, mica-schist, and gneiss systems	Granites and gneisses; metamorphic rocks	CAMBRIAN Sedgwick 1835 Wales
							PRECAMBRIAN

WERNER group labels: ALLUVIAL · FLOETZ or SECONDARY · TRANSITION · PRIMITIVE

RICHARDSON[16] group labels: ALLUVIAL · FLOETZ or SECONDARY · TRANSITION · PRIMITIVE

LYELL group labels: TERTIARY PERIOD · SECONDARY PERIOD · CARBONIFEROUS PERIOD · PRIMARY PERIOD

PHILLIPS group labels: SECONDARY STRATA · PRIMARY STRATA

RICHARDSON[17] group labels: PRIMITIVE or PALEOZOIC or hypogene igneous rocks

GENERAL USE group labels: CENOZOIC Phillips 1849 · MESOZOIC Phillips 1849 · PALEOZOIC Sedgwick 1838 stone, and the first organic remains. Precipitates or deposits from a universal ocean.

1 *Primitive Period* with the formations red granite, sienite, gneiss, mica slate, slate, primitive greenstone, hornblende rock, porphyry, etc. No organic fossil remains. Precipitates or deposits from a universal ocean.

The above detailed Wernerian classification clearly shows that the basalts (or the alternative "traps") which Richardson recognized in the Copper-mine Mountains were placed by him in the Floetz Formation in accordance with the modified Wernerian classification. Their true nature as volcanic rocks was briefly considered and then rejected by Richardson: "Many of these trap and porphyry rocks presented the columnar structure which has been considered as indicative of a volcanic origin, but their other characters and the horizontal strata upon which they reposed seemed to give them a still greater claim to Neptunian origin. Our opportunities of observation, however, were much too limited to permit us to offer a decided opinion upon this disputed point."[20] Richardson thus still accepted the Wernerian classification and Neptunism in 1823. He had been taught these theories by Jameson and carried them into the field as part of his intellectual baggage. They served him well because his priority was to observe rocks and minerals, not to speculate on their origin or their position on a historical scale. Richardson was not alone in his acceptance of outmoded ideas. In the United States such well-known early geologists as William Maclure in 1817 or Amos Eaton as late as 1820 were avowed Wernerians.[21] What is surprising is that the challenge to Werner had come from Dr James Hutton in Edinburgh in 1785, some thirty years before Richardson attended Jameson's lectures, also in Edinburgh. The reasons for the slow acceptance of Hutton's new ideas, including the ascendency of Volcanism, which recognized the volcanic origin of basalt, over Neptunism, which held basalt to be an oceanic precipitate, were many and varied for different scientists. One factor, often pointed out, was the unreadable style of Hutton's original writings. Only after his death in 1797 did his theories find a wider audience through the publication of John Playfair's book. Opposed to his acceptance was the charismatic influence of Werner, the outstanding teacher of his time, who received all the publicity. Also, some of the geological evidence was by no means clear in the absence of techniques of investigating minerals and rocks now available but then not yet developed. To many scientists, Hutton's sug-gestion that granite had once been molten seemed absurd.[22]

For Richardson it appears that the influence of his teacher Jameson was all-pervasive and that he made no special efforts to keep abreast of new developments in a field of natural science that lay outside his primary interests of zoology and botany. Perhaps his devout religious character kept him, like many of his contemporaries, from accepting Hutton's theories, which were regarded as atheistic. Richardson must have been unaware that Werner was also accused of being an atheist, but it is only recently that this irony has been pointed out.[23]

In 1823 Richardson could not be expected to use most of the names now applied to eras and periods of geological time for the simple reason that, except for Carboniferous (1779), Jurassic (1799), Cretaceous (1822), and Tertiary (1760), they were introduced some ten to twenty years later. However, Richardson kept reasonably up to date with nineteenth-century development of stratigraphic nomenclature and his 1861 column comes much closer to the modern one and reflects the thinking of the time (Table 8).

At present the term "formation" has a precise and well-defined meaning to a geologist. It is used to designate the fundamental unit in litho-stratigraphy: a body of rock strata that is lithologically distinctive from other such units lying above and below. Formations need to be extensive enough to be mapped. They are not necessarily of homogeneous lithology throughout. No such definition can be attached to "formation" as used by Werner, Jameson, or Richardson. They used the term for all rocks of one kind. All sandstones constituted a formation distinct from all limestones. Somewhat later than Werner, other Germans used "Formation" for a widely recognizable set of rocks that might comprise many local rock strata of different kinds of rocks. In France the word "terrain" had been used for the same concept, but in time both "Formation" and "terrain" became replaced by the English "system," and "formation" took on its modern meaning.

The term "vein" was used in the beginning of the nineteenth century for what are now called dykes (a tabular igneous intrusion that cuts across the bedding or other layering of the host rock) and for the present concept of veins (a tabular mineral deposit filling a fracture in the host rock).

It is surprising that Richardson did not use the term "schist". In its earlier form, "schistus," it had been used for both schist and, occasionally, gneiss by Hutton and Playfair.[24] Instead Richardson used slate, mica slate, or referred to schists as gneisses.

Once these peculiarities of terminology, and a few others of lesser importance, are understood, a geologist can begin to use Richardson's recorded observations. Such use may corroborate or refute modern observations. It may show the old observations to be in error or it may reveal insights by Richardson which were new and for which he should be credited.

In general, Richardson's record of minerals which he encountered in the field is accurate and has a modern ring to it (Table 6). He was well aware of the economic importance of some of his finds: he refers to a vein of galena as an important ore. He provides a detailed account of the Copper Mountains and the unsuccessful search conducted there to find native copper in a "vein in its original repository," rather than the plates of native copper the field party found in the loose soil of the valleys or the disseminated scales of native copper, green malachite, copper glance, and iron-shot copper green that were encountered in trap rock.[25]

The men of the expedition took the first step toward commercial exploitation of the lead discovered by Richardson when they, according to Franklin, "collected a quantity of it in the hope of adding to our stock of balls; but their endeavours to melt it, were, as may be supposed, ineffectual."[26] Richardson also pointed out some resource potential even where his knowledge was only second hand:[27] "The Esquimaux, that frequent the shores of the Arctic Sea, make their culinary utensils of potstone, but we did not discover the place from where they obtained it." Later, Richardson would make even more of the mineral wealth of the country through which he travelled three times: "It would be true economy in the Imperial Government, or in the Hudson's Bay Company, who are the virtual sovereigns of the vast territory which spreads northwards from Lake Superior, to ascertain without delay the mineral treasures it contains. I have little doubt of many of the accessible districts abounding in metallic wealth of far greater value than all the returns which the fur trade can ever yield."[28] Richardson's rock descriptions require the reader's understanding of the names attached to them by someone who confessed to insufficient knowledge of the subject, who worked in the field using only visual examination, and who had to apply an as yet poorly defined classification. Considering these constraints, Richardson did rather well (Table 9).[29]

Richardson sometimes provided further details, such as quite often the colour or less frequently the grain size – fine or compact. He also recorded, where possible, the attitude (strike and dip) of beds and any smaller-scale structures including the presence of local folds or the occurrence of columns in basalt. His observations on the structural attitude of rocks more often than not diverge considerably from those on modern maps. Perhaps this is the result of Richardson's uncritical acceptance of the theory of a world-wide structural trend which then held sway, and his attempt at substantiating this theory: "The observations of Werner, Humboldt, Von Buch, Saussure, Ebel, and Daubuisson, in many districts in the continent of Europe and in America, and by Jameson in Scotland, shew that the general direction of the primitive and transition strata, is nearly from N.E. to S.W. It is, therefore, interesting to find that the general result of my notes on the positions of these rocks which we traced (except in a few instances when our route lay to the westward of their boundary) through twelve degrees of latitude, also gives N.E. and S.W. as the average direction of their strata."[30] In the bewildering structural complexity of the Precambrian Shield it is notoriously difficult to differentiate structures of local from those of regional significance. This can only be done after a broad expanse of country has been mapped in detail and then generalized as a geological map, or, even better for structural trends, a tectonic map. Richardson's observations were made in the Kazan Region of the Precambrian Shield of which he travelled through the Bear-Slave Upland Division to the Coronation Hills and Bathurst Hills Divisions back to the Bear-Slave Upland. In none of these divisions are the regional structural trends in a northeast-southwest direction. In the Bear-Slave Upland a weakly developed north-south grain can be detected, whereas the numerous diabase dykes are oriented northwest to southeast. The Coronation Hills trend east-west and the Bathurst Hills show a northwest-southeast grain.[31]

TABLE 9 Richardson's observations compared to modern knowledge

Journal entry date (day/month 1821*)/locality/ minerals and rocks recorded	Modern interpretation	Remarks. References listed in note 29
21/8/1820 Fort Enterprise Gneiss	Precambrian (Archaean) granitic gneisses	Fraser et al. 1960: map Douglas 1960: map
12/9/1820 South shore (east half) of Point Lake Gneiss	Precambrian (Archaean) Yellowknife Group grey-wacke; minor slate, phyllite, conglomerate; derived mica-quartz schist, hornblende-biotite schist, knotted schist. West half of south shore: Precambrian (Archaean) granitic gneisses	East half of south shore. Fraser et al. 1960: map West half of south shore. Douglas 1960: map
1/5 and 4/5 1821 South of Snare Lake, west of Wecho Lake, 64° N lat. Gneiss	Precambrian (Archaean and/or Proterozoic) granitic gneiss, migmatite; undifferentiated plutonic, sedimentary, and volcanic rocks	Douglas 1960: map
6/6 Northwest of Big Lake Gneiss	Precambrian (Archaean) massive and gneissic granitic rock	Fraser et al. 1960: map
8/6 South of Point Lake Gneiss	Precambrian (Archaean) Yellowknife Group. See 12/9/1820	Fraser et al. 1960: map Richardson was to the east of the boundary between Archaean gneisses in the west and the Archaean Yellowknife Group in the east
21/6 West shore of Keskarrah Bay, Point Lake Slate, probably of the Transition Series Gneiss	West shore: Precambrian (Archaean) Yellowknife Supergroup, Point Lake Formation of granodiorite, adamellite, with abundant mafic dykes. Locally on the west shore and over most of the east shore there are exposures of basalt, andesite, local minor dacite lenses, black shale lenses with rare quartz feldspar sandstone beds East shore: Precambrian (Archaean) slate, phyllite, schist, greywacke, quartzite, conglomerate, chert, iron-formation, and carbonate rocks	Henderson and Easton 1977: map Richardson's observation was most likely made at 113°00′ W longitude, 65°12′ N latitude at a prominent point on the west shore of Keskarrah Bay where "slate" and "greywacke" can be expected to occur as they do on the east shore. Douglas 1969: map

TABLE 9 (continued)

Journal entry date (day/month 1821*)/locality/ minerals and rocks recorded	Modern interpretation	Remarks. References listed in note 29
25/6 North shore of Point Lake Probably trap-rocks Greenish-grey clay slate	Precambrian (Archaean) Yellowknife Supergroup, Point Lake Formation of thin-bedded mafic tuffs	Henderson and Easton 1977: map Richardson's observation was likely made on a promontory of the north shore located in 113°13′ W longitude and 65°16′ N latitude where there is a high cliff. Adjacent to the promontory are mixed gneisses, granites, and pegmatites
27/6 North side of west end of Point Lake Gneiss and sienite Pure chrystalline greenstone	Precambrian (Archaean) massive and gneissic granitic rocks, hornblende granite, granodiorite, and minor quartz diorite	Fraser et al. 1960: map Richardson's "pure chrystalline greenstone" probably refers to hornblende
28/6 Redrock Lake Blue or red clay slate	Precambrian (Proterozoic) Epworth Formation of white, grey, and reddish quartzite and sandstone; conglomeratic sandstone and dark red siltstone	Fraser et al. 1960: map Richardson's "clay slate" most likely refers to the siltstone
29/6 North shore of west end of Redrock Lake Greenish-grey clay slate with faintly glimmering lustre	Precambrian (Archaean) Yellowknife Group of intermediate to basic volcanic rocks and derived amphibolite; hornblende schist. In fault contact with these rocks is the Precambrian (Proterozoic) Epworth Formation of buff, grey, and brown dolomite	Fraser et al. 1960: map Richardson's "clay slates" may refer to the thin-bedded dolomite, the glimmering referred to caused by the crystals of dolomite
30/6 Coppermine River between Redrock Lake and Rocknest Lake Clay slate, having a colour intermediate between greenish-grey and clove brown, and a feebly glistening or glimmering lustre	Precambrian (Proterozoic) Epworth Formation of buff, grey, and brown dolomite	Fraser et al. 1960: map Richardson's "clay slate" likely refers to the grey and brown dolomite

TABLE 9 (continued)

Journal entry date (day/month 1821*)/locality/ minerals and rocks recorded	Modern interpretation	Remarks. References listed in note 29
1/7 Nest Rock (southern termination of Rocknest Lake) Trap rocks "of the Rock-nest which in one point of view bears an exact resemblance to the remarkable hill in the neighbourhood of Edinburgh named Salisbury Crags"	The only intrusive rock into the Precambrian (Proterozoic) Epworth Formation shown at the shores of Rocknest Lake is a pale green, massive, aphanitic dacite that locally contains lath-like feldspar phenocrysts	Fraser et al. 1960: map Salisbury Crag mentioned by Richardson is a sill of distinctively red basic intrusive rock of mid-Carboniferous age. It lies just south of Holyrood Castle, Edinburgh. At the base is a famous section described by James Hutton and interpreted by him to show evidence in favour of magmatic intrusion. Beneath the sill lie well-bedded Upper Red Sandstone strata, alternately red and white (Mitchell et al. 1960)
6/7 Coppermine River Syenite Green stone Clay-slate, greenish, with a continuous pearly lustre	After travelling through Precambrian (Proterozoic) Epworth Formation of thick-bedded greywacke; black and red argillite, slate, phyllite, and minor quartzite, Richardson reached Precambrian (Archaean) Yellowknife Group rocks of greywacke, minor slate, phyllite, conglomerate, derived mica-quartz schist, hornblende-biotite schist, and knotted schist. This in turn is followed by Pre-cambrian (Archaean) massive and gneissic granitic rocks	Fraser et al. 1960: map Richardson's "syenite" is likely a granite-type rock, the "green stone" a hornblende schist, and the "greenish clay-slate" with pearly lustre, a phyllite
7/7 Coppermine River (Hook's encampment) Clay Slate	Precambrian (Proterozoic) granite-gneiss and migmatite, drift-covered. Encampment at night was in an area of Precambrian (Archaean) Yellowknife Group of intermediate to basic volcanic rocks and derived amphibolite as well as hornblende schist, cut by a diabase sill	Fraser et al. 1960: map It is unclear to what "Clay Slate" refers

TABLE 9 (continued)

Journal entry date (day/month 1821*)/locality/ minerals and rocks recorded	Modern interpretation	Remarks. References listed in note 29
8/7 Coppermine River near Hook's encampment Gneiss and sienite	On the north bank of the river is Precambrian (Proterozoic) Hornby Bay Group intercalated sandstone, quartzite, and conglomerate. On the south bank are massive and gneissic granitic rocks, granite-gneiss, and migmatite of Precambrian (Archaean? Proterozoic) age. Encampment in the evening was in an area of felsite	Fraser et al. 1960: map Richardson's reference to "gneiss and sienite" pertains to the gneissic granitic rocks on the south bank Baragar and Donaldson 1973: map 1338A
9/7 Coppermine River west of 116° W longitude Syenite of the Transition Series Variegated and spotted red sandstone composed principally of feldspar. Quartzy sandstone, greyish-white, coarse texture. Brownish-red glistening porphyritic stone with chrystals of a bluish- or greenish-black mineral. Limestone, wine yellow, very compact with thin layers of flinty slate	Above Rocky Defile Rapids the river cuts through porphyritic felsite (Precambrian, Proterozoic, Echo Bay Group?); below the rapids through granites of an age similar to the Echo Bay Group or possibly earlier. On the west side of the Coppermine River from south to north and from the base of the section upward are Precambrian (Proterozoic) rocks: *Dismal Lakes Group* Tan-weathering dolomite, red mudstone Lower laminated dolomite Massive dolomite Upper laminated dolomite *Copper Creek Formation* Basalt flows with minor intercalated sandstone	Baragar and Donaldson 1973: map 1338A Richardson's "transition syenite" is likely a granite of the Echo Bay Group or possibly earlier. The "variegated sandstone" is possibly a weathered granite. The "porphyritic stone" is equated with the porphyritic felsite of the Echo Bay Group? The "limestone" is likely a dolomite
11/7 Coppermine River downstream of Mouse River Clay-stone, greyish Dark-reddish brown, feldspar rich, ferruginous clay stone or conglomerate with calcite in amygdules Greenstone Reddish sandstone	Precambrian (Proterozoic) Coppermine River Group of minor, poorly exposed, tan-weathering dolomite and red mudstone; laminated dolomite, with few exposures; well-exposed massive dolomite; a younger rather well-exposed laminated dolomite; and the very well-exposed Copper Creek Formation of basalt flows and minor intercalated sandstone	Baragar and Donaldson 1973: 8, map 1338A Richardson's "greyish claystone" may well refer to a local chalky layer in the upper laminated dolomite which has in places been slightly metamorphosed and bleached by the overlying Coppermine River basalt

TABLE 9 (continued)

Journal entry date (day/month 1821*)/locality/ minerals and rocks recorded	Modern interpretation	Remarks. References listed in note 29
12/7 Coppermine River east of 116° W longitude, near Muskox Rapids Sandstone, brownish-red Freestone, red	Precambrian (Proterozoic) Copper Creek Formation of basalt flows, with minor intercalated sandstone. Farther north is the Precambrian (Proterozoic) younger Husky Creek Formation of crossbedded red sandstone and siltstone with subordinate intercalated basalt flows. The sediments are mostly friable and rarely outcrop except along the Coppermine River and beneath cappings of lava. The sandstones are partly contemporaneous with Coppermine River flows but were deposited principally during the declining phase of volcanism and overlie the major part of the volcanic deposits. Intercalated basalt flows, mainly in the upper part of the red bed succession, are generally similar to those forming the bulk of the volcanic deposits in the Coppermine Creek Formation	Baragar and Donaldson 1973: 10, map 1337A The "trap hills" noticed by Richardson farther to the north are most likely the Coronation Sills
14/7 Coppermine River, north of Sandstone Rapids Red sandstone Trap	North of the Precambrian (Proterozoic) Husky Creek Formation is the Precambrian (Proterozoic) younger Rae Group of which the following units from the oldest to youngest can be recognized: Sandstone, siltstone, shale Red and green sandstone, siltstone, mudstone Shaly sandstone, siltstone, shale These rocks are intruded by gabbro of the Coronation Sills and associated dykes	Baragar and Donaldson 1973: map 1337A The range noted by Richardson was the second of three Coronation Sills and the "blue mountains" the third at Bloody Fall

TABLE 9 (continued)

Journal entry date (day/month 1821*)/locality/ minerals and rocks recorded	Modern interpretation	Remarks. References listed in note 29
15/7 Coppermine River, Escape Rapids-Bloody Fall Sandstone Slate clay	Both Escape Rapids and Bloody Fall are in Pre-cambrian (Proterozoic) Coronation Sills of gabbro. The sandstone between the sills is greenish-grey and greyish-brown, fine-grained, and interbedded with dark grey to black shale	Baragar and Donaldson 1973: 10, 14, map 1337A Richardson does not mention the presence of the basic intrusive rock but describes only the sandstone and shale
21/7 Couper Islands Greenstone Basalt, columnar	The Couper and Berabs Islands are part of the Precambrian (Proterozoic) Coronation Sills and associated dykes of gabbro	Baragar and Donaldson 1973: 14 named the sills that intrude the Precambrian (Proterozoic) sediments of the Rae Group the Coronation Sills after Coronation Gulf where they prominently appear as islands and cuesta ridges
23/7 Coronation Gulf, Port Epworth Trap, basalt, pumice	Precambrian (Proterozoic) Coppermine River Group of sandstone, shale, and argillite with cliffs of diabase dykes and sills, occurs on both the east and west shore of Port Epworth	Bostock et al. 1963: map The quoin (wedge) shape of the units is such that the thin edge is to the north, the steep cliff facing south
24/7 East of Grays Bay, Wentzel River Basalt	Hepburn Island and Jameson Island consist of Precambrian (Proterozoic) diabase dykes and sills of more than one age which may include minor undifferentiated basalt flows of the Coppermine River Group. In front of the sills are sandstones, shales, and argillites, also of the Coppermine River Group	Bostock et al. 1963: map The basaltic cliffs mentioned by Richardson extend along the coast only as far as the west side of Grays Bay from where they continue on to Hepburn Island and the Jameson Islands. From the south and east shore of Grays Bay farther to the east the terrain is underlain by Precambrian (Archaean) granites, gneisses, and allied rocks
25/7 Desbarets Inlet Red and grey granite traversed by veins of red feldspar	Along the coast are Precambrian (Archaean?) granite, granodiorite, and allied rocks, massive to foliated, of more than one age; also pegmatitic granite. West of Bathurst Inlet bodies of massive granite to quartz diorite, and locally diorite, intrude rocks of the Precambrian (Archaean) Yellowknife Group	Bostock et al. 1963: map Richardson's "veins of red feldspar" are pegmatite dykes Fraser et al. 1964: 8

TABLE 9 (continued)

Journal entry date (day/month 1821*)/locality/minerals and rocks recorded	Modern interpretation	Remarks. References listed in note 29
27/7 Galena Point on mainland, opposite Galena Island A small vein of Galena in syenite 28/7 Same locality A small vein of galena traversing granite or gneiss rocks	Precambrian (Archaean) granite with inclusions of mica-quartz schist or amphibolite	Bostock et al. 1963: map, show the local presence of galena and chalcopyrite-galena. Fraser et al. 1964: 19 state that "veinlets of galena and chalcopyrite cut massive granite and tourmaline-muscovite pegmatite at Galena Point." Richardson is to be credited with the first published description of the galena occurrences
31/7 Arctic Sound, mouth of Hood River Syenite	Precambrian (Proterozoic) Goulburn Group of quartzite, minor arkose, conglomerate, and sandstone	Bostock et al. 1963: map Richardson's "syenite" appears to be in error. No such rock or similar ones (granite, granodiorite) are exposed here. Perhaps Richardson observed an arkose
2/8 Bathurst Inlet, Barry Islands Granite Brown indurated clay with green copper ore Clinkstone, columnar Basalt, columnar	Iglorua and Algak Islands are composed of basalt flows of the Precambrian (Proterozoic) Coppermine River Group	Bostock et al. 1963: map, indicate the occurrence of copper on the northern tip of Iglorua Island as well as southeast of Wollaston Point. Richardson presents an accurate summary of the geology with granites along the coast from the east side of Gray Bay to Cape Barrow and from there south to Detention Harbour and Daniel Moore Bay where basalt flows of the Coppermine River Group are exposed. Between Daniel Moore Bay and Arctic Sound there are basalt flows cut by diabase dykes and sills
3/8 West shore of Bathurst Inlet Light-red sandstone Bluish-grey slate clay Basalt, amygdaloid, trap tuff	The west shore of Bathurst Inlet consists mainly of Precambrian (Proterozoic) Parry Bay Formation of quartzite, arkose, conglomerate	Bostock et al. 1963: map Richardson's cliffs of basalt are flows of the Coppermine River Group which overlie the Parry Bay Formation

TABLE 9 (continued)

Journal entry date (day/month 1821*)/locality/ minerals and rocks recorded	Modern interpretation	Remarks. References listed in note 29
7/8 Bathurst Inlet – Manning Point Conglomerate Red sandstone	Precambrian (Proterozoic) quartzite, with minor arkose, conglomerate, and sandstone	Bostock et al. 1963: map
9/8 Bathurst Inlet – Rideout Island Sandstone Greenstone and basalt	The west side of Bathurst Inlet is composed of Precambrian (Proterozoic) quartzite, with minor arkose, conglomerate, and sandstone as well as argillite with inter-laminated limestone and calcareous siltstone. Within these layered rocks occur basalt flows. Rideout Island and the east shore of Bathurst Inlet consist of Precambrian (Archaean?) granite, granodiorite, and allied rocks, massive to foliated	Bostock et al. 1963: map Richardson describes only the rocks from the west side of Bathurst Inlet, not those of Rideout Island
11/8 Bathurst Inlet – Everitt Point to Cape Croker Gneiss Syenite Hornblende Mica Light-red sandstone	Everitt Point: Precambrian (Archaean?) granitic gneiss, mafic gneiss, mixed gneiss, and mylonite with some massive granitic rock; also some hornblende gneiss, and biotite gneiss. Cape Croker: Precambrian (Proterozoic) Parry Bay Formation of quartzite, minor arkose, conglomerate, and sandstone	Bostock et al. 1963: map Richardson's "hornblende" may occur in hornblende gneiss which is part of a heterogeneous assemblage of gneisses and migmatite, and which also includes granite gneiss, biotite gneiss, garnet-pyroxene gneiss, and granulite (Fraser et al. 1964: 8)
12/8 Melville Sound Red sandstone	As for Cape Croker	Bostock et al. 1963: map The sandstone weathers and erodes easily, forming the shelving shore mentioned by Richardson
14/8 Melville Sound – Parry Bay Greenstone and basalt White sandstone	On the west shore of Parry Bay there are few or no outcrops but the country is underlain by the Precambrian (Proterozoic) Parry Bay Formation of dolomite, limestone, with minor sandstone and shale. In this sequence are diabase dykes and sills	Bostock et al. 1963: map

TABLE 9 (continued)

Journal entry date (day/month 1821*)/locality/minerals and rocks recorded	Modern interpretation	Remarks. References listed in note 29
16/8 Kent Peninsula from Slaty Clay Point opposite Cockburn Islands north beyond Cape Flinders Basalt, columnar Trap Slate clay	A cliff of Precambrian (Proterozoic) of diabase dykes and sills is indicated on the easternmost of the Cockburn Islands and trending north from there onto Kent Peninsula, on the east side of Walker Bay. Rounding Cape Flinders one comes to an area of few or no outcrops. Surficial deposits are underlain by basalt flows that are part of the Precambrian (Proterozoic) Coppermine River Group which also comprises sandstone, shale, and argillite	Bostock et al. 1963: map The farthest north Richardson reached (68°35′ N latitude), 12 miles beyond Turnagain Point, where the shore turns east, is the only place where the party left the Precambrian Shield and entered the Arctic Lowlands Region (Victoria Lowlands Division), but no bedrock is exposed here
22/8 Slaty Clay Point	See entry for 16/8	Richardson's "slate clay" is argillite
23/8 Bathurst Inlet – Everitt Point Mica slate Gneiss Syenite Hornblende	See entry for 11/8	Richardson's "mica slate" is mica schist
24/8 Bathurst Inlet – Barry Islands Trap rocks, mostly basalt, columnar Clay stone Amygdaloidal rock Jasper Chalcedony Carnelian Agate	Algak Island, the southernmost of the Barry Islands, comprises Precambrian (Proterozoic) basalt flows and diabase dykes and sills that are underlain by the Precambrian (Proterozoic) Parry Bay Formation consisting of dolomite, limestone, minor sandstone and shale, and includes some conglomerate	Bostock et al. 1963: map Musk-ox Island is one of the Barry Islands, likely the unnamed island between Ekalulia and Iglorua Islands

TABLE 9 (continued)

Journal entry date (day/month 1821*)/locality/ minerals and rocks recorded	Modern interpretation	Remarks. References listed in note 29
26/8 Hood River, 6 to 7 miles from mouth, just upstream from junction with James River Alluvial clay Floetz rocks Clay stone Red amygdaloid	The waterfall is caused by faulted rocks of the Precambrian (Proterozoic) Goulburn Group of quartzite, minor arkose, conglomerate, and sandstone, as well as siltstone, argillite, and sandstone. East of Hood River are basalt flows	Bostock et al. 1963: map Below the youngest Alluvial clay deposits Richardson placed rocks of the Floetz Period to which he assigned the "clay stone" (siltstone and argillite) and the "red amygdaloid basalt"
27/8 Hood River – Wilberforce Falls Sandstone, light red, fine-grained	Wilberforce Falls is in Precambrian (Proterozoic) quartzite and minor arkose	Bostock et al. 1963: map Richardson's "very fine sandstone" which is perhaps "a compact feldspar" could refer to the arkose, which contains feldspar, but more likely is a description of the quartzite, which does not
3/9 Barren grounds south of Hood River, east of Wright River Basalt with imbedded white chrystals	Precambrian (Archaean?) granite, granodiorite, and allied rocks, massive to foliated, of more than one age. Also a few diabase dykes near the lower reaches of the Wright River	Bostock et al. 1963: map Richardson may have encountered a small diabase dyke not shown on modern maps. The white chrystals may be calcite or a zeolite
9/9 South of Kathawachaga Lake Gneiss	Precambrian (Archaean?) granitic gneiss, mafic gneiss, mixed gneiss, mylonite and granite, granite diorite, and allied rocks	Bostock et al. 1963: map Richardson recognized the typical Shield country with which he had become familiar near Fort Enterprise
27/9 Point Lake Gneiss Syenite	The southernmost part of Point Lake near Obstruction Rapids is underlain by Precambrian (Archaean) granite, granodiorite, quartz diorite, pegmatite, and chloritized granite. The same rock types are found in the western part of Point Lake where they were described as gneisses, orthogneiss, paragneiss, granite, and pegmatite	Stockwell 1933: map Henderson and Easton 1977: map The area occupied by "gneiss" and "syenite" at the south-easternmost end of Point Lake is rather small in extent but was noticed correctly by Richardson

*All dates are 1821 except where indicated otherwise.

Physiography

John Richardson's field notes included frequent mention of the type of landscape through which the party travelled, the landforms within these landscapes, and an occasional short note of some particularly striking small feature.

The Bear-Slave Upland, a physiographic division of what geologists now refer to as the Kazan Region of the Precambrian Shield, was recognized by Richardson as a region in which "primitive" rocks, of mainly "gneiss formation," with subordinate granite and mica slate, predominate. These rocks are typically "round-backed," their summits are "most smooth and rounded, never peaked." In some places, "not frequent," there are small cliffs, "mural precipices," or steep "almost precipitous ... acclivities," a word then used for the upward slope of a hill. The hills of these primitive rocks are detached from each other "without forming connected ranges, and the bottom of every valley is occupied either by a small lake or a stony marsh." Separate hills have an "obtusely conical" form. Together they present a "tolerably even outline." The gneisses are characteristically "naked" or "barren elevations."[32]

Taken together, these characterizations provide a reasonable word picture of the typical Precambrian Shield in this area beyond the treeline. They would not evoke in the reader an Alpine landscape, particularly not to the attentive reader who notices that the greatest differential relief is given as 600–700 feet, that being from the north shore of Point Lake to the hills on each side.[33] Yet, as St Onge rightly pointed out, in the engravings that accompany Franklin's *Journey* a romanticized Alpine scene was depicted.[34] Of the examples presented by him the most striking is Robert Hood's sketch dated 1 September 1820, which shows the first sighting of the Coppermine River valley at the south shore of Point Lake which here occupies the valley. His comparison of the drawing with a recent photograph reveals a remarkable degree of artistic licence that over-emphasizes the ruggedness of the terrain mainly by increasing the slopes to much greater angles than they are in the small, rounded hills of the Shield. Although the sides of the valley are fairly steep they rise to a plateau, which is between 150 and 200 metres above Point Lake (a value remarkably in accord with the figure given by Richardson) but which presents a rolling terrain easily traversed on foot. Not content with just increasing slopes, Hood showed two caribou clambering up a cliff like mountain goats, two men with walking sticks ready for a hike, and with some dramatic cumulus clouds in the background. Speculating on why such a distortion of reality took place, St Onge mentions the training of artists to appreciate the picturesque during the Romantic period and perhaps a desire to make the land look as attractive as possible – from a Victorian point of view – to justify the expedition. Also, it has been shown that the engraver enhanced the original sketches of the Franklin expedition.[35]

Whatever the causes, the engravings in Franklin's *Journey*, having been looked at by many more people than would read the text, had a much greater impact than Richardson's verbal account. One cannot but agree with St Onge that through these engravings "several generations of Europeans and North Americans were presented with romanticized images of Canada's northland in general and the Coppermine Valley in particular."[36] Conversely, Franklin was quite misleading in his statement that "the annexed sketch, by Mr. Hood, of the party when they first got sight of Point Lake, conveys the most accurate presentation of their mode of travelling, and of the character of the country."[37]

Near Hook's encampment Franklin's party entered a physiographic region, the Coronation Hills, which presented a different landscape from that of the typical Precambrian Shield. Although it is now known that the rocks of the Coronation Hills are also Precambrian (Proterozoic) in age and are therefore included in the Shield, to Richardson the strikingly different appearance of a landscape dominated by bedded rocks including layers of basalt was sufficient evidence to assign those rocks to the Floetz Formation and no longer to the Primitive Country.[38] He noted:

> In the evening we approached several ranges of hills, which were from 12 to 1500 feet high and lay nearly parallel to the river or about NW true. These are the first hills which we have seen in this country that can be said to possess the form of a mountain range. They are in general rather round-backed, but the outline is not even being interrupted by craggy eminences rather obtusely conical ...[39]
>
> The hills in the neighbourhood of the Hook's encampment are more even in their outline than those we had previously passed but there are some high peaks in the direction of the river, some of them obtuse – others short pointed – conical. From this spot the river course lay for a considerable distance between two ranges of hills, pretty even in their outlines and round-backed but having rather steep acclivities.[40]

In one place Richardson assigned a syenite projecting through alluvial sand tentatively to the Transition Series, which in his classification lay between the Primitive Series below and the Floetz Series above.[41] Still farther down the Coppermine River the differences between the Bear-Slave Upland and the Coronation Hills become more obvious and in several places Richardson mentions "ranges of trap hills."

Turning from the mouth of the Coppermine River eastward along the coast, one at first stays in the Coronation Hills region but from near the mouth of the Tree River at Port Epworth the Archaean rocks of the Shield are re-entered. This too produces a change in landscape which did not escape Richardson's attention: on Franklin's chart the Floetz Formation is replaced by Gneiss. Richardson describes his last look at the Coronation Hills near Port Epworth very aptly: "One basaltic cliff succeeds another, with a tiresome uniformity and their debris intirely covers the narrow vallies that intervene to the exclusion of every kind of herbage. These trap cliffs, resembling in some points of view a pummice quoin, were productive of considerable delay in our voyage, by frequently leading us into the bays in search of passages where none existed."[42] The islands offshore and Kent Peninsula also show this bedded sequence of Proterozoic sediments and basalts. Again, this was noted by Richardson, although outcrops are sparse and extensively covered by marine deposits. "Cliffs of trap rocks with intervening low beaches" was his comment on the appearance of Kent Peninsula north beyond Cape Flinders.[43]

Besides making remarks about the landscape, Richardson occasionally also commented on some landforms and some other smaller features. His descriptions of "a small lake which washed the base of a ridge of sand about three hundred feet high,"[44] "a remarkable sandy ridge,"[45] or the "high ridge of sand hills"[46] all refer to what are now known to be eskers which are abundant in the area between Fort Enterprise and Point Lake.[47]

The long stay during the winter of 1820–1 at Fort Enterprise made the recording of physiographic detail possible:

> The country about Fort Enterprise consists of short and very obtuse conical, or sometimes round-backed, hills, of moderate elevations, never disposed in mountain ranges, but entirely unconnected and separated from each other by inclined valleys of moderate extent. Their summits are almost universally formed of naked smooth rock, and generally of a species of durable red granite that has been more than once mentioned as composed of well crystallized reddish felspar and grey quartz.
>
> ... The banks of Winter River are ... flanked on each side by an irregular marshy plain, varying in breadth from one to three or four miles and somewhat broken by abrupt elevations of coarse gravel and bounded by an amphitheatre of disconnected hills. The summits of these hills are generally ... a naked, smooth rounded mass of gneiss rocks; their sides are very thinly covered with a loose gravelly soil and often exhibit small mural precipices or more frequently accumulations of large cubical stones; whilst near their bases there is often a thin stratum of mountain peat ...[48]

A more recent description of the land near Fort Enterprise reads: ... the country is less rocky than that farther south, valleys are generally broad, rock hills have more gentle slopes, and some of them are isolated in broad, nearly flat, drift-covered lowlands ... Many boulders are common, and shorelines are mostly of drift."[49]

The Winter River lies in a broad valley comprising a flood plain and some higher terraces composed of fluviatile gravels. The valley walls are Precambrian granitic gneisses that are either exposed in steep cliffs or covered by coarse talus of massive blocks. Such blocks of cubical shape are a common characteristic of weathered granite, the well-developed joints of which determine the directions along which the weathering will proceed that produces the blocks. The flat faces of such joint-blocks, as are those of the joint-controlled columns of basalt, are by some people believed to be an indication that the blocks are giant crystals. Richardson made this common mistake. He then compounded it by believing a granite to be a bedded oceanic precipitate in the best of Wernerian tradition. "The very general, through rude, resemblance these blocks bore to large crystals is a remarkable circumstance, and seems to indicate a crystallization in the great of the red granite, of which they were very frequently composed, and of whose beds or strata they are perhaps the remains."[50]

Wray, in his account of travel along the Yellowknife River, which included a visit to the remnants of Fort Enterprise, shows some flat-faced, joint-controlled large boulders in a photograph taken on the shore of Upper Carp Lake, as well as one of the "Big Stone" across the Winter River from Fort Enterprise which also is nearly cubical. The latter boulder may well be the one that inspired the name Big Stone Hill:

> Large irregular, but somewhat cubical, fragments of this rock [red granite] are scattered over the surface of the hills, or rest upon their very summits, by two or three angular points, as if left exposed there by the decay of the less durable material that enclosed them [finer grained till matrix?]. A remarkable instance of this occurs about a mile and a half to the southward of Fort Enterprise, on a hill which is thence termed the *Big Stone Hill*. This hill, which is the highest for many miles, rises from six to eight hundred feet above Winter River. The acclivities of the hills, generally speaking, consist of gneiss wrapped in a mantle [talus] form round the granite. These acclivities are more or less thickly covered with a coarse gravelly soil, and very often exhibit accumulations of large cubical fragments of gneiss, which fall from small mural precipices.[51]

In several places Richardson makes mention of the terrain being "strewed with large stones" or the "soil gravelly and interspersed with large stones,"[52] but with little questioning of where these stones came from or how they had been transported. In his "Geognostical Observations" he clung to what even then had become an untenable theory, that they were deposited by the Deluge: "With regard to the large rolled blocks which are so plentifully scattered over the surface of some countries by the waters of the flood, we have no remarks of moment to make."[53] Those boulders encountered in stream valleys Richardson regarded as having been transported by running water, apparently without regard to size. Many of those on uplands he believed to be of local derivation:

> During our journey from York Factory to Fort Enterprise, we seldom had an opportunity of ascending out of the valley of the river through which our route lay, and any blocks of stone observed in such a situation may as readily be supposed to have been transported by the river as by a more general cause. On the Barren Grounds, where we adopted a different style of travelling, the loose stones which were very numerous, even in the most elevated situations, were,

as far as we observed, similar to the rocks on which they rested, and may be supposed to be the more durable remains of the covering strata, which have been destroyed by long-continued action of the atmosphere. Their angular forms and their resting-places, often upon the very summit of the hills, militate against their having travelled from a distance.[54]

Yet, the theory of glacial transport of erratic boulders had been proposed by James Hutton, and then popularized by John Playfair in 1802 when he stated that "for the moving of large masses of rock, the most powerful engines without doubt which nature employs are the glaciers."[55] This recognition, however, did not mean that geologists of the time were ready to extrapolate from observations made in glaciated mountainous terrain to the flat Precambrian terrains of either northern Europe or North America. Certainly, John Richardson did not take this step and as late as 1851, when he again directed himself to the question of the origin of the ubiquitous boulders, he had abandoned the Flood but stated that "... the surface soil, the beds of rivers, and sea-shore abound in them. I noticed them also in various places accumulated in clusters, forming small eminences of from 10 to 100 yards in diameter, and from 8 to 20 feet high. These may be ice-borne boulders [meaning carried by ice-bergs]. The usually circular forms of the heaps militates against their being glacier moraines."[56] Richardson was in good company in opting for iceberg transport as he adhered to Charles Lyell's theory advocated in 1833 in *Principles of Geology*, the most influential geological textbook of the time. After 1840 Louis Agassiz convinced a majority of geologists of the former existence of continental glaciers. The theory that "drift" was transported by floating icebergs in a sea (hence the word) survived into the last quarter of the nineteenth century. The concept is still valid today for certain boulder accumulations on the bottoms of former glacial lakes or the seabed.

Richardson's most important physiographic observation was no doubt his recognition of the existence of a former higher water level in the valley of the Coppermine River. He noticed the presence of high level sandy deposits along the Coppermine River when he wrote that "... the banks of the river were gravelly and latterly were bounded at a small distance by cliffs of fine sand of from one to two hundred feet high. Sandy plains on a level with the summits of these cliffs extended six or seven miles backward from the banks of the river and were terminated by ranges of hills ..."[57]

According to St Onge, who has studied the surficial deposits and the Quaternary history of the Coppermine River valley for several years now, Richardson described a series of high terraces. These terraces are composed of varved silts and clays, covered by one to two metres of coarse alluvial sand, and mark one of the levels of Glacial Lake Coppermine.[58]

At the Hook's encampment spectacular exposures of varved silts and clays of Glacial Lake Coppermine can be seen. Richardson's entry of a "lofty sand cliff" may refer to this exposure.[59] More revealing is his observation that "The immediate borders of the stream consisted either of high banks of fine sand or of steep gravelly cliffs and sometimes where the hills receded to a little distance the intervening space was occupied by high sandy ridges apparently the ancient banks of the river."[60] The above likely refers to the area north of the mouth of Quicksand Creek where large terraces mark a low level of Glacial Lake Coppermine.[61]

The most perceptive observation was made by Richardson when he recorded that "The form of the land here would lead one to suppose that the river, at some distant period, pent in by the rock formed a long narrow lake whose superfluous waters were discharged by a magnificent cascade, and this opinion is in some degree corroborated by the figure of various sandy ridges and peaks which rise immediately above the rapid to the height of 5 to 600 feet – and bear an exact resemblance to the banks of sand which are often found in the borders of a lake."[62] Thus Richardson noted the presence of an abandoned cascade or waterfall and deduced the former existence of a lake. In corroboration he remarked on the presence of abandoned lake beaches. All these features formed after the retreat of the last Pleistocene glacier from the area, the terraces relating to a lower level (Dismal Lakes Outlet) of Glacial Lake Coppermine. Richardson's suggestion of the possible existence of a lake in the Coppermine River valley is the first in the scientific literature.[63]

Collections

An important part, arguably the most important aspect, of a geologist's work is the collection of specimens of the minerals, rocks, and fossils encountered in the field. The proper study of these samples can only be done in the laboratory by experts in mineralogy, petrology, or palaeontology. Richardson was well aware of this and intended to make a representative collection. In this endeavour, however, he was frustrated: "Whilst we travelled in canoes, which includes the greatest part of our journey, and nearly the whole of the season in which the ground was uncovered, my opportunities of making collections in Natural History were limited to the short halts it was necessary to make for the needful refreshment or repose of the men – a further delay being incompatible with the attainment of the main object of the Expedition [geographical exploration and mapping]. The want of opportunity for observation it was impossible to remedy, but I was desirous of compensating for my own inexperience in geognosy, by making as extensive a collection of specimens as circumstances would permit. Beyond Fort Enterprise, however, the want of means of transport prevented one from even making an attempt at collection. Those specimens that were obtained to the southward of that place have been submitted to the inspection of Professor Jameson ..."[64]

From the above it could be concluded that Richardson did not make any attempts at collecting rock and mineral specimens during the journey described in his Journal. This, however, does not appear to have been the case. Franklin in his *Journey* wrote that on 11 July 1821:"We availed ourselves of this delay to visit the

Copper Mountains in search of specimens of ore, agreeable to my instructions; and a party of twenty-one persons, consisting of the officers, some of the voyagers [sic], and all the Indians, set off on that excursion. We travelled for nine hours over a considerable space of ground, but found only a few small pieces of native copper."[65] In his "Geognostical Observations" Richardson mentions the names of some minerals that were not recorded in his Journal. Examples from the Coppermine include copper glance, malachite, variegated copper ore, and, strangely enough, native copper, although he may have employed the term "copper," which he did use in his Journal, as a kind of shorthand designation for native copper (Table 6). Richardson in his Journal for 11 July 1821 states that "the minerals with which it [copper] is associated will appear from the specimens sent home." Wentzel and the four returning voyageurs carried the specimens from the Coppermine River back to Fort Enterprise. Through the Hudson's Bay Company they later reached the Edinburgh laboratory and museum of Professor Jameson. The latter's unpublished notes on the specimens are preserved in the Richardson Papers, Geological Society Collection, Mineralogical Department Library, British Museum of Natural History, London. Richardson relied on Jameson's notes when writing the "Geognostical Observations."

On 21 September "Dr. Richardson was obliged to deposit his specimens of plants and minerals, collected on the sea-coast, being unable to carry them any further."[66] Thereby no specimens from east of the Coppermine, collected after Wentzel's departure on 19 July, reached Britain.

THE REPORT AND MAP

Richardson's "Geognostical Observations," a report based on the field notes of his journal, is a disappointing document in that it provides the reader with little more than a rewritten chronological account of the observations recorded in the Journal. Only in the Concluding Remarks, which cover a mere four pages, is any attempt made at a synthesis. Even then there is no discussion of the origin of the features observed, or even a discussion of their significance. As Richardson remarked, his aim was "merely at a very general account of the different rock formations." He appears to have been conscious of his shortcomings as a geologist and the lack of opportunity for more thorough examination in the field: "To have given a satisfactory account of the structure of so large an extent of country, would have required not only a much better acquaintance with geognosy than I can lay any claim to, but that I should have turned my undivided attention to that object."[67] He would repeat this theme in several of his later publications, adding in some that his first interest was with plants and animals. His "Topographical and Geological Notices" which comprise Appendix 1 of the account of the second Franklin expedition start as follows:

> A very limited portion of my time could be allotted to geological inquiries. For eight months in the year the ground in the northern parts of America is covered

with snow; and during the short summer, the prosecution of the main object of the expedition rendered the slightest delay in our journey inadvisable. The few hours that could be stolen from the necessary halts, for rest and refreshment, were principally occupied in the collection of objects for the illustration of botany and zoology. It is evident,that an account of the rock formations, drawn up under such circumstances, cannot be otherwise than very imperfect; but I have been led to publish it from the belief that, in the absence of more precise information, even the slightest notice of the rocks of the extreme northern parts of the American continent would be useful to those employed in developing the structure of the crust of the earth; the more especially, as it is not probable that the same tract of country will soon be trod by an expert geologist.[68]

Even in his later writings, self-doubts about observations "with all their imperfections" as well as in an "imperfect acquaintance with the science of geology" appear to preoccupy his mind.[69] He merely hoped that his contribution would elicit "opinions from gentlemen more conversant with the science of geology" than himself.[70]

To illustrate how the same basic field data were rewritten several times with, perhaps, the results of laboratory investigations, no better example than the description of the geology of the Coppermine Mountains can be given. In this area the most intensive field work was done. The presence here of copper had already been reported by Samuel Hearne when he travelled to the Coppermine River in 1771 for the express purpose of finding the source of copper that Indians had brought in to the Hudson's Bay Company post at Fort Churchill.[71] In his Journal Richardson recorded the results of this work as follows:

> The Copper mountains seem to be composed principally of felspar much iron-shot and hence of a dark reddish brown appearance. This rock has very generally an amygdaloidal structure, the cavities filled with calcareous spar and other substances; at other times it occurs in form of a simple clay stone and sometimes it has a conglomerated appearance. There are many narrow vallies in this range of the Copper mountains which are generally bounded by perpendicular walls of greenstone. One or two beds of reddish-sandstone were also met with. It would appear that the Indians search in the vallies and when they see any sparry substance, green ore or copper projecting above the surface they dig in that neighbourhood – but they have no other rules to direct them and have never found the metal in its original repository. From the small fragments we picked up I am led to believe that it occurs in veins in the amygdaloid and perhaps also disseminated through it. The minerals with which it is associated will appear from the specimens sent home. The Indians report that they find Copper often in large pieces in every part of this range which they have examined for two days walk to the NW and that the Eskimaux come hither to search for that mineral.[72]

These notes were then rewritten by Richardson for his "Geognostical Observations":

The Copper Mountains consist principally of trap rocks, which seem to be imposed upon the new red sandstone or the floetz limestone which covers it. A short way below the influx of the Mouse, the Copper-Mine River washes the base of some bluish-grey claystone cliffs, having a somewhat slaty structure, dipping to the north at an angle of 20°. The Copper Mountains appear to form a range running s.e. and n.w. The great mass of rock in the mountains seems to consist of felspar in various conditions; sometimes in the form of felspar rock or claystone, sometimes coloured by hornblende, and approaching to greenstone, but most generally in the form of dark reddish-brown amygdaloid. The amygdaloidal masses, contained in the amygdaloid, are either entirely pistacite, or pistacite enclosing calc-spar. Scales of native copper are very generally disseminated through this rock, through a species of trap tuff which nearly resembled it, and also through a reddish sandstone on which it appears to rest. When the felspar assumed the appearance of a slaty clay-stone, which it did towards the base of the mountains on the banks of the river, we observed no copper in it. The rough, and in general rounded and more elevated parts of the mountain, are composed of the amygdaloid; but between the eminences there occur many narrow and deep valleys, which are bounded by perpendicular mural precipices of greenstone. It is in these valleys, amongst the loose soil, that the Indians search for copper. Amongst the specimens we picked up in these valleys, were plates of native copper; masses of pistacite containing native copper; of trap rock with associated native copper, green malachite, copper glance or variegated copper ore and iron-shot copper green, of greenish-grey prehnite in trap, (the trap is felspar, deeply coloured with hornblende) with disseminated native copper: the copper, in some specimens, was crystallized in rhomboidal dodecahedrons. We also found some large tabular fragments, evidently portions of a vein consisting of prehnite, associated with calcareous spar, and native copper. The Indians dig wherever they observe the prehnite lying on the soil, experience having taught them that the largest pieces of copper are found associated with it. We did not observe the vein in its original repository, nor does it appear that the Indians have found it, but judging from the specimens just mentioned, it most probably traverses felspathose trap. We also picked up some fragments of a greenish-grey coloured rock, apparently sandstone, with disseminated variegated copper ore and copper glance; likewise rhomboidal fragments of white calcareous spar, and some rock crystals. The Indians report that they have found copper in every part of this range, which they have examined for thirty or forty miles to the N.W., and that the Esquimaux come hither to search for that metal. We afterwards found some ice chisels in possession of the latter people twelve or fourteen inches long, and half an inch in diameter, formed of pure copper.[73]

Having lost his own notes, Franklin had to rely on Richardson's Journal. For details he made reference to the "Geognostical Observations." Franklin's account reads:

> The mountains varied in height from one thousand two hundred to one thousand five hundred feet. For a description of the character of the rocks I must refer the reader to Dr. Richardson's Mineralogical Observations. The uniformity of the mountains is interrupted by narrow valleys traversed by small streams. The best specimens of metal we procured were found among the stones in these valleys, and it was in such situations that our guides desired us to search most carefully. It would appear, that when the Indians see any sparry substance projecting above the surface, they dig there; but they have no other rule to direct them, and have never found the metal in its original repository. Our guides reported that they had found copper in large pieces in every part of this range, for two days' walk to the north-west, and that the Esquimaux come hither to search for it. The annual visits which the Copper Indians were accustomed to make to these mountains, when most of their weapons and utensils were made of copper, have been discontinued since they have been enabled to obtain a supply of ice chisels and other instruments of iron by the establishment of trading posts near to their hunting grounds. That none of those who accompanied us had visited them for many years was evident, from their ignorance of the spots most abundant in metal.[74]

Five years after his first geognostical description was published, Richardson repeated the previous observations in Appendix 1, "Topographical and Geological Notices," to Franklin's *Narrative of a Second Expedition*:

THE COPPER MOUNTAINS

> The Copper Mountains rise perhaps eight or nine hundred feet above the bed of the river, and at a distance present a somewhat soft outline, but on a nearer view they appear to be composed of ridges which have a direction from w.n.w. to e.s.e. Many of the ridges have precipitous sides, and their summits, which are uneven and stony, do not rise more than two hundred or two hundred and fifty feet above the vallies, which are generally swampy and full of small lakes. The only rocks noticed when we crossed these hills on the late journey, were clay-slate, greenstone, and dark red sandstone, sometimes containing white calcareous concretions, resembling an amygdaloidal rock. On our first journey down the Coppermine River, we visited a valley, where the Indians had been accustomed to look for native copper, and we found there many loose fragments of a trap rock, containing native copper, green malachite, copper glance, and iron-shot copper green; also trap containing greenish-gray prehnite with disseminated native copper, which, in some specimens, was crystallized in rhomboidal dodecahedrons. Tabular fragments of prehnite,

associated with calc-spar and native copper, were also picked up, evidently portions of a vein, but we did not discover the vein in its original repository. The traprock, whose fragments strewed the valley, consists of felspar, deeply coloured by hornblende. A few clumps of white spruce trees occur in the vallies of the Copper Mountains, but the country is in general naked. The Coppermine River makes a remarkable bend round the end of these hills.[75]

To evaluate all these versions of the original field observations and to put them into perspective, it is of benefit to quote here also from a recent report that contains a description of the Copper Creek Formation:

It consists of about 150 flows with thicknesses ranging from 10 to 300 feet. Most flows are in the range 25 to 75 feet thick. The flows are plateau basalts that maintain nearly constant thicknesses for many miles. Individual flows are typically composed of a massive base and a highly amygdaloidal top, commonly in a ratio of about 3 or 4 to 1. The base is formed of little-altered black or grey basalt. Upward it grades into a reddish altered top, rich in amygdules of red orthoclase, calcite, epidote, and chlorite ... The lower member is commonly about 2,000 feet thick but may be much less. It is distinguished from the rest of the lava sequence by the presence of sparse phenocrysts 1 to 2 mm long, of augite, still lesser amounts of plagioclase, and rare orthopyroxene or pigeonite. The upper flows contain no macrophenocrysts but are otherwise very similar and generally contain microphenocrysts of augite, plagioclase or both.

The flows are composed essentially of plagioclase, pyroxene, and magnetite; minor interstitial potash feldspar, iron oxides, and quartz. Native copper is a very minor constituent of many flows in the middle and, particularly upper parts of the succession but it has not been found in the lower member. It occurs both in tiny amygdules and in intimate association with the rock-forming minerals and undoubtedly is a primary constituent of the rock ... Thin beds of red sandstone are intercalated with the lavas of the Copper Creek Formation, particularly in its upper part, but because of their susceptibility to erosion they rarely outcrop ...

In the lavas, copper is present as sulphides, principally chalcocite and to lesser extent bornite, and as native copper. The sulphides are predominantly in fractures, but native copper is mainly a primary constituent of the lavas. Most copper prospects have to date been found in the upper parts of the volcanic succession where the lavas themselves are richest in copper.[76]

What mainly distinguishes Richardson's report from his field notes is the introduction of an attempt to fit the rocks to Werner's sequential order. References to a position in this scheme are sparse in the Journal, but pervasive in the "Geognostical Observations" where, for instance, the Transition rocks are mentioned in several places while the term was used only twice in the Journal.[77] This is an acceptable working method, for only in retrospect could Richardson assign a stratigraphic position to the rocks he had seen in the field. He realized that he had travelled "up section." This generalization still holds, although now geologists assign the rocks encountered along the route travelled only to the lower (Archaeozoic) and the upper (Proterozoic) part of the Precambrian. Richardson went much higher in the section and regarded his youngest bedrock as Floetz belonging to the New Red Sandstone (Table 8): "The secondary trap and porphyry rocks, which occur so abundantly on the coast of the Arctic Sea, and throughout the whole extent of the Copper Mountains, are to all appearance connected with the new red sandstone."[78]

In this manner, by putting various kinds of rocks together into the groupings of Primitive or Primary, Transition, and Floetz or Secondary, Richardson attempted to synthesize his field observations. Having made these distinctions it is hard to understand why Richardson failed to take the next logical step: to produce a geological map. All that was done was to put on Franklin's chart some remarks regarding the prevailing rock type or the character of the landscape. Only two of these verbal expressions of the geology along the route from Fort Enterprise northward and return have any stratigraphic significance: "Primitive Country, rock Chiefly feldspar with some quartz and mica" from Lower Carp Lake, past Fort Enterprise, to Point Lake and, in large print, "Floetz Formation" from the confluence of the Mouse and Coppermine rivers north to the Arctic Ocean.[79] There is no mention of Transition rocks on the map, nor are there any boundaries drawn between rock types such as gneiss, clay slate, or trap.

EVALUATION

A careful reading of Richardson's Journal against some background knowledge of geological theory and practice in the first quarter of the nineteenth century, combined with an understanding of the geology in the northeastern part of the District of Mackenzie, NWT, will convince any critic that John Richardson was a thorough, careful, and competent field geologist. Principally known for his work as a naturalist interested in plants and animals, his contribution to systematic geological inventory-taking and classification tends to be too easily overlooked. This neglect is understandable because Richardson failed to provide an easily grasped synthesis of his work. Perhaps he was reluctant to do so because he regarded himself not fully qualified, a sentiment which he expressed several times in his writings. Nowhere is this failing of synthesis more clearly shown than in the absence of a geological map. When he finally produced such a map, the first to cover all of what is now Canada, it showed only two geological units: "Metamorphic or Primitive Rocks" and "Fossiliferous Rocks from the Silurian Rocks upwards."[80] Through such gross generalization, the detail of Richardson's careful field work was lost. Only those who made the effort to read through and correlate the appendices to the narratives of both the first and second Franklin expeditions would be in a position to fill in that detail.

A comparison of Richardson's three original accounts of geological field work (the "Geognostical Observations," the "Topographical and Geological Notices," and the "Physical Geography") demonstrates that he kept himself reasonably well informed about recent developments in the science of geology. The "Topographical and Geological Notices," although they make for dull reading, are a serious attempt at a systematic investigation of minerals, rocks, and stratigraphic relationships. Numerous samples were taken and a number assigned to each. The report consists of a description of each sample in numerical order. It also contains several field sketches or profiles showing various rock units and their dispositions which were lacking in his "Geognostical Observations." Richardson's "Physical Geography" is even more advanced in that it was an attempt to relate the stratigraphy of the rocks with which he was familiar to what were then becoming standard sections, mainly those of James Hall in New York and other sections in Europe.

Because his writings lack analytical thought, Richardson does not appear to have contributed to geological theory. Where he deals with the origin of geological substance, features, or phenomena, he falls back to what he was taught or to what he had read about in the works of others. He did not introduce any new thoughts himself, perhaps, again, because he was not as comfortable with the science of geology as he was with zoology or botany. Behind all his observations is a fundamentally conservative and deeply religious mind not amenable to the introduction of revolutionary or even novel thought. He was comfortable with the idea that his work had revealed the world to consist of parts that made "a grand and harmonious whole, the production of infinite wisdom."[81]

Notes

Short-form notation is used in the notes for works cited in the Bibliography. Works not included in the Bibliography are cited in full at their first mention within each chapter, and in short form for any subsequent use.

PREFACE

1 Franklin, *Journey.*
2 Houston, ed., *To the Arctic by Canoe.*
3 Traill, *Franklin*, p. 104.
4 Two older brothers had died in childhood.
5 Letter of Robert E. Johnson to C.S. Houston, 8 Nov. 1982.
6 Johnson, *Richardson*, p. xii; Mary F. Curvey and Robert E. Johnson, "A Bibliography of Sir John Richardson (1787–1865)–printed books," *Journal of the Society for the Bibliography of Natural History* 5 (1969): 202–17.

INTRODUCTION

1 Franklin, *Journey*, second title page.
2 Ibid., pp. xi, xii.
3 John Richardson, "John Franklin," *Encyclopaedia Britannica* (8th ed., 1856), pp. 294–9.
4 Traill, *Franklin*, p. 437.
5 Stefansson, *Unsolved Mysteries of the Arctic*, p. 39.
6 Traill, *Franklin*, p. 443.
7 Johnson, *Richardson*, pp. 27, 28, 31, 32.
8 John McIlraith, *Life of Sir John Richardson* (London: Longmans, Green 1868), pp. 59–60.
9 Ibid., p. 64.
10 [Richard G. and Muriel E. Birch], *The Birch Tree* (Vancouver: published privately 1980), section 4, p. 7.
11 Houston, ed., *To the Arctic by Canoe.*
12 McIlraith, *Richardson*, p. 81.
13 Rich, ed., *Journal by George Simpson*, p. 243.
14 Houston, *To the Arctic by Canoe*, plates 1–24.
15 Hudson's Bay Company Archives [HBCA], Provincial Archives of Manitoba, B27/a/9, Fort Carlton journal, 1820–1.
16 During the second Arctic Land Expedition, Richardson made one of the most remarkable journeys of any birdwatcher

before or since. He left Fort Resolution on Great Slave Lake on Christmas Day 1826 (HBCA, B181/a/7), stopped at Fort Chipewyan on Lake Athabasca from 3 to 8 January (B39/a/25), and arrived at Carlton on 12 February (B27/a/15), well in advance of the spring migration he came to observe, after walking 900 miles, in the depth of winter, camping out in temperatures sometimes below −40°.

17 Franklin, *Journey*, p. 6.

18 Ibid., pp. 262, 297.

19 McIlraith, *Richardson*, pp. 79–80. For a modern investigation of the site see Timothy C. Losey, ed., *An Interdisciplinary Investigation of Fort Enterprise, Northwest Territories, 1970* (Edmonton: Boreal Institute for Northern Studies, Occasional Publication no. 9 1973).

20 Wentzel, "Letters to the Hon. Roderic McKenzie," p. 131. The Hon. Roderick McKenzie of Terrebonne, Lower Canada, had sold his shares in the North West Company for £10,000 in 1814.

21 A theodolite is a surveying telescope used for measuring horizontal and vertical angles and distances.

22 The magnetic inclination, or dip, is measured at right angles to the magnetic deviation or declination with a dipping needle.

23 Houston, *To the Arctic by Canoe*, p. 25.

24 Franklin, *Journey*, pp. 193, 208.

25 Ibid., p. 27.

26 Houston, *To the Arctic by Canoe*, p. 28.

27 Ibid., p. 118.

28 Ibid., p. 112.

29 Franklin, *Journey*, p. 193.

30 Ibid., p. 199.

31 Ibid., pp. 207–8.

32 Ibid., p. 207.

33 Ibid., pp. 250, 278.

34 Ibid., p. 278.

35 HBCA, B181/a/3, Fort Resolution journal, 1820–1; B39/a/16, Fort Chipewyan journal.

36 A slender, strong cord, including that later used to pull Richardson back when his brave attempt to swim across the Coppermine River failed.

37 Franklin, *Journey*, p. 487.

38 Booty, spoils, plunder, loot. Figuratively, harvest. Her belongings? Her baby?

39 Sheer misery (much misery, with the added sense of poverty, or many needs lacking), no cooking utensils, lots of swearing.

40 McIlraith, *Richardson*, pp. 83–5.

41 Houston, *To the Arctic by Canoe*, p. 27.

42 A hermaphrodite is a person with both male and female sex organs.

43 Houston, *To the Arctic by Canoe*, p. xxxii.

44 Rich, ed., *Colin Robertson's Correspondence Book*, pp. 116–17. Colin Robertson (1783–1842) played an important role in extending the Hudson's Bay Company trade into the Athabasca region.

45 Innis, *The Fur Trade in Canada*, pp. 239, 241.

46 En route, at Fort Enterprise, Wentzel picked up a box of journals, charts, and drawings left there on 14 June. He reached Slave Lake on 29 September and Fort Chipewan on 25 October. Wentzel, "Letters to the Hon. Roderick McKenzie," pp. 142–4.

COMMENTARY

1 Franklin, *Journey*, p. 362.

2 MacLeod and Glover, "Franklin's First Expedition."

3 Traill, *Franklin*, p. 424.

4 Franklin, *Journey*, pp. xv, xvi.

5 Andrew Graham's prior observation in

the 1770s was not published until 1969. Williams, ed., *Andrew Graham's Observations on Hudson's Bay*, pp. 96–7.

6 Richardson, "Zoological Appendix," pp. 287–379.

7 Houston, ed., *To the Arctic by Canoe*, p. 77.

8 George R. Johnson, "Physicians in Canadian History, III, Sir John Richardson (1787–1865)," *Calgary Associate Clinic Historical Bulletin* 7 (1942): 1–10.

9 Franklin, *Journey*, pp. 118–19.

10 Matovinovic and Ramalingaswami, "Therapy and Prophylaxis of Endemic Goitre."

11 Quoted in Franklin, *Journey*, pp. 118–19.

12 Franklin, *Journey*, p. 60. C. Stuart Houston, Robert L. Weiler, and Brian F. Habbick, "Severity of Lung Disease in Indian Children," *Canadian Medical Association Journal* 120 (1979): 1116–21.

13 Franklin, *Journey*, p. 47.

14 Ibid., p. 212.

15 Ibid., p. 297.

16 Ibid., p. 302.

17 Ibid., p. 336.

18 Ibid., pp. 157, 158.

19 MacLeod and Glover, "Franklin's First Expedition."

20 Robert Greenblatt, "Inappropriate Lactation in Men and Women," *Medical Aspects of Human Sexuality* (1972): 25–33. See also Cecil Slome, "Non-puerperal Lactation in Grandmothers," *Journal of Pediatrics* 49 (1956): 550–2.

21 John Knott, "Abnormal Lactation in the Virgin; in the Old Woman; in the Male; in the Newborn of Either Sex," *American Medicine* 13 (1907): 373–8; R.C. Creasy, "Lactation from the Mammary Gland in the Male," *Journal of the American Medical Association* 58 (1912): 747–8; Alexander von Humboldt, *Travels and Researches of Baron Humboldt* (New York: Harper 1833), p. 79; J.K. Kulski, P.E. Hartmann, and D.H. Gutteridge, "Composition of Breast Fluid of a Man with Galactorrhea and Hyperprolactinaemia," *Journal of Clinical Endocrinology and Metabolism* 52 (1981): 581–2.

22 Houston, *To the Arctic by Canoe*, p. 133.

23 Franklin, *Journey*, p. 202.

24 Ibid., p. 312.

25 Johnson, *Richardson*, p. 44.

26 William E. Swinton, "Physicians as Explorers. Sir John Richardson: Immense Journeys in Rupert's Land," *Canadian Medical Association Journal* 117 (1977): 1095–1100.

27 John McIlraith, *Life of Sir John Richardson* (London: Longmans Green 1868), p. 113.

28 Ibid., pp. 117–18.

29 Hearne, *Journey*, p. 21.

30 Vilhjalmur Stefansson, "Observations on Three Cases of Scurvy," *Journal of the American Medical Association* 71 (1918): 1715–18.

31 J. McGregor, *Historical and Descriptive Sketches of the Maritime Colonies of British America* (London: Longman 1828), p. 23. Quoted by Charlotte Erichsen-Brown, *Use of Plants for the Past 500 Years* (Aurora: Breezy Creeks Press 1979), p. 195; D.K. Brown, "Vitamin, Protein and Carbohydrate Content of Some Arctic Plants from the Fort Churchill, Manitoba Region," *Canadian Defence Research Board Paper* 23 (1954): 1–12.

32 Vilhjalmur Stefansson, "Original Observations on Scurvy and My Opinion of the Medical Profession," *Medical Review of Reviews* 24 (1918): 257–64; Vilhjalmur Stefansson, *The Fat of the Land* (New York: Macmillan 1956), p. 212.

33 Franklin, *Journey*, p. 248.

34 Ibid., p. 240.

35 Wentzel, "Letters to the Hon. Roderic McKenzie," pp. 138–41.

36 T.C. Dauphiné, Jr, *Biology of the Kaminuriak Population of Barren-ground Caribou*, Part 4. Canadian Wildlife Service Report Series no. 38 1976, pp. 7, 20–1.

37 John P. Kelsall, *The Migratory Barren-Ground Caribou of Canada* (Ottawa: Canadian Wildlife Service 1968), p. 278.

38 Horace Thornton, *Textbook of Meat Inspection* (London: Ballière, Tindall and Cox 1962), pp. 4, 9, 68.

39 Franklin, *Journey*, p. 117; Frank Gilbert Roe, *The North American Buffalo: A Critical Study of the Species in its Wild State* (Toronto: University of Toronto Press 1951), pp. 854–5.

40 Stefansson, *The Fat of the Land*, pp. 212–13.

41 Ruth Fremes and Zak Sabry, *NutriScore* (New York: Methuen 1976), pp. 216–37.

42 Johnson, *Richardson*, p. 176.

43 Thornton, *Textbook of Meat Inspection*, pp. 116–17.

44 J.V.G.A. Durnin and R. Passmore, *Energy, Work and Leisure* (London: Heinemann 1967), pp. 47–82.

45 McIlraith, *Richardson*, pp. 111–14.

46 Thor Arnason, Richard J. Hebda, and Timothy Johns, "Use of Plants for Food and Medicine by Native Peoples of Eastern Canada," *Canadian Journal of Botany* 59 (1981): 2240.

47 Stefansson, *Unsolved Mysteries*, p. 44.

48 When Dr Richardson was at Fort Carlton in May 1827, towards the end of the second Franklin expedition, an interesting example of eating clothing was encountered. The fur trade journal kept by J.P. Pruden (HBCA, PAM, B27/a/15) had the following entry for 6 May 1827, when the nights were still and cold: "Late in the evening came across from the opposite of the [river], a woman & 2 children almost starved to death and entirely naked, having eat all of their clothes, the poor woman had lost her youngest son by starvation 3 days ago. I gave them three leather skins to make clothes for themselves."

49 Capelle, "Myiasis," pp. 289–91.

50 Hearne, *Journey*, p. 128.

51 Warkentin, "Geological Lectures by Dr. John Richardson, 1825–26."

52 In Franklin, *Journey*, Appendix I, pp. 497–538.

53 Richardson, "Botanical Appendix."

54 George W. Scotter and John W. Thomson, personal communications.

55 Sabine, "Account of the Marmots of North America."

56 Ibid., p. 31.

57 Sabine, "Zoological Appendix."

58 Swainson and Richardson, *Birds*, pp. 380, 409.

59 Richardson, *Mammals*, p. xiii.

60 Franklin, *Journey*, pp. 243–4.

61 Richardson, *Mammals*, pp. 248–9.

62 Swainson and Richardson, *Birds*, p. 378.

63 Ibid., p. 340.

64 Richardson, *Mammals*, p. 217.

65 Ibid., p. xiii.

66 Richardson, "Botanical Appendix," p. 729.

67 Not until 1912 did white men again visit Bathurst Inlet; Harry V. Radford and Thomas G. Street were killed by the Eskimos there. The third white man to come was Inspector F.H. French of the RCMP in 1917; he determined that Radford had "provoked the Eskimos into the killings." Alan Cooke and Clive Holland, *The Exploration of Northern Canada, 500 to 1920: A Chronology* (Toronto: Arctic History Press 1978), pp. 327–8.

68 Thomson, *Men and Meridians*, Vol. 1, p. 21.

69 Franklin, *Journey*, p. 28.

70 Leslie H. Neatby, *In Quest of the North West Passage* (Toronto: Longmans Green 1958), p. 80.

71 Franklin, *Journey*, p. 440.

72 Letter of G.C. Jacoby to W.O. Kupsch, 17 Jan. 1983. Jacoby's tree-ring studies from the Yukon, which correlate strongly with temperatures, show that Franklin's ill-fated 1845 expedition encountered even colder temperatures, indeed among the coldest in 400 years. G.C. Jacoby and E.R. Cook, "Past Temperature Variations Inferred from a 400-year Tree-ring Chronology from Yukon Territory, Canada," *Arctic and Alpine Research* 13 (1981): 409–18.

73 Franklin, *Journey*, pp. 492–3.

74 McIlraith, *Richardson*, p. 112.

75 Ibid., p. 112.

76 Communication from Wentzel to Franklin, in Franklin, *Journey*, pp. 492–3.

77 McIlraith, *Richardson*, pp. 117–18.

78 Rich, ed., *Journal by George Simpson*, p. 243.

79 HBCA, B181/a/2, Fort Resolution journal, 1819–20, 14 Oct. 1819.

80 Rich, ed., *Colin Robertson's Correspondence Book*, p. 116.

81 HBCA, B181/a/2, Fort Resolution journal, 1 Dec. 1819, 11 and 20 Jan., 5 Feb., 17 March, and 22 April 1820; B181/a/3, 16 June and 26 July 1820.

82 Rich, ed., *Journal by George Simpson*, p. 244.

83 Franklin, *Journey*, p. 198.

84 HBCA, B181/a/3, Fort Resolution journal, 1 July 1820.

85 Ibid., 2 July 1820.

86 Franklin, *Journey*, p. 150; Rich, ed., *Colin Robertson's Correspondence Book*, p. 118; HBCA, B181/a/2, 22 April 1820.

87 Franklin, *Journey*, pp. 295–6.

88 Ibid., p. 296.

89 Ibid., p. 356.

90 Louis Melzack, Introduction to the reprint edition of Franklin, *Journey*, p. xiv.

91 J.M. Wordie and R.J. Cyriax, Introduction, *Rae's Arctic Correspondence, 1844–45*, ed., E.E. Rich (London: Hudson's Bay Record Society 1953), p. lxxxvii.

92 Wentzel, "Letters to the Hon. Roderic Mackenzie," pp. 148–51.

93 Joseph René Bellot, *Memoirs* (London: Hurst and Blackett 1855), I, p. 252.

94 HBCA, B181/a/7, copy of a letter of 26 June 1826 from John Franklin at Fort Norman to Robert McVicar at Fort Resolution, in Fort Resolution journal, 1826–7.

95 Wentzel, "Letters to the Hon. Roderic McKenzie," pp. 148–51.

96 Ibid., pp. 145–7.

97 Ibid., pp. 148–51.

98 Richard Glover, Introduction, Hearne, *Journey*, pp. xxx–xxxi.

99 Stefansson, *Unsolved Mysteries*, p. 53.

100 *Proceedings of the Royal Society of London* 15 (1867), pp. xxxvii–xliii.

101 Ibid., pp. xxxvii–xliii.

102 *Cygnus buccinator* Richardson; *Lagopus leucurus* (Richardson); *Sterna forsteri* Nuttall; *Picoides arcticus* (Swainson); *Contopus borealis* (Swainson); *Spizella pallida* (Swainson); and *Calcarius pictus* (Swainson), respectively.

103 *Branta canadensis hutchinsii* (Richardson); *Picoides villosus septentrionalis* (Nuttall); *Catharus ustulatus swainsoni* (Tschudi); *Ixoreus naevius meruloides* (Swainson); *Lanius ludovicianus excubitorides* Swainson; *Pipilo erythrophthalmus arcticus* (Swainson); and *Leucosticte arctoa tephrocotis* (Swainson), respectively.

104 *Empidonax pusillus* (Swainson), based on Richardson's specimen from Carlton House. Gale Monson and Allan R.

Phillips, *Annotated Checklist of the Birds of Arizona* (2nd ed., Tucson: University of Arizona Press 1981), p. 104.

105 *Buteo swainsoni* Bonaparte.

106 *Falco columbarius richardsonii* Ridgway.

107 *Aegolius funereus richardsoni* (Bonaparte).

108 In 1858 Spencer F. Baird hesitantly decided that the specimen from Cumberland House, named *Tyrannula richardsonii* by Swainson, was the Western Wood Pewee, when in fact Swainson's plate more closely resembles the Eastern Phoebe, *Sayornis phoebe*. The mistaken name of Richardson's Wood Pewee ceased to be used after the publication "Taxonomic Comments on the Western Wood Pewee" by Allan R. Phillips and Kenneth C. Parkes in *Condor* 57 (1955): 244-6.

109 J.H Coyne, "Edward Ermatinger's York Factory Express Journal, Being a Record of Journeys Made Between Fort Vancouver and Hudson Bay in the Years 1927-28," *Transactions Royal Society of Canada* 3rd series, 6 (1912): 87-8.

110 Richardson, *Mammals*, p. 281.

111 David Douglas, *Journal kept by David Douglas during his Travels in North America, 1823-1827* (London: William Wesley & Son 1914), p. 271.

112 HBCA, B27/a/16, Carlton House journal, 1827-8.

113 HBCA,B49/a/42, Cumberland House journal, 1826-7.

114 Richardson, *Mammals*, p. 281.

115 Royce MacGillivray and Ewan Ross, *A History of Glengarry* (Belleville: Mika Publishing 1979), pp. 49-50.

116 *Report of the 12th meeting of the British Association for the Advancement of Science* (London: John Murray 1843), pp. 106-21.

117 Paul Lawrence Farber, *The Emergence of Ornithology as a Scientific Discipline: 1760-1850.* Studies in the History of Modern Science, vol. 12 (Dordrecht: D. Reidel 1982), p. 115.

118 Lynn Barber, *The Heyday of Natural History 1820-1870* (London: Jonathan Cape 1980), pp. 22-3.

119 Farber, *Emergence of Ornithology,* p. 88.

120 Eric J. Hobsbawm, *The Age of Revolution, 1789-1848* (London: Weidenfeld and Nicolson 1962), p. 111.

121 Farber, *Emergence of Ornithology,* pp. 92, 100. As ornithology emerged as a scientific discipline, it was "characterized by an international group of recognized experts, working on a set of fruitful questions, using an accepted rigorous method, and holding a common goal." The British Association for the Advancement of Science was founded in 1831, museums began to spring up about this time, and local natural history societies soon followed.

122 David Starr Jordan, *The Genera of Fishes* (4 vols., Stanford: Stanford University Press 1917-20).

123 Johnson, *Richardson*, p. xi.

124 John Richardson, *Arctic Searching Expedition: A Journal of a Boat-Voyage through Ruperts Land and the Arctic Sea in Search of the Discovery Ships under Command of Sir John Franklin* (New York: Harper & Brothers 1852).

125 *Proceedings of the Royal Society of London* 15 (1867): xxxvii-xliii.

126 Gavin de Beer, "Darwin's Notebooks on Transmutation of Species," *Bulletin British Museum (Natural History) Historical Series* 2, part 5 (1960): 164.

127 David A. Stewart, "Sir John Richardson, Surgeon, Physician, Sailor, Explorer, Naturalist, Scholar," *British Medical Journal* 1 (17 Jan. 1931): 110-12.

APPENDIX A

1 C.S. Houston, "Birds First Described from Hudson Bay," *Canadian Field-Naturalist* 97 (1983): 95-8.
2 Swainson and Richardson, *Birds*, has a publication date of 1831, but in fact did not appear until February 1832.
3 The Appendix carries a date of 1825, whereas the frontispiece of the narrative itself is dated 1824.
4 *Proceedings of the Zoological Society of London* 27 (1859): 167.
5 Author of *The American Ornithology* in nine volumes (Philadelphia: Bradford and Inskeep 1808-14).
6 McIlraith, *Richardson*, p. 74.

APPENDIX B

1 C. Hart Merriam, "Descriptions of Twenty-six new Mammals from Alaska and British North America," *Proceedings Washington Academy of Science* 2 (1900): 26.
2 William Swainson, *Animals in Menageries* (London: Longman, Orme, Brown, Green & Longmans 1838), pp. 54-6.

APPENDIX C

1 When Richardson sent his specimen to Paris, Cuvier agreed that it was identical with the European *fluvialis*. Not until 1868 did Martens recognize the North Pacific form as a new species. Richardson's was the first North American record.
2 Although Richardson considered this a new species which he named *Salmo Hearnii*, it does not differ appreciably from the Lapland specimen first named by Linnaeus. Richardson's was the first description from North America.

3 Richardson in 1823 considered the tullibee conspecific with *artedi*, the "herring salmon" or "lake herring" of the Great Lakes, a viewpoint 100 years in advance of its time. In 1836 Richardson named it *Salmo (Coregonus) Tullibee*. As late as 1949 D.S. Rawson's *A Check List of the Fishes of Saskatchewan* (Regina: Department of Natural Resources) listed the tullibee as a subspecies, *Leucichthys artedi tullibee* (Richardson).
4 J.R. Dymond notes that Richardson's name of *quadrilateralis* was recognized until 1936, when Berg pointed out its similarity to the Asiatic *cylindraceum*. (J.R. Dymond, "A History of Ichthyology in Canada," *Copeia* 1 (1964): 2-33.)
5 Richardson considered this fish sufficiently different from the Caspian Sea variety, leucichthys, to warrant a new species name, which he gave in honour of Sir Alexander Mackenzie. It was Richardson who gave the new name, *Stenodus*, to this genus in 1836.
6 Richardson's name of *signifer* was used until 1948 when Berg proposed that it be considered conspecific with the Siberian form, *arcticus*, described by Pallas from the Ob River in 1776 (Dymond, "History of Ichthyology").
7 Because the original name given by Rafinesque was the inappropriate *alveoides*, not *alosoides*, the name used to correct a supposed "misprint,"some later authorities have reverted to use the next reliable name, *chrysopsis*, given by Richardson in 1823.
8 Scott and Crossman point out that Richardson's was the first record for what is now Canada.
9 Ichthyologists have long presumed that either the locality or the identification of the catfish was in error. However, E.L. Dean's "First Saskatchewan Record of

Channel Catfish," *Blue Jay* 41 (1983): 183–4, stimulated F.M. Atton to obtain a transcript of Peter Fidler's Cumberland House journal for 8 Nov. 1797 (HBCA B49/a/28) in which Fidler gives an unmistakeable description of a channel catfish, 2 feet, 7 inches long, with the statement that "1 is caught most every winter here" (F.M. Atton, "Early Records of the Channel Catfish, *Ictalurus punctatus*, in Cumberland Lake, Saskatchewan," *Canadian Field-Naturalist*, in press). These records give credibility to Richardson's record and extend the range of this species in Canada.

10 For this and the subsequent three marine species, the names are those used by the American Fisheries Society in their Special Publication No. 12, *A List of Common and Scientific Names of Fishes from the United States and Canada*, fourth edition (1980).

APPENDIX D

1 *American Journal of Science* 91 (1866): 265.
2 Hooker, *Flora Boreali-Americana.*
3 Stewart, "Sir John Richardson."

APPENDIX E

1 In the second edition, concluding the description of *Dufourea arctica*, Richardson adds: "Obs. For this beautiful additional plate I am indebted to the friendship and liberality of Dr. Hooker, who made the drawings, and had them engraved at his own expense."
2 W.A. Leighton, "Notes on Lichens collected by Sir John Richardson in Arctic America," *Journal of the Linnaean*

Society of London, Botany 9 (1867): 184–200.
3 J.W. Thomson, G.W. Scotter, and T. Ahti, "Lichens of the Great Slave Lake Region, Northwest Territories, Canada," *Bryologist* 72 (1969): 137–77.

APPENDIX F

1 Richardson, "Geognostical Observations." John Franklin, "A Chart of the Discoveries and Route of the Northern Land Expedition, under the Command of Captain Franklin, R.N. in the years 1820, 21, Laid down under his Inspection by the Officers Assisting in the Expedition," in Franklin, *Journey.*
2 Richardson, "Geognostical Observations," p. 534.
3 Tables 6 and 7 show some alternative spellings used by Richardson for names of minerals and rocks. In "Geognostical Observations," p. 537 he uses the archaic "deposite" for "deposit."
4 Journal, 1 July 1821.
5 Franklin, *Journey*, p. 328.
6 Richardson, "Geognostical Observations," p. 525.
7 The principal source of Tables 6 and 7 is R.L. Bates, and Julia A. Jackson, *Glossary of Geology* (Falls Church, VA: American Geological Institute 1980). Some definitions are based on D.G.A. Whitten with J.R.V. Brooks, *The Penguin Dictionary of Geology* (Penguin Books 1972). The *Oxford English Dictionary* [OED] provides much information on first usage and gives definitions of obsolete terms no longer included in modern glossaries.
8 *See* OED. The word is derived from the Greek *petra*, rock, and *-ology*. The erroneously formed "petralogy" was

subsequently replaced by the correct and current "petrology."

9 Richardson, "Geognostical Observations," p. 497.

10 Robert Jameson (1774–1854) attended natural history classes under John Walker of Edinburgh University, a centre of geological thought at the time. Geology and mineralogy were Jameson's chief interests and he became an advocate of the views of Abraham Gottlob Werner on these subjects. In September 1800 Jameson went to Freiberg, Saxony, to study under Werner. He stayed over a year, returning to Scotland early in 1802. Jameson was elected to the natural history chair occupied by John Walker soon after the latter's death on 31 December 1803. Although Jameson was known for his "dry manner," his lectures were attended by several hundreds of students a year, compared with the Bergakademie in Freiberg which accepted only twenty. In the first two decades of the nineteenth century, therefore, far more students were instructed in Wernerian doctrines in Edinburgh than in Freiberg from the master himself.

Between 1804 and 1808 Jameson published his three-volume *System of Mineralogy*. The third volume, *Elements of Geognosy*, contained the first detailed account in English of Werner's geognostic theories and his classification of the rock strata. It also made Jameson the acknowledged leader of the Scottish Wernerians or Neptunists. In 1808 he founded and became president of the Wernerian Natural History Society. It existed for nearly fifty years and Jameson remained its president until his death.

Jameson's "interpretations of various rock junctions in terms of Wernerian concepts present a strangely unreal picture to a modern geologist, just as the modern chemist finds it difficult to understand the chemical ideas of the phlogistic period" (Joan M. Eyles, "Robert Jameson," in Charles C. Gillispie, ed., *Dictionary of Scientific Biography* (New York: Charles Scribner's Sons 1973, VII, 69–71). This judgment, although correct in stating that the Wernerian classification of the bedded rocks is unreal to modern eyes, is unduly harsh in its comparison to the phlogiston theory. The basic tenet that younger strata overlie older ones, which is the principle of geologic succession, comprises the core of both Wernerian and modern historical geology. A Wernerian stratigraphic column can be placed side by side of a current one (Table 8). The phlogiston theory, in contrast, is based on a different paradigm from our modern concepts of combustion. The more controversial parts of Werner's teachings, such as the aqueous origin of basalt, were gradually abandoned by Jameson and replaced by new ideas, particularly after Werner's death in 1817.

11 Richardson, "Geognostical Observations," p. 497.

12 Franklin, *Journey*, 368.

13 The term geology was introduced in 1778, in the work of Jean André de Luc (a Swiss-born scientist who lived at Windsor, England, for much of his life as adviser to Queen Charlotte), and at much the same time in the work of the Swiss chemist S.B. de Saussure (Whitten with Brooks, *Dictionary of Geology*, 204). Richardson gives the impression that he used the title "Geognostical Observa-

tions" for his Appendix 1 in Franklin's *Journey* to please Jameson and thus to show his indebtedness to his teacher, but that he was ready to abandon a word that had become obsolete in 1823.

14 OED.

15 After Charles F. Berkstresser, "The Geological Time Scale: Application of European Terminology in the United States and California" (MA thesis, California State University, Sacramento 1980), tables 1 (p. 6), 2 (p. 16), and 3 (p. 84). See also William B.N. Berry, *Growth of a Prehistoric Time Scale* (San Francisco; W.H. Freeman 1968); John W. Harbaugh, *Stratigraphy and Geologic Time* (Dubuque, Iowa: Wm. C. Brown 1968), particularly chap. 1, "Geologic Time Scale."

16 Compiled from Journal, "Geognostical Observations," and Franklin, *Journey*, chart. This column is similar to, but less detailed than the one used by Richardson in his lectures at Fort Franklin described in Warkentin, "Geological Lectures."

17 Compiled from John Richardson, *The Polar Regions* (Edinburgh: Adam and Charles Black 1861).

18 Born into a financially well-off family living in what is presently southwestern Poland, Abraham Gottlob Werner (1749–1817) received his first formal education from his father who interested him in mineralogy. In 1769 Werner enrolled in the recently founded Bergakademie Freiberg (near Dresden in the south central part of what is now the German Democratic Republic), where he stayed for two years before entering the University of Leipzig which he left in 1774 without a degree. In 1775, after having written his first book on miner-

als, he joined the faculty of the Bergakademie Freiberg to remain there for the rest of his life. He made the little mining academy into one of the most famous schools in the world through his reputation as a mineralogist and his skill as a teacher. Werner came to be acknowledged as the foremost geologist of his day and he counted noted scientists such as Leopold von Buch, Alexander von Humboldt, and Robert Jameson among his students. Werner was a towering figure in his field and "probably no other geologist has ever been so extensively eulogized by followers and opponents alike as he was during the two decades following his death" (Alexander Ospovat, "Abraham Gottlob Werner,"in Gillispie, ed., *Dictionary of Scientific Biography* (1976), XIV, 263).

Abraham Werner considered mineralogy to be the basis for all study of the earth. He divided mineralogy into five branches, two of which were geognosy (historical geology-stratigraphy) and oryctognosy (descriptive mineralogy). Because he worked out a complete, universally applicable geological system, Werner has been called the father of historical geology. Moreover, because he based his theories on the evidence provided by the geological knowledge of his day, he made geology into a science and an academic discipline.

Werner became known as a Neptunist on account of his postulate that the earth was once enveloped by an universal ocean and that almost all rocks were either precipitates or sediments from that ocean. The waters of this universal ocean receded very slowly over a long period of time with the chemical precipitates, such as granite, laid down first.

Werner's theory included two general risings of the universal ocean as well as some local floods and storms which broke up previously deposited rocks. Werner, in a chapter on volcanic rocks in one of his books published in 1786, held that basalt is of aqueous origin, "thus precipitating the great basalt controversy" (Ospovat, "Werner," p. 261). In time he was to be proved wrong, but for many years the weight of evidence then available was in his favour. As new evidence came in, Werner shifted basalt from the Primitive to the Floetz Period, but this is as far as he went. He never accepted basalt as a volcanic rock.

19 Modified after Ospovat, "Werner," with details from Karl Alfred Von Zittel, *History of Geology and Palaeontology to the End of the Nineteenth Century*, translated by Maria M. Ogilvie-Gordon (London: Walter Scott 1901; reprinted Codicote, Herts.: J. Cramer-Weinheim, Wheldon and Wesley; New York: Hafner Publishing 1962). Terms not used by Richardson have been omitted from the formations listed as examples by Von Zittel.

20 Richardson, "Geognostical Observations," p. 537.

21 George W. White, ed., Introduction and biographical notes in John Playfair, *Illustrations of the Huttonian Theory of the Earth* (1802; facsimile reprint, Urbana: University of Illinois Press 1956).

22 Whitten with Brooks, *Dictionary of Geology*, p. 229.

23 Ospovat, "Werner," p. 259.

24 White, Introduction, p. ix.

25 Richardson, "Geognostical Observations," pp. 528–9.

26 Franklin, *Journey*, p. 370.

27 Richardson, "Geognostical Observations," p. 536.

28 John Richardson, *Arctic Searching Expedition: A Journal of a Boat Voyage through Rupert's Land and the Arctic Sea in Search of the Discovery Ships under Command of Sir John Franklin, with an Appendix on the Physical Geography of North America* (2 vols., London: Longman, Brown, Green, and Longmans 1851), p. 162.

29 W.R.A. Baragar, and J.A. Donaldson, *Coppermine and Dismal Lakes Map Areas* (Ottawa: Geological Survey of Canada 1973), Paper 71-39, maps 1337A (Coppermine) and 1338A (Dismal Lakes); H.H. Bostock, J.A. Donaldson, J.A. Fraser, W.H. Poole, and F.M.G. Williams, *Geology Northeastern District of Mackenzie, Northwest Territories* (Ottawa: Geological Survey of Canada, 1963), Map 45-1963; R.J.W. Douglas, comp., *Geological Map of Canada* (Ottawa: Geological Survey of Canada 1969), Map 1250A; J.A. Fraser, *Geological Notes on Northeastern District of Mackenzie, Northwest Territories* (Ottawa: Geological Survey of Canada 1964), Paper 63-40, Map 45-1963; J.A. Fraser, et al., *Geology North-Central District of Mackenzie, Northwest Territories* (Ottawa: Geological Survey of Canada 1960), Preliminary Map 18-1960; J.B. Henderson, and R.M. Easton, *Archaean Supracrustal-basement Rock Relationships in the Keskarrah Bay Map-area, Slave Structural Province, District of Mackenzie* (Ottawa: Geological Survey of Canada 1977), Open File 447; G.H. Mitchell, E.K. Walton, and Douglas Grant, eds., *Edinburgh Geology–An Excursion Guide* (Edinburgh and London: Oliver and Boyd 1960); C.H. Stockwell, *Great Slave Lake–Coppermine Area, Northwest Territories* (Ottawa: Geological Survey of Canada 1933), Summary Report 1932, part C, pp. 37C-63C.

30 Richardson, "Geognostical Observations," p. 534.

31 H.S. Bostock, comp., *Physiographic Regions of Canada* (Ottawa: Geological Survey of Canada 1967), Map 1254A; Douglas, *Geological Map*, Map 1250A; C.H. Stockwell, chairman, *Tectonic Map of Canada* (Ottawa: Geological Survey of Canada 1968), Map 1251A.

32 All quotes are from Richardson's Journal.

33 Journal, 25 June.

34 Denis A. St Onge, "The Coppermine River: Art and Reality," *Canadian Geographic*, Aug.–Sept.: 28–31.

35 A striking example is presented in Figure 5 (engraving) and Figure 6 (watercolour by Captain George Back) of the view of the Clearwater River valley from the end of Methy Portage (Portage La Loche) in Saskatchewan in W.O. Kupsch, "A Valley View in Verdant Prose: The Clearwater Valley from Portage La Loche," *Musk-Ox* 20, 1977: 28–49.

36 St Onge, "Coppermine River," p. 28.

37 Franklin, *Journey*, p. 237.

38 Richardson, "Geognostical Observations," chart.

39 Journal, 6 July.

40 Ibid., 8 July.

41 Ibid., 9 July.

42 Ibid., 23 July.

43 Ibid., 16 Aug.

44 Ibid., 9 Sept. 1820.

45 Ibid., 11 Sept. 1820.

46 Ibid., 6 June.

47 See map in B.G. Craig, *Surficial Geology of North-central District of Mackenzie, Northwest Territories* (Ottawa: Geological Survey of Canada 1960), Paper 60-18.

48 Richardson, "Geognostical Observations," p. 520; Journal, 21 Aug. 1820.

49 Stockwell, *Great Slave Lake–Coppermine Area*, p. 43C.

50 Richardson, "Geognostical Observations," p. 538.

51 O.R. Wray, "By Canoe up the Yellowknife River in 1932," *Musk-Ox* 26 (1980): 21–50 (part 1); 27 (1980): 36–59 (part 2). The photographs are Figures 12 and 26; Richardson, "Geognostical Observations," p. 521.

52 Journal, 17 and 19 Sept.

53 Richardson, "Geognostical Observations," pp. 537–8.

54 Ibid., p. 538.

55 Playfair, *Illustrations*, p. 388.

56 Richardson, *Arctic Searching Expedition*, p. 211.

57 Journal, 4 July.

58 D.A. St Onge, personal communication, 1982, and "Glacial Lake Coppermine, North-central District of Mackenzie, Northwest Territories," *Canadian Journal of Earth Sciences* 7 (1980): 1310–15; D.A. St Onge, et al., "Aspects of the Deglaciation of the Coppermine River Region, District of Mackenzie," *Current Research, Part A, Geological Survey of Canada, Paper 81–1A* (1981): 327–31; D.A. St Onge, and F. Guay, "Quaternary Geology of Upper Coppermine River Valley, District of Mackenzie," *Current Research, Part A, Geological Survey of Canada Paper 82-1A* (1982): 127–9.

59 St Onge, personal communication, 1982, and "Glacial Lake Coppermine"; Journal, 8 July.

60 Journal, 8 July.

61 St Onge, personal communication, 1982, and "Deglaciation."

62 Journal, 9 July.

63 St Onge, personal communication, 1982, and "Deglaciation."

64 Richardson, "Geognostical Observations," p. 497.

65 Franklin, *Journey*, p. 340.

66 Ibid., p. 415.

67 Richardson, "Geognostical Observations," p. 498.

68 John Richardson, "Topographical and Geological Notices," in Franklin, *Narrative of a Second Expedition*, Appendix I, p. (i).

69 Richardson, *Arctic Searching Expedition*, pp. 162, 180n.

70 John Richardson, "On Some Point of the Physical Geography of North America in Connection with its Geological Structure," *Quarterly Journal of the Geological Society London* 7 (1851): 214.

71 Samuel Hearne, *A Journey from Prince of Wales's Fort in Hudson's Bay to the Northern Ocean undertaken by Order of the Hudson's Bay Company for the Discovery of copper mines, a North-west Passage, etc. in the Years 1769, 1770, 1771, and 1772* (London: A. Strahan and T. Cadell 1795). Hearne describes his search for copper as follows (pp. 173–4):

... we arrived at one of the copper mines, which lies, from the river's mouth about South South East, distant about twenty-nine or thirty miles.

This mine, if it deserves that appelation, is no more than an entire jumble of rocks and gravel, which has been rent many ways by an earthquake. Through these ruins there runs a small river; but no part of it, at the time I was there [July 1771] was more than knee-deep.

The Indians who were the occasion of my undertaking this journey, represented this mine to be so rich and valuable, that if a factory were built at the river, a ship might be ballasted with the oar [sic], instead of stone; and that with the same ease and dispatch as is done with stones at Churchill River. By their account the hills were entirely composed of

that metal, all in handy lumps, like a heap of pebbles. But their account differed so much from the truth, that I and almost all my companions expended nearly four hours in search of some of this metal, with such poor success, that among us all, only one piece of any size could be found. This, however, was remarkably good, and weighed above four pounds. (This piece is now in the possession of the Hudson's Bay Company.) I believe the copper has formerly been in much greater plenty; for in many places, both on the surface and in the cavities and crevices of the rocks, the stones are much tinged with verdigrise [copper green or malachite].

Through Hearne's published record, the occurrence of copper at the lower Coppermine River had become common knowledge in Britain by the late eighteenth century. It is therefore not surprising that one of the instructions to John Franklin (*Journey*, p. xvii) was to explore this matter further: "I was instructed, on my arrival at, or near, the mouth of the Copper-Mine River, to make every inquiry as to the situation of the spot from whence native copper had been brought down by the Indians to the Hudson's Bay establishment, and to visit and explore the place in question; in order that Dr. Richardson might be enabled to make such observations as might be useful in a commercial point of view, or interesting to the science of mineralogy."

72 Journal, 11 July.

73 Richardson, "Geognostical Observations," pp. 528–9.

74 Franklin, *Journey*, pp. 340–1.

75 Richardson, "Topographical and Geological Notices," I, (50).

76 Baragar and Donaldson, *Coppermine and Dismal Lakes Map Areas*, 8–9, 16.

77 Richardson, "Geognostical Observations," pp. 520, 523, 524, 525, 527, 535, 536; Journal, 21 June, 9 July.

78 Richardson, "Geognostical Observations," p. 537.

79 Ibid., chart.

80 W.O. Kupsch, "Boundary of the Canadian Shield," in W.O. Kupsch, and W.A.S. Sarjeant, eds., *History of Concepts in Precambrian Geology* (Toronto: Geological Association of Canada Special Paper 19), pp. 119–31.

81 Richardson, "Geognostical Observations," p. 538.

Bibliography

Acharius, Erik. *Lichenographia Universalis.* Gottingae: I.F. Danckwerts 1810.

American Ornithologists'Union. *Check-list of North American Birds.* 6th ed. Lawrence, Kansas: Allen Press 1983.

Banfield, A.W.F. *The Mammals of Canada.* Toronto: University of Toronto Press 1974.

Capelle, K.J. "Myiasis," chapter 11 in *Parasitic Diseases of Wild Mammals*, ed. John W. Davis and Roy C. Anderson. Ames: Iowa State University Press 1971.

Cuvier, Georges. *Le Règne Animal, distribue d'après son organization.* 4 vols. Paris: Deterville 1817.

Franklin, John. *Narrative of a Journey to the Shores of the Polar Sea in the Years 1819, 20, 21 and 22.* London: John Murray 1823; Reprint, Edmonton: M.G. Hurtig 1969.

Franklin, John. *Narrative of a Second Expedition to the Shores of the Polar Sea in the Years 1825, 1826 and 1827.* London: John Murray 1828.

Godfrey, W. Earl. *The Birds of Canada.* Ottawa: National Museum of Canada Bulletin 203 1966.

Hearne, Samuel. *A Journey from Prince of Wales's Fort in Hudson's Bay to the Northern Ocean in the Years 1769, 1770, 1771 and 1772*, ed., R. Glover. Toronto: Macmillan 1958.

Hooker, William Jackson. *Flora Boreali-Americana;* or *the Botany of the Northern Parts of British America.* London: Henry G. Bohn 1840; Reprint, Weinheim: J. Cramer 1960.

Houston, C. Stuart, ed. *To the Arctic by Canoe, 1819–21: The Journal and Paintings of Robert Hood, Midshipman with Franklin.* Montreal: McGill-Queen's University Press 1974.

Houston, C. Stuart and Maurice G. Street. *The Birds of the Saskatchewan River, Carlton to Cumberland.* Regina: Saskatchewan Natural History Society, Special Publication No 2 1959.

Innis, Harold A. *The Fur Trade in Canada: An Introduction to Canadian Economic History.* Toronto: University of Toronto Press 1956.

Johnson, Robert E. *Sir John Richardson, Arctic Explorer, Natural Historian, Naval Surgeon.* London: Taylor and Francis 1976.

Kupsch, W.O. *Pioneer Geologists in Saskatchewan*. Regina: Department of Mineral Resources 1955.

Lacombe, Albert. *Dictionnaire de la Langue des Cris*. Montreal: Beauchemin et Valois 1874.

Looman, J. and K.F. Best. *Budd's Flora of the Canadian Prairie Provinces*. Ottawa: Research Branch Agriculture Canada Publication 1662 1979.

McIlraith, John. *Life of Sir John Richardson*. London: Longmans, Green 1868.

MacLeod, Margaret Arnett and Richard Glover. "Franklin's First Expedition as seen by the Fur Traders." *Polar Record* 15 (1971): 669–82.

Matovinovic, J. and V. Ramalingaswami. "Therapy and Prophylaxis of Endemic Goitre." *Bulletin World Health Organization* 18 (1958): 233–53.

Porsild, A.E. and W.J. Cody. *Vascular Plants of Continental Northwest Territories, Canada*. Ottawa: National Museums of Canada 1980.

Rich, Edwin Ernest, ed. *Journal of Occurrences in the Athabasca Department by George Simpson, 1820 and 1821, and Report*. Toronto: Champlain Society 1938.

Rich, Edwin Ernest, ed. *Colin Robertson's Correspondence Book, September 1817 to September 1822*. Toronto: Champlain Society 1939.

Richardson, John. "Geognostical Observations," Appendix I, pp. 497–538, in Franklin, *Journey* (1823).

Richardson, John. "Notices of the Fishes," Appendix VI, pp. 705–28, in Franklin, *Journey* (1823).

Richardson, John. "Botanical Appendix," Appendix VII, pp. 729–68, in Franklin, *Journey* (1823).

Richardson, John. "Account of the Quadrupeds and Birds," Zoological Appendix in William Edward Parry, *Journal of a Second Voyage for the Discovery of a North-West Passage* (London: John Murray 1825).

Richardson, John. *Fauna Boreali-Americana, or the Zoology of the Northern Parts of British America*. Part First: *The Mammals*. London: John Murray 1829.

Richardson, John. *Fauna Boreali-Americana, or the Zoology of the Northern Parts of British America*. Part Third: *The Fish*. London: Richard Bentley 1836.

Rydberg, Per Axel. *Flora of the Prairies and Plains of Central North America*. New York: New York Botanical Garden 1932.

Sabine, Joseph. "Account of the Marmots of North America hitherto known, with Notices and Descriptions of Three New Species." *Transactions Linnean Society* 13 (1822): 19–31. Separate printing, London: Richard Taylor 1822.

Sabine, Joseph. "Zoological Appendix. Appendix V": Quadrupeds, pp. 647–68; Birds, pp. 669–703, in Franklin, *Journey* (1823).

Scoggan, H.J. *Flora of Manitoba*. Ottawa: National Museum of Canada Bulletin 140, 1957.

Scott, W.B. and E.J. Crossman. *Freshwater Fishes of Canada*. Ottawa: Fisheries Research Board of Canada Bulletin 184 1973.

Stefansson, Vilhjalmur. *Unsolved Mysteries of the Arctic*. New York: Macmillan 1939.

Stephen, Leslie and Sidney Lee, eds. *The Dictionary of National Biography: From the Earliest Times to 1900*. London: Oxford University Press 1949–50.

Stewart, D.A. "Sir John Richardson: Surgeon, Physician, Sailor, Explorer, Naturalist, Scholar." *British Medical Journal* 1 (1931): 110–12.

Swainson, William and John Richardson. *Fauna Boreali-Americana, or the Zoology of the Northern Parts of British America.* Part Second: *The Birds.* London: John Murray 1831 (actual publication date, February 1832).

Thomson, Don W. *Men and Meridians, the History of Surveying and Mapping in Canada.* 2 vols. Ottawa: Queen's Printer 1966, 1967.

Traill, Henry Duff. *The Life of Sir John Franklin, R.N.* London: John Murray 1896.

Warkentin, John, "Geological Lectures by Dr. John Richardson, 1825–26." *Syllogeus* #22, National Museum of Canada 1979.

Wentzel, Willard-Ferdinand. "Letters to the Hon. Roderic McKenzie," pp. 67–153 in *Les Bourgeois de la Compagnie du Nord-Ouest, Récits de Voyages, Lettres et Rapports Inédits Relatifs au Nord-Ouest Canadian Publiés avec une Esquisse historique et des Annotations,* vol. 1, part 2, ed. L.F.R. Masson. Québec: A. Coté 1889–90.

Williams, Glyndwr, ed. *Andrew Graham's Observations on Hudson's Bay, 1767–91.* London: Hudson's Bay Record Society 1969.

"A wolf chased a stout buck-deer across the lake," 18 June 1821

Index

INSECTS

LICHENS

MAMMALS